Microsoft® OFFICE 2013

ESSENTIAL

Misty E. Vermaat

Contributing Authors

Steven M. Freund

Raymond E. Enger

Susan L. Sebok

Mali B. Jones

Philip J. Pratt

Mary Z. Last

Corinne L. Hoisington

CENGAGE
Learning®

SHELLY
CASHMAN
SERIES®

Australia • Brazil • Japan • Korea • Mexico • Singapore • Spain • United Kingdom • United States

Microsoft® Office 2013: Essential
Misty E. Vermaat

Executive Editor: Kathleen McMahon

Product Manager: Jon Farnham

Associate Product Manager: Crystal Parenteau

Editorial Assistant: Sarah Ryan

Print Buyer: Julio Esperas

Director of Production: Patty Stephan

Content Project Manager: Matthew Hutchinson

Development Editors: Lyn Markowicz, Deb Kaufmann, Amanda Brodkin, Lisa Ruffolo

Senior Brand Manager: Elinor Gregory

Market Development Manager: Kristie Clark

Market Development Manager: Gretchen Swann

Marketing Coordinator: Amy McGregor

QA Manuscript Reviewers: Jeffrey Schwartz, John Freitas, Serge Palladino, Susan Pedicini, Danielle Shaw, Susan Whalen

Art Director: GEX Publishing Services, Inc.

Text Design: Joel Sadagursky

Cover Design: Lisa Kuhn, Curio Press, LLC

Cover Photo: Tom Kates Photography

Compositor: PreMediaGlobal

Copyeditor: Foxxe Editorial

Proofreader: Kim Kosmatka

Indexer: Rich Carlson

For product information and technology assistance, contact us at
Cengage Learning Customer & Sales Support, 1-800-354-9706

For permission to use material from this text or product, submit all requests online at **cengage.com/permissions**
Further permissions questions can be emailed to
permissionrequest@cengage.com

Library of Congress Control Number: 2013935965

ISBN-13: 978-1-285-16611-7
ISBN-10: 1-285-16611-6

Cengage Learning
20 Channel Center Street
Boston, MA 02210
USA

Cengage Learning is a leading provider of customized learning solutions with office locations around the globe, including Singapore, the United Kingdom, Australia, Mexico, Brazil, and Japan. Locate your local office at:
international.cengage.com/region

Cengage Learning products are represented in Canada by Nelson Education, Ltd.

To learn more about Cengage Learning, visit **www.cengage.com**

Purchase any of our products at your local college bookstore or at our preferred online store at **www.CengageBrain.com**

Printed in the United States of America
2 3 4 5 6 7 14

Microsoft® OFFICE 2013

INTRODUCTORY

Contents

Microsoft **Office 365**

Microsoft **Word 2013**

CHAPTER ONE
Creating, Formatting, and Editing a Word Document with a Picture

Microsoft **PowerPoint 2013**

CHAPTER ONE
Creating and Editing a Presentation with Pictures

Microsoft **Excel 2013**

CHAPTER ONE
Creating a Worksheet and a Chart

Microsoft **Access 2013**

CHAPTER ONE
Databases and Database Objects: An Introduction

Preface

The Shelly Cashman Series® offers the finest textbooks in computer education. We are proud that since Microsoft Office 4.3, our series of Microsoft Office textbooks have been the most widely used books in education. With each new edition of our Office books, we make significant improvements based on the software and comments made by instructors and students. For this Microsoft Office 2013 text, the Shelly Cashman Series development team carefully reviewed our pedagogy and analyzed its effectiveness in teaching today's Office student. Students today read less, but need to retain more. They need not only to be able to perform skills, but to retain those skills and know how to apply them to different settings. Today's students need to be continually engaged and challenged to retain what they're learning.

With this Microsoft Office 2013 text, we continue our commitment to focusing on the users and how they learn best.

Objectives of This Textbook

Microsoft Office 2013: Essential is intended for a course that includes an essential introduction to Office 2013. No experience with a computer is assumed, and no mathematics beyond the high school freshman level is required. The objectives of this book are:

- To teach the fundamentals of Microsoft Windows 8, Microsoft Word 2013, Microsoft PowerPoint 2013, Microsoft Excel 2013, and Microsoft Access 2013

- To expose students to practical examples of the computer as a useful tool

- To acquaint students with the proper procedures to create documents, presentations, worksheets, and databases suitable for coursework, professional purposes, and personal use

- To help students discover the underlying functionality of Office 2013 so they can become more productive

- To develop an exercise-oriented approach that allows learning by doing

The Shelly Cashman Approach

A Proven Pedagogy with an Emphasis on Project Planning
Each chapter presents a practical problem to be solved within a project planning framework. The project orientation is strengthened by the use of the Roadmap, which provides a visual framework for the project. Step-by-step instructions with supporting screens guide students through the steps. Instructional steps are supported by the Q&A, Experimental Step, and BTW features.

A Visually Engaging Book that Maintains Student Interest
The step-by-step tasks, with supporting figures, provide a rich visual experience for the student. Call-outs on the screens that present both explanatory and navigational information provide students with information they need when they need to know it.

Supporting Reference Materials
With the Quick Reference, students can quickly look up information about a single task, such as keyboard shortcuts, and find page references to where in the book the task is illustrated.

Integration of the World Wide Web
The World Wide Web is integrated into the Office 2013 learning experience with (1) BTW annotations; (2) BTW, Q&A, and Quick Reference Summary Web pages; and (3) the Learn Online resources for each chapter.

End-of-Chapter Student Activities
Extensive end-of-chapter activities provide a variety of reinforcement opportunities for students to apply and expand their skills through individual and group work. To complete some of these assignments, you will be required to use the Data Files for Students. Visit www.cengage.com/ct/studentdownload for detailed access instructions or contact your instructor for information about accessing the required files.

New to this Edition

Enhanced Coverage of Critical Thinking Skills
A New Consider This element poses thought-provoking questions throughout each chapter, providing an increased emphasis on critical thinking and problem-solving skills. Also, every task in the project now includes a reason *why* the students are performing the task and *why* the task is necessary.

Enhanced Retention and Transference
A new Roadmap element provides a visual framework for each project, showing students where they are in the process of creating each project, and reinforcing the context of smaller tasks by showing how they fit into the larger project.

Integration of Office with Cloud and Web Technologies
A new Lab focuses entirely on integrating cloud and web technologies with Office 2013, using technologies like blogs, social networks, and SkyDrive.

More Personalization
Each chapter project includes an optional instruction for the student to personalize his or her solution, if required by an instructor, making each student's solution unique.

More Collaboration
A new Research and Collaboration project has been added to the Consider This: Your Turn assignment at the end of each chapter.

Instructor Resources

The Instructor Resources include both teaching and testing aids and can be accessed via CD-ROM or at www.cengage.com/login.

Instructor's Manual Includes lecture notes summarizing the chapter sections, figures and boxed elements found in every chapter, teacher tips, classroom activities, lab activities, and quick quizzes in Microsoft Word files.

Syllabus Easily customizable sample syllabi that cover policies, assignments, exams, and other course information.

Figure Files Illustrations for every figure in the textbook in electronic form.

Powerpoint Presentations A multimedia lecture presentation system that provides slides for each chapter. Presentations are based on chapter objectives.

Solutions to Exercises Includes solutions for all end-of-chapter and chapter reinforcement exercises.

Test Bank & Test Engine Test banks include 112 questions for every chapter, featuring objective-based and critical thinking question types, and including page number references and figure references, when appropriate. Also included is the test engine, ExamView, the ultimate tool for your objective-based testing needs.

Data Files for Students Includes all the files that are required by students to complete the exercises.

Additional Activities for Students Consists of Chapter Reinforcement Exercises, which are true/false, multiple-choice, and short answer questions that help students gain confidence in the material learned.

Learn Online

CengageBrain.com is the premier destination for purchasing or renting Cengage Learning textbooks, eBooks, eChapters, and study tools at a significant discount (eBooks up to 50% off Print). In addition, CengageBrain.com provides direct access to all digital products, including eBooks, eChapters, and digital solutions, such as CourseMate and SAM, regardless of where purchased. The following are some examples of what is available for this product on www.cengagebrain.com.

Student Companion Site The Student Companion Site reinforces chapter terms and concepts using true/false questions, multiple choice questions, short answer questions, flash cards, practice tests, and learning games, all available for no additional cost at www.cengagebrain.com.

SAM: Skills Assessment Manager Get your students workplace-ready with SAM, the market-leading proficiency-based assessment and training solution for Microsoft Office! SAM's active, hands-on environment helps students master Microsoft Office skills and computer concepts that are essential to academic and career success, delivering the most comprehensive online learning solution for your course! Through skill-based assessments, interactive trainings, business-centric projects, and comprehensive remediation, SAM engages students in mastering the latest Microsoft Office programs on their own, giving instructors more time to focus on teaching. Computer concepts labs supplement instruction of important technology-related topics and issues through engaging simulations and interactive, auto-graded assessments. With enhancements including streamlined course setup, more robust grading and reporting features, and the integration of fully interactive MindTap Readers containing Cengage Learning's premier textbook content, SAM provides the best teaching and learning solution for your course.

MindLinks MindLinks is a new Cengage Learning Service designed to provide the best possible user experience and facilitate the highest levels of learning retention and outcomes, enabled through a deep integration of Cengage Learning's digital suite into an instructor's Learning Management System (LMS). MindLinks works on any LMS that supports the IMS Basic LTI open standard. Advanced features, including gradebook exchange, are the result of active, enhanced LTI collaborations with industry-leading LMS partners to drive the evolving technology standards forward.

CourseNotes

course|notes™
quick reference guide

Cengage Learning's CourseNotes are six-panel quick reference cards that reinforce the most important and widely used features of a software application in a visual and user-friendly format. CourseNotes serve as a great reference tool during and after the course. CourseNotes are available for software applications, such as Microsoft Office 2013. There are also topic-based CourseNotes available, such as Best Practices in Social Networking, Hot Topics in Technology, and Web 2.0. Visit www.cengagebrain.com to learn more!

About Our Covers

The Shelly Cashman Series is continually updating our approach and content to reflect the way today's students learn and experience new technology. This focus on student success is reflected on our covers, which feature real students from The University of Rhode Island using the Shelly Cashman Series in their courses, and reflect the varied ages and backgrounds of the students learning with our books. When you use the Shelly Cashman Series, you can be assured that you are learning computer skills using the most effective courseware available.

Textbook Walk-Through

The Shelly Cashman Series Pedagogy: Project-Based — Step-by-Step — Variety of Assessments

Roadmaps provide a visual framework for each project, showing the students where they are in the process of creating each project.

Step-by-step instructions provide a context beyond the point-and-click. Each step provides information on why students are performing each task and what will occur as a result.

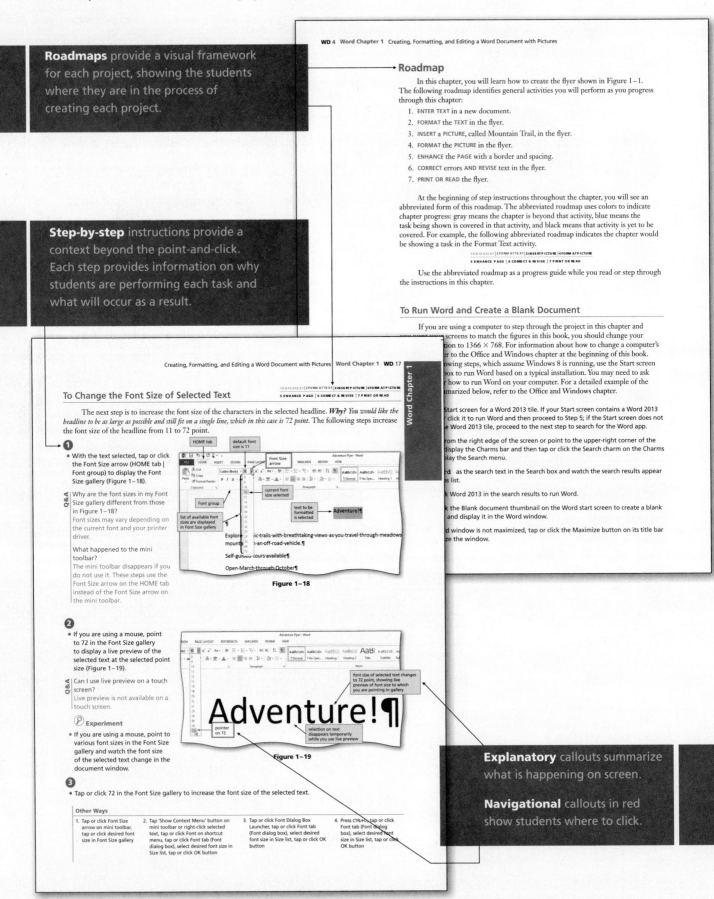

Roadmap

In this chapter, you will learn how to create the flyer shown in Figure 1–1. The following roadmap identifies general activities you will perform as you progress through this chapter:

1. ENTER TEXT in a new document.
2. FORMAT the TEXT in the flyer.
3. INSERT a PICTURE, called Mountain Trail, in the flyer.
4. FORMAT the PICTURE in the flyer.
5. ENHANCE the PAGE with a border and spacing.
6. CORRECT errors AND REVISE text in the flyer.
7. PRINT OR READ the flyer.

At the beginning of step instructions throughout the chapter, you will see an abbreviated form of this roadmap. The abbreviated roadmap uses colors to indicate chapter progress: gray means the chapter is beyond that activity, blue means the task being shown is covered in that activity, and black means that activity is yet to be covered. For example, the following abbreviated roadmap indicates the chapter would be showing a task in the Format Text activity.

1 ENTER TEXT | 2 FORM AT TE XT | 3 INSE RT P ICTURE | 4 FORM AT P ICTURE
5 ENHANCE PAGE | 6 CORRECT & REVISE | 7 PRINT OR READ

Use the abbreviated roadmap as a progress guide while you read or step through the instructions in this chapter.

To Run Word and Create a Blank Document

If you are using a computer to step through the project in this chapter and you want your screens to match the figures in this book, you should change your ...tion to 1366 × 768. For information about how to change a computer's ...er to the Office and Windows chapter at the beginning of this book. ...owing steps, which assume Windows 8 is running, use the Start screen ...box to run Word based on a typical installation. You may need to ask ...r how to run Word on your computer. For a detailed example of the ...marized below, refer to the Office and Windows chapter.

...Start screen for a Word 2013 tile. If your Start screen contains a Word 2013 ...click it to run Word and then proceed to Step 5; if the Start screen does not ...e Word 2013 tile, proceed to the next step to search for the Word app.

...rom the right edge of the screen or point to the upper-right corner of the ...display the Charms bar and then tap or click the Search charm on the Charms ...lay the Search menu.

...d   as the search text in the Search box and watch the search results appear ...s list.

...k Word 2013 in the search results to run Word.

...k the Blank document thumbnail on the Word start screen to create a blank ...and display it in the Word window.

...d window is not maximized, tap or click the Maximize button on its title bar ...ze the window.

To Change the Font Size of Selected Text

1 ENTER TE XT | 2 FORM AT TE XT | 3 INSE RT PICTURE | 4 FORM AT P ICTURE
5 ENHANCE PAGE | 6 CORRECT & REVISE | 7 PRINT OR READ

The next step is to increase the font size of the characters in the selected headline. **Why?** *You would like the headline to be as large as possible and still fit on a single line, which in this case is 72 point.* The following steps increase the font size of the headline from 11 to 72 point.

1

- With the text selected, tap or click the Font Size arrow (HOME tab | Font group) to display the Font Size gallery (Figure 1–18).

Q&A Why are the font sizes in my Font Size gallery different from those in Figure 1–18?
Font sizes may vary depending on the current font and your printer driver.

What happened to the mini toolbar?
The mini toolbar disappears if you do not use it. These steps use the Font Size arrow on the HOME tab instead of the Font Size arrow on the mini toolbar.

Figure 1–18

2

- If you are using a mouse, point to 72 in the Font Size gallery to display a live preview of the selected text at the selected point size (Figure 1–19).

Q&A Can I use live preview on a touch screen?
Live preview is not available on a touch screen.

Experiment

- If you are using a mouse, point to various font sizes in the Font Size gallery and watch the font size of the selected text change in the document window.

Figure 1–19

3

- Tap or click 72 in the Font Size gallery to increase the font size of the selected text.

Other Ways

1. Tap or click Font Size arrow on mini toolbar, tap or click desired font size in Font Size gallery	2. Tap 'Show Context Menu' button on mini toolbar or right-click selected text, tap or click Font on shortcut menu, tap or click Font tab (Font dialog box), select desired font size in Size list, tap or click OK button	3. Tap or click Font Dialog Box Launcher, tap or click Font tab (Font dialog box), select desired font size in Size list, tap or click OK button	4. Press CTRL+D, tap or click Font tab (Font dialog box), select desired font size in Size list, tap or click OK button

Explanatory callouts summarize what is happening on screen.

Navigational callouts in red show students where to click.

Q&A boxes anticipate questions students may have when working through the steps and provide additional information about what they are doing right where they need it.

Experiment Steps within the step-by-step instructions encourage students to explore, experiment, and take advantage of the features of the Office 2013 user interface. These steps are not necessary to complete the projects, but are designed to increase confidence with the software and build problem-solving skills.

---

1 ENTER TEXT | 2 FORMAT TEXT | 3 INSERT PICTURE | 4 FORMAT PICTURE
5 ENHANCE PAGE | 6 CORRECT & REVISE | 7 PRINT OR READ

To Change the Font Size of Selected Text

The next step is to increase the font size of the characters in the selected headline. *Why? You would like the headline to be as large as possible and still fit on a single line, which in this case is 72 point.* The following steps increase the font size of the headline from 11 to 72 point.

1
- With the text selected, tap or click the Font Size arrow (HOME tab | Font group) to display the Font Size gallery (Figure 1–18).

Q&A Why are the font sizes in my Font Size gallery different from those in Figure 1–18?
Font sizes may vary depending on the current font and your printer driver.

What happened to the mini toolbar?
The mini toolbar disappears if you do not use it. These steps use the Font Size arrow on the HOME tab instead of the Font Size arrow on the mini toolbar.

Figure 1–18

2
- If you are using a mouse, point to 72 in the Font Size gallery to display a live preview of the selected text at the selected point size (Figure 1–19).

Q&A Can I use live preview on a touch screen?
Live preview is not available on a touch screen.

Experiment
- If you are using a mouse, point to various font sizes in the Font Size gallery and watch the font size of the selected text change in the document window.

Adventure!¶

Figure 1–19

3
- Tap or click 72 in the Font Size gallery to increase the font size of the selected text.

Other Ways

1. Tap or click Font Size arrow on mini toolbar, tap or click desired font size in Font Size gallery
2. Tap or click 'Show Context Menu' button on mini toolbar or right-click selected text, tap or click Font on shortcut menu, tap or click Font tab (Font dialog box), select desired font size in Size list, tap or click OK button
3. Tap or click Font Dialog Box Launcher, tap or click Font tab (Font dialog box), select desired font size in Size list, tap or click OK button
4. Press CTRL+D, tap or click Font tab (Font dialog box), select desired font size in Size list, tap or click OK button

---

flyer before formatting

Adventure!

Explore scenic trails with breathtaking views as you travel through meadows, fores
mountains in an off-road vehicle.

Self-guided tours available
Open March through October
All vehicles and gear provided
To book your adventure, call 555-89281

(a) Unformatted Flyer

Figure 1

Font, Font Sizes, and Themes

Characters that appear on the screen are a specific shape and size. The **font**, or typeface, defines the appearance and shape of the letters, numbers, and special characters. In Word, the default font usually is Calibri (shown in Figure 1–14 on 15). You can leave characters in the default font or change them to a different font. **Font size** specifies the size of the characters and is determined by a measurement system called points. A single **point** is about 1/72 of one inch in height. The default font size in Word typically is 11 (Figure 1–14). Thus, a character with a font size of 11 is about 11/72 or a little less than 1/6 of one inch in height. You can increase or decrease the font size of characters in a document.

A document **theme** is a set of unified formats for fonts, colors, and graphics. Word includes a variety of document themes to assist you with coordinating these visual elements in a document. The default theme fonts are Calibri Light for headings and Calibri for body text. By changing the document theme, you quickly can give your document a new look. You also can define your own document themes.

Formatting Marks
With some fonts, the formatting marks will not be displayed properly on the screen. For example, the raised dot that signifies a blank space between words may be displayed behind a character instead of in the blank space, causing the characters to look incorrect.

CONSIDER THIS

How do I know which formats to use in a flyer?
In a flyer, consider the following formatting suggestions.

- **Increase the font size of characters.** Flyers usually are posted on a bulletin board or in a window. Thus, the font size should be as large as possible so that passersby easily can read the flyer. To give the headline more impact, its font size should be larger than the font size of the text in the body copy. If possible, make the font size of the signature line larger than the body copy but smaller than the headline.

- **Change the font of characters.** Use fonts that are easy to read. Try to use only two different fonts in a flyer; for example, use one for the headline and the other for all other text. Too many fonts can make the flyer visually confusing.

- **Change the paragraph alignment.** The default alignment for paragraphs in a document is **left-aligned**, that is, flush at the left margin of the document with uneven right edges. Consider changing the alignment of some of the paragraphs to add interest and variety to the flyer.

- **Highlight key paragraphs with bullets.** A bulleted paragraph is a paragraph that begins with a dot or other symbol. Use bulleted paragraphs to highlight important points in a flyer.

- **Emphasize important words.** To call attention to certain words or lines, you can underline them, italicize them, or bold them. Use these formats sparingly, however, because overuse will minimize their effect and make the flyer look too busy.

- **Use color.** Use colors that complement each other and convey the meaning of the flyer. Vary colors in terms of hue and brightness. Headline colors, for example, can be bold and bright. Signature lines should stand out more than body copy but less than headlines. Keep in mind that too many colors can detract from the flyer and make it difficult to read.

Consider This boxes pose thought-provoking questions with answers throughout each chapter, promoting critical thought along with immediate feedback.

Textbook Walk-Through

Chapter Summary A listing of the tasks completed within the chapter, grouped into major task categories in an outline format.

Chapter Summary

In this chapter you have learned to create an Access database, create tables and add records to a database, print the contents of tables, import data, create queries, create forms, create reports, and change database properties. You also have learned how to design a database. The items listed below include all the new Access skills you have learned in this chapter, with tasks grouped by activity.

Database Object Management
Delete a Table or Other Object in the Database (AC 58)
Rename an Object in the Database (AC 58)

Database Properties
Change Database Properties (AC 55)

File Management
Run Access (AC 5)
Create a Database (AC 6)
Create a Database Using a Template (AC 7)
Exit Access (AC 24)
Open a Database from Access (AC 25)
Back Up a Database (AC 56)
Compact and Repair a Database (AC 57)
Close a Database without Exiting Access (AC 57)
Save a Database with Another Name (AC 57)

Form Creation
Create a Form (AC 45)

Import Data
Import an Excel Worksheet (AC 33)

Print Objects
Preview and Print the Contents of a Table (AC 30)

Print the Results of a Query (AC 45)
Print a Report (AC 54)

Query Creation
Use the Simple Query Wizard to Create a Query (AC 40)
Use a Criterion in a Query (AC 43)

Report Creation
Create a Report (AC 48)
Modify Report Column Headings and Resize Columns (AC 50)
Add Totals to a Report (AC 53)

Table Creation
Modify the Primary Key (AC 11)
Define the Remaining Fields in a Table (AC 14)
Save a Table (AC 16)
View the Table in Design View (AC 17)
Change a Field Size in Design View (AC 18)
Close the Table (AC 20)
Resize Columns in a Datasheet (AC 28)
Modify a Table in Design View (AC 37)

Table Update
Add Records to a Table (AC 20)
Add Records to a Table that Contains Data (AC 26)

What decisions will you need to make when creating your next database?
Use these guidelines as you complete the assignments in this chapter and create your own databases outside of this class.

1. Identify the tables that will be included in the database.
2. Determine the primary keys for each of the tables.
3. Determine the additional fields that should be included in each of the tables.
4. Determine relationships between the tables.
   a) Identify the "one" table.
   b) Identify the "many" table.
   c) Include the primary key of the "one" table as a field in the "many" table.
5. Determine data types for the fields in the tables.
6. Determine additional properties for fields.
   a) Determine if a special caption is warranted.
   b) Determine if a special description is warranted.
   c) Determine field sizes.
   d) Determine formats.
7. Identify and remove any unwanted redundancy.
8. Determine a storage location for the database.
9. Determine the best method for distributing the database objects.

CONSIDER THIS

Apply Your Knowledge This exercise usually requires students to open and manipulate a file that parallels the activities learned in the chapter.

Databases and

How should you submit solutions to questions in the assi a ⊛ symbol?
Every assignment in this book contains one or more questions identified you to think beyond the assigned database. Present your solutions to th instructor. Possible formats may include one or more of these options: V contains the answer; present your answer to the class; discuss your ans or video using a webcam, smartphone, or portable media player; or pos

Apply Your Knowledge

Reinforce the skills and apply the concepts you learne

Adding a Caption, Changing a Data Type, Creating
Note: To complete this assignment, you will be required t
www.cengage.com/ct/studentdownload for detailed instruc
mation about accessing the required files.

Instructions: Cosmetics Naturally Inc. manufactures and sells beauty and skin care products made with only natural ingredients. The company's products do not contain any synthetic chemicals, artificial fragrances, or chemical preservatives. Cosmetics Naturally has a database that keeps track of its sales representatives and customers. Each customer is assigned to a single sales rep, but each sales rep may be assigned to many customers. The database has two tables. The Customer table contains data on the customers who purchase Cosmetics Naturally products. The Sales Rep table contains data on the sales reps. You will add a caption, change a data type, create two queries, a form, and a report, as shown in Figure 1–83 on the next page.

Perform the following tasks:

1. Start Access, open the Apply Cosmetics Naturally database from the Data Files for Students, and enable the content.
2. Open the Sales Rep table in Datasheet view, add SR # as the caption for the Sales Rep Number field, and resize all columns to best fit the data. Save the changes to the layout of the table and close the table.
3. Open the Customer table in Design view and change the data type for the Postal Code field to Short Text. Change the field size for the field to 5. Save the changes to the table and close the table.
4. Use the Simple Query Wizard to create a query for the Customer table that contains the Customer Number, Customer Name, Amount Paid, Balance, and Sales Rep Number. The query is a detail query. Use the name Customer Query for the query and close the query.
5. Create a simple form for the Sales Rep table. Save the form and use the name Sales Rep for the form. Close the form.
6. Create the report shown in Figure 1–83 for the Customer table. The report includes totals for both the Amount Paid and Balance fields. Be sure the totals appear completely. You might need to expand the size of the total controls. Move the page number so that it is within the margins. Save the report as Customer Financial Report.
7. If requested by your instructor, add your last name to the title of the report, that is, change the title to Customer Financial Report LastName where LastName is your actual last name.
8. Compact and repair the database.
9. Submit the revised database in the format specified by your instructor.
10. ⊛ How would you change the field name of the Balance field in the Customer table to Current Balance?

Continued >

Consider This: Plan Ahead box presents a single master planning guide that students can use as they create documents on their own.

Apply Your Knowledge *continued*

Customer Financial Report | Monday, September 15, 2014
9:24:56 PM

Customer Number	Customer Name	Amount Paid	Balance	Sales Rep Number
AS24	Ashley's Salon	$1,789.65	$236.99	34
UR23	U R Beautiful	$0.00	$1,235.00	39
		$14,786.17	$5,617.78	

Figure 1–83

Extend Your Knowledge

Extend the skills you learned in this chapter and experiment with new skills. You may need to use Help to complete the assignment.

Using a Database Template to Create a Contacts Database
Note: To complete this assignment, you will be required to use the Data Files for Students. Visit www.cengage.com/ct/studentdownload for detailed instructions or contact your instructor for information about accessing the required files.

Instructions: Access includes both desktop database templates and web-based templates. You can use a template to create a beginning database that can be modified to meet your specific needs. You will use a template to create a Contacts database. The database template includes sample tables, queries, forms, and reports. You will modify the database and create the Contacts Query shown in Figure 1–84.

Perform the following tasks:
1. Start Access.
2. Select the Desktop contacts template in the templ... file name Extend Contacts.
3. Enable the content. If requested to do so by your Started with Contacts dialog box. Close the Gett...
4. Close the Contact List form.
5. Open the Contacts table in Datasheet view and d... Attachments field in the table. The Attachments
6. Change the data type for the ID field to Short Te... and change the field size to 4. Change the colum... displayed.
7. Save the changes to the Contacts table and close
8. Use the Simple Query Wizard to create the Con... query.

Figure 1–

> **Extend Your Knowledge** projects at the end of each chapter allow students to extend and expand on the skills learned within the chapter. Students use critical thinking to experiment with new skills to complete each project.

9. Open the Phone Book report in Layout view. Delete the control containing the date. Change the title of the report to Contact Phone List.
10. Save the changes to the report.
11. If requested to do so by your instructor, add your first and last names to the end of the title and save the changes to the report.
12. Submit the revised database in the format specified by your instructor.
13. a. Why would you use a template instead of creating a database from scratch with just the fields you need?
    b. The Attachment data type allows you to attach files to a database record. If you were using this database for a job search, what specific documents might you attach to a Contacts record?

Analyze, Correct, Improve

Analyze a database, correct all errors, and improve the design.

Correcting Errors in the Table Structure
Note: To complete this assignment, you will be required to use the Data Files for Students. Visit www.cengage.com/ct/studentdownload for detailed instructions or contact your instructor for information about accessing the required files.

Instructions: Analyze SciFi Movies is a database containing information on classic science fiction movies that your film professor would like to use for teaching. The Movie table shown in Figure 1–85 contains errors to the table structure. Your professor has asked you to correct the errors and make some improvements to the database. Start Access and open the Analyze SciFi Movies database from the Data Files for Students.

Figure 1–85

1. Correct Movie Number should be the primary key for the Movie table. The ID field should not be a field in the table. The Rating field represents a numerical rating system of one to four to indicate the quality of the movie. Your instructor wants to be able to find the average rating for films directed by a particular director. Only integers should be stored in both the Rating and the Length (Minutes) fields.

2. Improve The default field size for Short Text fields is 255. Changing the field size to more accurately represent the maximum number of characters that can be stored in a field is one way to improve the accuracy of the data. The Movie Number, Director Number, and Awards fields should have a maximum size of 3 characters. The Year Made field should have a maximum field size of 4. The Movie Name and Studio fields should have a maximum field size of 50. If instructed to do so by your instructor, rename the Movie table as Movie Last Name where Last Name is your last name. Submit the revised database in the format specified by your instructor.

3. The Awards field currently has a data type of Short Text, but the only values that will be stored in that field are Yes and No to indicate whether the movie won any awards. What would be a more appropriate data type for this field?

> **Analyze, Correct, Improve** projects call on the students to analyze a file, discover errors in it, fix the errors, and then improve upon the file using the skills they learned in the chapter.

Textbook Walk-Through

STUDENT ASSIGNMENTS

In the Labs

Design, create, modify, and/or use a database following the guidelines, concepts, and skills presented in this chapter. Labs are listed in order of increasing difficulty. Labs 1 and 2, which increase in difficulty, require you to create solutions based on what you learned in the chapter; Lab 3 requires you to create a solution, which uses cloud and web technologies, by learning and investigating on your own from general guidance.

Lab 1: Creating Objects for the Dartt Offsite Services Database

Problem: Dartt Offsite Services is a local company that provides offsite data services and solutions. The company provides remote data backup, disaster recovery planning and services, website backup, and offsite storage of paper documents for small businesses and nonprofit organizations. Service representatives are responsible for communicating data solutions to the client, scheduling backups and other tasks, and resolving any conflicts. The company recently decided to store its client and service rep data in a database. Each client is assigned to a single service rep, but each service rep may be assigned many clients. The database and the Service Rep table have been created, but the Monthly Salary field needs to be added to the table. The records shown in Table 1–6 must be added to the Service Rep table. The company plans to import the Client table from the Excel worksheet shown in Figure 1–86. Dartt would like to finish storing this data in a database and has asked you to help.

	A	B	C	D	E	F	G	H	I	J	K
1	Client Number	Client Name	Street	City	State	Postal Code	Amount Paid	Balance Due	Service Rep Number		
2	BBF32	Babbage CPA Firm	464 Linnell Dr.	Austin	SC	28796	$3,524.00	$567.85	24		
15	WEC05	Walburg Energy Company	12 Polk St.	Walburg	NC	28819	$1,567.45	$1,100.50	24		
16	WSC01	Wood Sports Complex	578 Central Ave.	Walburg	NC	28819	$2,250.00	$1,600.00	24		
17											

Figure 1–86

Note: To complete this assignment, you will be required to use the Data Files for Students. Visit www.cengage.com/ct/studentdownload for detailed information about accessing the required files.

Instructions: Perform the following tasks:
1. Start Access and open the Lab 1 Dartt Offsite Services.
2. Open the Service Rep table in Datasheet view and the table. The field has the Currency data type. Number field.
3. Add the records shown in Table 1–6.
4. Resize the columns to best fit the data. Save the.

Table 1–6 Data for Service Rep Table

Service Rep Number	Last Name	First Name	Street	City
21	Kelly	Jonna	25 Paint St.	Kyle
45	Scott	Josh	1925 Pine Rd.	Byron
24	Liu	Mia	265 Marble Dr.	Kyle
37	Martinez	Mike	31 Steel St.	Georgetown

In the Lab Three in-depth assignments in each chapter that require students to apply the chapter concepts and techniques to solve problems. One Lab is devoted entirely to Cloud and Web 2.0 integration.

Consider This: Your Turn exercises call on students to apply creative thinking and problem solving skills to design and implement a solution.

STUDENT ASSIGNMENTS Word Chapter 1

✹ Consider This: Your Turn

Apply your creative thinking and problem solving skills to design and implement a solution.

Note: To complete these assignments, you may be required to use the Data Files for Students. Visit www.cengage.com/ct/studentdownload for detailed instructions or contact your instructor for information about accessing the required files.

1: Design and Create a Photography Club Flyer
Personal

Part 1: As secretary of your school's Photography Club, you are responsible for creating and distributing flyers announcing the club. The flyer should contain two digital pictures appropriately resized; the Data Files for Students contains two pictures called Photography 1 and Photography 2, or you can use your own digital pictures if they are appropriate for the topic of the flyer. The flyer should contain the headline, Photography Club, and this signature line: Questions? Call Emily at (883) 555-0901. The body copy consists of the following text, in any order: Do you love photography? This is the club for you! All skill levels are welcome. Meetings every Tuesday at 5:00 p.m. in the Student Center (room 232). Bring your camera. We look forward to seeing you at our next meeting!

Use the concepts and techniques presented in this chapter to create and format this flyer. Be sure to check spelling and grammar. Submit your assignment and answers to the critical thinking questions in the format specified by your instructor.

Part 2: ⚫ You made several decisions while creating the flyer in this assignment: where to place text, how to format the text (i.e., font, font size, paragraph alignment, bulleted paragraphs, underlines, italics, bold, color, etc.), which graphics to use, where to position the graphics, how to format the graphics, and which page enhancements to add (i.e., borders and spacing). What was the rationale behind each of these decisions? When you proofread the document, what further revisions did you make and why? How would you recommend distributing this flyer?

2: Design and Create a Hot Air Balloon Rides Flyer
Professional

Part 1: As a part-time employee at Galaxy Recreations, your boss has asked you to create and distribute flyers announcing hot air balloon rides. The flyer should contain two digital pictures appropriately resized; the Data Files for Students contains two pictures called Hot Air Balloon 1 and Hot Air Balloon 2, or you can use your own digital pictures if they are appropriate for the topic of the flyer. The flyer should contain the headline, Hot Air Balloon Rides, and this signature line: For reservations, call (485) 555-2295. The body copy consists of the following text, in any order: Amazing sights from incredible heights! The experience of a lifetime. Fun for the whole family. No pets. Bring your camera. Open seven days a week from 10:00 a.m. to 4:00 p.m. Book your private tour with Galaxy Recreations today!

Use the concepts and techniques presented in this chapter to create and format this flyer. Be sure to check spelling and grammar. Submit your assignment in the format specified by your instructor.

Part 2: ⚫ You made several decisions while creating the flyer in this assignment: where to place text, how to format the text (i.e., font, font size, paragraph alignment, bulleted paragraphs, underlines, italics, bold, color, etc.), which graphics to use, where to position the graphics, how to format the graphics, and which page enhancements to add (i.e., borders and spacing). What was the rationale behind each of these decisions? When you proofread the document, what further revisions did you make and why? How would you recommend distributing this flyer?

Continued >

Office 2013 and Windows 8: Essential Concepts and Skills

Microsoft product screen shots used with permission from Microsoft Corporation.

Objectives

You will have mastered the material in this chapter when you can:

- Use a touch screen
- Perform basic mouse operations
- Start Windows and sign in to an account
- Identify the objects in the Windows 8 desktop
- Identify the apps in and versions of Microsoft Office 2013
- Run an app
- Identify the components of the Microsoft Office ribbon

- Create folders
- Save files
- Change screen resolution
- Perform basic tasks in Microsoft Office apps
- Manage files
- Use Microsoft Office Help and Windows Help

Office 2013 and Windows 8: Essential Concepts and Skills

This introductory chapter covers features and functions common to Office 2013 apps, as well as the basics of Windows 8.

Roadmap

In this chapter, you will learn how to perform basic tasks in Windows and the Office apps. The following roadmap identifies general activities you will perform as you progress through this chapter:

1. SIGN IN to an account
2. USE WINDOWS
3. USE Office APPS
4. FILE and Folder MANAGEMENT
5. SWITCH between APPS
6. SAVE and Manage FILES
7. CHANGE SCREEN RESOLUTION
8. EXIT Office APPS
9. USE ADDITIONAL Office APPS
10. USE Office and Windows HELP

At the beginning of the step instructions throughout the chapter, you will see an abbreviated form of this roadmap. The abbreviated roadmap uses colors to indicate chapter progress: gray means the chapter is beyond that activity, blue means the task being shown is covered in that activity, and black means that activity is yet to be covered. For example, the following abbreviated roadmap indicates the chapter would be showing a task in the Use Apps activity.

1 SIGN IN | 2 USE WINDOWS | 3 USE APPS | 4 FILE MANAGEMENT | 5 SWITCH APPS | 6 SAVE FILES

7 CHANGE SCREEN RESOLUTION | 8 EXIT APPS | 9 USE ADDITIONAL APPS | 10 USE HELP

Use the abbreviated roadmap as a progress guide while you read or step through the instructions in this chapter.

Introduction to the Windows 8 Operating System

Windows 8 is the newest version of Microsoft Windows, which is a popular and widely used operating system. An **operating system** is a computer program (set of computer instructions) that coordinates all the activities of computer hardware, such as memory, storage devices, and printers, and provides the capability for you to communicate with the computer.

The Windows operating system simplifies the process of working with documents and apps by organizing the manner in which you interact with the computer. Windows is used to run apps. An **app** (short for application) consists of programs designed to make users more productive and/or assist them with personal tasks, such as word processing or browsing the web.

The Windows 8 interface begins with the **Start screen**, which shows tiles (Figure 1). A **tile** is a shortcut to an app or other content. The tiles on the Start screen include installed apps that you use regularly. From the Start screen, you can choose which apps to run using a touch screen, mouse, or other input device.

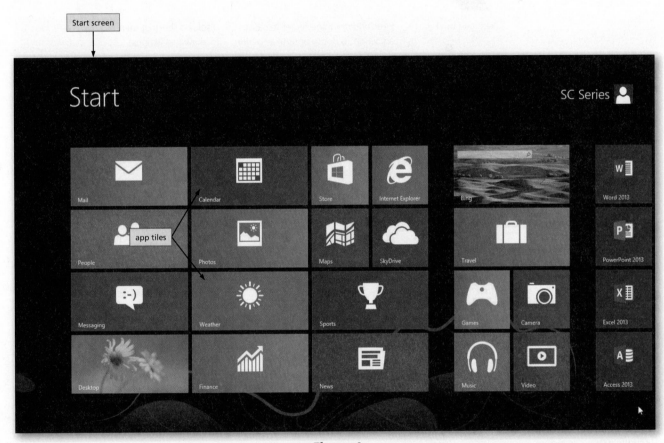

Figure 1

Using a Touch Screen and a Mouse

Windows users who have computers or devices with touch screen capability can interact with the screen using gestures. A **gesture** is a motion you make on a touch screen with the tip of one or more fingers or your hand. Touch screens are convenient because they do not require a separate device for input. Table 1 on the next page presents common ways to interact with a touch screen.

If you are using your finger on a touch screen and are having difficulty completing the steps in this chapter, consider using a stylus. Many people find it easier to be precise with a stylus than with a finger. In addition, with a stylus you see the pointer. If you still are having trouble completing the steps with a stylus, try using a mouse.

Table 1 Touch Screen Gestures

Motion	Description	Common Uses
Tap	Quickly touch and release one finger one time.	Activate a link (built-in connection) Press a button Run a program or an app
Double-tap	Quickly touch and release one finger two times.	Run a program or an app Zoom in (show a smaller area on the screen, so that contents appear larger) at the location of the double-tap
Press and hold	Press and hold one finger to cause an action to occur, or until an action occurs.	Display a shortcut menu (immediate access to allowable actions) Activate a mode enabling you to move an item with one finger to a new location
Drag, or slide	Press and hold one finger on an object and then move the finger to the new location.	Move an item around the screen Scroll
Swipe	Press and hold one finger and then move the finger horizontally or vertically on the screen.	Select an object Swipe from edge to display a bar such as the Charms bar, Apps bar, and Navigation bar (all discussed later)
Stretch	Move two fingers apart.	Zoom in (show a smaller area on the screen, so that contents appear larger)
Pinch	Move two fingers together.	Zoom out (show a larger area on the screen, so that contents appear smaller)

© 2014 Cengage Learning

BTW

BTWs

For a complete list of the BTWs found in the margins of this book, visit the BTW resource on the Student Companion Site located on www.cengagebrain.com. For detailed instructions about accessing available resources, visit www.cengage.com/ct/studentdownload or contact your instructor for information about accessing the required files.

BTW

Touch Screen Differences

The Office and Windows interfaces may vary if you are using a touch screen. For this reason, you might notice that the function or appearance of your touch screen differs slightly from this chapter's presentation.

CONSIDER THIS

Will your screen look different if you are using a touch screen?

The Windows and Microsoft Office interface varies slightly if you are using a touch screen. For this reason, you might notice that your screen looks slightly different from the screens in this chapter.

Windows users who do not have touch screen capabilities typically work with a mouse that has at least two buttons. For a right-handed user, the left button usually is the primary mouse button, and the right mouse button is the secondary mouse button. Left-handed people, however, can reverse the function of these buttons.

Table 2 explains how to perform a variety of mouse operations. Some apps also use keys in combination with the mouse to perform certain actions. For example, when you hold down the CTRL key while rolling the mouse wheel, text on the screen may become larger or smaller based on the direction you roll the wheel. The function of the mouse buttons and the wheel varies depending on the app.

Operation	Mouse Action	Example*
Point	Move the mouse until the pointer on the desktop is positioned on the item of choice.	Position the pointer on the screen.
Click	Press and release the primary mouse button, which usually is the left mouse button.	Select or deselect items on the screen or run an app or app feature.
Right-click	Press and release the secondary mouse button, which usually is the right mouse button.	Display a shortcut menu.
Double-click	Quickly press and release the primary mouse button twice without moving the mouse.	Run an app or app feature.
Triple-click	Quickly press and release the primary mouse button three times without moving the mouse.	Select a paragraph.
Drag	Point to an item, hold down the primary mouse button, move the item to the desired location on the screen, and then release the mouse button.	Move an object from one location to another or draw pictures.
Right-drag	Point to an item, hold down the right mouse button, move the item to the desired location on the screen, and then release the right mouse button.	Display a shortcut menu after moving an object from one location to another.
Rotate wheel	Roll the wheel forward or backward.	Scroll vertically (up and down).
Free-spin wheel	Whirl the wheel forward or backward so that it spins freely on its own.	Scroll through many pages in seconds.
Press wheel	Press the wheel button while moving the mouse.	Scroll continuously.
Tilt wheel	Press the wheel toward the right or left.	Scroll horizontally (left and right).
Press thumb button	Press the button on the side of the mouse with your thumb.	Move forward or backward through webpages and/or control media, games, etc.

Table 2 Mouse Operations

*Note: The examples presented in this column are discussed as they are demonstrated in this chapter.

© 2014 Cengage Learning

Scrolling

A **scroll bar** is a horizontal or vertical bar that appears when the contents of an area may not be visible completely on the screen (Figure 2). A scroll bar contains **scroll arrows** and a **scroll box** that enable you to view areas that currently cannot be seen on the screen. Tapping or clicking the up and down scroll arrows moves the screen content up or down one line. You also can tap or click above or below the scroll box to move up or down a section, or drag the scroll box up or down to move to a specific location.

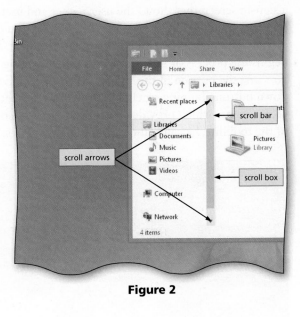

scroll bar

scroll arrows

scroll box

Figure 2

What should you do if you are running Windows 7 instead of Windows 8?
Although Windows 8 includes several user interface and feature enhancements, many of the steps in this chapter work in both Windows 7 and Windows 8. If you have any questions about differences between the two operating systems or how to perform tasks in an earlier version of Windows, contact your instructor.

CONSIDER THIS

Keyboard Shortcuts

In many cases, you can use the keyboard instead of the mouse to accomplish a task. To perform tasks using the keyboard, you press one or more keyboard keys, sometimes identified as a **keyboard shortcut**. Some keyboard shortcuts consist of a single key, such as the F1 key. For example, to obtain help in many apps, you can press the F1 key. Other keyboard shortcuts consist of multiple keys, in which case a plus sign separates the key names, such as CTRL+ESC. This notation means to press and hold down the first key listed, press one or more additional keys, and then release all keys. For example, to display the Start screen, press CTRL+ESC, that is, hold down the CTRL key, press the ESC key, and then release both keys.

Starting Windows

It is not unusual for multiple people to use the same computer in a work, educational, recreational, or home setting. Windows enables each user to establish a **user account**, which identifies to Windows the resources, such as apps and storage locations, a user can access when working with the computer.

Each user account has a user name and may have a password and an icon, as well. A **user name** is a unique combination of letters or numbers that identifies a specific user to Windows. A **password** is a private combination of letters, numbers, and special characters associated with the user name that allows access to a user's account resources. An icon is a small image that represents an object, thus a **user icon** is a picture associated with a user name.

When you turn on a computer, Windows starts and displays a **lock screen** consisting of the time and date (Figure 3a). To unlock the screen, swipe up or click the lock screen. Depending on your computer's settings, Windows may or may not display a sign-in screen that shows the user names and user icons for users who have accounts on the computer (Figure 3b). This **sign-in screen** enables you to sign in to your user account and makes the computer available for use. Tapping or clicking the user icon begins the process of signing in, also called logging on, to your user account.

At the bottom of the sign-in screen is the 'Ease of access' button and a Shut down button. Tapping or clicking the 'Ease of access' button displays the Ease of access menu, which provides tools to optimize a computer to accommodate the needs of the mobility, hearing, and vision impaired users. Tapping or clicking the Shut down

Figure 3a

Note: To help you locate screen elements that are referenced in the step instructions, such as buttons and commands, this book uses red boxes to point to these screen elements.

SC Series user icon

Figure 3b

BTW

Q&As

For a complete list of the Q&As found in many of the step-by-step sequences in this book, visit the Q&A resource on the Student Companion Site located on www.cengagebrain.com. For detailed instructions about accessing available resources, visit www.cengage.com/ct/studentdownload or contact your instructor for information about accessing the required files.

button displays a menu containing commands related to restarting the computer, putting it in a low-power state, and shutting it down. The commands available on your computer may differ.

- The Sleep command saves your work, turns off the computer fans and hard disk, and places the computer in a lower-power state. To wake the computer from sleep mode, press the power button or lift a laptop's cover, and sign in to your account.
- The Shut down command exits running apps, shuts down Windows, and then turns off the computer.
- The Restart command exits running apps, shuts down Windows, and then restarts Windows.

To Sign In to an Account

1 SIGN IN | 2 USE WINDOWS | 3 USE APPS | 4 FILE MANAGEMENT | 5 SWITCH APPS | 6 SAVE FILES
7 CHANGE SCREEN RESOLUTION | 8 EXIT APPS | 9 USE ADDITIONAL APPS | 10 USE HELP

The following steps, which use SC Series as the user name, sign in to an account based on a typical Windows installation. *Why? After starting Windows, you might be required to sign in to an account to access the computer's resources.* You may need to ask your instructor how to sign in to your account. If you are using Windows 7, skip these steps and instead perform the steps in the yellow box that immediately follows these Windows 8 steps.

1

- Swipe up or click the lock screen (shown in Figure 3a) to display a sign-in screen (shown in Figure 3b).
- Tap or click the user icon (for SC Series, in this case) on the sign-in screen, which depending on settings, either will display a second sign-in screen that contains a Password text box (Figure 4) or will display the Windows Start screen (shown in Figure 5 on the next page).

Q&A

Why do I not see a user icon?
Your computer may require you to type a user name instead of tapping or clicking an icon.

What is a text box?
A text box is a rectangular box in which you type text.

Why does my screen not show a Password text box?
Your account does not require a password.

password text box

SC Series

Submit button

'Ease of access' button

Shut down button

Figure 4

- If Windows displays a sign-in screen with a Password text box, type your password in the text box.

2

- Tap or click the Submit button (shown in Figure 4 on the previous page) to sign in to your account and display the Windows Start screen (Figure 5).

Q&A

Why does my Start screen look different from the one in Figure 5?
The Windows Start screen is customizable, and your school or employer may have modified the screen to meet its needs. Also, your screen resolution, which affects the size of the elements on the screen, may differ from the screen resolution used in this book. Later in this chapter, you learn how to change screen resolution.

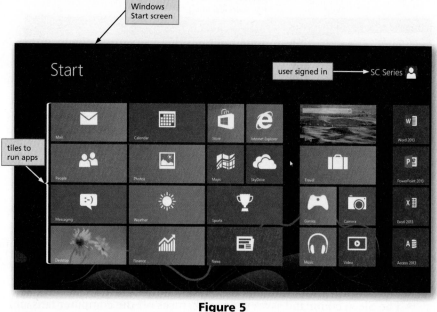

Figure 5

How do I type if my tablet has no keyboard?
You can use your fingers to press keys on a keyboard that appears on the screen, called an on-screen keyboard, or you can purchase a separate physical keyboard that attaches to or wirelessly communicates with the tablet.

TO SIGN IN TO AN ACCOUNT USING WINDOWS 7

If you are using Windows 7, perform these steps to sign in to an account instead of the previous steps that use Windows 8.

1. Click the user icon on the Welcome screen; depending on settings, this either will display a password text box or will sign in to the account and display the Windows 7 desktop.

2. If Windows 7 displays a password text box, type your password in the text box and then click the arrow button to sign in to the account and display the Windows 7 desktop.

The Windows Start Screen

BTW

Modern UI
The new Windows 8 user interface also is referred to as the Modern UI (user interface).

The Windows Start screen provides a scrollable space for you to access apps that have been pinned to the Start screen (shown in Figure 5). Pinned apps appear as tiles on the Start screen. In addition to running apps, you can perform tasks such as pinning apps (placing tiles) on the Start screen, moving the tiles around the Start screen, and unpinning apps (removing tiles) from the Start screen.

If you swipe up from the bottom of or right-click an open space on the Start screen, the App bar will appear. The **App bar** includes a button that enables you to display all of your apps. When working with tiles, the App bar also provides options for manipulating the tiles, such as resizing them.

CONSIDER THIS

How do you pin apps, move tiles, and unpin apps?

- To pin an app, swipe up from the bottom of the Start screen or right-click an open space on the Start screen to display the App bar, tap or click the All apps button on the App bar to display the Apps list, swipe down on or right-click the app you want to pin, and then tap or click the 'Pin to Start' button on the App bar. One way to return to the Start screen is to swipe up from the bottom or right-click an open space in the Apps list and then tap or click the All apps button again.

- To move a tile, drag the tile to the desired location.

- To unpin an app, swipe down on or right-click the app to display the App bar and then tap or click the 'Unpin from Start' button on the App bar.

Introduction to Microsoft Office 2013

Microsoft Office 2013 is the newest version of Microsoft Office, offering features that provide users with better functionality and easier ways to work with the various files they create. These features include enhanced design tools, such as improved picture formatting tools and new themes, shared notebooks for working in groups, mobile versions of Office apps, broadcast presentations for the web, and a digital notebook for managing and sharing multimedia information.

Microsoft Office 2013 Apps

Microsoft Office 2013 includes a wide variety of apps such as Word, PowerPoint, Excel, Access, Outlook, Publisher, OneNote, InfoPath, SharePoint Workspace, and Lync:

- **Microsoft Word 2013**, or Word, is a full-featured word processing app that allows you to create professional-looking documents and revise them easily.
- **Microsoft PowerPoint 2013**, or PowerPoint, is a complete presentation app that enables you to produce professional-looking presentations and then deliver them to an audience.
- **Microsoft Excel 2013**, or Excel, is a powerful spreadsheet app that allows you to organize data, complete calculations, make decisions, graph data, develop professional-looking reports, publish organized data to the web, and access real-time data from websites.
- **Microsoft Access 2013**, or Access, is a database management system that enables you to create a database; add, change, and delete data in the database; ask questions concerning the data in the database; and create forms and reports using the data in the database.
- **Microsoft Outlook 2013**, or Outlook, is a communications and scheduling app that allows you to manage email accounts, calendars, contacts, and access to other Internet content.
- **Microsoft Publisher 2013**, or Publisher, is a desktop publishing app that helps you create professional-quality publications and marketing materials that can be shared easily.
- **Microsoft OneNote 2013**, or OneNote, is a note taking app that allows you to store and share information in notebooks with other people.
- **Microsoft InfoPath Designer 2013**, or InfoPath, is a form development app that helps you create forms for use on the web and gather data from these forms.
- **Microsoft SharePoint Workspace 2013**, or SharePoint, is a collaboration app that allows you to access and revise files stored on your computer from other locations.
- **Microsoft Lync 2013** is a communications app that allows you to use various modes of communications such as instant messaging, videoconferencing, and sharing files and apps.

Microsoft Office 2013 Suites

A **suite** is a collection of individual apps available together as a unit. Microsoft offers a variety of Office suites, including a stand-alone desktop app (boxed software), Microsoft Office 365, and Microsoft Office Web Apps. **Microsoft Office 365**, or Office 365, provides plans that allow organizations to use Office in a mobile setting while also being able to communicate and share files, depending upon the type of plan selected by the organization. **Microsoft Office Web Apps**, or Web Apps, are apps that allow you to edit and share files on the web using the familiar Office interface. Table 3 on the next page outlines the differences among these Office suites.

Apps/ Licenses	Office 365 Home Premium	Office 365 Small Business Premium	Office Home & Student	Office Home & Business	Office Professional
Word	✔	✔	✔	✔	✔
PowerPoint	✔	✔	✔	✔	✔
Excel	✔	✔	✔	✔	✔
Access	✔	✔			✔
Outlook	✔	✔		✔	✔
Publisher	✔	✔			✔
Lync		✔			
OneNote			✔	✔	✔
InfoPath		✔			
Licenses	5	5	1	1	1

Table 3 Office Suites

© 2014 Cengage Learning

During the Office 365 installation, you select a plan, and depending on your plan, you receive different apps and services. Office Web Apps do not require a local installation and are accessed through SkyDrive and your browser. **SkyDrive** is a cloud storage service that provides storage and other services, such as Office Web Apps, to computer users.

How do you sign up for a SkyDrive account?

• Use your browser to navigate to skydrive.live.com.

• Create a Microsoft account by tapping or clicking the 'Sign up now' link and then entering your information to create the account.

• Sign in to SkyDrive using your new account or use it in Office to save your files on SkyDrive.

Apps in a suite, such as Microsoft Office, typically use a similar interface and share features. Once you are comfortable working with the elements and the interface and performing tasks in one app, the similarity can help you apply the knowledge and skills you have learned to another app(s) in the suite. For example, the process for saving a file in Word is the same in PowerPoint, Excel, and the other Office apps. While briefly showing how to use several Office apps, this chapter illustrates some of the common functions across the apps and identifies the characteristics unique to these apps.

Running and Using an App

To use an app, you must instruct the operating system to run the app. Windows provides many different ways to run an app, one of which is presented in this section (other ways to run an app are presented throughout this chapter). After an app is running, you can use it to perform a variety of tasks. The following pages use Word to discuss some elements of the Office interface and to perform tasks that are common to other Office apps.

Word

Word is a full-featured word processing app that allows you to create many types of personal and business documents, including flyers, letters, memos, resumes, reports, fax cover sheets, mailing labels, and newsletters. Word also provides tools that enable you to create webpages and save these webpages directly on a web server. Word has many features designed to simplify the production of documents and add visual appeal. Using Word, you easily can change the shape, size, and color of text. You also can include borders, shading, tables, images, pictures, charts, and web addresses in documents.

To Run an App from the Start Screen

The Start screen contains tiles that allow you to run apps, some of which may be stored on your computer.
Why? When you install an app, for example, tiles are added to the Start screen for the various Office apps included in the suite.

The following steps, which assume Windows is running, use the Start screen to run an Office app based on a typical installation. You may need to ask your instructor how to run an Office app on your computer. Although the steps illustrate running the Word app, the steps to run any Office app are similar. If you are using Windows 7, skip these steps and instead perform the steps in the yellow box that immediately follows these Windows 8 steps.

1

- If necessary, scroll to display the Word tile on the Start screen (Figure 6).

Q&A
Why does my Start screen look different?
It may look different because of your computer's configuration. The Start screen may be customized for several reasons, such as usage requirements or security restrictions.

What if the app I want to run is not on the Start screen?
You can display all installed apps by swiping up from the bottom of the Start screen or right-clicking an open space on the Start screen and then tapping or clicking the All apps button on the App bar.

How do I scroll on a touch screen?
Use the slide gesture; that is, press and hold your finger on the screen and then move your finger in the direction you wish to scroll.

Figure 6

2

- Tap or click the Word 2013 tile to run the Word app and display the Word start screen (Figure 7).

Figure 7

❸

● Tap or click the Blank document thumbnail on the Word start screen to create a blank Word document in the Word window (Figure 8).

Q&A | What happens when you run an app?
| Some apps provide a means for you to create a blank document, as shown in Figure 7 on the previous page; others immediately display a blank document in an app window, such as the Word window shown in Figure 8. A **window** is a rectangular area that displays data and information. The top of a window has a **title bar**, which is a horizontal space that contains the window's name.

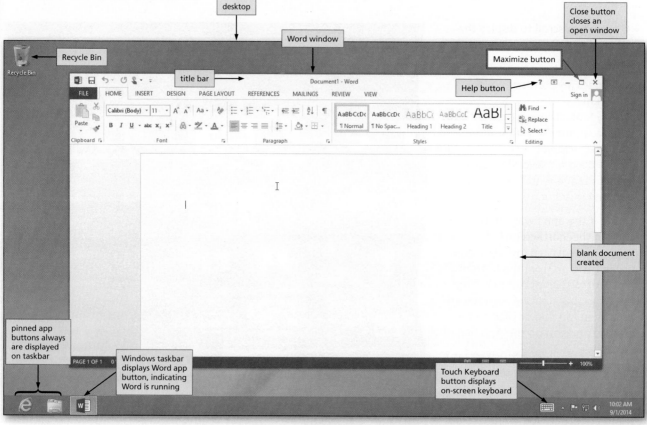

Figure 8

Other Ways
1. Tap or click Search charm on Charms bar, type app name in search box, tap or click app name in results list   2. Double-tap or double-click file created in app you want to run

BTW

Touch Keyboard
To display the on-screen touch keyboard, tap the Touch Keyboard button on the Windows taskbar. When finished using the touch keyboard, tap the X button on the touch keyboard to close the keyboard.

TO RUN AN APP USING THE START MENU USING WINDOWS 7

If you are using Windows 7, perform these steps to run an app using the Start menu instead of the previous steps that use Windows 8.

1. Click the Start button on the Windows 7 taskbar to display the Start menu.

2. Click All Programs at the bottom of the left pane on the Start menu to display the All Programs list.

3. If the app you wish to start is located in a folder, click, or scroll to and then click, the folder in the All Programs list to display a list of the folder's contents.

4. Click, or scroll to and then click, the app name in the list to run the selected app.

Windows Desktop

When you run an app in Windows, it may appear in an on-screen work area app, called the **desktop** (shown in Figure 8). You can perform tasks such as placing objects in the desktop, moving the objects around the desktop, and removing items from the desktop.

Some icons also may be displayed in the desktop. For instance, the icon for the **Recycle Bin**, the location of files that have been deleted, appears in the desktop by default. A **file** is a named unit of storage. Files can contain text, images, audio, and video. You can customize your desktop so that icons representing apps and files you use often appear in the desktop.

To Switch between an App and the Start Screen

1 SIGN IN | 2 USE WINDOWS | 3 USE APPS | 4 FILE MANAGEMENT | 5 SWITCH APPS | 6 SAVE FILES
7 CHANGE SCREEN RESOLUTION | 8 EXIT APPS | 9 USE ADDITIONAL APPS | 10 USE HELP

While working with an app or in the desktop, you easily can return to the Start screen. The following steps switch from the desktop to the Start screen. *Why? Returning to the Start screen allows you to run any of your other apps.* If you are using Windows 7, read these steps without performing them because Windows 7 does not have a Start screen.

❶
- Swipe in from the left edge of the screen, and then back to the left, or point to the lower-left corner of the desktop to display a thumbnail of the Start screen (Figure 9).

Figure 9

❷
- Tap or click the thumbnail of the Start screen to display the Start screen (Figure 10).

❸
- Tap or click the Desktop tile to redisplay the desktop (shown in Figure 8).

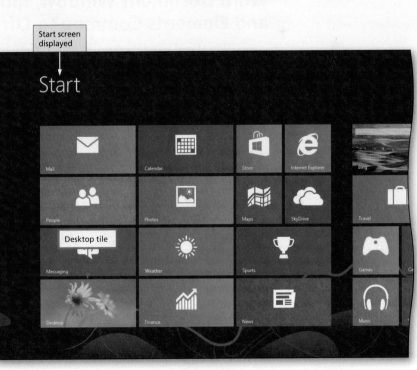

Figure 10

Other Ways

1. Press WINDOWS key to display Start screen

To Maximize a Window

Sometimes content is not visible completely in a window. One method of displaying the entire contents of a window is to **maximize** it, or enlarge the window so that it fills the entire screen. The following step maximizes the Word window; however, any Office app's window can be maximized using this step. *Why?* *A maximized window provides the most space available for using the app.*

1

- If the app window is not maximized already, tap or click the Maximize button (shown in Figure 8 on page OFF 12) next to the Close button on the window's title bar (the Word window title bar, in this case) to maximize the window (Figure 11).

Q&A What happened to the Maximize button?
It changed to a Restore Down button, which you can use to return a window to its size and location before you maximized it.

How do I know whether a window is maximized?
A window is maximized if it fills the entire display area and the Restore Down button is displayed on the title bar.

Figure 11

Other Ways

1. Double-tap or double-click title bar	2. Drag title bar to top of screen

Word Document Window, Ribbon, and Elements Common to Office Apps

The Word window consists of a variety of components to make your work more efficient and documents more professional. These include the document window, ribbon, mini toolbar, shortcut menus, Quick Access Toolbar, and Microsoft Account area. Most of these components are common to other Microsoft Office apps; others are unique to Word.

You view a portion of a document on the screen through a **document window** (Figure 12). The default (preset) view is **Print Layout view**, which shows the document on a mock sheet of paper in the document window.

Scroll Bars You use a scroll bar to display different portions of a document in the document window. At the right edge of the document window is a vertical scroll bar. If a document is too wide to fit in the document window, a horizontal scroll bar also appears at the bottom of the document window. On a scroll bar, the position of the scroll box reflects the location of the portion of the document that is displayed in the document window.

Status Bar The **status bar**, located at the bottom of the document window above the Windows taskbar, presents information about the document, the progress of current tasks, and the status of certain commands and keys; it also provides controls for viewing the document. As you type text or perform certain tasks, various indicators and buttons may appear on the status bar.

Figure 12

The left side of the status bar in Figure 12 shows the current page followed by the total number of pages in the document, the number of words in the document, and an icon to check spelling and grammar. The right side of the status bar includes buttons and controls you can use to change the view of a document and adjust the size of the displayed document.

Ribbon The ribbon, located near the top of the window below the title bar, is the control center in Word and other Office apps (Figure 13). The ribbon provides easy, central access to the tasks you perform while creating a document. The ribbon consists of tabs, groups, and commands. Each **tab** contains a collection of groups, and each **group** contains related commands. When you run an Office app, such as Word, it initially displays several main tabs, also called default or top-level tabs. All Office apps have a HOME tab, which contains the more frequently used commands.

Figure 13

In addition to the main tabs, the Office apps display **tool tabs**, also called contextual tabs (Figure 14), when you perform certain tasks or work with objects such as pictures or tables. If you insert a picture in a Word document, for example, the PICTURE TOOLS tab and its related subordinate FORMAT tab appear, collectively referred to as the PICTURE TOOLS FORMAT tab. When you are finished working with the picture, the PICTURE TOOLS FORMAT tab disappears from the ribbon. Word and other Office apps determine when tool tabs should appear and disappear based on tasks you perform. Some tool tabs, such as the TABLE TOOLS tab, have more than one related subordinate tab.

Figure 14

SEE THE ELEPHANT HABITAT

Figure 15

Items on the ribbon include buttons, boxes, and galleries (shown in Figure 13 on the previous page). A **gallery** is a set of choices, often graphical, arranged in a grid or in a list. You can scroll through choices in an in-ribbon gallery by tapping or clicking the gallery's scroll arrows. Or, you can tap or click a gallery's More button to view more gallery options on the screen at a time.

Some buttons and boxes have arrows that, when tapped or clicked, also display a gallery; others always cause a gallery to be displayed when tapped or clicked. Most galleries support **live preview**, which is a feature that allows you to point to a gallery choice and see its effect in the document — without actually selecting the choice (Figure 15). Live preview works only if you are using a mouse; if you are using a touch screen, you will not be able to view live previews.

Some commands on the ribbon display an image to help you remember their function. When you point to a command on the ribbon, all or part of the command glows in a shade of blue, and a ScreenTip appears on the screen. A **ScreenTip** is an on-screen note that provides the name of the command, available keyboard shortcut(s), a description of the command, and sometimes instructions for how to obtain help about the command (Figure 16).

Figure 16

Some groups on the ribbon have a small arrow in the lower-right corner, called a **Dialog Box Launcher**, that when tapped or clicked, displays a dialog box or a task pane with additional options for the group (Figure 17). When presented with a dialog box, you make selections and must close the dialog box before returning to the document. A **task pane**, in contrast to a dialog box, is a window that can remain open and visible while you work in the document.

BTW
Touch Mode
The Office and Windows interfaces may vary if you are using Touch mode. For this reason, you might notice that the function or appearance of your touch screen differs slightly from this chapter's presentation.

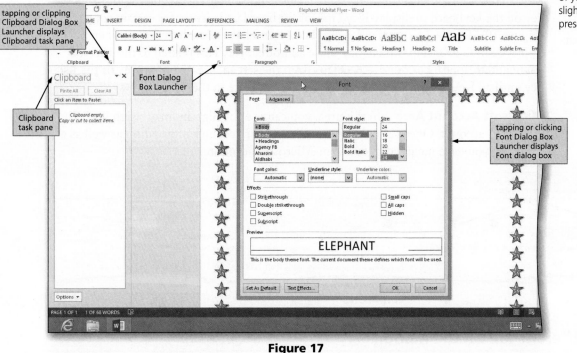

Figure 17

Mini Toolbar   The **mini toolbar**, which appears automatically based on tasks you perform, contains commands related to changing the appearance of text in a document (Figure 18). If you do not use the mini toolbar, it disappears from the screen. The buttons, arrows, and boxes on the mini toolbar vary, depending on whether you are using Touch mode versus Mouse mode. If you press and hold or right-click an item in the document window, Word displays both the mini toolbar and a shortcut menu, which is discussed in a later section in this chapter.

All commands on the mini toolbar also exist on the ribbon. The purpose of the mini toolbar is to minimize hand or mouse movement.

Figure 18

Quick Access Toolbar   The **Quick Access Toolbar**, located initially (by default) above the ribbon at the left edge of the title bar, provides convenient, one-tap or one-click access to frequently used commands (shown in Figure 16). The commands on the Quick Access Toolbar always are available, regardless of the task you are performing. The Touch/Mouse Mode button on the Quick Access Toolbar allows you to switch between Touch mode and Mouse mode. If you primarily are using touch gestures, Touch mode will add

BTW
Turning Off the Mini Toolbar
If you do not want the mini toolbar to appear, tap or click FILE on the ribbon to open the Backstage view, tap or click Options in the Backstage view, tap or click General (Options dialog box), remove the check mark from the 'Show Mini Toolbar on selection' check box, and then tap or click the OK button.

more space between commands in menus and on the ribbon so that they are easier to tap. While touch gestures are convenient ways to interact with Office apps, not all features are supported when you are using Touch mode. If you are using a mouse, Mouse mode will not add the extra space between buttons and commands. The Quick Access Toolbar is discussed in more depth later in the chapter.

KeyTips   If you prefer using the keyboard instead of the mouse, you can press the ALT key on the keyboard to display **KeyTips**, or keyboard code icons, for certain commands (Figure 19). To select a command using the keyboard, press the letter or number displayed in the KeyTip, which may cause additional KeyTips related to the selected command to appear. To remove KeyTips from the screen, press the ALT key or the ESC key until all KeyTips disappear, or tap or click anywhere in the app window.

Microsoft Account Area   In this area, you can use the Sign in link to sign in to your Microsoft account. Once signed in, you will see your account information as well as a picture if you have included one in your Microsoft account.

Figure 19

To Display a Different Tab on the Ribbon

1 SIGN IN | 2 USE WINDOWS | 3 USE APPS | 4 FILE MANAGEMENT | 5 SWITCH APPS | 6 SAVE FILES
7 CHANGE SCREEN RESOLUTION | 8 EXIT APPS | 9 USE ADDITIONAL APPS | 10 USE HELP

When you run Word, the ribbon displays nine main tabs: FILE, HOME, INSERT, DESIGN, PAGE LAYOUT, REFERENCES, MAILINGS, REVIEW, and VIEW. The tab currently displayed is called the **active tab**.

The following step displays the INSERT tab, that is, makes it the active tab. *Why? When working with an Office app, you may need to switch tabs to access other options for working with a document.*

1
• Tap or click INSERT on the ribbon to display the INSERT tab (Figure 20).

Experiment
• Tap or click the other tabs on the ribbon to view their contents. When you are finished, tap or click INSERT on the ribbon to redisplay the INSERT tab.

Q&A If I am working in a different Office app, such as PowerPoint or Access, how do I display a different tab on the ribbon?
Follow this same procedure; that is, tap or click the desired tab on the ribbon.

Figure 20

To Collapse and Expand the Ribbon and Use Full Screen Mode

To display more of a document or other item in the window of an Office app, some users prefer to collapse the ribbon, which hides the groups on the ribbon and displays only the main tabs, or to use **Full Screen mode**, which hides all the commands and just displays the document. Each time you run an Office app, the ribbon appears the same way it did the last time you used that Office app. The chapters in this book, however, begin with the ribbon appearing as it did at the initial installation of the software.

The following steps collapse, expand, and restore the ribbon in an Office app and then switch to Full Screen mode. *Why? If you need more space on the screen to work with your document, you may consider collapsing the ribbon or switching to Full Screen mode to gain additional workspace.*

1

- Tap or click the 'Collapse the Ribbon' button on the ribbon (shown in Figure 20) to collapse the ribbon (Figure 21).

Q&A What happened to the groups on the ribbon?
When you collapse the ribbon, the groups disappear so that the ribbon does not take up as much space on the screen.

What happened to the 'Collapse the Ribbon' button?
The 'Pin the ribbon' button replaces the 'Collapse the Ribbon' button when the ribbon is collapsed. You will see the 'Pin the ribbon' button only when you expand a ribbon by tapping or clicking a tab.

Figure 21

2

- Tap or click HOME on the ribbon to expand the HOME tab (Figure 22).

Q&A Why would I click the HOME tab?
If you want to use a command on a collapsed ribbon, tap or click the main tab to display the groups for that tab. After you select a command on the ribbon, the groups will be collapsed once again. If you decide not to use a command on the ribbon, you can collapse the groups by tapping or clicking the same main tab or tapping or clicking in the app window.

Experiment

- Tap or click HOME on the ribbon to collapse the groups again. Tap or click HOME on the ribbon to expand the HOME tab.

Figure 22

3

• Tap or click the 'Pin the ribbon' button on the expanded HOME tab to restore the ribbon.

• Tap or click the 'Ribbon Display Options' button to display the Ribbon Display Options menu (Figure 23).

Figure 23

4

• Tap or click Auto-hide Ribbon to hide all the commands from the screen (Figure 24).

• Tap or click the ellipsis to temporarily display the ribbon.

• Tap or click the 'Ribbon Display Options' button to display the Ribbon Display Options menu (shown in Figure 23).

• Tap or click 'Show Tabs and Commands' to exit Full Screen mode.

Figure 24

Other Ways

1. Double-tap or double-click a main tab on the ribbon   2. Press CTRL+F1

To Use a Shortcut Menu to Relocate the Quick Access Toolbar

1 SIGN IN | 2 USE WINDOWS | 3 USE APPS | 4 FILE MANAGEMENT | 5 SWITCH APPS | 6 SAVE FILES
7 CHANGE SCREEN RESOLUTION | 8 EXIT APPS | 9 USE ADDITIONAL APPS | 10 USE HELP

When you press and hold or right-click certain areas of the Word and other Office app windows, a shortcut menu will appear. A **shortcut menu** is a list of frequently used commands that relate to an object. *Why? You can use shortcut menus to access common commands quickly.* When you press and hold or right-click the status bar, for example, a shortcut menu appears with commands related to the status bar. When you press and hold or right-click the Quick Access Toolbar, a shortcut menu appears with commands related to the Quick Access Toolbar. The following steps use a shortcut menu to move the Quick Access Toolbar, which by default is located on the title bar.

1

- Press and hold or right-click the Quick Access Toolbar to display a shortcut menu that presents a list of commands related to the Quick Access Toolbar (Figure 25).

Q&A What if I cannot make the shortcut menu appear using the touch instruction?

When you use the press and hold technique, be sure to release your finger when the circle appears on the screen to display the shortcut menu. If the technique still does not work, you might need to add more space around objects on the screen, making it easier for you to press or tap them. Click the 'Customize Quick Access Toolbar' button and then click Touch/Mouse Mode on the menu.

Figure 25

2

- Tap or click 'Show Quick Access Toolbar Below the Ribbon' on the shortcut menu to display the Quick Access Toolbar below the ribbon (Figure 26).

Figure 26

3

- Press and hold or right-click the Quick Access Toolbar to display a shortcut menu (Figure 27).

4

- Tap or click 'Show Quick Access Toolbar Above the Ribbon' on the shortcut menu to return the Quick Access Toolbar to its original position (shown in Figure 25).

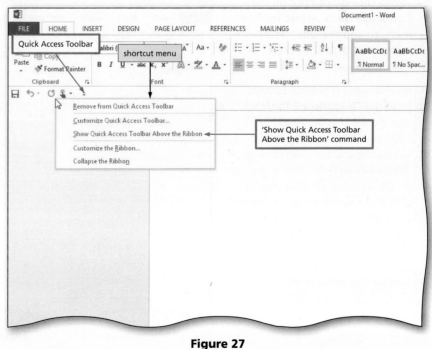

Figure 27

Other Ways

1. Tap or click 'Customize Quick Access Toolbar' button on Quick Access Toolbar, tap or click 'Show Below the Ribbon' or 'Show Above the Ribbon'

To Customize the Quick Access Toolbar

The Quick Access Toolbar provides easy access to some of the more frequently used commands in the Office apps. By default, the Quick Access Toolbar contains buttons for the Save, Undo, and Redo commands. You can customize the Quick Access Toolbar by changing its location in the window, as shown in the previous steps, and by adding more buttons to reflect commands you would like to access easily. The following steps add the Quick Print button to the Quick Access Toolbar. *Why? Adding the Quick Print button to the Quick Access Toolbar speeds up the process of printing.*

1

- Tap or click the 'Customize Quick Access Toolbar' button to display the Customize Quick Access Toolbar menu (Figure 28).

Q&A Which commands are listed on the Customize Quick Access Toolbar menu?
It lists commands that commonly are added to the Quick Access Toolbar.

What do the check marks next to some commands signify?
Check marks appear next to commands that already are on the Quick Access Toolbar. When you add a button to the Quick Access Toolbar, a check mark will be displayed next to its command name.

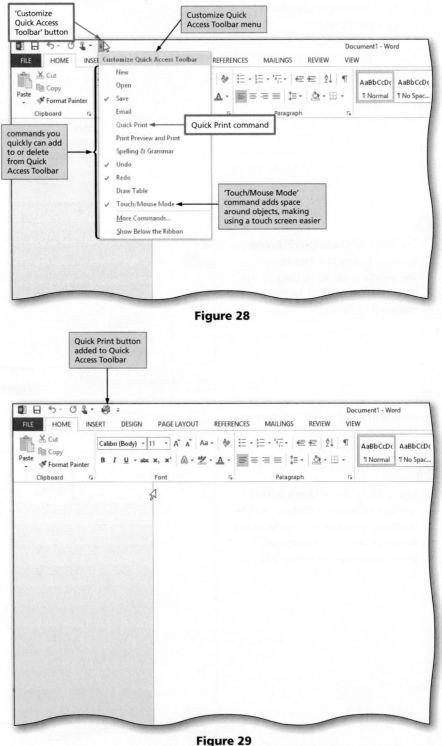

Figure 28

Figure 29

2

- Tap or click Quick Print on the Customize Quick Access Toolbar menu to add the Quick Print button to the Quick Access Toolbar (Figure 29).

Q&A How would I remove a button from the Quick Access Toolbar?
You would press and hold or right-click the button you wish to remove and then tap or click 'Remove from Quick Access Toolbar' on the shortcut menu or tap or click the 'Customize Quick Access Toolbar' button on the Quick Access Toolbar and then click the button name in the Customize Quick Access Toolbar menu to remove the check mark.

To Enter Text in a Document

The first step in creating a document is to enter its text by typing on the keyboard. By default, Word positions text at the left margin as you type. The following steps type this first line of a flyer. *Why? To begin creating a flyer, for example, you type the headline in the document window.*

1

- Type **SEE THE ELEPHANT HABITAT** as the text (Figure 30).

Q&A What is the blinking vertical bar to the right of the text?
The blinking bar is the insertion point, which indicates where text, graphics, and other items will be inserted in the document. As you type, the insertion point moves to the right, and when you reach the end of a line, it moves down to the beginning of the next line.

What if I make an error while typing?
You can press the BACKSPACE key until you have deleted the text in error and then retype the text correctly.

Why does a circle appear below the insertion point?
If you are using a touch screen, a selection handle (small circle) appears below the text so that you can format the text easily.

Figure 30

2

- Press the ENTER key to move the insertion point to the beginning of the next line (Figure 31).

Q&A Why did blank space appear between the entered text and the insertion point?
Each time you press the ENTER key, Word creates a new paragraph and inserts blank space between the two paragraphs. Depending on your settings, Office may or may not insert a blank space between the two paragraphs.

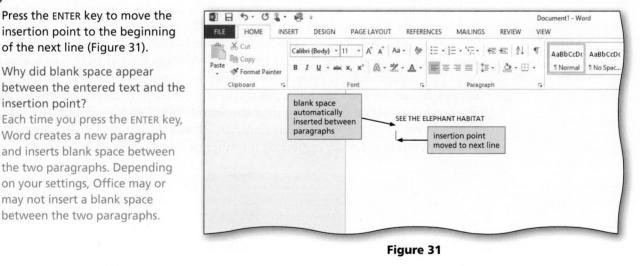

Figure 31

Saving and Organizing Files

While you are creating a document, the computer stores it in memory. When you save a document, the computer places it on a storage medium such as a hard disk, solid state drive (SSD), USB flash drive, or optical disc. The storage medium can be permanent in your computer, may be portable where you remove it from your computer, or may be on a web server you access through a network or the Internet.

BTW
File Type
Depending on your Windows settings, the file type .docx may be displayed immediately to the right of the file name after you save the file. The file type .docx is a Word 2013 document.

A saved document is referred to as a file. A **file name** is the name assigned to a file when it is saved. When saving files, you should organize them so that you easily can find them later. Windows provides tools to help you organize files.

CONSIDER THIS

How often should you save a document?

It is important to save a document frequently for the following reasons:

• The document in memory might be lost if the computer is turned off or you lose electrical power while an app is running.

• If you run out of time before completing a project, you may finish it at a future time without starting over.

Organizing Files and Folders

A file contains data. This data can range from a research paper to an accounting spreadsheet to an electronic math quiz. You should organize and store files in folders to avoid misplacing a file and to help you find a file quickly.

If you are taking an introductory computer class (CIS 101, for example), you may want to design a series of folders for the different subjects covered in the class. To accomplish this, you can arrange the folders in a hierarchy for the class, as shown in Figure 32.

The hierarchy contains three levels. The first level contains the storage medium, such as a hard disk. The second level contains the class folder (CIS 101, in this case), and the third level contains seven folders, one each for a different Office app that will be covered in the class (Word, PowerPoint, Excel, Access, Outlook, Publisher, and OneNote).

When the hierarchy in Figure 32 is created, the storage medium is said to contain the CIS 101 folder, and the CIS 101 folder is said to contain the separate Office folders (i.e., Word, PowerPoint, Excel, etc.). In addition, this hierarchy easily can be expanded to include folders from other classes taken during additional semesters.

The vertical and horizontal lines in Figure 32 form a pathway that allows you to navigate to a drive or folder on a computer or network. A **path** consists of a drive letter (preceded by a drive name when necessary) and colon, to identify the storage device, and one or more folder names. A hard disk typically has a drive letter of C. Each drive or folder in the hierarchy has a corresponding path.

By default, Windows saves documents in the Documents library, music in the Music library, photos in the Pictures library, and videos in the Videos library. A **library** helps you manage multiple folders stored in various locations on a computer and devices. It does not store the folder contents; rather, it keeps track of their locations so that you can access the folders and their contents quickly. For example, you can save pictures from a digital camera in any folder on any storage location on a computer. Normally, this would make organizing the different folders difficult. If you add

Figure 32

the folders to a library, however, you can access all the pictures from one location regardless of where they are stored.

The following pages illustrate the steps to organize the folders for this class and save a file in one of those folders:

1. Create the folder identifying your class.

2. Create the Word folder in the folder identifying your class.

3. Create the remaining folders in the folder identifying your class (one each for PowerPoint, Excel, Access, Outlook, Publisher, and OneNote).

4. Save a file in the Word folder.

5. Verify the location of the saved file.

To Create a Folder

1 SIGN IN | 2 USE WINDOWS | 3 USE APPS | 4 FILE MANAGEMENT | 5 SWITCH APPS | 6 SAVE FILES
7 CHANGE SCREEN RESOLUTION | 8 EXIT APPS | 9 USE ADDITIONAL APPS | 10 USE HELP

When you create a folder, such as the CIS 101 folder shown in Figure 32, you must name the folder. A folder name should describe the folder and its contents. A folder name can contain spaces and any uppercase or lowercase characters, except a backslash (\), slash (/), colon (:), asterisk (*), question mark (?), quotation marks ("), less than symbol (<), greater than symbol (>), or vertical bar (|). Folder names cannot be CON, AUX, COM1, COM2, COM3, COM4, LPT1, LPT2, LPT3, PRN, or NUL. The same rules for naming folders also apply to naming files.

The following steps create a class folder (CIS 101, in this case) in the Documents library. *Why? When storing files, you should organize the files so that it will be easier to find them later.* If you are using Windows 7, skip these steps and instead perform the steps in the yellow box that immediately follows these Windows 8 steps.

1

- Tap or click the File Explorer app button on the taskbar to run the File Explorer app (Figure 33).

Q&A Why does the title bar say Libraries?
File Explorer, by default, displays the name of the selected library or folder on the title bar.

Figure 33

2

- Tap or click the Documents library in the navigation pane to display the contents of the Documents library in the file list (Figure 34).

Q&A What if my screen does not show the Documents, Music, Pictures, and Videos libraries?
Double-tap or double-click Libraries in the navigation pane to expand the list.

Figure 34

3

- Tap or click the New folder button on the Quick Access Toolbar to create a new folder with the name, New folder, selected in a text box (Figure 35).

Q&A Why is the folder icon displayed differently on my computer?
Windows might be configured to display contents differently on your computer.

Figure 35

4

- Type CIS 101 (or your class code) in the text box as the new folder name.

  If requested by your instructor, add your last name to the end of the folder name.

- Press the ENTER key to change the folder name from New folder to a folder name identifying your class (Figure 36).

Q&A What happens when I press the ENTER key?
The class folder (CIS 101, in this case) is displayed in the file list, which contains the folder name, date modified, type, and size.

Figure 36

Other Ways

1. Press CTRL+SHIFT+N   2. Tap or click the New folder button (Home tab | New group)

To Create a Folder Using Windows 7

If you are using Windows 7, perform these steps to create a folder instead of the previous steps that use Windows 8.

1. Click the Windows Explorer button on the taskbar to run Windows Explorer.
2. Click the Documents library in the navigation pane to display the contents of the Documents library in the file list.
3. Click the New folder button on the toolbar to display a new folder icon with the name, New folder, selected in a text box.
4. Type `CIS 101` (or your class code) in the text box to name the folder.
5. Press the ENTER key to create the folder.

Folder Windows

The Documents window (shown in Figure 36) is called a folder window. Recall that a folder is a specific named location on a storage medium that contains related files. Most users rely on **folder windows** for finding, viewing, and managing information on their computers. Folder windows have common design elements, including the following (shown in Figure 36).

- The **address bar** provides quick navigation options. The arrows on the address bar allow you to visit different locations on the computer.
- The buttons to the left of the address bar allow you to navigate the contents of the navigation pane and view recent pages.
- The **Previous Locations arrow** displays the locations you have visited.
- The **Refresh button** on the right side of the address bar refreshes the contents of the folder list.
- The **search box** contains the dimmed words, Search Documents. You can type a term in the search box for a list of files, folders, shortcuts, and elements containing that term within the location you are searching. A **shortcut** is an icon on the desktop that provides a user with immediate access to an app or file.
- The **ribbon** contains five tabs used to accomplish various tasks on the computer related to organizing and managing the contents of the open window. This ribbon works similarly to the ribbon in the Office apps.
- The **navigation pane** on the left contains the Favorites area, Libraries area, Homegroup area, Computer area, and Network area.
- The **Favorites area** shows your favorite locations. By default, this list contains only links to your Desktop, Downloads, and Recent places.
- The **Libraries area** shows folders included in a library.

1 SIGN IN | 2 USE WINDOWS | 3 USE APPS | 4 FILE MANAGEMENT | 5 SWITCH APPS | 6 SAVE FILES
7 CHANGE SCREEN RESOLUTION | 8 EXIT APPS | 9 USE ADDITIONAL APPS | 10 USE HELP

To Create a Folder within a Folder

With the class folder created, you can create folders that will store the files you create using each Office app. The following steps create a Word folder in the CIS 101 folder (or the folder identifying your class). *Why?* *To be able to organize your files, you should create a folder structure.* If you are using Windows 7, skip these steps and instead perform the steps in the yellow box that immediately follows these Windows 8 steps.

1

- Double-tap or double-click the icon or folder name for the CIS 101 folder (or the folder identifying your class) in the file list to open the folder (Figure 37).

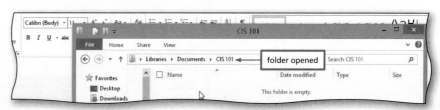

Figure 37

2

- Tap or click the New folder button on the Quick Access Toolbar to create a new folder with the name, New folder, selected in a text box folder.

- Type **Word** in the text box as the new folder name.

- Press the ENTER key to rename the folder (Figure 38).

New folder button

Word folder created

Figure 38

Other Ways

1. Press CTRL+SHIFT+N   2. Tap or click the New folder button (Home tab | New group)

TO CREATE A FOLDER WITHIN A FOLDER USING WINDOWS 7

If you are using Windows 7, perform these steps to create a folder within a folder instead of the previous steps that use Windows 8.

1. Double-click the icon or folder name for the CIS 101 folder (or the folder identifying your class) in the file list to open the folder.

2. Click the New folder button on the toolbar to display a new folder icon and text box for the folder.

3. Type **Word** in the text box to name the folder.

4. Press the ENTER key to create the folder.

To Create the Remaining Folders

The following steps create the remaining folders in the folder identifying your class (in this case, CIS 101). If you are using Windows 7, skip these steps and instead perform the steps in the yellow box that immediately follows these Windows 8 steps.

1 Tap or click New folder button on the Quick Access Toolbar to create a new folder with the name, New folder, selected in a text box.

2 Type **PowerPoint** in the text box as the new folder name.

3 Press the ENTER key to rename the folder.

4 Repeat Steps 1 through 3 to create each of the remaining folders, using Excel, Access, Outlook, Publisher, and OneNote as the folder names (Figure 39).

folders created in CIS 101 folder

Figure 39

TO CREATE THE REMAINING FOLDERS USING WINDOWS 7

If you are using Windows 7, perform these steps to create the remaining folders instead of the previous steps that use Windows 8.

1. Click the New folder button on the toolbar to create a new folder with the name, New folder, selected in a text box.

2. Type **PowerPoint** in the text box as the new folder name.

3. Press the ENTER key to rename the folder.

4. Repeat Steps 1 through 3 to create each of the remaining folders, using Excel, Access, Outlook, Publisher, and OneNote as the folder names.

To Expand a Folder, Scroll through Folder Contents, and Collapse a Folder

1 SIGN IN | 2 USE WINDOWS | 3 USE APPS | 4 FILE MANAGEMENT | 5 **SWITCH APPS** | 6 **SAVE FILES**
7 CHANGE SCREEN RESOLUTION | 8 EXIT APPS | 9 USE ADDITIONAL APPS | 10 USE HELP

Folder windows display the hierarchy of items and the contents of drives and folders in the file list. You might want to expand a library or folder in the navigation pane to view its contents, slide or scroll through its contents, and collapse it when you are finished viewing its contents. *Why? When a folder is expanded, you can see all the folders it contains. By contrast, a collapsed folder hides the folders it contains.* The following steps expand, slide or scroll through, and then collapse the folder identifying your class (CIS 101, in this case).

1

- Double-tap or double-click the Documents library in the navigation pane, which expands the library to display its contents and displays a black arrow to the left of the Documents library icon (Figure 40).

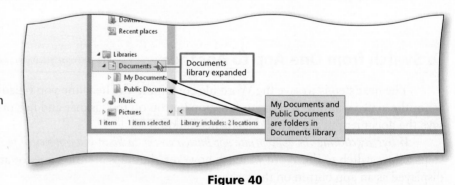

Figure 40

2

- Double-tap or double-click the My Documents folder, which expands the folder to display its contents and displays a black arrow to the left of the My Documents folder icon.

Q&A What is the My Documents folder? When you save files on your hard disk, the My Documents folder is the default save location.

- Double-tap or double-click the CIS 101 folder, which expands the folder to display its contents and displays a black arrow to the left of the folder icon (Figure 41).

Figure 41

Experiment

- Slide the scroll bar down or click the down scroll arrow on the vertical scroll bar to display additional folders at the bottom of the navigation pane. Slide the scroll bar up or click the scroll bar above the scroll box to move the scroll box to the top of the navigation pane. Drag the scroll box down the scroll bar until the scroll box is halfway down the scroll bar.

③

- Double-tap or double-click the folder identifying your class (CIS 101, in this case) to collapse the folder (Figure 42).

Q&A Why are some folders indented below others?
A folder contains the indented folders below it.

Figure 42

Other Ways
1. Point to display arrows in navigation pane, tap or click white arrow to expand or tap or click black arrow to collapse   2. Select folder to expand or collapse using arrow keys, press RIGHT ARROW to expand; press LEFT ARROW to collapse.

1 SIGN IN | 2 USE WINDOWS | 3 USE APPS | 4 FILE MANAGEMENT | 5 **SWITCH APPS** | 6 **SAVE FILES**
7 **CHANGE SCREEN RESOLUTION** | 8 **EXIT APPS** | 9 **USE ADDITIONAL APPS** | 10 **USE HELP**

To Switch from One App to Another

The next step is to save the Word file containing the headline you typed earlier. Word, however, currently is not the active window. You can use the app button on the taskbar and live preview to switch to Word and then save the document in the Word document window.

Why? *By clicking the appropriate app button on the taskbar, you can switch to the open app you want to use.* The steps below switch to the Word window; however, the steps are the same for any active Office app currently displayed as an app button on the taskbar.

①

- If you are using a mouse, point to the Word app button on the taskbar to see a live preview of the open document(s) or the window title(s) of the open document(s), depending on your computer's configuration (Figure 43).

Figure 43

2

- Tap or click the app button or the live preview to make the app associated with the app button the active window (Figure 44).

Q&A What if multiple documents are open in an app?
Tap or click the desired live preview to switch to the window you want to use.

Figure 44

To Save a File in a Folder

With the folders for storing your files created, you can save the Word document. **Why?** *Without saving a file, you may lose all the work you have done and will be unable to reuse or share it with others later.* The following steps save a file in the Word folder contained in your class folder (CIS 101, in this case) using the file name, Elephant Habitat.

1

- Tap or click the Save button (shown in Figure 44) on the Quick Access Toolbar, which depending on settings, will display either the Save As gallery in the Backstage view (Figure 45) or the Save As dialog box (Figure 46 on the next page).

Q&A What is the Backstage view?
The **Backstage view** contains a set of commands that enable you to manage documents and data about the documents.

What if the Save As gallery is not displayed in the Backstage view?
Tap or click the Save As tab to display the Save As gallery.

How do I close the Backstage view?
Tap or click the Back button in the upper-left corner of the Backstage view to return to the app window.

Figure 45

2

- If your screen displays the Backstage view, tap or click Computer, if necessary, to display options in the right pane related to saving on your computer; if your screen already displays the Save As dialog box, proceed to Step 3.

Q&A What if I wanted to save on SkyDrive instead?

You would tap or click SkyDrive. Saving on SkyDrive is discussed in a later section in this chapter.

- Tap or click the Browse button in the right pane to display the Save As dialog box (Figure 46).

Q&A Why does a file name already appear in the File name box?

Word automatically suggests a file name the first time you save a document. The file name normally consists of the first few words contained in the document. Because the suggested file name is selected, you do not need to delete it; as soon as you begin typing, the new file name replaces the selected text.

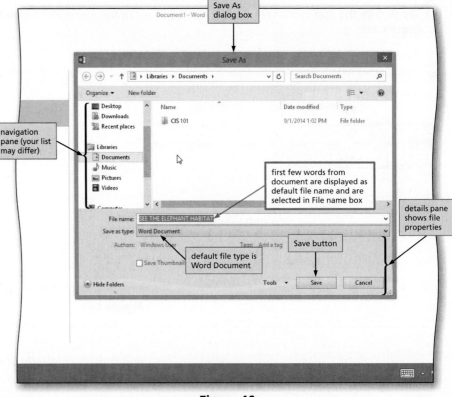

Figure 46

3

- Type **Elephant Habitat** in the File name box (Save As dialog box) to change the file name. Do not press the ENTER key after typing the file name because you do not want to close the dialog box at this time (Figure 47).

Q&A What characters can I use in a file name?

The only invalid characters are the backslash (\), slash (/), colon (:), asterisk (*), question mark (?), quotation mark ("), less than symbol (<), greater than symbol (>), and vertical bar (|).

Figure 47

4

- Navigate to the desired save location (in this case, the Word folder in the CIS 101 folder [or your class folder] in the My Documents folder in the Documents library) by performing the tasks in Steps 4a and 4b.

4a

- If the Documents library is not displayed in the navigation pane, slide to scroll or drag the scroll bar in the navigation pane until Documents appears.

- If the Documents library is not expanded in the navigation pane, double-tap or double-click Documents to display its folders in the navigation pane.

- If the My Documents folder is not expanded in the navigation pane, double-tap or double-click My Documents to display its folders in the navigation pane.

Figure 48

- If your class folder (CIS 101, in this case) is not expanded, double-tap or double-click the CIS 101 folder to select the folder and display its contents in the navigation pane (Figure 48).

Q&A | What if I do not want to save in a folder?
Although storing files in folders is an effective technique for organizing files, some users prefer not to store files in folders. If you prefer not to save this file in a folder, select the storage device on which you wish to save the file and then proceed to Step 5.

4b

- Tap or click the Word folder in the navigation pane to select it as the new save location and display its contents in the file list (Figure 49).

Figure 49

5

- Tap or click the Save button (Save As dialog box) to save the document in the selected folder in the selected location with the entered file name (Figure 50).

Q&A

How do I know that the file is saved?

While an Office app is saving a file, it briefly displays a message on the status bar indicating the amount of the file saved. In addition, the file name appears on the title bar.

Figure 50

Other Ways
1. Tap or click FILE on ribbon, tap or click Save As in Backstage view, tap or click Computer, tap or click Browse button, type file name (Save As dialog box), navigate to desired save location, tap or click Save button	2. Press F12, type file name (Save As dialog box), navigate to desired save location, tap or click Save button

Navigating in Dialog Boxes

Navigating is the process of finding a location on a storage device. While saving the Elephant Habitat file, for example, Steps 4a and 4b on the previous page navigated to the Word folder located in the CIS 101 folder in the My Documents folder in the Documents library. When performing certain functions in Windows apps, such as saving a file, opening a file, or inserting a picture in an existing document, you most likely will have to navigate to the location where you want to save the file or to the folder containing the file you want to open or insert. Most dialog boxes in Windows apps requiring navigation follow a similar procedure; that is, the way you navigate to a folder in one dialog box, such as the Save As dialog box, is similar to how you might navigate in another dialog box, such as the Open dialog box. If you chose to navigate to a specific location in a dialog box, you would follow the instructions in Steps 4a and 4b.

To Minimize and Restore a Window

1 SIGN IN | 2 USE WINDOWS | 3 USE APPS | 4 FILE MANAGEMENT | 5 SWITCH APPS | 6 SAVE FILES
7 CHANGE SCREEN RESOLUTION | 8 EXIT APPS | 9 USE ADDITIONAL APPS | 10 USE HELP

Before continuing, you can verify that the Word file was saved properly. To do this, you will minimize the Word window and then open the CIS 101 window so that you can verify the file is stored in the CIS 101 folder on the hard disk. A **minimized window** is an open window that is hidden from view but can be displayed quickly by clicking the window's app button on the taskbar.

In the following example, Word is used to illustrate minimizing and restoring windows; however, you would follow the same steps regardless of the Office app you are using. *Why? Before closing an app, you should make sure your file saved correctly so that you can find it later.*

The following steps minimize the Word window, verify that the file is saved, and then restore the minimized window. If you are using Windows 7, skip these steps and instead perform the steps in the yellow box that immediately follows these Windows 8 steps.

1

- Tap or click the Minimize button on the app's title bar (shown in Figure 50) to minimize the window (Figure 51).

Q&A Is the minimized window still available?

The minimized window, Word in this case, remains available but no longer is the active window. It is minimized as an app button on the taskbar.

- If the File Explorer window is not open on the screen, tap or click the File Explorer app button on the taskbar to make the File folder window the active window.

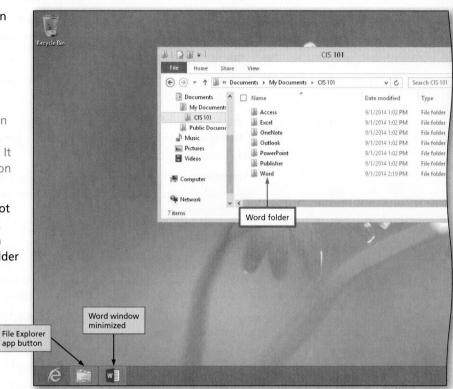

Figure 51

2

- Double-tap or double-click the Word folder in the file list to select the folder and display its contents (Figure 52).

Q&A Why does the File Explorer app button on the taskbar change?

A selected app button indicates that the app is active on the screen. When the button is not selected, the app is running but not active.

3

- After viewing the contents of the selected folder, tap or click the Word app button on the taskbar to restore the minimized window (as shown in Figure 50).

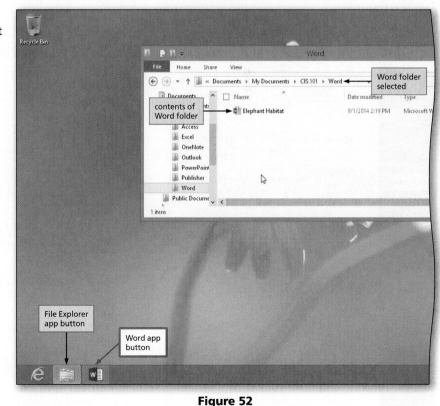

Figure 52

Other Ways

1. Press and hold or right-click title bar, tap or click Minimize on shortcut menu, tap or click taskbar button in taskbar button area

2. Press WINDOWS+M, press WINDOWS+SHIFT+M

TO MINIMIZE AND RESTORE A WINDOW USING WINDOWS 7

If you are using Windows 7, perform these steps to minimize and restore a window instead of the previous steps that use Windows 8.

1. Click the Minimize button on the app's title bar to minimize the window.
2. If the Windows Explorer window is not open on the screen, click the Windows Explorer button on the taskbar to make the Windows Explorer window the active window.
3. Double-click the Word folder in the file list to select the folder and display its contents.
4. After viewing the contents of the selected folder, click the Word button on the taskbar to restore the minimized window.

To Save a File on SkyDrive

1 SIGN IN | 2 USE WINDOWS | 3 USE APPS | 4 FILE MANAGEMENT | 5 SWITCH APPS | 6 SAVE FILES
7 CHANGE SCREEN RESOLUTION | 8 EXIT APPS | 9 USE ADDITIONAL APPS | 10 USE HELP

One of the features of Office is the capability to save files on SkyDrive so that you can use the files on multiple computers without having to use external storage devices such as a USB flash drive. Storing files on SkyDrive also enables you to share files more efficiently with others, such as when using Office Web Apps and Office 365.

In the following example, Word is used to save a file to SkyDrive. *Why? Storing files on SkyDrive provides more portability options than are available from storing files in the Documents library.*

You can save files directly to SkyDrive from within Word, PowerPoint, and Excel. The following steps save the current Word file to the SkyDrive. These steps require you have a Microsoft account and an Internet connection.

1

● Tap or click FILE on the ribbon to open the Backstage view (Figure 53).

Q&A | What is the purpose of the FILE tab?
The FILE tab opens the Backstage view for each Office app.

Figure 53

2

- Tap or click the Save As tab in the Backstage view to display the Save As gallery.

- Tap or click SkyDrive to display SkyDrive saving options or a Sign In button, if you are not signed in already to your Microsoft account (Figure 54).

Q&A What if my Save As gallery does not display SkyDrive as a save location?
Tap or click 'Add a Place' and proceed to Step 3.

Figure 54

3

- If your screen displays a Sign In button, tap or click it to display the Sign in dialog box (Figure 55).

Q&A What if the Sign In button does not appear?
If you already are signed into your Microsoft account, the Sign In button will not be displayed. In this case, proceed to Step 5.

Figure 55

4
- Type your Microsoft account user name and password in the text boxes and then tap or click the Sign in button (Sign in dialog box) to sign in to SkyDrive.

5
- Tap or click your SkyDrive to select your SkyDrive as the storage location (Figure 56).

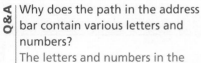

Figure 56

6
- Tap or click the Browse button to contact the SkyDrive server (which may take some time, depending on the speed of your Internet connection) and then display the Save As dialog box (Figure 57).

Q&A Why does the path in the address bar contain various letters and numbers?
The letters and numbers in the address bar uniquely identify the location of your SkyDrive files and folders.

7
- Tap or click the Save button (Save As dialog box) to save the file on SkyDrive.

Figure 57

To Sign Out of a Microsoft Account

If you are using a public computer or otherwise wish to sign out of your Microsoft account, you should sign out of the account from the Accounts gallery in the Backstage view. Signing out of the account is the safest way to make sure that nobody else can access online files or settings stored in your Microsoft account. *Why? For security reasons, you should sign out of your Microsoft account when you are finished using a public or shared computer. Staying signed in to your Microsoft account might enable others to access your files.*

The following steps sign out of a Microsoft account from Word. You would use the same steps in any Office app. If you do not wish to sign out of your Microsoft account, read these steps without performing them.

1 Tap or click FILE on the ribbon to open the Backstage view.

2 Tap or click the Account tab to display the Account gallery (Figure 58).

3 Tap or click the Sign out link, which displays the Remove Account dialog box. If a Can't remove Windows accounts dialog box appears instead of the Remove Account dialog box, click the OK button and skip the remaining steps.

Q&A | Why does a Can't remove Windows accounts dialog box appear?
If you signed in to Windows using your Microsoft account, then you also must sign out from Windows, rather than signing out from within Word. When you are finished using Windows, be sure to sign out at that time.

4 Tap or click the Yes button (Remove Account dialog box) to sign out of your Microsoft account on this computer.

Q&A | Should I sign out of Windows after removing my Microsoft account?
When you are finished using the computer, you should sign out of Windows for maximum security.

5 Tap or click the Back button in the upper-left corner of the Backstage view to return to the document.

Figure 58

Screen Resolution

Screen resolution indicates the number of pixels (dots) that the computer uses to display the letters, numbers, graphics, and background you see on the screen. When you increase the screen resolution, Windows displays more information on the screen, but the information decreases in size. The reverse also is true: as you decrease the screen resolution, Windows displays less information on the screen, but the information increases in size.

Screen resolution usually is stated as the product of two numbers, such as 1366 × 768 (pronounced "thirteen sixty-six by seven sixty-eight"). A 1366 × 768 screen resolution results in a display of 1366 distinct pixels on each of 768 lines, or about 1,050,624 pixels. Changing the screen resolution affects how the ribbon appears in Office apps and some Windows dialog boxes. Figure 59 shows the Word ribbon at screen resolutions of 1366 × 768 and 1024 × 768. All of the same commands are available regardless of screen resolution. The app (Word, in this case), however, makes changes to the groups and the buttons within the groups to accommodate the various screen resolutions. The result is that certain commands may need to be accessed differently depending on the resolution chosen. A command that is visible on the ribbon and available by tapping or clicking a button at one resolution may not be visible and may need to be accessed using its Dialog Box Launcher at a different resolution.

Comparing the two ribbons in Figure 59, notice the changes in content and layout of the groups and galleries. In some cases, the content of a group is the same in each resolution, but the layout of the group differs. For example, the same gallery and buttons appear in the Styles groups in the two resolutions, but the layouts differ. In other cases, the content and layout are the same across the resolution, but the level of detail differs with the resolution.

Figure 59a

Figure 59b

1 SIGN IN | 2 USE WINDOWS | 3 USE APPS | 4 FILE MANAGEMENT | 5 SWITCH APPS | 6 SAVE FILES
7 CHANGE SCREEN RESOLUTION | 8 EXIT APPS | 9 USE ADDITIONAL APPS | 10 USE HELP

To Change the Screen Resolution

If you are using a computer to step through the chapters in this book and you want your screen to match the figures, you may need to change your screen's resolution. *Why? The figures in this book use a screen resolution of 1366 × 768.* The following steps change the screen resolution to 1366 × 768. Your computer already may be set to 1366 × 768. Keep in mind that many computer labs prevent users from changing the screen resolution; in that case, read the following steps for illustration purposes.

1

● Tap or click the Show desktop button, which is located at the far-right edge of the taskbar, to display the Windows desktop.

Q&A I cannot see the Show desktop button. Why not?
When you point to the far-right edge of the taskbar, a small outline appears to mark the Show desktop button.

● Press and hold or right-click an empty area on the Windows desktop to display a shortcut menu that contains a list of commands related to the desktop (Figure 60).

Q&A Why does my shortcut menu display different commands?
Depending on your computer's hardware and configuration, different commands might appear on the shortcut menu.

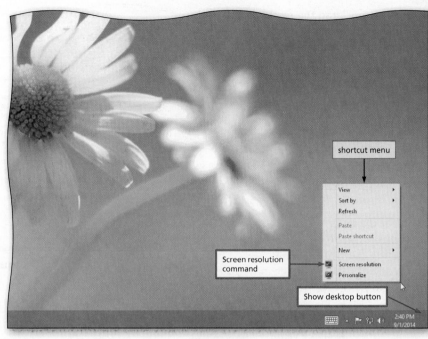

Figure 60

2

● Tap or click Screen resolution on the shortcut menu to open the Screen Resolution window (Figure 61).

3

● Tap or click the Resolution button in the Screen Resolution window to display the resolution slider.

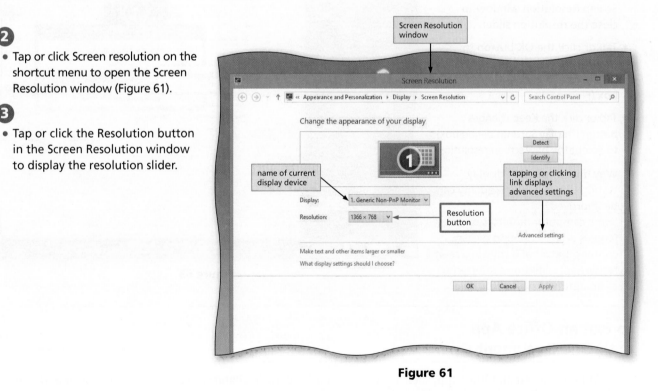

Figure 61

4

- If necessary, drag the resolution slider until the desired screen resolution (in this case, 1366 × 768) is selected (Figure 62).

Q&A What if my computer does not support the 1366 × 768 resolution?

Some computers do not support the 1366 ×768 resolution. In this case, select a resolution that is close to the 1366 × 768 resolution.

What is a slider?

A **slider** is an object that allows users to choose from multiple predetermined options. In most cases, these options represent some type of numeric value. In most cases, one end of the slider (usually the left or bottom) represents the lowest of available values, and the opposite end (usually the right or top) represents the highest available value.

Figure 62

5

- Tap or click an empty area of the Screen Resolution window to close the resolution slider.

- Tap or click the OK button to change the screen resolution and display the Display Settings dialog box (Figure 63).

- Tap or click the Keep changes button (Display Settings dialog box) to accept the new screen resolution.

Q&A Why does a message display stating that the image quality can be improved?

Some computer monitors or screens are designed to display contents better at a certain screen resolution, sometimes referred to as an optimal resolution.

Figure 63

To Exit an Office App with One Document Open

1 SIGN IN | 2 USE WINDOWS | 3 USE APPS | 4 FILE MANAGEMENT | 5 SWITCH APPS | 6 SAVE FILES
7 CHANGE SCREEN RESOLUTION | 8 EXIT APPS | 9 USE ADDITIONAL APPS | 10 USE HELP

When you exit an Office app, such as Word, if you have made changes to a file since the last time the file was saved, the Office app displays a dialog box asking if you want to save the changes you made to the file before it closes the app window. **Why?** *The dialog box contains three buttons with these resulting actions: the Save button saves the changes and then exits the Office app, the Don't Save button exits the Office app without saving changes, and the Cancel button closes the dialog box and redisplays the file without saving the changes.*

If no changes have been made to an open document since the last time the file was saved, the Office app will close the window without displaying a dialog box.

The following steps exit an Office app. In the following example, Word is used to illustrate exiting an Office app; however, you would follow the same steps regardless of the Office app you were using.

1

- If necessary, tap or click the Word app button on the taskbar to display the Word window on the desktop.

- If you are using a mouse, point to the Close button on the right side of the app's title bar, Word in this case (Figure 64).

Figure 64

2

- Tap or click the Close button to close the document and exit Word.

Q&A What if I have more than one document open in an Office app?
You could click the Close button for each open document. When you click the last open document's Close button, you also exit the Office app. As an alternative that is more efficient, you could press and hold or right-click the app button on the taskbar and then tap or click 'Close all windows' on the shortcut menu, or press ALT+F4 to close all open documents and exit the Office app.

3

- If a Microsoft Word dialog box appears, tap or click the Save button to save any changes made to the document since the last save.

Other Ways

1. Press and hold or right-click the Office app button on Windows taskbar, click Close window on shortcut menu   2. Press ALT + F4

To Copy a Folder to a USB Flash Drive

1 SIGN IN | 2 USE WINDOWS | 3 USE APPS | **4 FILE MANAGEMENT** | 5 SWITCH APPS | 6 SAVE FILES
7 CHANGE SCREEN RESOLUTION | 8 EXIT APPS | **9 USE ADDITIONAL APPS** | 10 USE HELP

To store files and folders on a USB flash drive, you must connect the USB flash drive to an available USB port on a computer. The following steps copy your CIS 101 folder to a USB flash drive. *Why? It often is good practice to have a backup of your files. Besides SkyDrive, you can save files to a portable storage device, such as a USB flash drive.* If you are using Windows 7, skip these steps and instead perform the steps in the yellow box that immediately follows these Windows 8 steps.

1

- Insert a USB flash drive in an available USB port on the computer to connect the USB flash drive.

Q&A How can I ensure the USB flash drive is connected?
In File Explorer, you can use the navigation bar to find the USB flash drive. If it is not showing, then it is not connected properly.

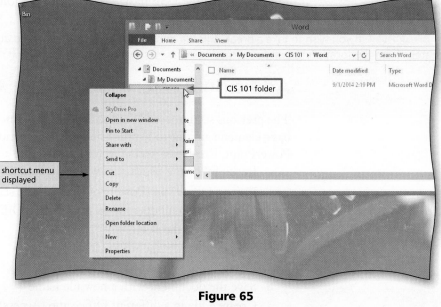

2

- Tap or click the File Explorer app button on the taskbar to make the folder window the active window.

- If necessary, navigate to the CIS 101 folder in the File Explorer window (see Step 4a on page OFF 33 for instructions about navigating to a folder location).

Figure 65

- Press and hold or right-click the CIS 101 folder to display a shortcut menu (Figure 65).

3

- Tap or point to Send to, which causes a submenu to appear (Figure 66).

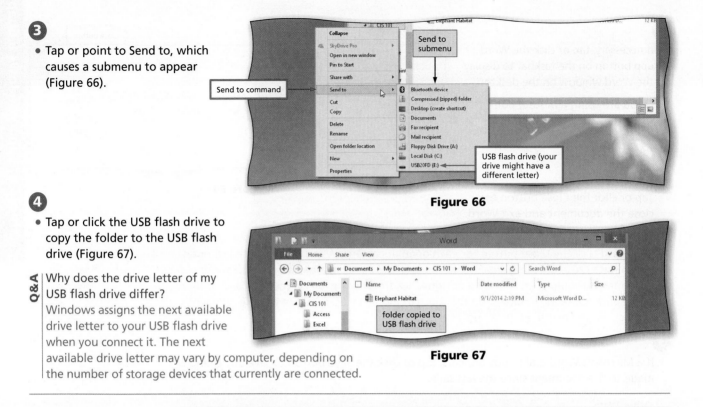

Figure 66

4

- Tap or click the USB flash drive to copy the folder to the USB flash drive (Figure 67).

Q&A Why does the drive letter of my USB flash drive differ?

Windows assigns the next available drive letter to your USB flash drive when you connect it. The next available drive letter may vary by computer, depending on the number of storage devices that currently are connected.

Figure 67

TO COPY A FOLDER TO A USB FLASH DRIVE USING WINDOWS 7

If you are using Windows 7, perform these steps to copy a folder to a USB flash drive instead of the previous steps that use Windows 8.

1. Insert a USB flash drive in an available USB port on the computer to open the AutoPlay window.
2. Click the 'Open folder to view files' link in the AutoPlay window to open the Windows Explorer window.
3. Navigate to the Documents library.
4. Right-click the CIS 101 folder to display a shortcut menu.
5. Point to Send to, which causes a submenu to appear.
6. Click the USB flash drive to copy the folder to the USB flash drive.

Break Point: If you wish to take a break, this is a good place to do so. To resume at a later time, continue to follow the steps from this location forward.

Additional Microsoft Office Apps

The previous section used Word to illustrate common features of Office and some basic elements unique to Word. The following sections present elements unique to PowerPoint, Excel, and Access, as well as illustrate additional common features of Office.

In the following pages, you will learn how to do the following:

1. Run an Office app (PowerPoint) using the search box.
2. Create two small documents in the same Office app (PowerPoint).
3. Close one of the documents.
4. Reopen the document just closed.
5. Create a document in a different Office app (Excel).
6. Save the document with a new file name.
7. Create a file in a different Office app (Access).
8. Close the file and then open the file.

PowerPoint

PowerPoint is a full-featured presentation app that allows you to produce compelling presentations to deliver and share with an audience (Figure 68). A PowerPoint **presentation** also is called a **slide show**. PowerPoint contains many features to design, develop, and organize slides, including formatting text, adding and editing video and audio clips, creating tables and charts, applying artistic effects to pictures, animating graphics, and collaborating with friends and colleagues. You then can turn your presentation into a video, broadcast your slide show on the web, or create a photo album.

Figure 68

(a) Slide 1 (Title)

Product Listing

Hand Blown Glass

Sea Shell Sculptures

Custom Jewelry

Rustic Wood Art

(b) Slide 2 (Text and Diagram)

Delivery Options

(c) Slide 3 (Text and Picture)

Figure 68 (Continued)

1 SIGN IN | 2 USE WINDOWS | 3 USE APPS | 4 FILE MANAGEMENT | 5 SWITCH APPS | 6 SAVE FILES
7 CHANGE SCREEN RESOLUTION | 8 EXIT APPS | 9 USE ADDITIONAL APPS | 10 USE HELP

To Run an App Using the Search Box

The following steps, which assume Windows is running, use the search box to run the PowerPoint app based on a typical installation; however, you would follow similar steps to run any Office app. *Why? Sometimes an app does not appear on the Start screen, so you can find it quickly by searching.* You may need to ask your instructor how to run apps for your computer. If you are using Windows 7, skip these steps and instead perform the steps in the yellow box that immediately follows these Windows 8 steps.

1

- Swipe in from the right edge of the screen or point to the upper-right corner of the screen to display the Charms bar (Figure 69).

upper-right corner

Charms bar

Search charm

Figure 69

②

- Tap or click the Search charm on the Charms bar to display the Search menu (Figure 70).

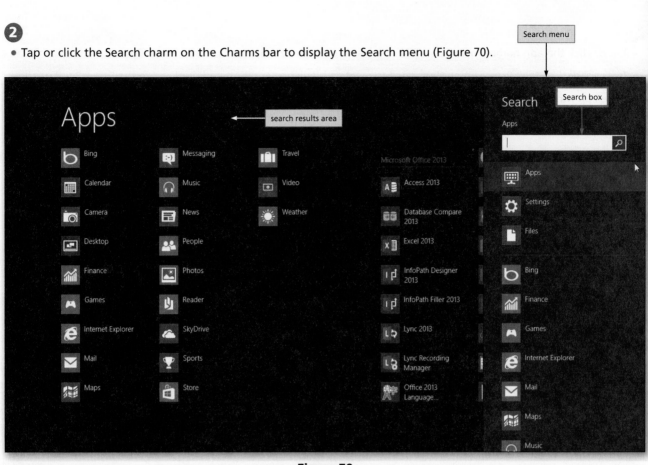

Figure 70

③

- Type **PowerPoint 2013** as the search text in the Search box and watch the search results appear in the Apps list (Figure 71).

Q&A Do I need to type the complete app name or use correct capitalization?
No, you need to type just enough characters of the app name for it to appear in the Apps list. For example, you may be able to type PowerPoint or powerpoint, instead of PowerPoint 2013.

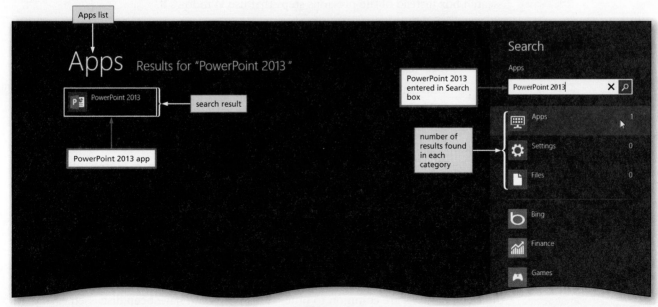

Figure 71

4

- Tap or click the app name, PowerPoint 2013 in this case, in the search results to run PowerPoint.

- Tap or click the Blank Presentation thumbnail to create a blank presentation and display it in the PowerPoint window.

- If the app window is not maximized, tap or click the Maximize button on its title bar to maximize the window (Figure 72).

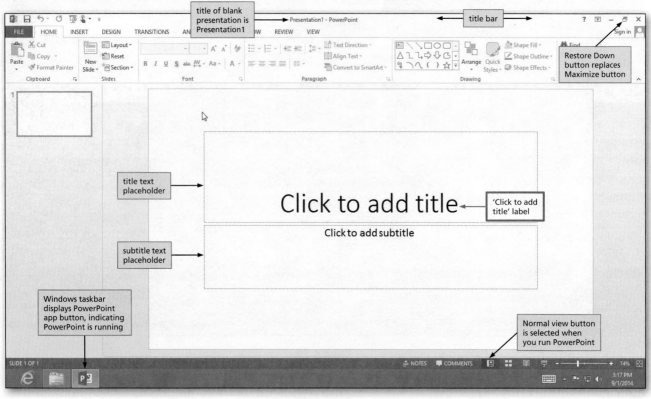

Figure 72

TO RUN AN APP USING THE SEARCH BOX USING WINDOWS 7

If you are using Windows 7, perform these steps to run an app using the search box instead of the previous steps that use Windows 8.

1. Click the Start button on the Windows 7 taskbar to display the Start menu.

2. Type **PowerPoint 2013** as the search text in the 'Search programs and files' text box and watch the search results appear on the Start menu.

3. Click the app name, PowerPoint 2013 in this case, in the search results on the Start menu to run PowerPoint.

4. Click the Blank Presentation thumbnail to create a blank presentation and display it in the PowerPoint window.

5. If the app window is not maximized, click the Maximize button on its title bar to maximize the window.

The PowerPoint Window and Ribbon

The PowerPoint window consists of a variety of components to make your work more efficient and documents more professional: the window, ribbon, mini toolbar, shortcut menus, Quick Access Toolbar, and Microsoft Account area. Many of these components are common to other Office apps and have been discussed earlier in this chapter. Other components, discussed in the following paragraphs and later in subsequent chapters, are unique to PowerPoint.

The basic unit of a PowerPoint presentation is a **slide**. A slide may contain text and objects, such as graphics, tables, charts, and drawings. **Layouts** are used to position this content on the slide. When you create a new presentation, the default **Title Slide** layout appears (shown in Figure 72). The purpose of this layout is to introduce the presentation to the audience. PowerPoint includes several other built-in standard layouts.

The default slide layouts are set up in **landscape orientation**, where the slide width is greater than its height. In landscape orientation, the slide size is preset to 10 inches wide and 7.5 inches high when printed on a standard sheet of paper measuring 11 inches wide and 8.5 inches high.

Placeholders   **Placeholders** are boxes with dashed or solid borders that are displayed when you create a new slide. All layouts except the Blank slide layout contain placeholders. Depending on the particular slide layout selected, title and subtitle placeholders are displayed for the slide title and subtitle; a content placeholder is displayed for text or a table, chart, picture, graphic, or movie. The title slide in Figure 73 has two text placeholders for the main heading, or title, and the subtitle.

Figure 73

Ribbon   The ribbon in PowerPoint is similar to the one in Word and the other Microsoft Office apps. When you run PowerPoint, the ribbon displays nine main tabs: FILE, HOME, INSERT, DESIGN, TRANSITIONS, ANIMATIONS, SLIDE SHOW, REVIEW, and VIEW.

To Enter Content in a Title Slide

1 SIGN IN | 2 USE WINDOWS | 3 USE APPS | 4 FILE MANAGEMENT | 5 SWITCH APPS | 6 SAVE FILES
7 CHANGE SCREEN RESOLUTION | 8 EXIT APPS | 9 USE ADDITIONAL APPS | 10 USE HELP

With the exception of a blank slide, PowerPoint assumes every new slide has a title. Many of PowerPoint's layouts have both a title text placeholder and at least one content placeholder. To make creating a presentation easier, any text you type after a new slide appears becomes title text in the title text placeholder. As you begin typing text in the title text placeholder, the title text also is displayed in the Slide 1 thumbnail in the Thumbnail pane. The title for this presentation is Kelitestone Crafts. The steps on the next page enter a presentation title on the title slide. *Why? In general, every presentation should have a title to describe what the presentation will be covering.*

1

- Tap or click the 'Click to add title' label located inside the title text placeholder (shown in Figure 72 on page OFF 48) to select the placeholder (Figure 74).

Q&A

What are the white squares that appear around the title text placeholder as I type the presentation title?
The white squares are sizing handles, which you can drag to change the size of the title text placeholder. Sizing handles also can be found around other placeholders and objects within an Office app.

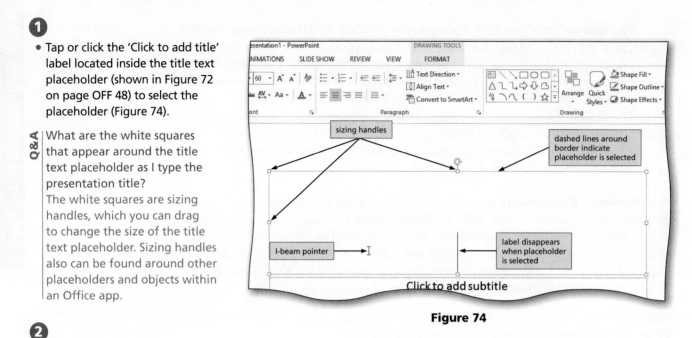

Figure 74

2

- Type **Kelitestone Crafts** in the title text placeholder. Do not press the ENTER key because you do not want to create a new line of text (Figure 75).

Figure 75

To Save a File in a Folder

The following steps save the presentation in the PowerPoint folder in the class folder (CIS 101, in this case) in the My Documents folder in the Documents library using the file name, Kelitestone Crafts.

1 Tap or click the Save button on the Quick Access Toolbar (shown in Figure 75), which depending on settings will display either the Save As gallery in the Backstage view or the Save As dialog box.

2 If your screen displays the Backstage view, tap or click Computer, if necessary, to display options in the right pane related to saving on your computer; if your screen already displays the Save As dialog box, proceed to Step 4.

3 Tap or click the Browse button in the right pane to display the Save As dialog box.

④ If necessary, type `Kelitestone Crafts` in the File name box (Save As dialog box) to change the file name. Do not press the ENTER key after typing the file name because you do not want to close the dialog box at this time.

⑤ Navigate to the desired save location (in this case, the PowerPoint folder in the CIS 101 folder [or your class folder] in the My Documents folder in the Documents library). For specific instructions, perform the tasks in Steps 5a through 5e.

⑤ₐ If the Documents library is not displayed in the navigation pane, slide to scroll or drag the scroll bar in the navigation pane until Documents appears.

⑤ᵦ If the Documents library is not expanded in the navigation pane, double-tap or double-click Documents to display its folders in the navigation pane.

⑤ᵧ If the My Documents folder is not expanded in the navigation pane, double-tap or double-click My Documents to display its folders in the navigation pane.

⑤ᵨ If your class folder (CIS 101, in this case) is not expanded, double-tap or double-click the CIS 101 folder to select the folder and display its contents in the navigation pane.

⑤ₑ Tap or click the PowerPoint folder in the navigation pane to select it as the new save location and display its contents in the file list.

⑥ Tap or click the Save button (Save As dialog box) to save the presentation in the selected folder in the selected location with the entered file name.

To Create a New Office Document from the Backstage View

1 SIGN IN | 2 USE WINDOWS | 3 USE APPS | 4 FILE MANAGEMENT | 5 SWITCH APPS | 6 SAVE FILES
7 CHANGE SCREEN RESOLUTION | 8 EXIT APPS | 9 USE ADDITIONAL APPS | 10 USE HELP

As discussed earlier, the Backstage view contains a set of commands that enable you to manage documents and data about the documents. *Why? From the Backstage view in PowerPoint, for example, you can create, open, print, and save presentations. You also can share documents, manage versions, set permissions, and modify document properties. In other Office 2013 apps, the Backstage view may contain features specific to those apps.* The following steps create a file, a blank presentation in this case, from the Backstage view.

①

• Tap or click FILE on the ribbon to open the Backstage view (Figure 76).

Q&A What is the purpose of the Info tab in the Backstage view?

The Info tab, which is selected by default when you click FILE on the ribbon, allows you to protect your document, inspect your document, and manage versions of your document as well as view all the file properties such as when the file was created.

Figure 76

2

- Tap or click the New tab in the Backstage view to display the New gallery (Figure 77).

Q&A Can I create documents through the Backstage view in other Office apps?
Yes. If the Office app has a New tab in the Backstage view, the New gallery displays various options for creating a new file.

Figure 77

3

- Tap or click the Blank Presentation thumbnail in the New gallery to create a new presentation (Figure 78).

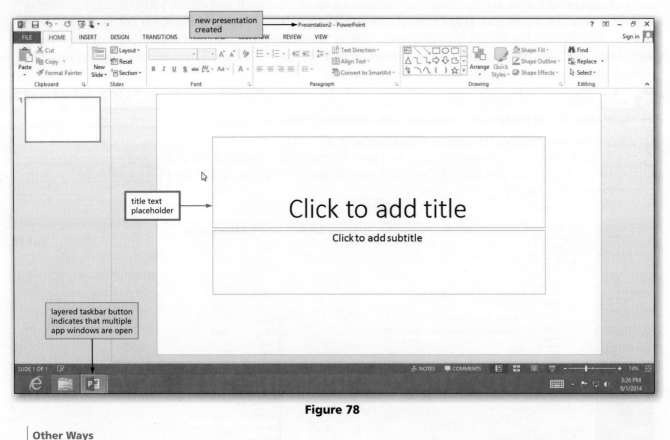

Figure 78

Other Ways

1. Press CTRL+N

To Enter Content in a Title Slide of a Second PowerPoint Presentation

The presentation title for this presentation is Elephant Habitat Opening. The following steps enter a presentation title on the title slide.

1 Tap or click the title text placeholder (shown in Figure 78) to select it.

2 Type **Elephant Habitat Opening** in the title text placeholder. Do not press the ENTER key (Figure 79).

Figure 79

To Save a File in a Folder

The following steps save the second presentation in the PowerPoint folder in the class folder (CIS 101, in this case) in the My Documents folder in the Documents library using the file name, Elephant Habitat Opening.

1 Tap or click the Save button on the Quick Access Toolbar (shown in Figure 79), which depending on settings will display either the Save As gallery in the Backstage view or the Save As dialog box.

2 If your screen displays the Backstage view, tap or click Computer, if necessary, to display options in the right pane related to saving on your computer; if your screen already displays the Save As dialog box, proceed to Step 4.

3 Tap or click the Browse button in the right pane to display the Save As dialog box.

4 If necessary, type **Elephant Habitat Opening** in the File name box (Save As dialog box) to change the file name. Do not press the ENTER key after typing the file name because you do not want to close the dialog box at this time.

5 If necessary, navigate to the desired save location (in this case, the PowerPoint folder in the CIS 101 folder [or your class folder] in the My Documents folder in the Documents library). For specific instructions, perform the tasks in Steps 5a through 5e on page OFF 51.

6 Tap or click the Save button (Save As dialog box) to save the presentation in the selected folder on the selected drive with the entered file name.

To Close an Office File Using the Backstage View

Sometimes, you may want to close an Office file, such as a PowerPoint presentation, entirely and start over with a new file. **Why else would I close a file?** *You also may want to close a file when you are finished working with it so that you can begin a new file.* The following steps close the current active Office file, that is, the Elephant Habitat Opening presentation, without exiting the active app (PowerPoint, in this case).

1
- Tap or click FILE on the ribbon (shown in Figure 79 on the previous page) to open the Backstage view (Figure 80).

2
- Tap or click Close in the Backstage view to close the open file (Elephant Habitat Opening, in this case) without exiting the active app.

Q&A What if the Office app displays a dialog box about saving?
Tap or click the Save button if you want to save the changes, tap or click the Don't Save button if you want to ignore the changes since the last time you saved, and tap or click the Cancel button if you do not want to close the document.

Can I use the Backstage view to close an open file in other Office apps, such as Word and Excel?
Yes.

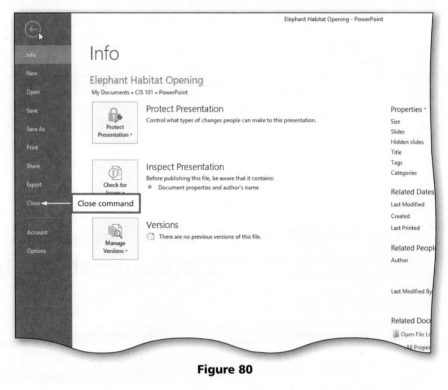

Figure 80

Other Ways

1. Press CTRL+F4

To Open a Recent Office File Using the Backstage View

You sometimes need to open a file that you recently modified. **Why?** *You may have more changes to make such as adding more content or correcting errors.* The Backstage view allows you to access recent files easily. The following steps reopen the Elephant Habitat Opening file just closed.

1
- Tap or click FILE on the ribbon to open the Backstage view.
- Tap or click the Open tab in the Backstage view to display the Open gallery (Figure 81).

2
- Tap or click the desired file name in the Recent Presentations list, Elephant Habitat Opening in this case, to open the file (shown in Figure 79 on the previous page).

Q&A Can I use the Backstage view to open a recent file in other Office apps, such as Word and Excel?
Yes, as long as the file name appears in the list of recent files.

Figure 81

Other Ways
1. Tap or click FILE on ribbon, tap or click Open in Backstage view, tap or click Computer, tap or click Browse, navigate to file (Open dialog box), tap or click Open button

To Exit an Office App

You are finished using PowerPoint. Thus, you should exit this Office app. The following steps exit PowerPoint.

1 If you have one Office document open, tap or click the Close button on the right side of the title bar to close the document and exit the Office app; or if you have multiple Office documents open, press and hold or right-click the app button on the taskbar and then tap or click 'Close all windows' on the shortcut menu, or press ALT+F4 to close all open documents and exit the Office app.

Q&A If I am using a touch screen, could I press and hold the Close button until all windows close and the app exits?
Yes.

2 If a dialog box appears, tap or click the Save button to save any changes made to the document since the last save.

Excel

Excel is a powerful spreadsheet app that allows users to organize data, complete calculations, make decisions, graph data, develop professional-looking reports (Figure 82), publish organized data to the web, and access real-time data from websites. The four major parts of Excel are:

- **Workbooks and Worksheets:** A **workbook** is like a notebook. Inside the workbook are sheets, each of which is called a **worksheet**. Thus, a workbook is a collection of worksheets. Worksheets allow users to enter, calculate, manipulate, and analyze data such as numbers and text. The terms worksheet and spreadsheet are interchangeable.

- **Charts:** Excel can draw a variety of charts such as column charts and pie charts.

- **Tables:** Tables organize and store data within worksheets. For example, once a user enters data into a worksheet, an Excel table can sort the data, search for specific data, and select data that satisfies defined criteria.

• **Web Support:** Web support allows users to save Excel worksheets or parts of a worksheet in a format that a user can view in a browser, so that a user can view and manipulate the worksheet using a browser. Excel web support also provides access to real-time data, such as stock quotes, using web queries.

Figure 82

To Create a New Blank Office Document from File Explorer

1 SIGN IN | 2 USE WINDOWS | 3 USE APPS | 4 FILE MANAGEMENT | 5 SWITCH APPS | 6 SAVE FILES
7 CHANGE SCREEN RESOLUTION | 8 EXIT APPS | 9 USE ADDITIONAL APPS | 10 USE HELP

File Explorer provides a means to create a blank Office document without running an Office app. The following steps use File Explorer to create a blank Excel document. *Why? Sometimes you might need to create a blank document and then return to it later for editing.* If you are using Windows 7, skip these steps and instead perform the steps in the yellow box that immediately follows these Windows 8 steps.

1

- If necessary, double-tap or double-click the File Explorer app button on the taskbar to make the folder window the active window.
- If necessary, double-tap or double-click the Documents library in the navigation pane to expand the Documents library.
- If necessary, double-tap or double-click the My Documents folder in the navigation pane to expand the My Documents folder.
- If necessary, double-tap or double-click your class folder (CIS 101, in this case) in the navigation pane to expand the folder.
- Tap or click the Excel folder in the navigation pane to display its contents in the file list.
- With the Excel folder selected, press and hold or right-click an open area in the file list to display a shortcut menu.
- Tap or point to New on the shortcut menu to display the New submenu (Figure 83).

Figure 83

2

• Tap or click 'Microsoft Excel Worksheet' on the New submenu to display an icon and text box for a new file in the current folder window with the file name, New Microsoft Excel Worksheet, selected (Figure 84).

Figure 84

3

• Type `Iverstonit Electronics` in the text box and then press the ENTER key to assign a new name to the new file in the current folder (Figure 85).

Figure 85

TO CREATE A NEW BLANK OFFICE DOCUMENT FROM WINDOWS EXPLORER USING WINDOWS 7

If you are using Windows 7, perform these steps to create a new blank Office document from Windows Explorer instead of the previous steps that use Windows 8.

1. If necessary, click the Windows Explorer button on the taskbar to make the folder window the active window.

2. If necessary, double-click the Documents library in the navigation pane to expand the Documents library.

3. If necessary, double-click the My Documents folder in the navigation pane to expand the My Documents folder.

4. If necessary, double-click your class folder (CIS 101, in this case) in the navigation pane to expand the folder.

5. Click the Excel folder in the navigation pane to display its contents in the file list.

6. With the Excel folder selected, right-click an open area in the file list to display a shortcut menu.

7. Point to New on the shortcut menu to display the New submenu.

8. Click 'Microsoft Excel Worksheet' on the New submenu to display an icon and text box for a new file in the current folder window with the name, New Microsoft Excel Worksheet, selected.

9. Type `Iverstonit Electronics` in the text box and then press the ENTER key to assign a new name to the new file in the current folder.

To Run an App from File Explorer and Open a File

1 SIGN IN | 2 USE WINDOWS | 3 USE APPS | 4 FILE MANAGEMENT | 5 SWITCH APPS | 6 SAVE FILES
7 CHANGE SCREEN RESOLUTION | 8 EXIT APPS | 9 USE ADDITIONAL APPS | **10 USE HELP**

Previously, you learned how to run an Office app using the Start screen and the Search charm. The steps on the next page, which assume Windows is running, use File Explorer to run the Excel app based on a typical installation. *Why? Another way to run an Office app is to open an existing file from File Explorer, which causes the app in which the file was created to run and then open the selected file.* You may need to ask your instructor how to run Office apps for your computer. If you are using Windows 7, follow the steps in the yellow box that immediately follows these Windows 8 steps.

1

- If necessary, display the file to open in the folder window in File Explorer (shown in Figure 85 on the previous page).

- Press and hold or right-click the file icon or file name (Iverstonit Electronics, in this case) to display a shortcut menu (Figure 86).

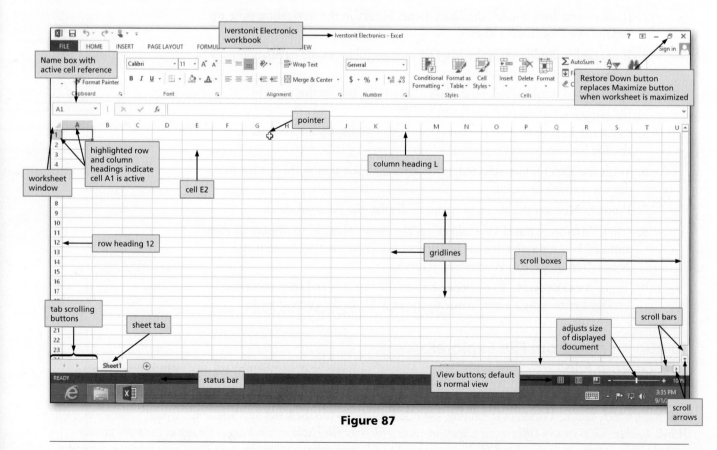

Figure 86

2

- Tap or click Open on the shortcut menu to open the selected file in the app used to create the file, Excel in this case (Figure 87).

- If the app window is not maximized, tap or click the Maximize button on the title bar to maximize the window.

Q&A Instead of using File Explorer, can I run Excel using the same method shown previously for Word and PowerPoint?
Yes, you can use any method of running an Office app to run Excel.

Figure 87

TO RUN AN APP FROM WINDOWS EXPLORER AND OPEN A FILE USING WINDOWS 7

If you are using Windows 7, perform these steps to run an app from Windows Explorer and open a file instead of the previous steps that use Windows 8.

1. Display the file to open in the folder window in Windows Explorer.
2. Right-click the file icon or file name (Iverstonit Electronics, in this case) to display a shortcut menu.
3. Click Open on the shortcut menu to open the selected file in the app used to create the file, Excel in this case.
4. If the app window is not maximized, click the Maximize button on the title bar to maximize the window.

Unique Features of Excel

The Excel window consists of a variety of components to make your work more efficient and worksheets more professional. These include the document window, ribbon, mini toolbar and shortcut menus, Quick Access Toolbar, and Microsoft Account area. Some of these components are common to other Office apps; others are unique to Excel.

Excel opens a new workbook with one worksheet. If necessary, you can add additional worksheets as long as your computer has enough memory to accommodate them.

Each worksheet has a sheet name that appears on a **sheet tab** at the bottom of the workbook. For example, Sheet1 is the name of the active worksheet displayed in the Iverstonit Electronics workbook. You can add more sheets to the workbook by clicking the New sheet button.

The Worksheet The worksheet is organized into a rectangular grid containing vertical columns and horizontal rows. A column letter above the grid, also called the **column heading**, identifies each column. A row number on the left side of the grid, also called the **row heading**, identifies each row. With the screen resolution set to 1366 × 768 and the Excel window maximized, Excel displays 20 columns (A through T) and 23 rows (1 through 23) of the worksheet on the screen, as shown in Figure 87.

The intersection of each column and row is a cell. A **cell** is the basic unit of a worksheet into which you enter data. Each worksheet in a workbook has 16,384 columns and 1,048,576 rows for a total of 17,179,869,180 cells. Only a small fraction of the active worksheet appears on the screen at one time.

A cell is referred to by its unique address, or **cell reference**, which is the coordinates of the intersection of a column and a row. To identify a cell, specify the column letter first, followed by the row number. For example, cell reference E2 refers to the cell located at the intersection of column E and row 2 (Figure 87).

One cell on the worksheet, designated the **active cell**, is the one into which you can enter data. The active cell in Figure 87 is A1. The active cell is identified in three ways. First, a heavy border surrounds the cell; second, the active cell reference shows immediately above column A in the Name box; and third, the column heading A and row heading 1 are highlighted so that it is easy to see which cell is active (Figure 87).

The horizontal and vertical lines on the worksheet itself are called **gridlines**. Gridlines make it easier to see and identify each cell in the worksheet. If desired, you can turn the gridlines off so that they do not show on the worksheet. While learning Excel, gridlines help you to understand the structure of the worksheet.

BTW

The Worksheet Size and Window

The 16,384 columns and 1,048,576 rows in Excel make for a huge worksheet that — if you could imagine — takes up the entire side of a building to display in its entirety. Your computer screen, by comparison, is a small window that allows you to view only a minute area of the worksheet at one time. While you cannot see the entire worksheet, you can move the window over the worksheet to view any part of it.

BTW

Customizing the Ribbon

In addition to customizing the Quick Access Toolbar, you can add items to and remove items from the ribbon. To customize the ribbon, click FILE on the ribbon to open the Backstage view, click Options in the Backstage view, and then click Customize Ribbon in the left pane of the Options dialog box. More information about customizing the ribbon is presented in a later chapter.

The pointer in Figure 87 on page OFF 58 has the shape of a block plus sign. The pointer appears as a block plus sign whenever it is located in a cell on the worksheet. Another common shape of the pointer is the block arrow. The pointer turns into the block arrow when you move it outside the worksheet or when you drag cell contents between rows or columns. The other pointer shapes are described when they appear on the screen.

Ribbon When you run Excel, the ribbon displays eight main tabs: FILE, HOME, INSERT, PAGE LAYOUT, FORMULAS, DATA, REVIEW, and VIEW. The FORMULAS and DATA tabs are specific to Excel. The FORMULAS tab allows you to work with Excel formulas, and the DATA tab allows you to work with data processing features such as importing and sorting data.

Formula Bar As you type, Excel displays the entry in the **formula bar**, which appears below the ribbon (Figure 88). You can make the formula bar larger by dragging the sizing handle at the bottom of the formula bar or tapping or clicking the expand button to the right of the formula bar. Excel also displays the active cell reference in the **Name box** on the left side of the formula bar.

Figure 88

To Enter a Worksheet Title

1 SIGN IN | 2 USE WINDOWS | 3 USE APPS | 4 FILE MANAGEMENT | 5 SWITCH APPS | 6 SAVE FILES
7 CHANGE SCREEN RESOLUTION | 8 EXIT APPS | 9 USE ADDITIONAL APPS | 10 USE HELP

To enter data into a cell, you first must select it. The easiest way to select a cell (make it active) is to tap the cell or use the mouse to move the block plus sign pointer to the cell and then click. An alternative method is to use the arrow keys that are located just to the right of the typewriter keys on the keyboard. An arrow key selects the cell adjacent to the active cell in the direction of the arrow on the key.

In Excel, any set of characters containing a letter, hyphen (as in a telephone number), or space is considered text. **Text** is used to place titles, such as worksheet titles, column titles, and row titles, on the worksheet. The following steps enter the worksheet title in cell A1. *Why? A title informs others as to the contents of the worksheet, such as information regarding a company.*

1
- If it is not already the active cell, tap or click cell A1 to make it the active cell (Figure 89).

Figure 89

2

- Type `Inverstonit Electronics` in cell A1 (Figure 90).

Q&A

Why did the appearance of the formula bar change?

Excel displays the title in the formula bar and in cell A1. When you begin typing a cell entry, Excel displays two additional boxes in the formula bar: the Cancel box and the Enter box. Tapping or clicking the Enter box completes an entry. Tapping or clicking the Cancel box cancels an entry.

Figure 90

3

- Tap or click the Enter box to complete the entry and enter the worksheet title in cell A1 (Figure 91).

Q&A

Why do some commands on the ribbon appear dimmed?

Excel dims the commands that are unavailable for use at the current time.

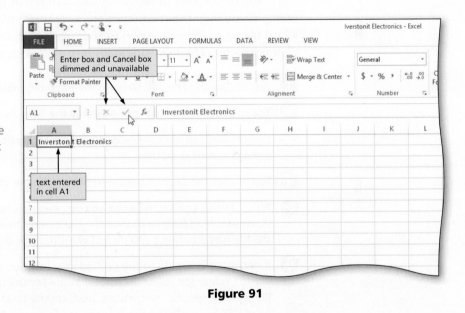

Figure 91

Other Ways

1. To complete entry, tap or click any cell other than active cell

2. To complete entry, press ENTER, HOME, PAGE UP, PAGE DOWN, END, UP ARROW, DOWN ARROW, LEFT ARROW, or RIGHT ARROW

To Save an Existing Office File with the Same File Name

1 SIGN IN | 2 USE WINDOWS | 3 USE APPS | 4 FILE MANAGEMENT | 5 SWITCH APPS | 6 SAVE FILES
7 CHANGE SCREEN RESOLUTION | 8 EXIT APPS | 9 USE ADDITIONAL APPS | 10 USE HELP

Saving frequently cannot be overemphasized. *Why? You have made modifications to the file (spreadsheet) since you created it. Thus, you should save again. Similarly, you should continue saving files frequently so that you do not lose the changes you have made since the time you last saved the file.* You can use the same file name, such as Iverstonit Electronics, to save the changes made to the document. The step on the next page saves a file again with the same file name.

- Tap or click the Save button on the Quick Access Toolbar to overwrite the previously saved file (Iverstonit Electronics, in this case) in the Excel folder (Figure 92).

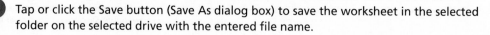

Figure 92

Other Ways

1. Press CTRL+S or press SHIFT+F12

To Save a File with a New File Name

You might want to save a file with a different name or to a different location. For example, you might start a homework assignment with a data file and then save it with a final file name for submission to your instructor, saving it to a location designated by your instructor. The following steps save a file with a different file name.

1 Tap or click the FILE tab to open the Backstage view.

2 Tap or click the Save As tab to display the Save As gallery.

3 If necessary, tap or click Computer to display options in the right pane related to saving on your computer.

4 Tap or click the Browse button in the right pane to display the Save As dialog box.

5 Type **Iverstonit Electronics Rental Summary** in the File name box (Save As dialog box) to change the file name. Do not press the ENTER key after typing the file name because you do not want to close the dialog box at this time.

6 If necessary, navigate to the desired save location (in this case, the Excel folder in the CIS 101 folder [or your class folder] in the My Documents folder in the Documents library). For specific instructions, perform the tasks in Steps 5a through 5e on page OFF 51, replacing the PowerPoint folder with the Excel folder.

7 Tap or click the Save button (Save As dialog box) to save the worksheet in the selected folder on the selected drive with the entered file name.

To Exit an Office App

You are finished using Excel. The following steps exit Excel.

1 If you have one Office document open, tap or click the Close button on the right side of the title bar to close the document and exit the Office app; or if you have multiple Office documents open, press and hold or right-click the app button on the taskbar and then tap or click 'Close all windows' on the shortcut menu, or press ALT+F4 to close all open documents and exit the Office app.

2 If a dialog box appears, tap or click the Save button to save any changes made to the file since the last save.

Access

The term **database** describes a collection of data organized in a manner that allows access, retrieval, and use of that data. **Access** is a database management system. A **database management system** is software that allows you to use a computer to create a database; add, change, and delete data in the database; create queries that allow you to ask questions concerning the data in the database; and create forms and reports using the data in the database.

To Run an App

The following steps, which assume Windows is running, run the Access app based on a typical installation. You may need to ask your instructor how to run apps for your computer. If you are using Windows 7, skip these steps and instead perform the steps in the yellow box that immediately follows these Windows 8 steps.

 Swipe in from the right edge of the screen or point to the upper-right corner of the screen to display the Charms bar.

 Tap or click the Search charm on the Charms bar to display the Search menu.

 Type **Access 2013** as the search text in the Search box and watch the search results appear in the Apps list.

 Tap or click the app name, Access 2013 in this case, in the search results to run Access.

Figure 93

 If the app window is not maximized, tap or click the Maximize button on its title bar to maximize the window (Figure 93).

Q&A Do I have to run Access using these steps?

No. You can use any previously discussed method of running an Office app to run Access.

TO RUN AN APP USING WINDOWS 7

If you are using Windows 7, perform these steps to run an app instead of the previous steps that use Windows 8.

1. Click the Start button on the Windows 7 taskbar to display the Start menu.

2. Type **Access 2013** as the search text in the 'Search programs and files' text box and watch the search results appear on the Start menu.

3. Click the app name, Access 2013 in this case, in the search results on the Start menu to run Access.

4. If the app window is not maximized, click the Maximize button on its title bar to maximize the window.

Unique Elements in Access

You work on objects such as tables, forms, and reports in the **Access work area**. Figure 94 shows a work area with multiple objects open. **Object tabs** for the open objects appear at the top of the work area. You select an open object by tapping or clicking its tab. In the figure, the Asset List table is the selected object. To the left of the work area is the Navigation Pane, which contains a list of all the objects in the database. You use this pane to open an object. You also can customize the way objects are displayed in the Navigation Pane.

Because the Navigation Pane can take up space in the window, you may not have as much open space for working as you would with Word or Excel. You can use the 'Shutter Bar Open/Close Button' to minimize the Navigation Pane when you are not using it, which allows more space to work with tables, forms, reports, and other database elements.

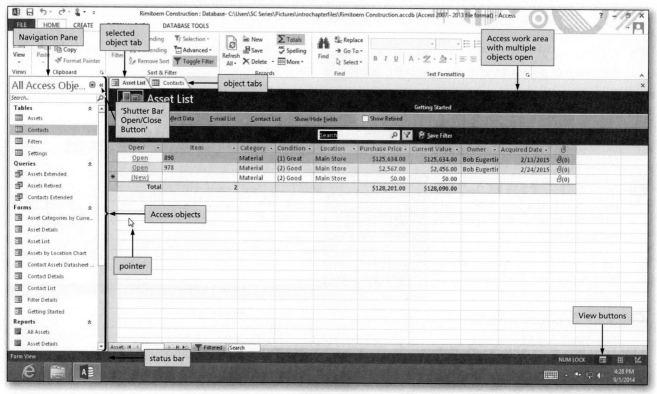

Figure 94

Ribbon When you run Access, the ribbon displays five main tabs: FILE, HOME, CREATE, EXTERNAL DATA, and DATABASE TOOLS. Access has unique groupings such as Sort & Filter and Records that are designed specifically for working with databases. Many of the formatting options are reserved for the tool tabs that appear when you are working with forms and reports.

To Create an Access Database

1 SIGN IN | 2 USE WINDOWS | 3 USE APPS | 4 FILE MANAGEMENT | 5 SWITCH APPS | 6 SAVE FILES
7 CHANGE SCREEN RESOLUTION | 8 EXIT APPS | 9 USE ADDITIONAL APPS | 10 USE HELP

Unlike the other Office apps, Access saves a database when you first create it. When working in Access, you will add data to an Access database. As you add data to a database, Access automatically saves your changes rather than waiting until you manually save the database or exit Access. Recall that in Word and Excel, you entered the data first and then saved it.

Because Access automatically saves the database as you add and change data, you do not always have to click the Save button on the Quick Access Toolbar. Instead, the Save button in Access is used for saving the objects (including tables, queries, forms, reports, and other database objects) a database contains. You can use either the 'Blank desktop database' option or a template to create a new database. If you already know the organization of your database, you would use the 'Blank desktop database' option. If not, you can use a template. Templates can guide you by suggesting some commonly used database organizations.

The following steps use the 'Blank desktop database' option to create a database named Rimitoein Construction in the Access folder in the class folder (CIS 101, in this case) in the Documents library. *Why? You have decided to use Microsoft Access to maintain large amounts of data.*

1

- Tap or click the 'Blank desktop database' thumbnail (shown in Figure 93 on page OFF 63) to select the database type.

- Type **Rimitoein Construction** in the File Name box to enter the new file name. Do not press the ENTER key after typing the file name because you do not want to create the database at this time (Figure 95).

Figure 95

2

- Tap or click the 'Browse for a location to put your database' button to display the File New Database dialog box.

- Navigate to the location for the database, that is, the Documents library, the My Documents folder, then to the folder identifying your class (CIS 101, in this case), and then to the Access folder (Figure 96). For specific instructions, perform the tasks in Steps 5a through 5e on page OFF 51, replacing the PowerPoint folder with the Access folder.

Q&A Why does the 'Save as type' box say Microsoft Access 2007-2013 Databases?
Microsoft Access database formats change with some new versions of Microsoft Access. The most recent format is the Microsoft Access 2007-2013 Databases format, which was released with Access 2007 and Access 2013.

Figure 96

3

- Tap or click the OK button (File New Database dialog box) to select the Access folder as the location for the database and close the dialog box (Figure 97).

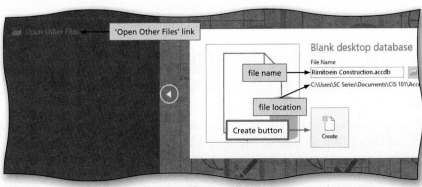

Figure 97

4

- Tap or click the Create button to create the database on the selected drive in the selected folder with the file name, Rimitoein Construction (Figure 98).

Q&A How do I know that the Rimitoein Construction database is created?
The file name of the database appears on the title bar.

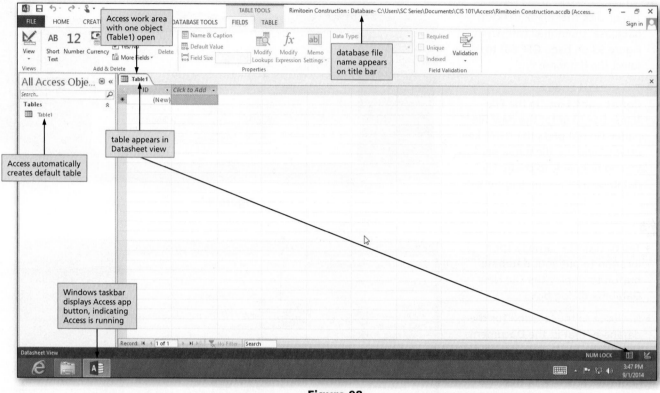

Figure 98

To Close an Office File

Assume you need to close the Access database and return to it later. The following step closes an Office file.

1 Tap or click FILE on the ribbon to open the Backstage view and then tap or click Close in the Backstage view to close the open file (Rimitoein Construction, in this case) without exiting the active app.

Q&A Why is Access still on the screen?
When you close a database, the app remains running.

To Open an Existing Office File

1 SIGN IN | 2 USE WINDOWS | 3 USE APPS | 4 FILE MANAGEMENT | 5 SWITCH APPS | 6 SAVE FILES
7 CHANGE SCREEN RESOLUTION | 8 EXIT APPS | **9 USE ADDITIONAL APPS** | **10 USE** HELP

Assume you wish to continue working on an existing file, that is, a file you previously saved. Earlier in this chapter, you learned how to open a recently used file through the Backstage view. The following step opens a database, specifically the Rimitoein Construction database, that recently was saved. **Why?** *Because the file has been created already, you just need to reopen it.*

1

- Tap or click FILE on the ribbon to open the Backstage view and then tap or click Open in the Backstage view to display the Open gallery in the Backstage view.

- Tap or click Computer to display recent folders accessed on your computer.

- Tap or click the Browse button to display the Open dialog box.

- If necessary, navigate to the location of the file to open.

- Tap or click the file to open, Rimitoein Construction in this case, to select the file.

- Tap or click the Open button (Open dialog box) to open the file. If necessary, tap or click the Enable Content button (Figure 99).

Q&A

Why did the Security Warning appear?

The Security Warning appears when you open an Office file that might contain harmful content. The files you create in this chapter are not harmful, but you should be cautious when opening files from other people.

Figure 99

Other Ways
1. Press CTRL+O   2. Navigate to file in File Explorer window, double-tap or double-click file

To Exit an Office App

You are finished using Access. The following step exits Access.

1 Tap or click the Close button on the right side of the title bar to close the file and exit the Office app.

Other Office Apps

In addition to the Office apps discussed thus far, three other apps are useful when collaborating and communicating with others: Outlook, Publisher, and OneNote.

Outlook

Outlook is a powerful communications and scheduling app that helps you communicate with others, keep track of contacts, and organize your calendar. Apps such as Outlook provide a way for individuals and workgroups to organize, find, view, and share information easily. Outlook allows you to send and receive email messages and provides a means to organize contacts. Users can track email messages, meetings, and notes related to a particular contact. Outlook's Calendar, People, Tasks, and Notes components aid in this organization. Contact information readily is available from the Outlook Calendar, Mail, People, and Task components by accessing the Search Contacts feature.

Email is the transmission of messages and files over a computer network. Email has become an important means of exchanging information and files between business associates, classmates and instructors, friends, and family. Businesses find that using email to send documents electronically saves both time and money. Parents with students away at college or relatives who live across the country find that communicating by email is an inexpensive and easy way to stay in touch with their family members. Exchanging email messages is a widely used service of the Internet.

The Outlook Window Figure 100 shows an Outlook window, which is divided into three panes: the Folder pane, the Inbox message pane to the left of center, and the Reading Pane to the right of center.

When an email message is open in Outlook, it is displayed in a Message window (Figure 101). When you open a message, the Message tab on the ribbon appears, which contains the more frequently used commands.

Figure 100

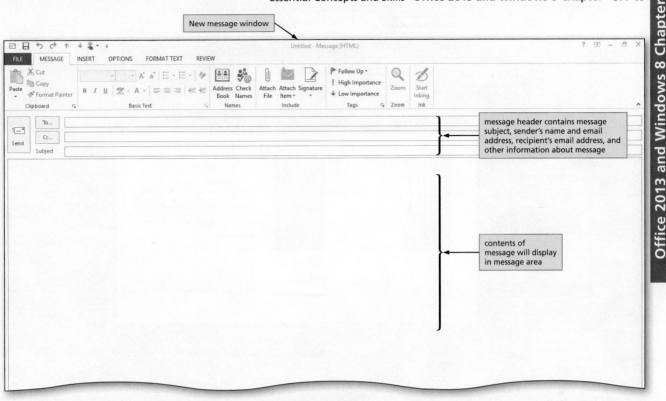

New message window

message header contains message subject, sender's name and email address, recipient's email address, and other information about message

contents of message will display in message area

Figure 101

Publisher

Publisher is a powerful desktop publishing (DTP) app that assists you in designing and producing professional-quality documents that combine text, graphics, illustrations, and photos. DTP software provides additional tools beyond those typically found in word processing apps, including design templates, graphic manipulation tools, color schemes or libraries, advanced layout and printing tools, and web components. For large jobs, businesses use DTP software to design publications that are camera ready, which means the files are suitable for outside commercial printing. In addition, DTP software can be used to create webpages and interactive web forms.

Publisher is used by people who regularly produce high-quality color publications, such as newsletters, brochures, flyers, logos, signs, catalogs, cards, and business forms. Saving publications as webpages or complete websites is a powerful component of Publisher. All publications can be saved in a format that easily is viewed and manipulated using a browser.

Publisher has many features designed to simplify production and make publications visually appealing. Using Publisher, you easily can change the shape, size, and color of text and graphics. You can include many kinds of graphical objects, including mastheads, borders, tables, images, pictures, charts, and web objects in publications, as well as integrate spreadsheets and databases.

The Publisher Window Publisher initially displays a list of publication types. **Publication types** are typical publications used by desktop publishers. The more popular types are displayed in the center of the window.

Once you select a publication type, a dialog box is displayed to allow you to create the publication (Figure 102 on the next page). Some templates are installed with Publisher, and others are available online. In Figure 102, the Brochure publication dialog box is displayed.

BTW

Running Publisher
When you first run Publisher, the New templates gallery usually is displayed in the Backstage view. If it is not displayed, click FILE on the ribbon, click Options in the Backstage view, click General (Publisher Options dialog box), and then click 'Show the New template gallery when starting Publisher' to select the check box in the right pane.

Figure 102

When you click the template, Publisher creates the document and sets it up for you to edit. Figure 103 shows the Brochure document that Publisher creates when default options are selected.

Figure 103

OneNote

OneNote is a note taking app that assists you in entering, saving, organizing, searching, and using notes. It enables you to create pages, which are organized in sections, just as in a physical notebook. In OneNote, you can type notes anywhere on a page and then easily move the notes around on the page. You can create lists and outlines, use handwriting to enter notes, and create drawings. If you use a tablet to add handwritten notes to a document, OneNote can convert the handwriting to text. It also can perform searches on the handwritten entries. Pictures and data from other apps easily are incorporated in your notes.

In addition to typing and handwriting, you can take audio notes. For example, you could record conversations during a meeting or lecture. As you record, you can take additional notes. When you play back the audio notes, you can synchronize the additional notes you took; that is, OneNote will show you during playback the exact points at which you added the notes. A variety of note flags, which are symbols that call your attention to notes on a page, enable you to flag notes as being important. You then can use the Note Flags summary to view the flagged notes, which can be sorted in a variety of ways.

OneNote includes tools to assist you with organizing a notebook and navigating its contents. It also includes a search feature, making it easy to find the specific notes in which you are interested. For short notes that you always want to have available readily, you can use Side Notes, which are used much like the sticky notes that you might use in a physical notebook.

OneNote Window All activity in OneNote takes place in the **notebook** (Figure 104). Like a physical notebook, the OneNote notebook consists of notes that are placed on **pages**. The pages are grouped into **sections**, which can be further grouped into **folders**. (No folders are shown in the notebook in the figure.) You can use the Search box to search for specific text in your notes.

You can add pages to the notebook using the Add Page button in the Page Tabs pane. If Page Tabs are displayed, you can switch to a page by tapping or clicking its tab. Figure 104 shows the Quick Notes page being displayed for the notebook.

Figure 104

Break Point: If you wish to take a break, this is a good place to do so. To resume at a later time, continue to follow the steps from this location forward.

Renaming, Moving, and Deleting Files

Earlier in this chapter, you learned how to organize files in folders, which is part of a process known as **file management**. The following sections cover additional file management topics including renaming, moving, and deleting files.

To Rename a File

1 SIGN IN | 2 USE WINDOWS | 3 USE APPS | **4 FILE MANAGEMENT** | 5 SWITCH APPS | 6 SAVE FILES
7 CHANGE SCREEN RESOLUTION | 8 EXIT APPS | 9 USE ADDITIONAL APPS | **10 USE HELP**

In some circumstances, you may want to change the name of, or rename, a file or a folder. *Why? You may want to distinguish a file in one folder or drive from a copy of a similar file, or you may decide to rename a file to better identify its contents.* The Word folder shown in Figure 67 on page OFF 44 contains the Word document, Elephant Habitat. The following steps change the name of the Elephant Habitat file in the Word folder to Elephant Habitat Flyer. If you are using Windows 7, skip these steps and instead perform the steps in the yellow box that immediately follows these Windows 8 steps.

1

- If necessary, tap or click the File Explorer app button on the taskbar to make the folder window the active window.

- Navigate to the location of the file to be renamed (in this case, the Word folder in the CIS 101 [or your class folder] folder in the My Documents folder in the Documents library) to display the file(s) it contains in the file list.

- Press and hold or right-click the Elephant Habitat icon or file name in the file list to select the Elephant Habitat file and display a shortcut menu that presents a list of commands related to files (Figure 105).

Figure 105

2

- Tap or click Rename on the shortcut menu to place the current file name in a text box.

- Type **Elephant Habitat Flyer** in the text box and then press the ENTER key (Figure 106).

Q&A Are any risks involved in renaming files that are located on a hard disk?
If you inadvertently rename a file that is associated with certain apps, the apps may not be able to find the file and, therefore, may not run properly. Always use caution when renaming files.

Can I rename a file when it is open?
No, a file must be closed to change the file name.

Figure 106

Other Ways

1. Select file, press F2, type new file name, press ENTER   2. Select file, tap or click Rename (Home tab | Organize group), type new file name, press ENTER

TO RENAME A FILE USING WINDOWS 7

If you are using Windows 7, perform these steps to rename a file instead of the previous steps that use Windows 8.

1. If necessary, click the Windows Explorer app button on the taskbar to make the folder window the active window.

2. Navigate to the location of the file to be renamed (in this case, the Word folder in the CIS 101 [or your class folder] folder in the My Documents folder in the Documents library) to display the file(s) it contains in the file list.

3. Right-click the Elephant Habitat icon or file name in the file list to select the Elephant Habitat file and display a shortcut menu that presents a list of commands related to files.

4. Click Rename on the shortcut menu to place the current file name in a text box.

5. Type **Elephant Habitat Flyer** in the text box and then press the ENTER key.

To Move a File

1 SIGN IN | 2 USE WINDOWS | 3 USE APPS | **4 FILE MANAGEMENT** | 5 SWITCH APPS | 6 SAVE FILES
7 CHANGE SCREEN RESOLUTION | 8 EXIT APPS | 9 USE ADDITIONAL APPS | **10 USE HELP**

Why? *At some time, you may want to move a file from one folder, called the source folder, to another, called the destination folder.* When you move a file, it no longer appears in the original folder. If the destination and the source folders are on the same media, you can move a file by dragging it. If the folders are on different media, then you will need to press and hold and then drag, or right-drag the file, and then click Move here on the shortcut menu. The following step moves the Iverstonit Electronics Rental Summary file from the Excel folder to the OneNote folder. If you are using Windows 7, skip these steps and instead perform the steps in the yellow box that immediately follows these Windows 8 steps.

1

- In File Explorer, navigate to the location of the file to be moved (in this case, the Excel folder in the CIS 101 folder [or your class folder] in the Documents library).

- Tap or click the Excel folder in the navigation pane to display the files it contains in the right pane (Figure 107).

- Drag the Iverstonit Electronics Rental Summary file in the right pane to the OneNote folder in the navigation pane.

Experiment

- Click the OneNote folder in the navigation pane to verify that the file was moved.

Figure 107

Other Ways

1. Press and hold or right-click file to move, tap or click Cut on shortcut menu, press and hold or right-click destination folder, tap or click Paste on shortcut menu

2. Select file to move, press CTRL+X, select destination folder, press CTRL+V

To Move a File Using Windows 7

If you are using Windows 7, perform these steps to move a file instead of the previous steps that use Windows 8.

1. In Windows Explorer, navigate to the location of the file to be moved (in this case, the Excel folder in the CIS 101 folder [or your class folder] in the Documents library).
2. Click the Excel folder in the navigation pane to display the files it contains in the right pane.
3. Drag the Iverstonit Electronics Rental Summary file in the right pane to the OneNote folder in the navigation pane.

To Delete a File

1 SIGN IN | 2 USE WINDOWS | 3 USE APPS | **4 FILE MANAGEMENT** | 5 SWITCH APPS | 6 SAVE FILES
7 CHANGE SCREEN RESOLUTION | 8 EXIT APPS | 9 USE ADDITIONAL APPS | **10 USE HELP**

A final task you may want to perform is to delete a file. Exercise extreme caution when deleting a file or files. When you delete a file from a hard disk, the deleted file is stored in the Recycle Bin where you can recover it until you empty the Recycle Bin. If you delete a file from removable media, such as a USB flash drive, the file is deleted permanently. The next steps delete the Elephant Habitat Opening file from the PowerPoint folder. *Why? When a file no longer is needed, you can delete it to conserve space in your storage location.* If you are using Windows 7, skip these steps and instead perform the steps in the yellow box that immediately follows these Windows 8 steps.

1

- In File Explorer, navigate to the location of the file to be deleted (in this case, the PowerPoint folder in the CIS 101 folder [or your class folder] in the Documents library).

- Press and hold or right-click the Elephant Habitat Opening icon or file name in the right pane to select the file and display a shortcut menu (Figure 108).

2

- Tap or click Delete on the shortcut menu to delete the file.

- If a dialog box appears, tap or click the Yes button to delete the file.

Q&A

Can I use this same technique to delete a folder?

Yes. Right-click the folder and then click Delete on the shortcut menu. When you delete a folder, all of the files and folders contained in the folder you are deleting, together with any files and folders on lower hierarchical levels, are deleted as well.

Figure 108

Other Ways

1. Select icon, press DELETE

TO DELETE A FILE USING WINDOWS 7

If you are using Windows 7, perform these steps to delete a file instead of the previous steps that use Windows 8.

1. In Windows Explorer, navigate to the location of the file to be deleted (in this case, the PowerPoint folder in the CIS 101 folder [or your class folder] in the Documents library).

2. Right-click the Elephant Habitat Opening icon or file name in the right pane to select the file and display a shortcut menu.

3. Click Delete on the shortcut menu to delete the file.

4. If a dialog box appears, click the Yes button to delete the file.

Microsoft Office and Windows Help

At any time while you are using one of the Office apps, you can use Office Help to display information about all topics associated with the app. To illustrate the use of Office Help, this section uses Word. Help in other Office apps operates in a similar fashion.

In Office, Help is presented in a window that has browser-style navigation buttons. Each Office app has its own Help home page, which is the starting Help page that is displayed in the Help window. If your computer is connected to the Internet, the contents of the Help page reflect both the local help files installed on the computer and material from Microsoft's website.

To Open the Help Window
in an Office App

1 SIGN IN | 2 USE WINDOWS | 3 USE APPS | **4 FILE MANAGEMENT** | 5 SWITCH APPS | 6 SAVE FILES
7 CHANGE SCREEN RESOLUTION | 8 EXIT APPS | 9 USE ADDITIONAL APPS | **10 USE HELP**

The following step opens the Word Help window. **Why?** *You might not understand how certain commands or operations work in Word, so you can obtain the necessary information using help.*

1

- Run an Office app, in this case Word.

- Tap or click the Office app's Help button near the upper-right corner of the app window (the 'Microsoft Word Help' button, in this case) to open the app's Help window (Figure 109).

Figure 109

Other Ways

1. Press F1

Moving and Resizing Windows

At times, it is useful, or even necessary, to have more than one window open and visible on the screen at the same time. You can resize and move these open windows so that you can view different areas of and elements in the window. In the case of the Help window, for example, it could be covering document text in the Word window that you need to see.

To Move a Window by Dragging

You can move any open window that is not maximized to another location on the desktop by dragging the title bar of the window. *Why? You might want to have a better view of what is behind the window or just want to move the window so that you can see it better.* The following step drags the Word Help window to the upper-left corner of the desktop.

1

- Drag the window title bar (the Word Help window title bar, in this case) so that the window moves to the upper-left corner of the desktop, as shown in Figure 110.

Figure 110

To Resize a Window by Dragging

A method used to change the size of the window is to drag the window borders. The following step changes the size of the Word Help window by dragging its borders. *Why? Sometimes, information is not visible completely in a window, and you want to increase the size of the window.*

1

- If you are using a mouse, point to the lower-right corner of the window (the Word Help window, in this case) until the pointer changes to a two-headed arrow.

- Drag the bottom border downward to display more of the active window (Figure 111).

Q&A

Can I drag other borders on the window to enlarge or shrink the window?
Yes, you can drag the left, right, and top borders and any window corner to resize a window.

Will Windows remember the new size of the window after I close it?
Yes. When you reopen the window, Windows will display it at the same size it was when you closed it.

Figure 111

Using Office Help

Once an Office app's Help window is open, several methods exist for navigating Help. You can search for help by using any of the three following methods from the Help window:

1. Enter search text in the 'Search online help' text box.

2. Click the links in the Help window.

3. Use the Table of Contents.

To Obtain Help Using the 'Search online help' Text Box

1 SIGN IN | 2 USE WINDOWS | 3 USE APPS | 4 FILE MANAGEMENT | 5 SWITCH APPS | 6 SAVE FILES
7 CHANGE SCREEN RESOLUTION | 8 EXIT APPS | 9 USE ADDITIONAL APPS | **10 USE HELP**

Assume for the following example that you want to know more about fonts. The following steps use the 'Search online help' text box to obtain useful information about fonts by entering the word, fonts, as search text. *Why? You may not know the exact help topic you are looking to find, so using keywords can help narrow your search.*

1

- Type **fonts** in the 'Search online help' text box at the top of the Word Help window to enter the search text.

- Tap or click the 'Search online help' button to display the search results (Figure 112).

Q&A Why do my search results differ?
If you do not have an Internet connection, your results will reflect only the content of the Help files on your computer. When searching for help online, results also can change as material is added, deleted, and updated on the online Help webpages maintained by Microsoft.

Why were my search results not very helpful?
When initiating a search, be sure to check the spelling of the search text; also, keep your search specific to return the most accurate results.

Figure 112

2

- Tap or click the 'Change the default font' link to display the Help information associated with the selected topic (Figure 113).

Figure 113

3

- Tap or click the Home button in the Help window to clear the search results and redisplay the Help home page (Figure 114).

Figure 114

To Obtain Help Using Help Links

1 SIGN IN | 2 USE WINDOWS | 3 USE APPS | 4 FILE MANAGEMENT | 5 SWITCH APPS | 6 SAVE FILES
7 CHANGE SCREEN RESOLUTION | 8 EXIT APPS | 9 USE ADDITIONAL APPS | 10 USE HELP

If your topic of interest is listed in the Help window, you can click the link to begin browsing the Help categories instead of entering search text. *Why? You browse Help just as you would browse a website. If you know which category contains your Help information, you may wish to use these links.* The following step finds the Resume information using the Resume link from the Word Help home page.

1

- Tap or click the Resume link on the Help home page (shown in Figure 114) to display the Resume help links (Figure 115).

2

- After reviewing the page, tap or click the Close button to close the Help window.

- Tap or click the Office app's Close button (Word, in this case) to exit the Office app.

Figure 115

Obtaining Help while Working in an Office App

Help in the Office apps provides you with the ability to obtain help directly, without opening the Help window and initiating a search. For example, you may be unsure about how a particular command works, or you may be presented with a dialog box that you are not sure how to use.

Figure 116 shows one option for obtaining help while working in an Office app. If you want to learn more about a command, point to its button and wait for the ScreenTip to appear. If the Help icon appears in the ScreenTip, press the F1 key while pointing to the button to open the Help window associated with that command.

Figure 117 shows a dialog box that contains a Help button. Pressing the F1 key while the dialog box is displayed opens a Help window. The Help window contains help about that dialog box, if available. If no help file is available for that particular dialog box, then the main Help window opens.

Figure 116

Figure 117

Using Windows Help and Support

One of the more powerful Windows features is Windows Help and Support. **Windows Help and Support** is available when using Windows or when using any Microsoft app running in Windows. The same methods used for searching Microsoft Office Help can be used in Windows Help and Support. The difference is that Windows Help and Support displays help for Windows, instead of for Microsoft Office.

To Use Windows Help and Support

The following steps use Windows Help and Support and open the Windows Help and Support window, which contains links to more information about Windows. *Why? This feature is designed to assist you in using Windows or the various apps.* If you are using Windows 7, skip these steps and instead perform the steps in the yellow box that immediately follows these Windows 8 steps.

1

- Swipe in from the right edge of the screen or point to the upper-right corner of the screen to display the Charms bar (Figure 118).

Figure 118

2

- Tap or click the Settings charm on the Charms bar to display the Settings menu (Figure 119).

Figure 119

3

- Tap or click Help to open the Windows Help and Support window (Figure 120).

4

- After reviewing the Windows Help and Support window, tap or click the Close button to close the Windows Help and Support window.

Figure 120

Other Ways

1. Press WINDOWS + F1

To Use Windows Help and Support with Windows 7

If you are using Windows 7, perform these steps to start Windows Help and Support instead of the previous steps that use Windows 8.

1. Click the Start button on the taskbar to display the Start menu.

2. Click Help and Support on the Start menu to open the Windows Help and Support window.

3. After reviewing the Windows Help and Support window, click the Close button to exit Windows Help and Support.

Chapter Summary

In this chapter, you learned how to use the Windows interface, several touch screen and mouse operations, file and folder management, some basic features of some Microsoft Office apps, including Word, PowerPoint, Excel, and Access, and discovered the common elements that exist among these different Office apps, and additional Office apps, including Office, Publisher, and OneNote. The items listed on the next page include all of the new Windows and Office apps skills you have learned in this chapter, with the tasks grouped by activity.

BTW

Certification
The Microsoft Office Specialist (MOS) program provides an opportunity for you to obtain a valuable industry credential — proof that you have the Microsoft Office 2013 skills required by employers. For more information, visit the Certification resource on the Student Companion Site located on www.cengagebrain.com. For detailed instructions about accessing available resources, visit www.cengage .com/ct/studentdownload or contact your instructor for information about accessing the required files.

BTW

Quick Reference
For a table that lists how to complete the tasks covered in this book using touch gestures, the mouse, ribbon, shortcut menu, and keyboard, see the Quick Reference Summary at the back of this book, or visit the Quick Reference resource on the Student Companion Site located on www.cengagebrain.com. For detailed instructions about accessing available resources, visit www.cengage .com/ct/studentdownload or contact your instructor for information about accessing the required files.

CONSIDER THIS: PLAN AHEAD

What guidelines should you follow to plan your projects?

The process of communicating specific information is a learned, rational skill. Computers and software, especially Microsoft Office 2013, can help you develop ideas and present detailed information to a particular audience and minimize much of the laborious work of drafting and revising projects. No matter what method you use to plan a project, it is beneficial to follow some specific guidelines from the onset to arrive at a final product that is informative, relevant, and effective. Use some aspects of these guidelines every time you undertake a project, and others as needed in specific instances.

1. Determine the project's purpose.
    a) Clearly define why you are undertaking this assignment.
    b) Begin to draft ideas of how best to communicate information by handwriting ideas on paper; composing directly on a laptop, tablet, or mobile device; or developing a strategy that fits your particular thinking and writing style.

2. Analyze your audience.
    a) Learn about the people who will read, analyze, or view your work.
    b) Determine their interests and needs so that you can present the information they need to know and omit the information they already possess.
    c) Form a mental picture of these people or find photos of people who fit this profile so that you can develop a project with the audience in mind.

3. Gather possible content.
    a) Locate existing information that may reside in spreadsheets, databases, or other files.
    b) Conduct a web search to find relevant websites.
    c) Read pamphlets, magazine and newspaper articles, and books to gain insights of how others have approached your topic.
    d) Conduct personal interviews to obtain perspectives not available by any other means.
    e) Consider video and audio clips as potential sources for material that might complement or support the factual data you uncover.

4. Determine what content to present to your audience.
   a) Write three or four major ideas you want an audience member to remember after reading or viewing your project.
   b) Envision your project's endpoint, the key fact you wish to emphasize, so that all project elements lead to this final element.
   c) Determine relevant time factors, such as the length of time to develop the project, how long readers will spend reviewing your project, or the amount of time allocated for your speaking engagement.
   d) Decide whether a graph, photo, or artistic element can express or enhance a particular concept.
   e) Be mindful of the order in which you plan to present the content, and place the most important material at the top or bottom of the page, because readers and audience members generally remember the first and last pieces of information they see and hear.

CONSIDER THIS

How should you submit solutions to questions in the assignments identified with a ✳ symbol?
Every assignment in this book contains one or more questions identified with a ✳ symbol. These questions require you to think beyond the assigned file. Present your solutions to the questions in the format required by your instructor. Possible formats may include one or more of these options: write the answer; create a document that contains the answer; present your answer to the class; discuss your answer in a group; record the answer as audio or video using a webcam, smartphone, or portable media player; or post answers on a blog, wiki, or website.

Apply Your Knowledge

Reinforce the skills and apply the concepts you learned in this chapter.

Creating a Folder and a Document

Instructions: You will create a Word folder and then create a Word document and save it in the folder.

Perform the following tasks:

1. Open the File Explorer window and then double-tap or double-click to open the Documents library.

2. Tap or click the New folder button on the Quick Access Toolbar to display a new folder icon and text box for the folder name.

3. Type **Word** in the text box to name the folder. Press the ENTER key to create the folder in the Documents library.

4. Run Word.

5. Enter the text shown in Figure 121 in a new blank document.

6. Tap or click the Save button on the Quick Access Toolbar. Navigate to the Word folder in the Documents library and then save the document using the file name, Apply 1 Class List.

7. If your Quick Access Toolbar does not show the Quick Print button, add the Quick Print button to the Quick Access Toolbar. Print the document using the Quick Print button on the Quick Access Toolbar. When you are finished printing, remove the Quick Print button from the Quick Access Toolbar.

8. Submit the printout to your instructor.

9. Exit Word.

10. ✳ What other commands might you find useful to include on the Quick Access Toolbar?

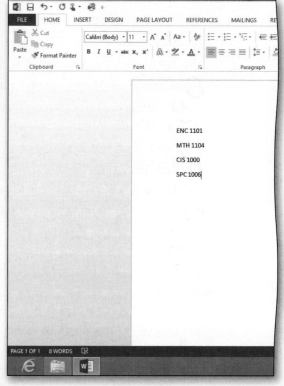

Figure 121

Extend Your Knowledge

Extend the skills you learned in this chapter and experiment with new skills. You will use Help to complete the assignment.

Using Help

Instructions: Use Office Help to perform the following tasks.

Perform the following tasks:

1. Run Word.

2. Tap or click the Microsoft Word Help button to open the Word Help window (Figure 122).

3. Search Word Help to answer the following questions.

   a. What are the steps to add a new group to the ribbon?

   b. What are Quick Parts?

4. With the Word app still running, run PowerPoint.

5. Tap or click the Microsoft PowerPoint Help button on the title bar to open the PowerPoint Help window.

6. Search PowerPoint Help to answer the following questions.

   a. What is a slide master?

   b. How do you copy slides from another presentation into the existing presentation?

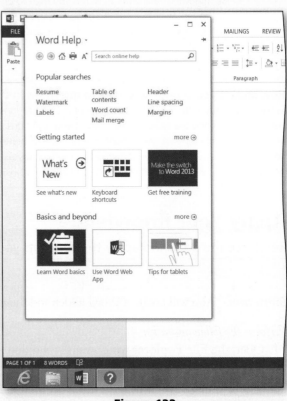

Figure 122

7. Exit PowerPoint.

8. Run Excel.

9. Tap or click the Microsoft Excel Help button to open the Excel Help window.

10. Search Excel Help to answer the following questions.

    a. What are three different functions available in Excel?

    b. What are sparklines?

11. Exit Excel.

12. Run Access.

13. Tap or click the Microsoft Access Help button to open the Access Help window.

14. Search Access Help to answer the following questions.

    a. What is SQL?

    b. What is a data macro?

15. Exit Access.

16. Type the answers from your searches in a new blank Word document. Save the document with a new file name and then submit it in the format specified by your instructor.

17. Exit Word.

18. What search text did you use to perform the searches above? Did it take multiple attempts to search and locate the exact information for which you were searching?

Analyze, Correct, Improve

Analyze a file structure, correct all errors, and improve the design.

Organizing Vacation Photos

Note: To complete this assignment, you will be required to use the Data Files for Students. Visit www.cengage.com/ct/studentdownload for detailed instructions or contact your instructor for information about accessing the required files.

Instructions: Traditionally, you have stored photos from past vacations together in one folder. The photos are becoming difficult to manage, and you now want to store them in appropriate folders. You will create the folder structure shown in Figure 123. You then will move the photos to the folders so that they will be organized properly.

1. Correct Create the folder structure in Figure 123 so that you are able to store the photos in an organized manner.

2. Improve View each photo and drag it to the appropriate folder to improve the organization.

3. ✺ Think about the files you have stored on your computer. What folder hierarchy would be best to manage your files?

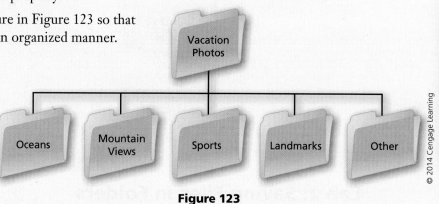

Figure 123

© 2014 Cengage Learning

In the Labs

Use the guidelines, concepts, and skills presented in this chapter to increase your knowledge of Windows 8 and Office 2013. Labs 1 and 2, which increase in difficulty, require you to create solutions based on what you learned in the chapter; Lab 3 requires you to create a solution, which uses cloud and web technologies, by learning and investigating on your own from general guidance.

Lab 1: **Creating Folders for a Video Store**

Problem: Your friend works for Ebaird Video. He would like to organize his files in relation to the types of videos available in the store. He has six main categories: drama, action, romance, foreign, biographical, and comedy. You are to create a folder structure similar to Figure 124 on the next page.

Instructions: Perform the following tasks:
1. Insert a USB flash drive in an available USB port and then open the USB flash drive window.
2. Create the main folder for Ebaird Video.
3. Navigate to the Ebaird Video folder.
4. Within the Ebaird Video folder, create a folder for each of the following: Drama, Action, Romance, Foreign, Biographical, and Comedy.
5. Within the Action folder, create two additional folders, one for Science Fiction and the second for Western.
6. Submit the assignment in the format specified by your instructor.
7. ✺ Think about how you use your computer for various tasks (consider personal, professional, and academic reasons). What folders do you think will be required on your computer to store the files you save?

Continued >

In the Labs *continued*

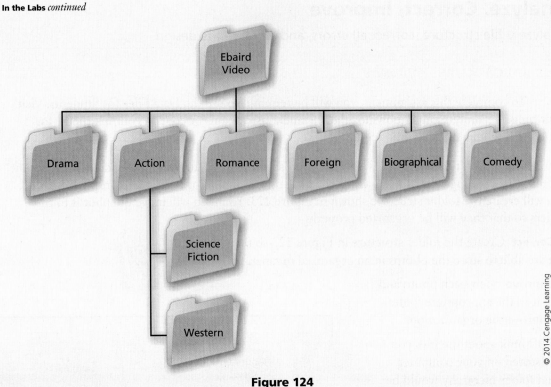

Figure 124

© 2014 Cengage Learning

Lab 2: **Saving Files in Folders**

Creating Office Documents

Problem: You are taking a class that requires you to create a Word, PowerPoint, Excel, and Access file. You will save these files to folders named for four different Office apps (Figure 125).

Instructions: Create the folders shown in Figure 125. Then, using the respective Office app, create a small file to save in each folder (i.e., create a Word document to save in the Word folder, a PowerPoint presentation to save in the PowerPoint folder, and so on).

1. Create a Word document containing the text, First Word Assignment.

2. In the Backstage view, tap or click Save As and then tap or click Computer.

3. Tap or click the Browse button to display the Save As dialog box.

4. Tap or click Documents to open the Documents library. Next, create the folder structure shown in Figure 125 using the New folder button.

5. Navigate to the Word folder and then save the file in the Word folder.

6. Create a PowerPoint presentation with one slide containing the title text, Sample PowerPoint Presentation, and then save it in the PowerPoint folder.

Figure 125

© 2014 Cengage Learning

7. Create an Excel spreadsheet containing the text, My First Budget Excel Spreadsheet, in cell A1 and then save it in the Excel folder.

8. Save an Access database named, My Music Database, in the Access folder.

9. Submit the assignment in the format specified by your instructor.

10. ✹ Based on your current knowledge of Word, PowerPoint, Excel, and Access, which app do you think you will use most frequently? Why?

Lab 3: Expand Your World: Cloud and Web Technologies
Creating Office Web App Documents

Problem: You are taking a class that requires you to create a file in Word, PowerPoint, and Excel. You will save these files to folders named for three different Office Web apps (Figure 126).

Instructions: Create the folders shown in Figure 126. Then, using the respective Office Web app, create a small file to save in each folder (i.e., create a Word document to save in the Word folder, a PowerPoint presentation to save in the PowerPoint folder, and so on).

1. Sign in to SkyDrive in your browser.
2. Use the Create button to create the folder structure shown in Figure 126.
3. In the Word folder, use the Create button to create a Word document with the file name, Notes, and containing the text, Important Test on Tuesday.
4. Save the document and then exit the app.
5. Navigate to the PowerPoint folder.
6. Create a PowerPoint presentation called Kirek Sales with one slide containing the title text, Online Presentation, and then exit the app.
7. Navigate to the Excel folder.
8. Create an Excel spreadsheet, called Kirek Sales Analysis, containing the text, Sales Cost Analysis, in cell A1, and then exit the app.
9. Submit the assignment in the format specified by your instructor.
10. ✸ Based on your current knowledge of SkyDrive, do you think you will use it? What about the Web apps?

© 2014 Cengage Learning

Figure 126

✸ Consider This: Your Turn

Apply your creative thinking and problem solving skills to design and implement a solution.

1: Creating Beginning Files for Classes

Personal

You are taking the following classes: Introduction to Sociology, Chemistry, Calculus, and Marketing. Create folders for each of the classes. Create a folder structure that will store the documents for each of these classes. Use Word to create a Word document with the name of each class and the class meeting locations and times. Use PowerPoint to begin creating a simple lab presentation for your chemistry class. It should begin with a title slide containing the text, Chemical Reactions. Create and save a database named Companies for your marketing class. The database does not need to contain any data. In the Calculus folder, create an Excel spreadsheet with the text, Excel Formulas, in cell A1. Use the concepts and techniques presented in this chapter to create the folders and files, and store the files in their respective locations. Submit your assignment in the format specified by your instructor.

✸ You made several decisions while determining the folder structure in this assignment. What was the rationale behind these decisions? Are there any other decisions that also might have worked?

Continued >

Consider This: Your Turn *continued*

2: Creating Folders
Professional

Your boss at the music store where you work part-time has asked for help with organizing his files. After looking through the files, you decided upon a file structure for her to use, including the following folders: CDs, DVDs, and general merchandise. Think about the different types of CDs, DVDs, and general merchandise that might be sold at your store, and create a folder structure that will be used to store information about the three types of items (CDs, DVDs, and general merchandise), and also can organize the different types of each item. For example, general merchandise might include items such as clothing, portable media players, and accessories. Use the concepts and techniques presented in this chapter to create the folders. Submit your assignment in the format specified by your instructor.

✳ You made several decisions while determining the folder structure in this assignment. What was the rationale behind these decisions? Justify why you feel this folder structure will help your boss organize her files.

3: Using Help
Research and Collaboration

You have just installed a new computer with the Windows operating system and want to be sure that it is protected from the threat of viruses, so you ask two of your friends to help research computer viruses, virus prevention, and virus removal. In a team of three people, each person should choose a topic (computer viruses, virus prevention, and virus removal) to research. Use the concepts and techniques presented in this chapter to use Help to find information regarding these topics. Create a Word document that contains steps to properly safeguard a computer from viruses, ways to prevent viruses, as well as the different ways to remove a virus should your computer become infected. Submit your assignment in the format specified by your instructor.

✳ You made several decisions while searching Windows Help and Support for this assignment. What decisions did you make? What was the rationale behind these decisions? How did you locate the required information about viruses in help?

Learn Online

Reinforce what you learned in this chapter with games, exercises, training, and many other online activities and resources.

Student Companion Site Reinforcement activities and resources are available at no additional cost on www.cengagebrain.com. Visit www.cengage.com/ct/studentdownload for detailed instructions about accessing the resources available at the Student Companion Site.

SAM Put your skills into practice with SAM Projects! If you have a SAM account, go to www.cengage.com/sam2013 to access SAM assignments for this chapter.

Office 365 Essentials

Microsoft product screen shots used with permission from Microsoft Corporation.

Objectives

You will have mastered the material in this chapter when you can:

- Describe the components of Office 365

- Compare Office 2013 to Office 365 subscription plans

- Understand the productivity tools of Office 365

- Sync multiple devices using Office 365

- Describe how business teams collaborate using SharePoint

- Describe how to use a SharePoint template to design a public website

- Describe how to conduct an online meeting with Lync

Explore Office 365

Introduction to Office 365

Microsoft Office 365 uses the cloud to deliver a subscription-based service offering the newest Office suite and much more. The Microsoft cloud provides Office software and information stored on remote servers all over the world. Your documents are located online or on the cloud, which provides you access to your information anywhere using a PC, Mac, tablet, mobile phone, or other device with an Internet connection. For businesses and students alike, Office 365 offers significant cost savings compared to the traditional cost of purchasing Microsoft Office 2013. In addition to the core desktop Office suite, Office 365 provides access to email, calendars, conferencing, file sharing, and website design, which sync across multiple devices.

Cloud Computing

Cloud computing refers to a collection of computer servers that house resources users access through the Internet (Figure 1). These resources include email messages, schedules, music, photos, videos, games, websites, programs, apps, servers, storage, and more. Instead of accessing these resources on your computer or mobile device, you access them on the cloud.

Figure 1

Cloud computing can help businesses be more efficient and save them money by shifting usage and the consumption of resources, such as servers and programs, from a local environment to the Internet. For example, an employee working during the day in California could use computing resources located in an office in London that is closed for the evening. When the company in California uses the computing resources, it pays a fee that is based on the amount of computing time and other resources it consumes, much in the same way that consumers pay utility companies for the amount of electricity they use.

Cloud computing is changing how users access and pay for software applications. Fading fast are the days when software packages were sold in boxes at a physical store location with a one-time purchase software license fee. Instead, the new pricing structure is a subscription-based model, where users pay a monthly or annual fee for the software that you can use on multiple devices. The cloud-based Office 365 offers the Office suite with added features that allow you to communicate and collaborate with others in real time.

When you create a free Microsoft account, do you get free cloud storage space?
Yes, when you create a free Microsoft account at Outlook.com, you have access to 7 GB of cloud storage for any type of files.

CONSIDER THIS

What Is Office 365?

Office 365 (Office365.com) is a collection of programs and services, which includes the Microsoft Office 2013 suite, file storage, online collaboration, and file synchronization, as shown in Figure 2 on the next page. You can access these services using your computer, browser, or supported mobile device. For example, a business has two options for providing Office to their employees. A business could purchase Office 2013 and install the software on company computers and servers; however, this traditional Office 2013 package with perpetual licensing does not include the communication and collaboration tools. Employees could not access the Office software if they were not using their work computers. In contrast, if the business purchases a monthly subscription to Office 365, each employee has access to the Office suite on up to five different computers, whether at home or work; company-wide email; web conferencing; website creation capabilities; cloud storage; and shared files. For a lower price, Office 365 provides many more features. In addition, a business may prefer a subscription plan with predictable monthly costs and no up-front infrastructure costs.

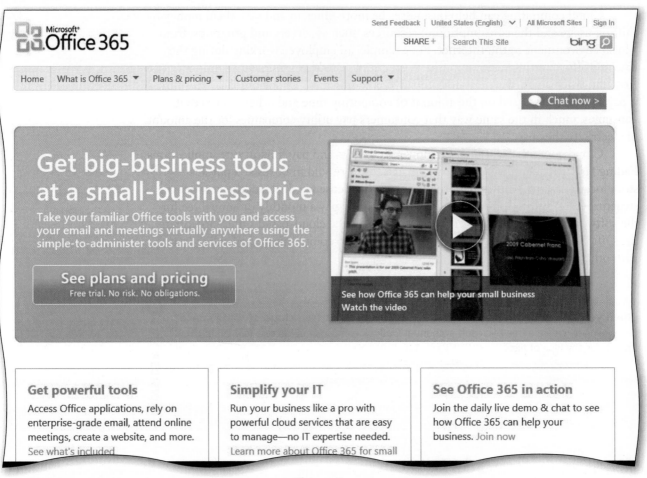

Figure 2

Office 2013 and Office 365 Features Comparison

Office 2013 is the name of the perpetual software package that includes individual applications that can be installed on a single computer. An Office 365 subscription comes with a license to install the software on multiple PCs or Macs at the same time, giving you more flexibility to use your Office products in your home, school, or workplace, whether on a computer or a mobile device. Office 365 provides the Office 2013 programs as part of a subscription service that includes online storage, sharing, and syncing via Microsoft cloud services as shown in Table 1.

Office 365 is available in business, consumer, education, and government editions. Office 365 combines the full version of the Microsoft Office desktop suite with cloud-based versions of Microsoft's communications and collaboration services. The subscription package includes:

- Microsoft Exchange online for shared email and calendars
- Microsoft SharePoint Online for shared file access and public website creation
- Microsoft Office Web apps for browser viewing
- Microsoft Lync Online for communication services

Table 1 Office 2013 and Office 365 Feature Comparison	
Office 2013 Professional (Installed on a single device)	**Office 365 Subscription (Installed on 2 to 5 devices)**
Microsoft Word	Microsoft Word
Microsoft Excel	Microsoft Excel
Microsoft PowerPoint	Microsoft PowerPoint
Microsoft Access	Microsoft Access
Microsoft Outlook	Microsoft Outlook
Microsoft Publisher	Microsoft Publisher
Microsoft OneNote	Microsoft OneNote
	email and calendars (Exchange Online)
	file sharing (SharePoint Online)
	public website design and publishing (SharePoint Online)
	browser-based Office Web Apps
	instant messaging (Lync Online)
	audio and video web conferencing (Lync Online)
	screen sharing with shared control (Lync Online)
	technical support

© 2014 Cengage Learning

Subscription-Based Office 365 Plans

Microsoft provides various subscription plans for Office 365 with different benefits for each individual or organization. Subscription plans include Office 365 Home Premium for home users, Office 365 University for students, Office 365 Small Business, Office 365 Small Business Premium, Office 365 Midsize Business, and Office 365 Enterprise and Government. During the Office 365 sign-up process, you create a Microsoft email address and password to use on your multiple devices. A single subscription to an Office 365 Home Premium account can cover an entire household. The Office 365 Home Premium subscription allows up to five concurrent installations by using the same email address and password combination. This means that your mother could be on the main family computer while you use your tablet and smartphone at the same time. You each can sign in with your individual Microsoft accounts using your settings and accessing your own documents using a single Office 365 subscription.

The Office 365 University subscription plan is designed for higher-education full-time and part-time students, faculty, and staff. By submitting the proper credentials, such as a school email address, students and faculty can purchase Office 365 University, including Word, PowerPoint, Excel, Access, Outlook, Publisher, and OneNote. A one-time payment covers a four-year subscription. In addition, Office 365 University provides users with 27 GB of SkyDrive cloud storage rather than the free 7 GB provided by a Microsoft account, and 60 Skype world minutes per month for videoconferencing. Students have the option of renewing for another four years, for a total of eight years. The Office 365 University edition is limited to two computers (PC or Mac).

The Microsoft Office 365 Business Plans can provide full support for employees to work from any location, whether they are in their traditional business office, commuting to and from work across the country, or working from a home office. Office 365 small business plans (Small Business and Small Business Premium) are best for companies with up to 10 employees, but can accommodate up to 25 users. Office 365 Midsize Business accommodates from 11 to 300 users. Office 365 Enterprise Plan fits organizations ranging in size from a single employee to 50,000-plus users. Each employee can install Microsoft Office 365 on five different computers.

First Look at Office 365

Microsoft Office 365 subscription plans offer all the same applications that are available in the Microsoft Office Professional 2013 suite in addition to multiple communication and collaboration tools. With Office 365 you can retrieve, edit, and save Office documents on the Office 365 cloud, coauthor documents in real time with others, and quickly initiate computer-based calls, instant messages, and web conferences with others.

Productivity Tools

Whether you are inserting audio and video into a Word document to create a high-impact business plan proposal or utilizing the visualization tools in Excel to chart the return on investment of a new mobile marketing program, Office 365 premium plans deliver the full Office product with the same features as the latest version of Microsoft Office. Office 365 uses a quick-start installation technology, called **Click-to-Run**, that downloads and installs the basics within minutes, so that users are able to start working almost immediately. It also includes **Office on Demand**, which streams Office to Windows 7- and Windows 8-based PCs for work performed on public computers. The single-use copy that is installed temporarily on the Windows computer does not count toward the device limit. No installation is necessary when using Office on Demand, and the applications disappear from the computer once you are finished using them. If you have a document on a USB drive or on SkyDrive that you need to edit on another PC, you can use Office on Demand to get the full version of Word in just a few minutes.

In effect, the Office 365 subscription provides access to the full Office applications wherever you are working. When you access your Office 365 account management panel, three choices are listed: 32- and 64-bit versions of Office 2013, and Office for Mac. Selecting the third option will initiate a download of an installer that must be run in the standard OS X fashion. When you install Office 365 on a Mac, the most current Mac version of Office is installed.

CONSIDER THIS

Unlike Google, which offers online documents, spreadsheets, and presentations called Google Docs, Microsoft Office 365 installs locally on your computer in addition to being available online. Google Docs is entirely browser based, which means if you are not connected to the Internet, you cannot access your Google Docs files.

Email and Calendars

In business, sharing information is essential to meeting the needs of your customers and staff. Office 365 offers shared access to business email, calendars, and contacts using **Exchange Online** from a computer, tablet, phone, and browser. The cloud-based Exchange Online enables business people to access Outlook information from anywhere at any time, while eliminating the cost of purchasing and maintaining servers to store data. If you need to meet with a colleague about a new project, you can compare calendars to view availability, confirm conference room availability, share project contacts, search email messages related to the project, and send email invitations to the project meeting. Exchange Online also allows you to search and access your company's address list.

Online Meetings

When you are working with a team on a project that requires interaction, email and text communications can slow the communications process. Microsoft Lync connects you with others by facilitating real-time, interactive presentations and meetings over the Internet using both video and audio calling. As shown in Figure 3, you can conduct an online meeting with a team member or customer that includes an instant messaging conversation, audio, high-definition video, virtual whiteboards, and screen sharing. If the customer does not have an Office 365 subscription, they still can join the meeting through the invitation link, which runs the Lync Web App.

Skype is another tool in the Office 365 subscription, which enables users to place video calls to computers and smartphones and voice calls to landlines. Skype also supports instant message and file sharing to computers and mobile devices. While Skype may be adequate for simple communication, Lync provides for more robust, comprehensive communications. These robust features include high-definition (HD) videoconferencing capabilities, a whiteboard, and a larger audience. Using Lync, meeting attendees simultaneously can view up to five participants' video, identify the active speaker, and associate names with faces. Lync supports up to 250 attendees per meeting. Unlike Skype, Lync meetings can be recorded for replaying at a later time. This enables businesses and schools to schedule meetings or organize online classes using Lync capabilities.

File Sharing

Office 365 includes a team site, which is a password-protected portal that supports sharing of large, difficult-to-email files and provides a single location for the latest versions of documents. In business, for example, colleagues working on common projects can save valuable time by being able to access instantly the latest master copy of each document. Security can be managed through different

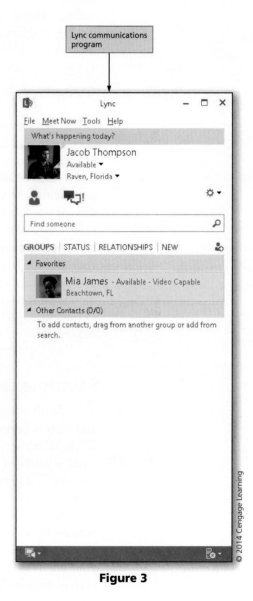

Lync communications program

Figure 3

© 2014 Cengage Learning

levels of user access so that users see only what they are supposed to see. Office 365 provides access to shared files using the cloud, making writing, editing, and sharing documents easier. If a construction company creates a commercial bid for a building project, the customers can be invited to view an Excel spreadsheet bid, construction timetable with a shared calendar, and an Access database of all the materials needed using the file sharing feature online.

Website Creation

Office 365 business plan subscriptions include a built-in hosted public website, where customers and clients can find an online storefront of a company. This public website, called the Website, can be customized to market a company by using various templates within the Office 365 cloud. The website creation tools include those for adding a theme, graphics, fonts, maps, directions, blogs, stock tickers, slide shows, PayPal, weather, and videos to interact with the website's visitors.

Synchronization

Office 365 subscription plans provide a central place to store and access your documents and business information. A feature of Office 365 ensures the original and backup computer files in two or more locations are identical through a process called **Active Directory Synchronization**. For example, if you open a PowerPoint presentation on your smartphone while you are riding a city bus and then add a new slide as you head to school, the PowerPoint presentation automatically is synced with Office 365. When you arrive on campus and open the PowerPoint presentation on a school computer, your new slide already is part of the finished slide show. By storing your files in Office 365, you can access your files on another computer if your home computer fails, with no loss of time or important information. When using your mobile phone's data plan, you do not need to search for a Wi-Fi hot spot to connect to the Office 365 cloud. Computer labs in schools can be configured to synchronize automatically all student files to Office 365 online.

Multiple Device Access to Office 365

With a single sign-in process, Office 365 provides access to multiple computers and mobile devices, including Android smartphones and tablets, Apple iPhones and iPads, Windows phones, and Blackberry phones. After you configure your devices' email settings, you can view your Microsoft account calendar, contacts, and email. Your personalized settings, preferences, and documents can be synchronized among all the different devices included in your Office 365 premium subscription. With the mobility of Office 365, students and employees can work anywhere, accessing information and responding to email requests immediately. If you lose your phone, Office 365 includes a feature that allows you to remotely wipe your phone clean of any data. By wiping your phone's data, you can prevent any unauthorized access to sensitive information, such as your banking information, passwords, and contacts, as well as discourage identity theft. Because your phone contacts and other information are stored on the Microsoft cloud, damaged or lost equipment is never a problem.

CONSIDER THIS

A thief can be quite resourceful if he or she steals your phone. Before you can alert your parents or spouse to the theft, they might receive a text from "you" asking for your ATM or credit card PIN number. Your parents or spouse might then reply with the PIN number. Your bank account could be emptied in minutes.

Teams Using Office 365 in Business

In the business world, rarely does an employee work in isolation. Companies need their employees to collaborate, whether they work in the same office or in locations around the world. Telecommuters working from home can communicate as if they were on-site by using a common team website and conferencing software. SharePoint Online and Lync Online provide seamless communication.

Small business subscription plans as low as $6.00 per user per month allow employees to create and store Word documents, Excel spreadsheets, and PowerPoint presentations online and communicate with one another via email, instant messaging, or video chat as they work on projects together. As shown in Figure 4, a team portal page is shown when you subscribe at https://portal.microsoftonline.com. Larger companies and those requiring more features can take advantage of the Office 365 business premium package, which, in addition to the features listed above, provides access to the Office 365 portal website and eliminates the effort and cost of the users maintaining their own costly computer servers.

Figure 4

Email Communication Using Exchange

Office 365 includes Exchange Online, an email-based collaborative communications server for business. Exchange enables employees to be more productive by effectively managing email across multiple devices and facilitating teamwork.

Collaboration Using SharePoint

SharePoint Online, a part of Office 365 subscription plans, allows employees to collaborate with one another, share documents, post announcements, and track tasks, as shown in Table 2.

Table 2 Office 365 SharePoint Features	
Team Site Feature	**Description**
Calendar	Track important dates
Shared Document Library	Store related documents according to topic; picture, report, and slide libraries often are included
Task List	Track team tasks according to who is responsible for completion
Team Discussion Board	Discuss the topics at hand in an open forum
Contacts List	Share contact lists of employees, customers, contractors, and suppliers

Office 365 provides the tools to plan meetings. Users can share calendars side by side, view availability, and suggest meeting times from shared calendars. Typically, a SharePoint team administrator or website owner establishes a folder structure to share and manage documents. The team website is fully searchable online, making locating and sharing data more efficient than using a local server. With a team website, everyone on the team has a central location to store and find all the information for a project, client, or department, as shown in Figure 5.

Figure 5

Website Design Using SharePoint

SharePoint provides templates to create a professional looking, public website for an online presence to market your business. As shown in Figure 6, a local pet sitting business is setting up a business website by customizing a SharePoint template. SharePoint Public Website includes features within the Design Manager that you use to customize and design your website by adding your own images, forms, style sheets, maps, themes, and social networking tools. When you finish customizing your business site, you can apply your own domain name to the site. A **domain** is a unique web address that identifies where your website can be found. Office 365 SharePoint hosts your website as part of your subscription. Your customers easily can find your business online and learn about your services.

BTW
Creating SharePoint Intranet Sites
A SharePoint website also can be customized to serve as an internal company website for private communications within the company.

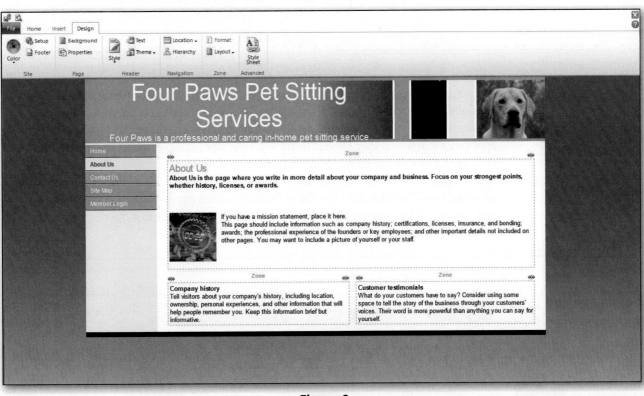

Figure 6

Real-Time Communications Using Lync

Lync Online is Microsoft's server platform for online team communications and comes bundled with Office 365 business subscriptions. As shown in Figure 7, Lync connects in real time to allow instant messaging, videoconferencing, and voice communications; it also integrates with email and Microsoft Office applications.

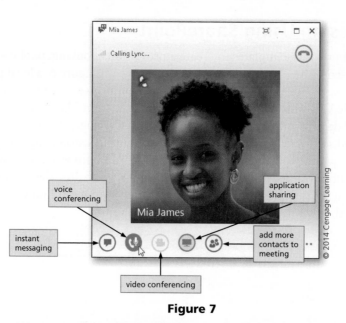

Figure 7

Lync allows you to connect with staff at remote locations using instant messaging capabilities, desktop sharing, videoconferencing, and shared agendas or documents. Lync is integrated into Office 365, which allows staff to start communicating from within the applications in which they currently are working. For example, while an employee is creating a PowerPoint presentation for a new product line, as shown in Figure 8, Lync enables him or her to collaborate with the entire team about the details of the product presentation. The team can view the presenter's screen displaying the PowerPoint presentation. The presenter can share control with any member of the team and can share his or her screen at any time during the Lync meeting.

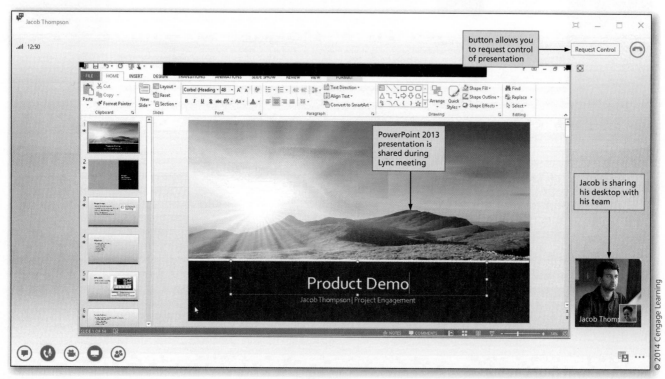

Figure 8

Users can send a Lync meeting request to schedule a team meeting, or an impromptu conversation can be started immediately using the Meet Now feature. Participants receive a Lync meeting request link via an email message, and when they click the meeting request link, Lync automatically connects them to the online conference. If the participant does not have Lync installed, the Lync Web App automatically connects to the Lync meeting through the user's PC or Mac OS X browser. If a participant is away from his or her computer, he or she still can participate using the Lync Mobile apps for Windows Phone, iOS, and Android. As shown in Figure 9, Lync utilizes **instant messaging** (IM), allowing two or more people to share text messages. They can communicate in real time, similar to a voice conversation. In addition to a simple instant message, Lync provides a feature called **persistent chat**, which allows end-users to participate in a working session of instant messages that is persistent or sustained over a specified amount of time in a moderated chat room. Consider having an instant messaging session with a group of colleagues in different parts of your organization, regardless of geographic region, where you all are working on the same project. Over the course of the project, different people post questions and concerns, and others are able to respond to all those who have subscribed to your topic or been admitted to the chat room. Instead of a long trail of email messages, a team can keep information in a controlled environment with a full history of the discussion in one location.

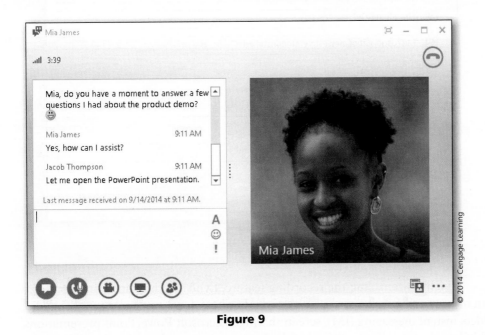

Figure 9

Lync also delivers support for full high-definition (HD) videoconferencing, so that a team can have a clear view of the participants, products, and demos. Before you join the video feed, you can preview your video feed to make sure your video camera is at the correct angle, your image is centered within the video frame, and that your room lighting provides for a clear image. The Lync preview option is important in creating a positive first impression over video. Your audio devices can be tested for clarity to make sure your headset, microphone, and speakers are functioning properly.

Lync provides a polling feature that presenters can use to ask the participants' opinions during a meeting (Figure 10). The poll question can consist of up to seven possible choices. The presenter has the option to view the results privately or share the results with the entire group.

Create a Poll

Poll name:

Office 365 Features

Question:

What is your favorite feature of Office 365?

Choices:

Lync Online video conferencing

SharePoint Online sites

Microsoft Office newest version installed

Microsoft SkyDrive storage

Microsoft Exchange email unlimited access

Lync Online polling

Lync Online screen sharing

Create   Cancel

© 2014 Cengage Learning

Figure 10

Finally, by enabling the recording feature, Lync meetings and conversations can be captured for viewing at a later time. For instance, you can capture the audio, video, instant messaging (IM), screen sharing, Microsoft PowerPoint presentations, whiteboard, and polling portions of the Lync session and then play them back just as they transpired during the live Lync event. The meeting recordings can be made available to others so that they can view all or part of the Lync event. Instructors can record Lync online class sessions for students who were unable to attend the original presentation. The recording starts in Microsoft Lync; recordings then can be viewed within the Recording Manager feature.

Chapter Summary

In this chapter, you have learned how to subscribe to Office 365, which provides local and online access to Office applications, email, document sharing, web conferencing, and business websites. You also learned how a business can utilize Office 365 features on the cloud to facilitate teamwork. Finally, you learned about the features of SharePoint and Lync, which provide collaboration and communications for business teams using Office 365.

✳ Consider This: Your Turn

Apply your creative thinking and problem solving skills to design and implement a solution.

1: Comparing Office 365 Personal Plans

Personal

Part 1:   You are a freshman in college living at home with your family. You are considering if it would be a better value to subscribe to Office 365 University or Office 365 Home Premium. Write a one-page document comparing the pros and cons of the two subscription plans. Research the different subscriptions in detail at Office365.com. Submit your assignment in the format specified by your instructor.

Part 2:   ✳ Which type of computer and/or devices would you use with your Office 365 subscription? If you are at a friend's home that does not have Office 365, how could you access your Office files if you do not have your computer or mobile device with you?

2: Upgrading a Local Business to Office 365

Professional

Part 1:   You are an employee at Impact Digital Marketing, a small marketing firm with 12 employees. The firm is setting up an Office 365 Small Business subscription next week, and you need to compose an email message with multiple paragraphs to explain the features of this new subscription plan to the members of your firm. Research the Office 365 Small Business subscription plan in detail at Office365.com, and compile your findings in an email message. Submit your assignment in the format specified by your instructor.

Part 2:   ✳ Give three examples of how a marketing firm could use Lync. How could a marketing firm use the SharePoint Websites feature?

3: Conducting a Lync Meeting

Research and Collaboration

* Students need an Office 365 subscription to complete the following assignment.

Part 1:   Using your Office 365 subscription, conduct a meeting using Lync. Working with a partner, use your Office 365 subscription to research how to use Lync. Then, conduct a 15-minute Lync meeting, including instant messaging, to discuss the features of Lync. Use the concepts and techniques presented in this chapter to create the Lync meeting. Submit your assignment in the format specified by your instructor.

Part 2:   ✳ When using Lync in business, when would the video feature best be utilized?

1 Creating, Formatting, and Editing a Word Document with a Picture

Microsoft product screen shots used with permission from Microsoft Corporation.

Objectives

You will have mastered the material in this chapter when you can:

- Enter text in a Word document
- Check spelling as you type
- Format paragraphs
- Format text
- Undo and redo commands or actions
- Change theme colors
- Insert digital pictures in a Word document
- Format pictures
- Add a page border
- Adjust spacing
- Change document properties
- Correct errors and revise a document
- Print and read a document

1 | Creating, Formatting, and Editing a Word Document with a Picture

Introduction

To advertise a sale, promote a business, publicize an event, or convey a message to the community, you may want to create a flyer and hand it out in person or post it in a public location. Libraries, schools, religious organizations, grocery stores, coffee shops, and other places often provide bulletin boards or windows for flyers. You also see flyers posted on webpages or as email messages.

Flyers announce personal items for sale or rent (car, boat, apartment); garage or block sales; services being offered (animal care, housecleaning, lessons, tours); membership, sponsorship, or donation requests (club, religious organization, charity); and other messages, such as a lost or found pet.

Project — Flyer with a Picture

Individuals and businesses create flyers to gain public attention. Flyers, which usually are a single page in length, are an inexpensive means of reaching the community. Many flyers, however, go unnoticed because they are designed poorly.

The project in this chapter follows general guidelines and uses Word to create the flyer shown in Figure 1–1. This colorful, eye-catching flyer announces tour adventures. The picture of the tour group on the mountain trail, taken with a digital camera, entices passersby or viewers to stop and look at the flyer. The headline on the flyer is large and colorful to draw attention into the text. The body copy below the picture briefly describes the tours, along with a bulleted list that concisely highlights important tour information. The signature line of the flyer calls attention to the contact phone number. The word, breathtaking, and the signature line are in a different color so that they stand apart from the rest of the text on the flyer. Finally, the graphical page border nicely frames and complements the contents of the flyer.

For an introduction to Office and instruction about how to perform basic tasks in Office apps, read the Office and Windows chapter at the beginning of this book, where you can learn how to run an application, use the ribbon, save a file, open a file, exit an application, use Help, and much more.

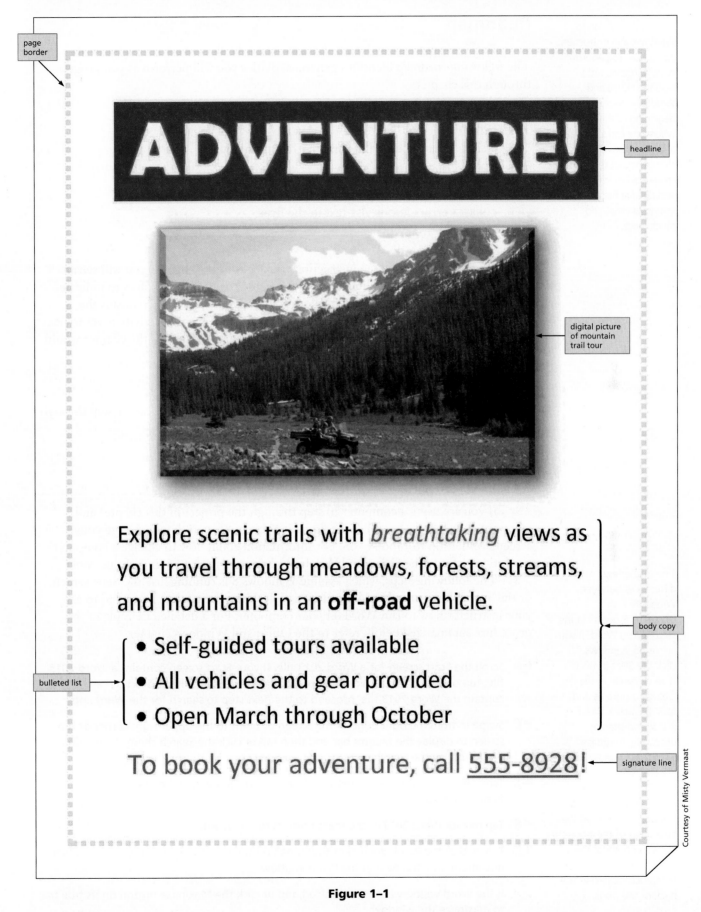

page border

ADVENTURE!

headline

digital picture of mountain trail tour

Explore scenic trails with *breathtaking* views as you travel through meadows, forests, streams, and mountains in an **off-road** vehicle.

body copy

bulleted list

- Self-guided tours available
- All vehicles and gear provided
- Open March through October

To book your adventure, call 555-8928!

signature line

Figure 1–1

For an introduction to Windows and instruction about how to perform basic Windows tasks, read the Office and Windows chapter at the beginning of this book, where you can learn how to resize windows, change screen resolution, create folders, move and rename files, use Windows Help, and much more.

Roadmap

In this chapter, you will learn how to create the flyer shown in Figure 1–1. The following roadmap identifies general activities you will perform as you progress through this chapter:

1. ENTER TEXT in a new document.
2. FORMAT the TEXT in the flyer.
3. INSERT a PICTURE, called Mountain Trail, in the flyer.
4. FORMAT the PICTURE in the flyer.
5. ENHANCE the PAGE with a border and spacing.
6. CORRECT errors AND REVISE text in the flyer.
7. PRINT OR READ the flyer.

At the beginning of step instructions throughout the chapter, you will see an abbreviated form of this roadmap. The abbreviated roadmap uses colors to indicate chapter progress: gray means the chapter is beyond that activity, blue means the task being shown is covered in that activity, and black means that activity is yet to be covered. For example, the following abbreviated roadmap indicates the chapter would be showing a task in the 2 FORMAT TEXT activity.

| 1 ENTER TEXT | 2 FORMAT TEXT | 3 INSERT PICTURE | 4 FORMAT PICTURE |

| 5 ENHANCE PAGE | 6 CORRECT & REVISE | 7 PRINT OR READ |

Use the abbreviated roadmap as a progress guide while you read or step through the instructions in this chapter.

To Run Word and Create a Blank Document

If you are using a computer to step through the project in this chapter and you want your screens to match the figures in this book, you should change your screen's resolution to 1366×768. For information about how to change a computer's resolution, refer to the Office and Windows chapter at the beginning of this book.

The following steps, which assume Windows 8 is running, use the Start screen or the Search box to run Word based on a typical installation. You may need to ask your instructor how to run Word on your computer. For a detailed example of the procedure summarized below, refer to the Office and Windows chapter.

One of the few differences between Windows 7 and Windows 8 occurs in the steps to run Word. If you are using Windows 7, click the Start button, type **Word** in the 'Search programs and files' box, click Word 2013, and then, if necessary, maximize the Word window. For detailed steps to run Word in Windows 7, refer to the Office and Windows chapter at the beginning of this book. For a summary of the steps, refer to the Quick Reference located at the back of this book.

1 Scroll the Start screen for a Word 2013 tile. If your Start screen contains a Word 2013 tile, tap or click it to run Word and then proceed to Step 5; if the Start screen does not contain the Word 2013 tile, proceed to the next step to search for the Word app.

2 Swipe in from the right edge of the screen or point to the upper-right corner of the screen to display the Charms bar and then tap or click the Search charm on the Charms bar to display the Search menu.

3 Type **Word** as the search text in the Search box and watch the search results appear in the Apps list.

4 Tap or click Word 2013 in the search results to run Word.

5 Tap or click the Blank document thumbnail on the Word start screen to create a blank document and display it in the Word window.

6 If the Word window is not maximized, tap or click the Maximize button on its title bar to maximize the window.

7 If the Print Layout button on the status bar is not selected (shown in Figure 1–2), tap or click it so that your screen is in Print Layout view.

Q&A What is Print Layout view?
The default (preset) view in Word is **Print Layout view**, which shows the document on a mock sheet of paper in the document window.

8 If Normal (HOME tab | Styles group) is not selected in the Styles gallery (shown in Figure 1–2), tap or click it so that your document uses the Normal style.

Q&A What is the Normal style?
When you create a document, Word formats the text using a particular style. The default style in Word is called the **Normal style**, which is discussed later in this book.

What if rulers appear on my screen?
Tap or click VIEW on the ribbon to display the VIEW tab and then remove the check mark from the View Ruler check box (VIEW tab | Show group).

Entering Text

The first step in creating a document is to enter its text. With the projects in this book, you enter text by typing on the keyboard. By default, Word positions text you type at the left margin. In a later section of this chapter, you will learn how to format, or change the appearance of, the entered text.

BTW
The Word Window
The chapters in this book begin with the Word window appearing as it did at the initial installation of the software. Your Word window may look different depending on your screen resolution and other Word settings.

To Type Text

1 ENTER TEXT | 2 FORMAT TEXT | 3 INSERT PICTURE | 4 FORMAT PICTURE
5 ENHANCE PAGE | 6 CORRECT & REVISE | 7 PRINT OR READ

To begin creating the flyer in this chapter, type the headline in the document window. *Why? The headline is the first line of text in the Adventure Flyer.* The following steps type the first line of text in the document.

1
• Type **Adventure!** as the headline (Figure 1–2).

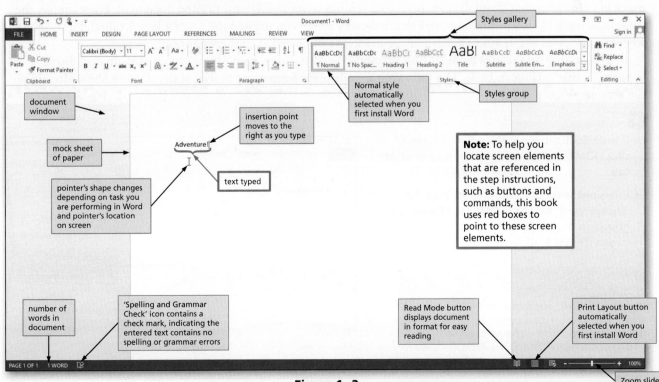

Figure 1–2

Q&A What if I make an error while typing?
You can press the BACKSPACE key until you have deleted the text in error and then retype the text correctly.

What is the purpose of the Spelling and Grammar Check icon on the status bar?
The **Spelling and Grammar Check icon** displays either a check mark to indicate the entered text contains no spelling or grammar errors, or an X to indicate that it found potential errors. Word flags potential errors in the document with a red, green, or blue wavy underline. Later in this chapter, you will learn how to fix flagged errors.

2

- Press the ENTER key to move the insertion point to the beginning of the next line (Figure 1–3).

Q&A Why did blank space appear between the headline and the insertion point?
Each time you press the ENTER key, Word creates a new paragraph and inserts blank space between the two paragraphs. Later in this chapter, you will learn how to increase and decrease the spacing between paragraphs.

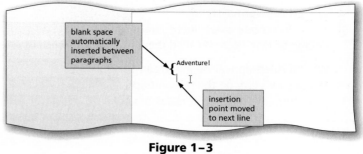

Figure 1–3

CONSIDER THIS

How do you use the touch keyboard with a touch screen?
To display the on-screen touch keyboard, tap the Touch Keyboard button on the Windows taskbar. When finished using the touch keyboard, tap the X button on the touch keyboard to close the keyboard.

To Display Formatting Marks

1 ENTER TEXT | 2 FORMAT TEXT | 3 INSERT PICTURE | 4 FORMAT PICTURE
5 ENHANCE PAGE | 6 CORRECT & REVISE | 7 PRINT OR READ

You may find it helpful to display formatting marks while working in a document. *Why? Formatting marks indicate where in a document you press the ENTER key, SPACEBAR, and other nonprinting characters.* A **formatting mark** is a character that Word displays on the screen but is not visible on a printed document. For example, the paragraph mark (¶) is a formatting mark that indicates where you pressed the ENTER key. A raised dot (·) shows where you pressed the SPACEBAR. Formatting marks are discussed as they appear on the screen.

Depending on settings made during previous Word sessions, your Word screen already may display formatting marks (Figure 1–4). The following step displays formatting marks, if they do not show already on the screen.

1

- If the HOME tab is not the active tab, tap or click HOME on the ribbon to display the HOME tab.

- If it is not selected already, tap or click the 'Show/Hide ¶' button (HOME tab | Paragraph group) to display formatting marks on the screen (Figure 1–4).

BTW
Zooming
If text is too small for you to read on the screen, you can zoom the document by dragging the Zoom slider on the status bar or tapping or clicking the Zoom Out or Zoom In buttons on the status bar. Changing the zoom has no effect on the printed document.

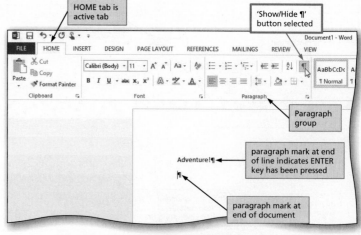

Figure 1–4

Q&A What if I do not want formatting marks to show on the screen?

You can hide them by tapping or clicking the 'Show/Hide ¶' button (HOME tab | Paragraph group) again. It is recommended that you display formatting marks so that you visually can identify when you press the ENTER key, SPACEBAR, and other keys associated with nonprinting characters. Most of the document windows presented in this book, therefore, show formatting marks.

Other Ways

1. Press CTRL+SHIFT+*

---

1 ENTER TEXT | 2 FORMAT TEXT | 3 INSERT PICTURE | 4 FORMAT PICTURE
5 ENHANCE PAGE | 6 CORRECT & REVISE | 7 PRINT OR READ

To Insert a Blank Line

In the flyer, the digital picture of the mountain trail appears between the headline and body copy. You will not insert this picture, however, until after you enter and format all text. *Why? Although you can format text and insert pictures in any order, for illustration purposes, this chapter formats all text first before inserting the picture. Thus, you leave a blank line in the document as a placeholder for the picture.*

To enter a blank line in a document, press the ENTER key without typing any text on the line. The following step inserts one blank line below the headline.

1

• Press the ENTER key to insert a blank line in the document (Figure 1–5).

Figure 1–5

---

1 ENTER TEXT | 2 FORMAT TEXT | 3 INSERT PICTURE | 4 FORMAT PICTURE
5 ENHANCE PAGE | 6 CORRECT & REVISE | 7 PRINT OR READ

To Zoom Page Width

The next step in creating this flyer is to enlarge the contents that appear on the screen. *Why? You would like the text on the screen to be larger so that it is easier to read.* The document currently displays at 100% (shown in Figure 1–6). With Word, you can zoom page width, which zooms (enlarges or shrinks) the mock sheet of paper on the screen so that it is the width of the Word window. The following steps zoom page width.

1

• Tap or click VIEW on the ribbon to display the VIEW tab.

Figure 1–6

2

- Tap or click the Page Width button (VIEW tab | Zoom group) to display the page the same width as the document window (Figure 1–7).

Q&A If I change the zoom, will the document print differently?
Changing the zoom has no effect on the printed document.

What are the other predefined zoom options?
Through the VIEW tab | Zoom group or the Zoom dialog box (Zoom button in Zoom group), you can zoom to one page (an entire single page appears in the document window), many pages (multiple pages appear at once in the document window), page width, text width, and a variety of set percentages. Whereas page width zoom places the edges of the page at the edges of the document window, text width zoom places the document contents at the edges of the document window.

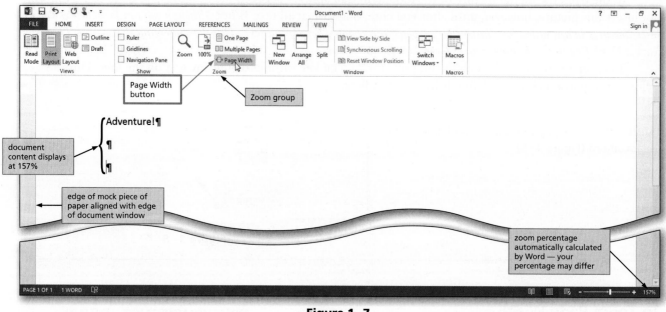

Figure 1–7

Other Ways

1. Tap or click Zoom button (VIEW tab | Zoom group), tap or click Page width (Zoom dialog box), tap or click OK button

BTW

The Ribbon and Screen Resolution
Word may change how the groups and buttons within the groups appear on the ribbon, depending on the computer's screen resolution. Thus, your ribbon may look different from the ones in this book if you are using a screen resolution other than 1366 × 768.

Wordwrap

Wordwrap allows you to type words in a paragraph continually without pressing the ENTER key at the end of each line. As you type, if a word extends beyond the right margin, Word also automatically positions that word on the next line along with the insertion point.

Word creates a new paragraph each time you press the ENTER key. Thus, as you type text in the document window, do not press the ENTER key when the insertion point reaches the right margin. Instead, press the ENTER key only in these circumstances:

1. To insert a blank line(s) in a document (as shown in the previous steps)
2. To begin a new paragraph
3. To terminate a short line of text and advance to the next line
4. To respond to questions or prompts in Word dialog boxes, task panes, and other on-screen objects

To Wordwrap Text as You Type

The next step in creating the flyer is to type the body copy. ***Why?*** *In many flyers, the body copy text appears below the headline.* The following steps illustrate how the body copy text wordwraps as you enter it in the document.

1

- Type the first sentence of the body copy: `Explore scenic trails with breathtaking views as you travel through meadows, forests, streams, and mountains in an off-road vehicle.`

Q&A Why does my document wrap on different words?
The printer connected to a computer is one factor that can control where wordwrap occurs for each line in a document. Thus, it is possible that the same document could wordwrap differently if printed on different printers.

2

- Press the ENTER key to position the insertion point on the next line in the document (Figure 1–8).

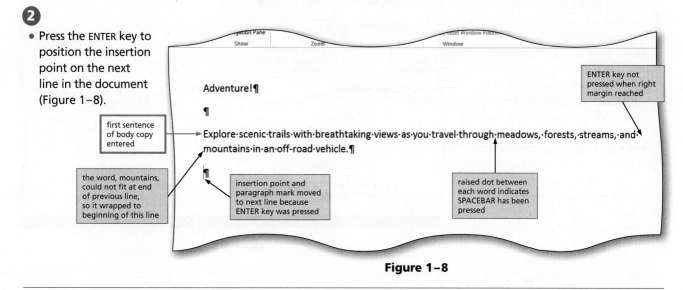

Figure 1–8

Spelling and Grammar Check

As you type text in a document, Word checks your typing for possible spelling and grammar errors. If all of the words you have typed are in Word's dictionary and your grammar is correct, as mentioned earlier, the Spelling and Grammar Check icon on the status bar displays a check mark. Otherwise, the icon shows an X. In this case, Word flags the potential error in the document window with a red, green, or blue wavy underline. A red wavy underline means the flagged text is not in Word's dictionary (because it is a proper name or misspelled). A green wavy underline indicates the text may be incorrect grammatically. A blue wavy underline indicates the text may contain a contextual spelling error, such as the misuse of homophones (words that are pronounced the same but that have different spellings or meanings, such as one and won). Although you can check the entire document for spelling and grammar errors at once, you also can check flagged errors as they appear on the screen.

A flagged word is not necessarily misspelled. For example, many names, abbreviations, and specialized terms are not in Word's main dictionary. In these cases, you can instruct Word to ignore the flagged word. As you type, Word also detects duplicate words while checking for spelling errors. For example, if your document contains the phrase, to the the store, Word places a red wavy underline below the second occurrence of the word, the.

BTW
Automatic Spelling Correction
As you type, Word automatically corrects some misspelled words. For example, if you type recieve, Word automatically corrects the misspelling and displays the word, receive, when you press the SPACEBAR or type a punctuation mark. To see a complete list of automatically corrected words, click FILE on the ribbon to open the Backstage view, click Options in the Backstage view, click Proofing in the left pane (Word Options dialog box), click the AutoCorrect Options button, and then scroll through the list near the bottom of the dialog box.

To Check Spelling and Grammar as You Type

1 ENTER TEXT | 2 FORMAT TEXT | 3 INSERT PICTURE | 4 FORMAT PICTURE
5 ENHANCE PAGE | 6 CORRECT & REVISE | 7 PRINT OR READ

In the following steps, the word, tours, has been misspelled intentionally as tuors. *Why?* *These steps illustrate Word's check spelling as you type feature. If you are completing this project on a computer, your flyer may contain different or no misspelled words, depending on the accuracy of your typing.*

1

- Type **Self-guided tuors** and then press the SPACEBAR, so that a red wavy line appears below the misspelled word (Figure 1–9).

Q&A What if Word does not flag my spelling and grammar errors with wavy underlines?

To verify that the check spelling and grammar as you type features are enabled, tap or click FILE on the ribbon to open the Backstage view and then tap or click Options in the Backstage view. When the Word Options dialog box is displayed, tap or click Proofing in the left pane, and then ensure the 'Check spelling as you type' and 'Mark grammar errors as you type' check boxes contain check marks. Also ensure the 'Hide spelling errors in this document only' and 'Hide grammar errors in this document only' check boxes do not contain check marks. Tap or click the OK button.

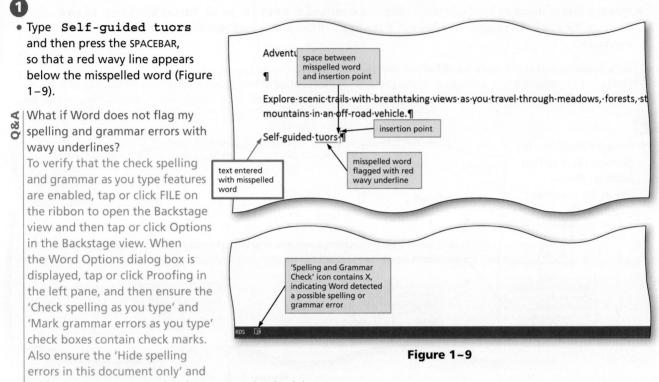

Figure 1–9

2

- Press and hold or right-click the flagged word (tuors, in this case) to display a shortcut menu that presents a list of suggested spelling corrections for the flagged word (Figure 1–10).

Q&A What if, when I press and hold or right-click the misspelled word, my desired correction is not in the list on the shortcut menu?

You can tap or click outside the shortcut menu to close the shortcut menu and then retype the correct word.

What if a flagged word actually is, for example, a proper name and spelled correctly?

Press and hold or right-click it and then tap or click Ignore All on the shortcut menu to instruct Word not to flag future occurrences of the same word in this document.

Figure 1–10

3

- Tap or click tours on the shortcut menu to replace the misspelled word in the document with a correctly spelled word (Figure 1–11).

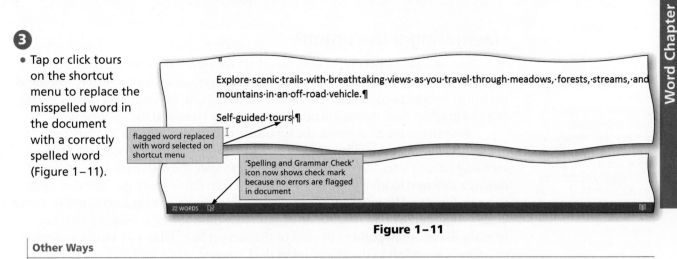

Figure 1–11

Other Ways
1. Tap or click 'Spelling and Grammar Check' icon on status bar, tap or click desired word in Spelling pane, tap or click Change button, tap or click OK button

To Enter More Text

In the flyer, the text yet to be entered includes the remainder of the body copy, which will be formatted as a bulleted list, and the signature line. The next steps enter the remainder of text in the flyer.

1 Press the END key to move the insertion point to the end of the current line.

2 Type **available** and then press the ENTER key.

3 Type **Open March through October** and then press the ENTER key.

4 Type **All vehicles and gear provided** and then press the ENTER key.

5 Type the signature line in the flyer (Figure 1–12): **To book your adventure, call 555-8928!**

If requested by your instructor, enter your phone number instead of 555-8928 in the signature line.

BTW
Character Widths
Many word processing documents use variable character fonts, where some characters are wider than others; for example, the letter w is wider than the letter i.

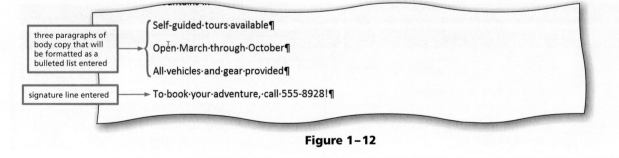

Figure 1–12

CONSIDER THIS

How should you organize text in a flyer?
The text in a flyer typically is organized into three areas: headline, body copy, and signature line.

- The **headline** is the first line of text on the flyer. It conveys the product or service being offered, such as a car for sale, personal lessons, or sightseeing tours, or the benefit that will be gained, such as a convenience, better performance, greater security, higher earnings, or more comfort, or it can contain a message, such as a lost or found pet.

- The **body copy** consists of text between the headline and the signature line. This text highlights the key points of the message in as few words as possible. It should be easy to read and follow. While emphasizing the positive, the body copy must be realistic, truthful, and believable.

- The **signature line**, which is the last line of text on the flyer, contains contact information or identifies a call to action.

Navigating a Document

BTW
Minimize Wrist Injury
Computer users frequently switch among touch gestures, the keyboard, and the mouse during a word processing session; such switching strains the wrist. To help prevent wrist injury, minimize switching. For instance, if your fingertips already are on the screen, use your finger to slide the document to a new location. If your fingers are already on the keyboard, use keyboard keys to scroll. If your hand already is on the mouse, use the mouse to scroll.

You view only a portion of a document on the screen through the document window. At some point when you type text or insert graphics, Word probably will **scroll** the top or bottom portion of the document off the screen. Although you cannot see the text and graphics once they scroll off the screen, they remain in the document.

You can use touch gestures, the keyboard, or a mouse to scroll to a different location in a document and/or move the insertion point around a document. If you are using a touch screen, simply use your finger to slide the document up or down to display a different location in the document and then tap to move the insertion point to a new location. When you use the keyboard, the insertion point automatically moves when you press the desired keys. For example, the previous steps used the END key to move the insertion point to the end of the current line. Table 1–1 outlines various techniques to navigate a document using the keyboard.

With the mouse, you can use the scroll arrows or the scroll box on the scroll bar to display a different portion of the document in the document window and then click the mouse to move the insertion point to that location. Table 1–2 explains various techniques for using the scroll bar to scroll vertically with the mouse.

Table 1–1 Moving the Insertion Point with the Keyboard

Insertion Point Direction	Key(s) to Press	Insertion Point Direction	Key(s) to Press
Left one character	LEFT ARROW	Up one paragraph	CTRL+UP ARROW
Right one character	RIGHT ARROW	Down one paragraph	CTRL+DOWN ARROW
Left one word	CTRL+LEFT ARROW	Up one screen	PAGE UP
Right one word	CTRL+RIGHT ARROW	Down one screen	PAGE DOWN
Up one line	UP ARROW	To top of document window	ALT+CTRL+PAGE UP
Down one line	DOWN ARROW	To bottom of document window	ALT+CTRL+PAGE DOWN
To end of line	END	To beginning of document	CTRL+HOME
To beginning of line	HOME	To end of document	CTRL+END

© 2014 Cengage Learning

Table 1–2 Using the Scroll Bar to Scroll Vertically with the Mouse

Scroll Direction	Mouse Action	Scroll Direction	Mouse Action
Up	Drag the scroll box upward.	Down one screen	Click anywhere below the scroll box on the vertical scroll bar.
Down	Drag the scroll box downward.	Up one line	Click the scroll arrow at the top of the vertical scroll bar.
Up one screen	Click anywhere above the scroll box on the vertical scroll bar.	Down one line	Click the scroll arrow at the bottom of the vertical scroll bar.

© 2014 Cengage Learning

To Save a Document

You have performed many tasks while creating this document and do not want to risk losing work completed thus far. Accordingly, you should save the document on your hard disk, SkyDrive, or a location that is most appropriate to your situation.

The following steps assume you already have created folders for storing your files, for example, a CIS 101 folder (for your class) that contains a Word folder (for your assignments). Thus, these steps save the document in the Word folder in the

CIS 101 folder on your desired save location. For a detailed example of the procedure for saving a file in a folder or saving a file on SkyDrive, refer to the Office and Windows chapter at the beginning of this book.

1 Tap or click the Save button on the Quick Access Toolbar, which depending on settings, will display either the Save As gallery in the Backstage view or the Save As dialog box.

2 To save on a hard disk or other storage media on your computer, proceed to Step 2a. To save on SkyDrive, proceed to Step 2b.

2a If your screen opens the Backstage view and you want to save on storage media on your computer, tap or click Computer in the left pane, if necessary, to display options in the right pane related to saving on your computer. If your screen already displays the Save As dialog box, proceed to Step 4.

2b If your screen opens the Backstage view and you want to save on SkyDrive, tap or click SkyDrive in the left pane to display SkyDrive saving options or a Sign In button. If your screen displays a Sign In button, tap or click it and then sign in to SkyDrive.

3 Tap or click the Browse button in the right pane to display the Save As dialog box associated with the selected save location (i.e., Computer or SkyDrive).

4 Type **Adventure Flyer** in the File name box to change the file name. Do not press the ENTER key after typing the file name because you do not want to close the dialog box at this time.

5 Navigate to the desired save location (in this case, the Word folder in the CIS 101 folder [or your class folder] on your computer or SkyDrive).

6 Tap or click the Save button (Save As dialog box) to save the document in the selected folder on the selected save location with the entered file name.

> **BTW**
> **Organizing Files and Folders**
> You should organize and store files in folders so that you easily can find the files later. For example, if you are taking an introductory computer class called CIS 101, a good practice would be to save all Word files in a Word folder in a CIS 101 folder. For a discussion of folders and detailed examples of creating folders, refer to the Office and Windows chapter at the beginning of this book.

Formatting Paragraphs and Characters

With the text for the flyer entered, the next step is to **format**, or change the appearance of, its text. A paragraph encompasses the text from the first character in the paragraph up to and including its paragraph mark (¶). **Paragraph formatting** is the process of changing the appearance of a paragraph. For example, you can center or add bullets to a paragraph. Characters include letters, numbers, punctuation marks, and symbols. **Character formatting** is the process of changing the way characters appear on the screen and in print. You use character formatting to emphasize certain words and improve readability of a document. For example, you can color, italicize, or underline characters. Often, you apply both paragraph and character formatting to the same text. For example, you may center a paragraph (paragraph formatting) and underline some of the characters in the same paragraph (character formatting).

Although you can format paragraphs and characters before you type, many Word users enter text first and then format the existing text. Figure 1–13a on the next page shows the flyer in this chapter before formatting its paragraphs and characters. Figure 1–13b on the next page shows the flyer after formatting. As you can see from the two figures, a document that is formatted is easier to read and looks more professional. The following pages discuss how to format the flyer so that it looks like Figure 1–13b.

> If you are using your finger on a touch screen and are having difficulty completing the steps in this chapter, consider using a stylus. Many people find it easier to be precise with a stylus than with a finger. In addition, with a stylus you see the pointer. If you still are having trouble completing the steps with a stylus, try using a mouse.

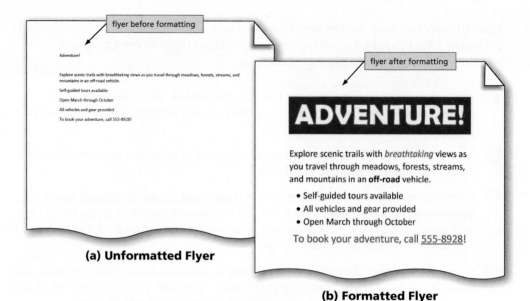

(a) Unformatted Flyer

(b) Formatted Flyer

Figure 1–13

Font, Font Sizes, and Themes

Characters that appear on the screen are a specific shape and size. The **font**, or typeface, defines the appearance and shape of the letters, numbers, and special characters. In Word, the default font usually is Calibri (shown in Figure 1–14). You can leave characters in the default font or change them to a different font. **Font size** specifies the size of the characters and is determined by a measurement system called points. A single **point** is about 1/72 of one inch in height. The default font size in Word typically is 11 (Figure 1–14). Thus, a character with a font size of 11 is about 11/72 or a little less than 1/6 of one inch in height. You can increase or decrease the font size of characters in a document.

A document **theme** is a set of unified formats for fonts, colors, and graphics. Word includes a variety of document themes to assist you with coordinating these visual elements in a document. The default theme fonts are Calibri Light for headings and Calibri for body text. By changing the document theme, you quickly can give your document a new look. You also can define your own document themes.

BTW
Formatting Marks
With some fonts, the formatting marks will not be displayed properly on the screen. For example, the raised dot that signifies a blank space between words may be displayed behind a character instead of in the blank space, causing the characters to look incorrect.

CONSIDER THIS

How do I know which formats to use in a flyer?
In a flyer, consider the following formatting suggestions.

- **Increase the font size of characters.** Flyers usually are posted on a bulletin board or in a window. Thus, the font size should be as large as possible so that passersby easily can read the flyer. To give the headline more impact, its font size should be larger than the font size of the text in the body copy. If possible, make the font size of the signature line larger than the body copy but smaller than the headline.

- **Change the font of characters.** Use fonts that are easy to read. Try to use only two different fonts in a flyer; for example, use one for the headline and the other for all other text. Too many fonts can make the flyer visually confusing.

- **Change the paragraph alignment.** The default alignment for paragraphs in a document is **left-aligned**, that is, flush at the left margin of the document with uneven right edges. Consider changing the alignment of some of the paragraphs to add interest and variety to the flyer.

- **Highlight key paragraphs with bullets.** A bulleted paragraph is a paragraph that begins with a dot or other symbol. Use bulleted paragraphs to highlight important points in a flyer.

- **Emphasize important words.** To call attention to certain words or lines, you can underline them, italicize them, or bold them. Use these formats sparingly, however, because overuse will minimize their effect and make the flyer look too busy.

- **Use color.** Use colors that complement each other and convey the meaning of the flyer. Vary colors in terms of hue and brightness. Headline colors, for example, can be bold and bright. Signature lines should stand out more than body copy but less than headlines. Keep in mind that too many colors can detract from the flyer and make it difficult to read.

To Center a Paragraph

1 ENTER TEXT | 2 FORMAT TEXT | 3 INSERT PICTURE | 4 FORMAT PICTURE
5 ENHANCE PAGE | 6 CORRECT & REVISE | 7 PRINT OR READ

The headline in the flyer currently is left-aligned (Figure 1–14). *Why? Word, by default left-aligns text, unless you specifically change the alignment.* You want the headline to be **centered**, that is, positioned horizontally between the left and right margins on the page. Recall that Word considers a single short line of text, such as the one-word headline, a paragraph. Thus, you will center the paragraph containing the headline. The following steps center a paragraph.

1

- Tap or click HOME on the ribbon to display the HOME tab.

- Tap or click somewhere in the paragraph to be centered (in this case, the headline) to position the insertion point in the paragraph to be formatted (Figure 1–14).

Figure 1–14

2

- Tap or click the Center button (HOME tab | Paragraph group) to center the paragraph containing the insertion point (Figure 1–15).

Q&A What if I want to return the paragraph to left-aligned?
You would tap or click the Center button again or tap or click the Align Left button (HOME tab | Paragraph group).

Figure 1–15

Other Ways

1. Tap 'Show Context Menu' button on mini toolbar or right-click paragraph, tap or click Paragraph on shortcut menu, tap or click Indents and Spacing tab (Paragraph dialog box), tap or click Alignment arrow, tap or click Centered, tap or click OK button

2. Tap or click Paragraph Settings Dialog Box Launcher (HOME tab or PAGE LAYOUT tab | Paragraph group), tap or click Indents and Spacing tab (Paragraph dialog box), tap or click Alignment arrow, tap or click Centered, tap or click OK button

3. Press CTRL+E

To Center Another Paragraph

In the flyer, the signature line is to be centered to match the paragraph alignment of the headline. The following steps center the signature line.

 Tap or click somewhere in the paragraph to be centered (in this case, the signature line) to position the insertion point in the paragraph to be formatted.

2 Tap or click the Center button (HOME tab | Paragraph group) to center the paragraph containing the insertion point (shown in Figure 1–16 on the next page).

BTW

File Type
Depending on your Windows settings, the file type .docx may be displayed on the title bar immediately to the right of the file name after you save the file. The file type .docx identifies a Word 2013 document.

BTW
Touch Screen
Differences
The Office and Windows interfaces may vary if you are using a touch screen. For this reason, you might notice that the function or appearance of your touch screen differs slightly from this chapter's presentation.

Formatting Single versus Multiple Paragraphs and Characters

As shown on the previous pages, to format a single paragraph, simply move the insertion point in the paragraph to make it the current paragraph, and then format the paragraph. Similarly, to format a single word, position the insertion point in the word to make it the current word, and then format the word.

To format multiple paragraphs or words, however, you first must select the paragraphs or words you want to format and then format the selection.

To Select a Line

1 ENTER TEXT | 2 FORMAT TEXT | 3 INSERT PICTURE | 4 FORMAT PICTURE
5 ENHANCE PAGE | 6 CORRECT & REVISE | 7 PRINT OR READ

The default font size of 11 point is too small for a headline in a flyer. To increase the font size of the characters in the headline, you first must select the line of text containing the headline. *Why? If you increase font size of text without selecting any text, Word will increase the font size only of the word containing the insertion point.* The following steps select a line.

1
- If you are using a mouse, move the pointer to the left of the line to be selected (in this case, the headline) until the pointer changes to a right-pointing block arrow (Figure 1–16).

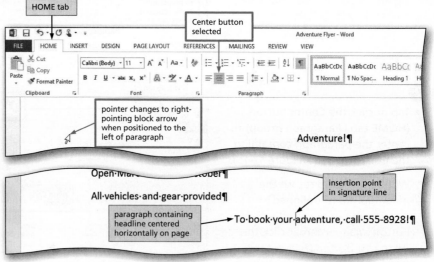

Figure 1–16

2
- If you are using a touch screen, double-tap to the left of the line to be selected to select the line; if you are using a mouse, while the pointer is a right-pointing block arrow, click the mouse to select the entire line to the right of the pointer (Figure 1–17).

Figure 1–17

Q&A Why is the selected text shaded gray?
If your screen normally displays dark letters on a light background, which is the default setting in Word, then selected text displays with a light shading color, such as gray, on the dark letters. Note that the selection that appears on the text does not print.

Other Ways

1. Drag pointer through line

2. With insertion point at beginning of desired line, press SHIFT+DOWN ARROW

To Change the Font Size of Selected Text

1 ENTER TEXT | 2 FORMAT TEXT | 3 INSERT PICTURE | 4 FORMAT PICTURE
5 ENHANCE PAGE | 6 CORRECT & REVISE | 7 PRINT OR READ

The next step is to increase the font size of the characters in the selected headline. *Why? You would like the headline to be as large as possible and still fit on a single line, which in this case is 72 point.* The following steps increase the font size of the headline from 11 to 72 point.

①

- With the text selected, tap or click the Font Size arrow (HOME tab | Font group) to display the Font Size gallery (Figure 1–18).

Q&A Why are the font sizes in my Font Size gallery different from those in Figure 1–18?
Font sizes may vary depending on the current font and your printer driver.

What happened to the mini toolbar?
The mini toolbar disappears if you do not use it. These steps use the Font Size arrow on the HOME tab instead of the Font Size arrow on the mini toolbar.

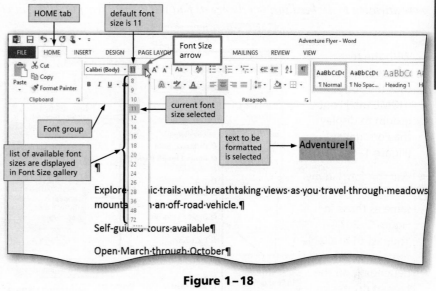

Figure 1–18

②

- If you are using a mouse, point to 72 in the Font Size gallery to display a live preview of the selected text at the selected point size (Figure 1–19).

Q&A Can I use live preview on a touch screen?
Live preview is not available on a touch screen.

Experiment

- If you are using a mouse, point to various font sizes in the Font Size gallery and watch the font size of the selected text change in the document window.

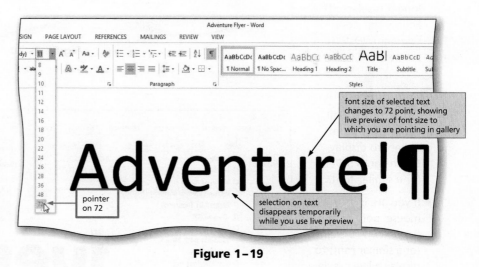

Figure 1–19

③

- Tap or click 72 in the Font Size gallery to increase the font size of the selected text.

Other Ways

1. Tap or click Font Size arrow on mini toolbar, tap or click desired font size in Font Size gallery

2. Tap 'Show Context Menu' button on mini toolbar or right-click selected text, tap or click Font on shortcut menu, tap or click Font tab (Font dialog box), select desired font size in Size list, tap or click OK button

3. Tap or click Font Dialog Box Launcher, tap or click Font tab (Font dialog box), select desired font size in Size list, tap or click OK button

4. Press CTRL+D, tap or click Font tab (Font dialog box), select desired font size in Size list, tap or click OK button

To Change the Font of Selected Text

The default theme font for headings is Calibri Light and for all other text, called body text in Word, is Calibri. Many other fonts are available, however, so that you can add variety to documents.

The following steps change the font of the headline from Calibri to Berlin Sans FB Demi. *Why? To draw more attention to the headline, you change its font so that it differs from the font of other text in the flyer.*

1

- With the text selected, tap or click the Font arrow (HOME tab | Font group) to display the Font gallery (Figure 1–20).

Q&A Will the fonts in my Font gallery be the same as those in Figure 1–20?
Your list of available fonts may differ, depending on the type of printer you are using and other settings.

What if the text no longer is selected?
Follow the steps on page WD 16 to select a line.

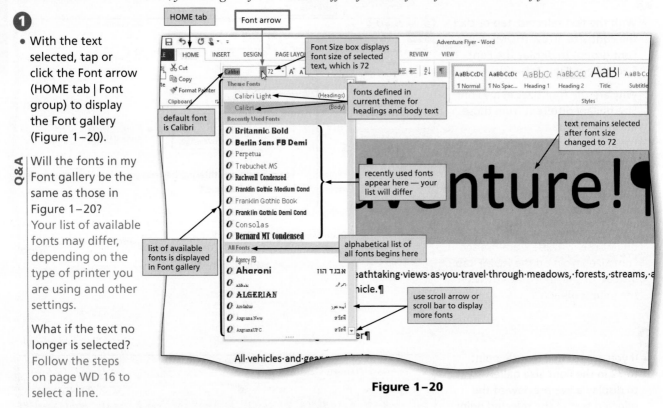

Figure 1–20

2

- If necessary, scroll through the Font gallery to display Berlin Sans FB Demi (or a similar font).

- If you are using a mouse, point to Berlin Sans FB Demi (or a similar font) to display a live preview of the selected text in the selected font (Figure 1–21).

Experiment

- If you are using a mouse, point to various fonts in the Font gallery and watch the font of the selected text change in the document window.

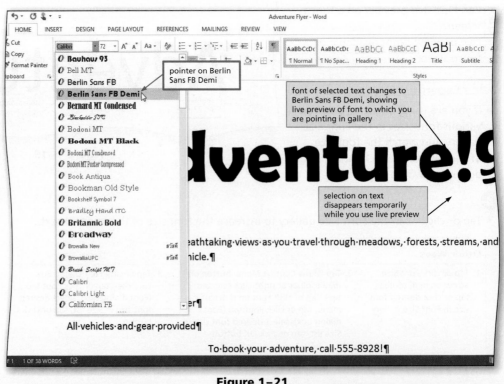

Figure 1–21

❸

● Tap or click Berlin Sans FB Demi (or a similar font) to change the font of the selected text.

Q&A If the font I want to use appears in the Recently Used Fonts list in the Font gallery, could I tap or click it there instead?
Yes.

Other Ways

1. Tap or click Font arrow on mini toolbar, tap or click desired font in Font gallery

2. Tap 'Show Context Menu' button on mini toolbar or right-click selected text, tap or click Font on shortcut menu, tap or click Font tab (Font dialog box), select desired font in Font list, tap or click OK button

3. Tap or click Font Dialog Box Launcher (HOME tab | Font group), tap or click Font tab (Font dialog box), select desired font in Font list, tap or click OK button

4. Press CTRL+D, tap or click Font tab (Font dialog box), select desired font in Font list, tap or click OK button

To Change the Case of Selected Text

1 ENTER TEXT | 2 FORMAT TEXT | 3 INSERT PICTURE | 4 FORMAT PICTURE
5 ENHANCE PAGE | 6 CORRECT & REVISE | 7 PRINT OR READ

The headline currently shows the first letter in each word capitalized, which sometimes is referred to as initial cap. The following steps change the headline to uppercase. *Why? To draw more attention to the headline, you would like the entire line of text to be capitalized, or in uppercase letters.*

❶

● With the text selected, tap or click the Change Case button (HOME tab | Font group) to display the Change Case gallery (Figure 1–22).

Figure 1–22

❷

● Tap or click UPPERCASE in the Change Case gallery to change the case of the selected text (Figure 1–23).

Q&A What if a ruler appears on the screen or the pointer shape changes?
If you are using a mouse, depending on the position of your pointer and locations you click on the screen, a ruler may automatically appear or the pointer's shape may change. Simply move the mouse and the ruler should disappear and/or the pointer shape will change.

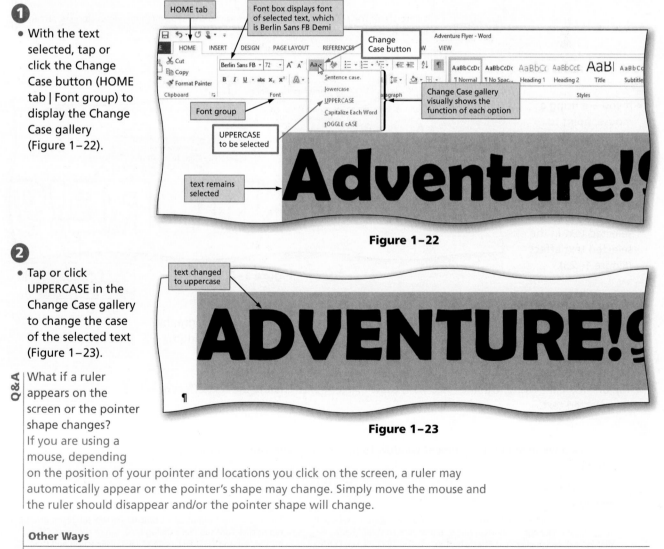

Figure 1–23

Other Ways

1. Tap 'Show Context Menu' button on mini toolbar or right-click selected text, tap or click Font on shortcut menu, tap or click Font tab (Font dialog box), select All caps in Effects area, tap or click OK button

2. Tap or click Font Dialog Box Launcher (HOME tab | Font group), tap or click Font tab (Font dialog box), select All caps in Effects area, tap or click OK button

3. Press SHIFT+F3 repeatedly until text is desired case

To Apply a Text Effect to Selected Text

Word provides many text effects to add interest and variety to text. The following steps apply a text effect to the headline. *Why? You would like the text in the headline to be even more noticeable.*

1
- With the text selected, tap or click the 'Text Effects and Typography' button (HOME tab | Font group) to display the Text Effects and Typography gallery (Figure 1–24).

Figure 1–24

2
- If you are using a mouse, point to 'Fill - White, Outline - Accent 1, Glow - Accent 1' (fourth text effect in second row) to display a live preview of the selected text in the selected text effect (Figure 1–25).

Figure 1–25

Experiment
- If you are using a mouse, point to various text effects in the Text Effects and Typography gallery and watch the text effects of the selected text change in the document window.

3
- Tap or click 'Fill - White, Outline - Accent 1, Glow - Accent 1' to change the text effect of the selected text.

4
- Tap or click anywhere in the document window to remove the selection from the selected text.

Other Ways

1. Tap 'Show Context Menu' button on mini toolbar or right-click selected text, tap or click Font on shortcut menu, tap or click Font tab (Font dialog box), tap or click Text Effects button, expand TEXT FILL or TEXT OUTLINE section and then select the desired text effect(s) (Format Text Effects dialog box), tap or click OK button, tap or click OK button

2. Tap or click Font Dialog Box Launcher (HOME tab | Font group), tap or click Font tab (Font dialog box), tap or click Text Effects button, expand TEXT FILL or TEXT OUTLINE section and then select desired text effect (Format Text Effects dialog box), tap or click OK button, tap or click OK button

To Shade a Paragraph

1 ENTER TEXT | 2 FORMAT TEXT | 3 INSERT PICTURE | 4 FORMAT PICTURE
5 ENHANCE PAGE | 6 CORRECT & REVISE | 7 PRINT OR READ

When you **shade** text, Word colors the rectangular area behind any text or graphics. If the text to shade is a paragraph, Word shades the area from the left margin to the right margin of the current paragraph. To shade a paragraph, place the insertion point in the paragraph. To shade any other text, you must first select the text to be shaded.

This flyer uses green as the shading color for the headline. ***Why?*** *To make the headline of the flyer more eye-catching, you shade it.* The following steps shade a paragraph.

1

- Tap or click somewhere in the paragraph to be shaded (in this case, the headline) to position the insertion point in the paragraph to be formatted.

- Tap or click the Shading arrow (HOME tab | Paragraph group) to display the Shading gallery (Figure 1–26).

Figure 1–26

Q&A If I am using a mouse, what if I click the Shading button by mistake?
Click the Shading arrow and proceed with Step 2. If you are using a touch screen, you may not have a separate Shading button.

 Experiment

- If you are using a mouse, point to various colors in the Shading gallery and watch the shading color of the current paragraph change.

2

- Tap or click 'Green, Accent 6, Darker 25%' (rightmost color in fifth row) to shade the current paragraph (Figure 1–27).

Q&A What if I apply a dark shading color to dark text?
When the font color of text is Automatic, it usually is black. If you select a dark shading color, Word automatically may change the text color to white so that the shaded text is easier to read.

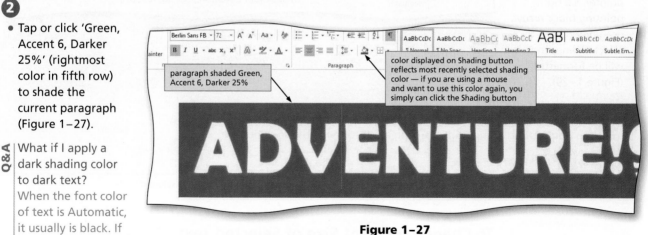

Figure 1–27

Other Ways

1. Tap or click Borders arrow (HOME tab | Paragraph group), tap or click Borders and Shading, tap or click Shading tab (Borders and Shading dialog box), tap or click Fill arrow, select desired color, tap or click OK button

To Select Multiple Lines

The next formatting step for the flyer is to increase the font size of the characters between the headline and the signature line. *Why? You want this text to be easier to read from a distance.*

To change the font size of the characters in multiple lines, you first must select all the lines to be formatted. The following steps select multiple lines.

1

- Scroll, if necessary, so that all text below the headline is displayed on the screen.

- If you are using a touch screen, tap to position the insertion point in the text to select; if you are using a mouse, move the pointer to the left of the first paragraph to be selected until the pointer changes to a right-pointing block arrow (Figure 1–28).

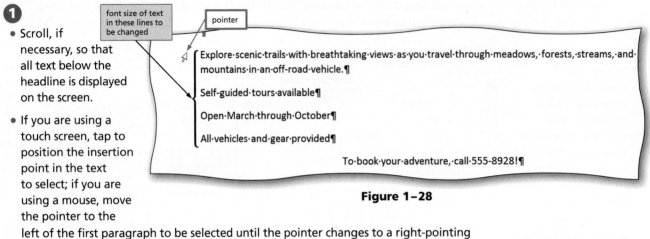

Figure 1–28

2

- If you are using a touch screen, drag the selection handle(s) as necessary to select the text that will be formatted; if you are using a mouse, while the pointer is a right-pointing block arrow, drag downward to select all lines that will be formatted (Figure 1–29).

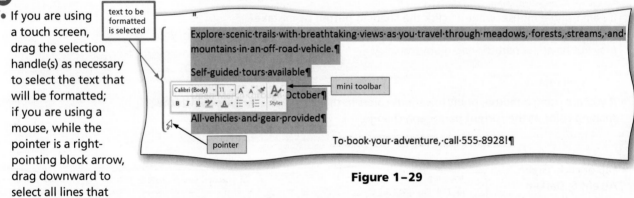

Figure 1–29

Q&A

What is a selection handle?

When working on a touch screen, a **selection handle** (small circle) appears below the insertion point. Using a fingertip, you drag a selection handle to select text.

Other Ways

1. With insertion point at beginning of desired line, press SHIFT+DOWN ARROW repeatedly until all lines are selected

To Change the Font Size of Selected Text

The characters between the headline and the signature line in the flyer currently are 11 point. To make them easier to read from a distance, this flyer uses a 24-point font size for these characters. The following steps change the font size of the selected text.

1 With the text selected, tap or click the Font Size arrow (HOME tab | Font group) to display the Font Size gallery.

2 Tap or click 24 in the Font Size gallery to increase the font size of the selected text.

3 Tap or click anywhere in the document window to remove the selection from the text.

4 If necessary, scroll so that you can see all the resized text on the screen (Figure 1–30).

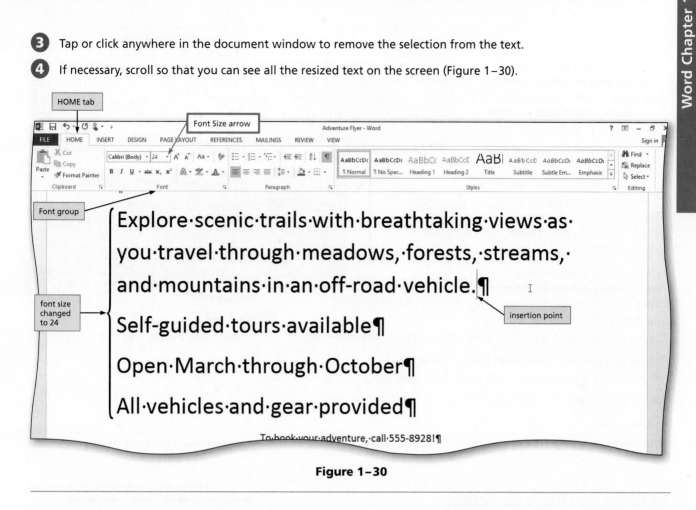

Figure 1–30

To Bullet a List of Paragraphs

1 ENTER TEXT | 2 FORMAT TEXT | 3 INSERT PICTURE | 4 FORMAT PICTURE
5 ENHANCE PAGE | 6 CORRECT & REVISE | 7 PRINT OR READ

A **bulleted list** is a series of paragraphs, each beginning with a bullet character. The next step is to format the three paragraphs about the tours that are above the signature line in the flyer as a bulleted list.

To format a list of paragraphs with bullets, you first must select all the lines in the paragraphs. *Why? If you do not select all paragraphs, Word will place a bullet only in the paragraph containing the insertion point.* The following steps bullet a list of paragraphs.

1

• If you are using a touch screen, tap to position the insertion point in the text to select; if you are using a mouse, move the pointer to the left of the first paragraph to be selected until the pointer changes to a right-pointing block arrow.

Figure 1–31

• If you are using a touch screen, drag the selection handle(s) as necessary to select the text that will be formatted; if you are using a mouse, drag downward until all paragraphs that will be formatted with a bullet character are selected (Figure 1–31).

2

- Tap or click the Bullets button (HOME tab | Paragraph group) to place a bullet character at the beginning of each selected paragraph (Figure 1–32).

Q&A What if my screen displays a Bullets gallery?

If you are using a touch screen, you may not have a separate Bullets button and Bullets arrow. In this case, select the desired bullet style in the Bullets gallery.

If I am using a mouse, what if I accidentally click the Bullets arrow? Press the ESCAPE key to remove the Bullets gallery from the screen and then repeat Step 2. If you are using a touch screen, you may not have a separate Bullets button and Bullets arrow.

How do I remove bullets from a list or paragraph? Select the list or paragraph and then tap or click the Bullets button again.

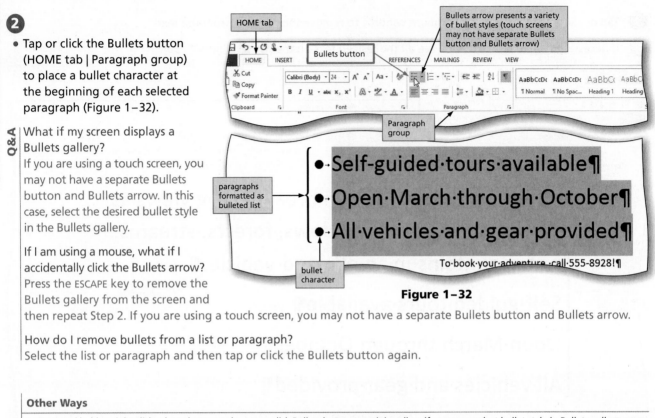

Figure 1–32

Other Ways

1. Press and hold or right-click selected paragraphs, tap or click Bullets button on mini toolbar, if necessary select bullet style in Bullets gallery

To Undo and Redo an Action

1 ENTER TEXT | 2 FORMAT TEXT | 3 INSERT PICTURE | 4 FORMAT PICTURE
5 ENHANCE PAGE | 6 CORRECT & REVISE | 7 PRINT OR READ

Word provides a means of canceling your recent command(s) or action(s). For example, if you format text incorrectly, you can undo the format and try it again. When you point to the Undo button, Word displays the action you can undo as part of a ScreenTip.

If, after you undo an action, you decide you did not want to perform the undo, you can redo the undone action. Word does not allow you to undo or redo some actions, such as saving or printing a document. The following steps undo the bullet format just applied and then redo the bullet format. *Why? These steps illustrate the undo and redo actions.*

1

- Tap or click the Undo button on the Quick Access Toolbar to reverse your most recent action (in this case, remove the bullets from the paragraphs) (Figure 1–33).

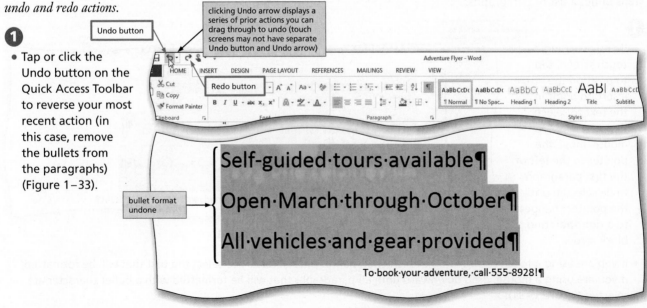

Figure 1–33

2

- Tap or click the Redo button on the Quick Access Toolbar to reverse your most recent undo (in this case, place a bullet character on the paragraphs again) (shown in Figure 1–32).

Other Ways
1. Press CTRL+Z to undo; press CTRL+Y to redo

To Italicize Text

1 ENTER TEXT | 2 FORMAT TEXT | 3 INSERT PICTURE | 4 FORMAT PICTURE
5 ENHANCE PAGE | 6 CORRECT & REVISE | 7 PRINT OR READ

Italic text has a slanted appearance. The next step is to italicize the word, breathtaking, in the flyer to further emphasize it. As with a single paragraph, if you want to format a single word, you do not need to select it. *Why? To format a single word, you simply position the insertion point somewhere in the word and apply the desired format.* The following step italicizes a word.

1

- Tap or click somewhere in the word to be italicized (breathtaking, in this case) to position the insertion point in the word to be formatted.

- Tap or click the Italic button (HOME tab | Font group) to italicize the word containing the insertion point (Figure 1–34).

Q&A
How would I remove an italic format?
You would tap or click the Italic button a second time, or you immediately could tap or click the Undo button on the Quick Access Toolbar or press CTRL+Z.

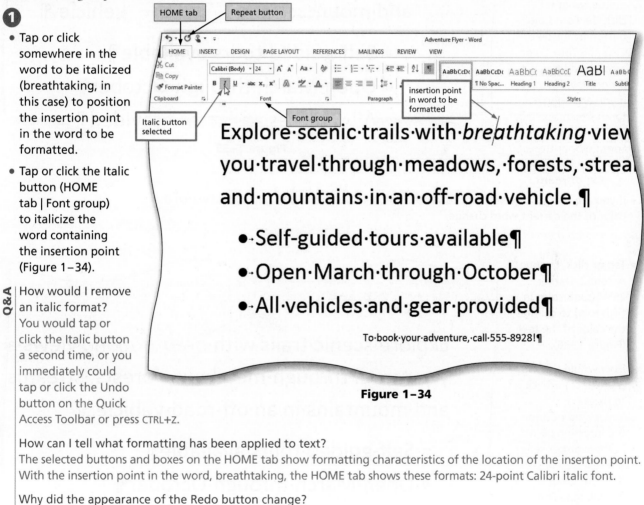

Figure 1–34

How can I tell what formatting has been applied to text?
The selected buttons and boxes on the HOME tab show formatting characteristics of the location of the insertion point. With the insertion point in the word, breathtaking, the HOME tab shows these formats: 24-point Calibri italic font.

Why did the appearance of the Redo button change?
It changed to a Repeat button. When it is a Repeat button, you can tap or click it to repeat your last action. For example, you can select different text and then click the Repeat button to apply (repeat) the italic format to the selected text.

Other Ways			
1. Tap or click Italic button on mini toolbar	2. Tap 'Show Context Menu' button on mini toolbar or right-click selected text, tap or click Font on shortcut menu, tap or click Font tab (Font dialog box), tap or click Italic in Font style list, tap or click OK button	3. Tap or click Font Dialog Box Launcher (HOME tab | Font group), tap or click Font tab (Font dialog box), tap or click Italic in Font style list, tap or click OK button	4. Press CTRL+I

To Color Text

The following steps change the color of the word, breathtaking. *Why? To emphasize the word even more, you change its color to a shade of orange.*

1

- With the insertion point in the word to format, tap or click the Font Color arrow (HOME tab | Font group) to display the Font Color gallery (Figure 1–35).

Q&A If I am using a mouse, what if I click the Font Color button by mistake? Click the Font Color arrow and then proceed with Step 2. If you are using a touch screen, you may not have a separate Font Color button.

Figure 1–35

Experiment

- If you are using a mouse, point to various colors in the Font Color gallery and watch the color of the current word change.

2

- Tap or click 'Orange, Accent 2, Darker 25%' (sixth color in fifth row) to change the color of the text (Figure 1–36).

Q&A How would I change the text color back to black? You would position the insertion point in the word or select the text, tap or click the Font Color arrow (HOME tab | Font group) again, and then tap or click Automatic in the Font Color gallery.

Figure 1–36

Other Ways

1. Tap or click Font Color arrow on mini toolbar, tap or click desired color

2. Tap 'Show Context Menu' button on mini toolbar or right-click selected text, tap or click Font on shortcut menu, tap or click Font tab (Font dialog box), tap or click Font color arrow, tap or click desired color, tap or click OK button

3. Tap or click Font Dialog Box Launcher (HOME tab | Font group), tap or click Font tab (Font dialog box), tap or click Font color arrow, tap or click desired color, tap or click OK button

To Use the Mini Toolbar to Format Text

1 ENTER TEXT | 2 FORMAT TEXT | 3 INSERT PICTURE | 4 FORMAT PICTURE
5 ENHANCE PAGE | 6 CORRECT & REVISE | 7 PRINT OR READ

Recall from the Office and Windows chapter at the beginning of this book that the mini toolbar automatically appears based on certain tasks you perform. *Why? Word places commonly used buttons and boxes on the mini toolbar for your convenience. If you do not use the mini toolbar, it disappears from the screen.* All commands on the mini toolbar also exist on the ribbon.

The following steps use the mini toolbar to change the color and font size of text in the signature line of the flyer.

1

- If you are using a touch screen, double-tap to the left of the line to be selected to select the line, and then tap the selection to display the mini toolbar; if you are using a mouse, move the pointer to the left of the line to be selected until the pointer changes to a right-pointing block arrow and then click to select the line and display the mini toolbar (Figure 1–37).

Q&A Why does my mini toolbar look different than the one in Figure 1–37?
If you are using a touch screen, the buttons and boxes on the mini toolbar differ. For example, it contains a 'Show Context Menu' button at the far-right edge, which you tap to display a shortcut menu.

2

- Tap or click the Font Size arrow on the mini toolbar to display the Font Size gallery.

- If you are using a mouse, point to 28 in the Font Size gallery to display a live preview of the selected font size (Figure 1–38).

3

- Tap or click 28 in the Font Size gallery to increase the font size of the selected text.

Figure 1–37

Figure 1–38

4

- With the text still selected and the mini toolbar still displayed, tap or click the Font Color arrow on the mini toolbar to display the Font Color gallery.

- If you are using a mouse, point to 'Orange, Accent 2, Darker 25%' (sixth color in the fifth row) to display a live preview of the selected font color (Figure 1–39).

5

- Tap or click 'Orange, Accent 2, Darker 25%' to change the color of the selected text.

- Tap or click anywhere in the document window to remove the selection from the text.

Figure 1–39

To Select a Group of Words

1 ENTER TEXT | 2 FORMAT TEXT | 3 INSERT PICTURE | 4 FORMAT PICTURE
5 ENHANCE PAGE | 6 CORRECT & REVISE | 7 PRINT OR READ

To emphasize the contact phone number (555-8928), this text is underlined in the flyer. Because the phone number is separated with a hyphen, Word considers it a group of words. To format a group of words, you first must select them. **Why?** *If you underline text without selecting any text first, Word will underline only the word containing the insertion point.* The following steps select a group of words.

1

- If you are using a touch screen, tap to position the insertion point in the text you want to select; if you are using a mouse, position the pointer immediately to the left of the first character of the text to be selected, in this case, the 5 in 555 (Figure 1–40).

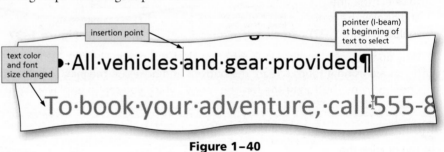

Figure 1–40

Q&A Why did the shape of the pointer change?
The pointer's shape is an I-beam when positioned in unselected text in the document window.

2

- If you are using a touch screen, drag the selection handle(s) to select the text to be formatted; if you are using a mouse, drag the pointer through the last character of the text to be selected, in this case, the 8 in the phone number (Figure 1–41).

Figure 1–41

Q&A Why did the pointer shape change again?
When the pointer is positioned in selected text, its shape is a left-pointing block arrow.

Other Ways

1. With insertion point at beginning of first word in group, press CTRL+SHIFT+RIGHT ARROW repeatedly until all words are selected

To Underline Text

1 ENTER TEXT | 2 FORMAT TEXT | 3 INSERT PICTURE | 4 FORMAT PICTURE

5 ENHANCE PAGE | 6 CORRECT & REVISE | 7 PRINT OR READ

Underlined text prints with an underscore (_) below each character. In the flyer, the contact phone number, 555-8928, in the signature line is underlined. *Why? Underlines are used to emphasize or draw attention to specific text.* The following step formats selected text with an underline.

1

- With the text selected, tap or click the Underline button (HOME tab | Font group) to underline the selected text (Figure 1–42).

Q&A What if my screen displays an Underline gallery?
If you are using a touch screen, you may not have a separate Underline button and Underline arrow. In this case, select the desired underline style in the Underline gallery.

If a button exists on the mini toolbar, can I tap or click that instead of using the ribbon?
Yes.

How would I remove an underline?
You would tap or click the Underline button a second time, or you immediately could tap or click the Undo button on the Quick Access Toolbar.

Figure 1–42

Other Ways

1. Tap or click Underline button on mini toolbar	2. Tap 'Show Context Menu' button on mini toolbar or right-click text, tap or click Font on shortcut menu, tap or click Font tab (Font dialog box), tap or click Underline style box arrow, tap or click desired underline style, tap or click OK button	3. Tap or click Font Dialog Box Launcher (HOME tab | Font group), tap or click Font tab (Font dialog box), tap or click Underline style arrow, tap or click desired underline style, tap or click OK button	4. Press CTRL+U

To Bold Text

1 ENTER TEXT | 2 FORMAT TEXT | 3 INSERT PICTURE | 4 FORMAT PICTURE

5 ENHANCE PAGE | 6 CORRECT & REVISE | 7 PRINT OR READ

Bold characters appear somewhat thicker and darker than those that are not bold. The steps on the next page format the text, off-road, in bold characters. *Why? To further emphasize this text, it is bold in the flyer.* Recall that if you want to format a single word, you simply position the insertion point in the word and then format the word. To format text that consists of more than one word, as you have learned previously, you select the text first.

1

- Select the text to be formatted (the text, off-road, in this case); that is, if you are using a touch screen, tap to position the insertion point in the text you want to select and then drag the selection handle(s) to select the text to be formatted; if you are using a mouse, position the pointer immediately to the left of the first character of the text to be selected and then drag the pointer through the last character of the text to be selected.

2

- With the text selected, tap or click the Bold button (HOME tab | Font group) to bold the selected text (Figure 1–43).

Q&A

How would I remove a bold format?

You would tap or click the Bold button a second time, or you immediately could tap or click the Undo button on the Quick Access Toolbar.

3

- Tap or click anywhere in the document window to remove the selection from the screen.

Figure 1–43

Other Ways

1. Tap or click Bold button on mini toolbar
2. Tap 'Show Context Menu' button on mini toolbar or right-click selected text, tap or click Font on shortcut menu, tap or click Font tab (Font dialog box), tap or click Bold in Font style list, tap or click OK button
3. Tap or click Font Dialog Box Launcher (HOME tab | Font group), tap or click Font tab (Font dialog box), tap or click Bold in Font style list, tap or click OK button
4. Press CTRL+B

To Zoom One Page

1 ENTER TEXT | 2 FORMAT TEXT | 3 INSERT PICTURE | 4 FORMAT PICTURE
5 ENHANCE PAGE | 6 CORRECT & REVISE | 7 PRINT OR READ

Earlier in this chapter, you changed the zoom to page width so that the text on the screen was larger and easier to read. In the next set of steps, you want to see the entire page (mock sheet of paper) on the screen at once. *Why? You want be able to see the effect of adjusting colors in the document as a whole.* The next step displays a single page in its entirety in the document window as large as possible.

1

- Tap or click VIEW on the ribbon to display the VIEW tab.

- Tap or click the One Page button (VIEW tab | Zoom group) to display the entire page in the document window as large as possible (Figure 1–44).

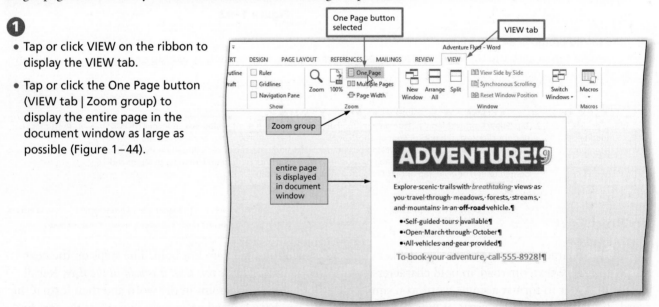

Figure 1–44

Other Ways

1. Tap or click Zoom button (VIEW tab | Zoom group), tap or click Whole page (Zoom dialog box), tap or click OK button

What colors should I choose when creating documents?

When choosing color, associate the meaning of the color with your message:

- Red expresses danger, power, or energy and often is associated with sports or physical exertion.

- Brown represents simplicity, honesty, and dependability.

- Orange denotes success, victory, creativity, and enthusiasm.

- Yellow suggests sunshine, happiness, hope, liveliness, and intelligence.

- Green symbolizes growth, healthiness, harmony, blooming, and healing and often is associated with safety or money.

- Blue indicates integrity, trust, importance, confidence, and stability.

- Purple represents wealth, power, comfort, extravagance, magic, mystery, and spirituality.

- White stands for purity, goodness, cleanliness, precision, and perfection.

- Black suggests authority, strength, elegance, power, and prestige.

- Gray conveys neutrality and, thus, often is found in backgrounds and other effects.

To Change Theme Colors

| 1 ENTER TEXT | 2 FORMAT TEXT | 3 INSERT PICTURE | 4 FORMAT PICTURE |
| 5 ENHANCE PAGE | 6 CORRECT & REVISE | 7 PRINT OR READ |

A **color scheme** in Word is a document theme that identifies 12 complementary colors for text, background, accents, and links in a document. With more than 20 predefined color schemes, Word provides a simple way to coordinate colors in a document.

The default color scheme is called Office. In the flyer, you will change the color scheme from Office to Green. *Why? You want the colors in the flyer to suggest growth, harmony, blooming, trust, and stability, which are conveyed by shades of greens and blues. In Word, the Green color scheme uses these colors.* The following steps change theme colors.

1

- Tap or click DESIGN on the ribbon to display the DESIGN tab.

- Tap or click the Theme Colors button (DESIGN tab | Document Formatting group) to display the Theme Colors gallery.

- If you are using a mouse, point to Green in the Theme Colors gallery to display a live preview of the selected theme color (Figure 1–45).

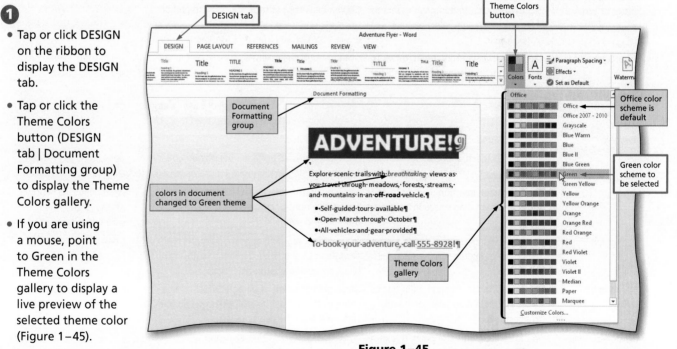

Figure 1–45

Experiment

- If you are using a mouse, point to various color schemes in the Theme Colors gallery and watch the colors change in the document.

2

- Tap or click Green in the Colors gallery to change the document theme colors.

Q&A

What if I want to return to the original color scheme?
You would tap or click the Theme Colors button again and then tap or click Office in the Theme Colors gallery.

BTW
Selecting Nonadjacent Items
In Word, you can use keyboard keys to select nonadjacent items, that is, items not next to each other. This is helpful when you are applying the same formatting to multiple items. To select nonadjacent items (text or graphics), select the first item, such as a word or paragraph, as usual; then, press and hold down the CTRL key. While holding down the CTRL key, select additional items.

To Zoom Page Width

Because the document contents are small when displayed at one page, the next steps zoom page width again.

1 Tap or click VIEW on the ribbon to display the VIEW tab.

2 Tap or click the Page Width button (VIEW tab | Zoom group) to display the page the same width as the document window (shown in Figure 1–46 on page WD 34).

Selecting Text

In many of the previous steps, you have selected text. Table 1–3 summarizes the techniques used to select various items.

Table 1–3 Techniques for Selecting Text			
Item to Select	**Touch**	**Mouse**	**Keyboard (where applicable)**
Block of text	Tap to position insertion point in text to select and then drag selection handle(s) to select text.	Click at beginning of selection, scroll to end of selection, position pointer at end of selection, hold down SHIFT key, and then click; or drag through text.	
Character(s)	Tap to position insertion point in text to select and then drag selection handle(s) to select text.	Drag through character(s).	SHIFT+RIGHT ARROW or SHIFT+LEFT ARROW
Document		Move pointer to left of text until pointer changes to right-pointing block arrow and then triple-click.	CTRL+A
Graphic	Tap the graphic.	Click the graphic.	
Line	Double-tap to left of line to be selected.	Move pointer to left of line until pointer changes to right-pointing block arrow and then click.	HOME, then SHIFT+END or END, then SHIFT+HOME
Lines	Tap to position insertion point in text to select and then drag selection handle(s) to select text.	Move pointer to left of first line until pointer changes to right-pointing block arrow and then drag up or down.	HOME, then SHIFT+DOWN ARROW or END, then SHIFT+UP ARROW
Paragraph	Tap to position insertion point in text to select and then drag selection handle(s) to select text.	Triple-click paragraph; or move pointer to left of paragraph until pointer changes to right-pointing block arrow and then double-click.	CTRL+SHIFT+DOWN ARROW or CTRL+SHIFT+UP ARROW
Paragraphs	Tap to position insertion point in text to select and then drag selection handle(s) to select text.	Move pointer to left of paragraph until pointer changes to right-pointing block arrow, double-click, and then drag up or down.	CTRL+SHIFT+DOWN ARROW or CTRL+SHIFT+UP ARROW repeatedly
Sentence	Tap to position insertion point in text to select and then drag selection handle(s) to select text.	Press and hold down CTRL key and then click sentence.	
Word	Double-tap word.	Double-click word.	CTRL+SHIFT+RIGHT ARROW or CTRL+SHIFT+LEFT ARROW
Words	Tap to position insertion point in text to select and then drag selection handle(s) to select text.	Drag through words.	CTRL+SHIFT+RIGHT ARROW or CTRL+SHIFT+LEFT ARROW repeatedly

To Save an Existing Document with the Same File Name

You have made several modifications to the document since you last saved it. Thus, you should save it again. The following step saves the document again. For an example of the step listed below, refer to the Office and Windows chapter at the beginning of this book.

1 Tap or click the Save button on the Quick Access Toolbar to overwrite the previously saved file.

Break Point: If you wish to take a break, this is a good place to do so. You can exit Word now (refer to page WD 46 for instructions). To resume at a later time, run Word (refer to pages WD 46 to WD 47 for instructions), open the file called Adventure Flyer (refer to page WD 47 for instructions), and continue following the steps from this location forward.

Inserting and Formatting a Picture in a Word Document

With the text formatted in the flyer, the next step is to insert a digital picture in the flyer and format the picture. Flyers usually contain a graphical image(s), such as a picture, to attract the attention of passersby. In the following pages, you will perform these tasks:

1. Insert a digital picture into the flyer and then reduce its size.
2. Enlarge the size of the picture.
3. Change the look of the picture.

How do I locate a graphic file to use in a document?

To use a graphic in a Word document, the image must be stored digitally in a file. Files containing graphics are available from a variety of sources:

• Microsoft has free digital images on the web for use in a document. Other websites also have images available, some of which are free, while others require a fee.

• You can take a picture with a digital camera or camera phone and **download** it, which is the process of copying the digital picture from the camera or phone to your computer.

• With a scanner, you can convert a printed picture, drawing, or diagram to a digital file.

If you receive a picture from a source other than yourself, do not use the file until you are certain it does not contain a virus. A **virus** is a computer program that can damage files and programs on your computer. Use an antivirus program to verify that any files you use are virus free.

CONSIDER THIS

To Center Another Paragraph

In the flyer, the digital picture of a mountain trail tour group should be centered on the blank line below the headline. The blank paragraph below the headline currently is left-aligned. The following steps center this paragraph.

 1 Tap or click HOME on the ribbon to display the HOME tab.

2 Tap or click somewhere in the paragraph to be centered (in this case, the blank line below the headline) to position the insertion point in the paragraph to be formatted.

3 Tap or click the Center button (HOME tab | Paragraph group) to center the paragraph containing the insertion point (shown in Figure 1–46 on the next page).

BTW

BTWs

For a complete list of the BTWs found in the margins of this book, visit the BTW resource on the Student Companion Site located on www.cengagebrain.com. For detailed instructions about accessing available resources, visit www.cengage.com/ct/studentdownload or contact your instructor for information about accessing the required files.

To Insert a Picture

1 ENTER TEXT | 2 FORMAT TEXT | 3 INSERT PICTURE | 4 FORMAT PICTURE
5 ENHANCE PAGE | 6 CORRECT & REVISE | 7 PRINT OR READ

The next step in creating the flyer is to insert a digital picture of a mountain trail tour group in the flyer on the blank line below the headline. The picture, which was taken with a digital camera, is available on the Data Files for Students. Visit www.cengage.com/ct/studentdownload for detailed instructions or contact your instructor for information about accessing the required files.

The following steps insert a picture, which, in this example, is located in the Chapter 01 folder in the Word folder in the Data Files for Students folder. *Why? It is good practice to organize and store files in folders so that you easily can find the files at a later date.*

1

- If necessary, position the insertion point at the location where you want to insert the picture (in this case, on the centered blank paragraph below the headline).

- Tap or click INSERT on the ribbon to display the INSERT tab (Figure 1–46).

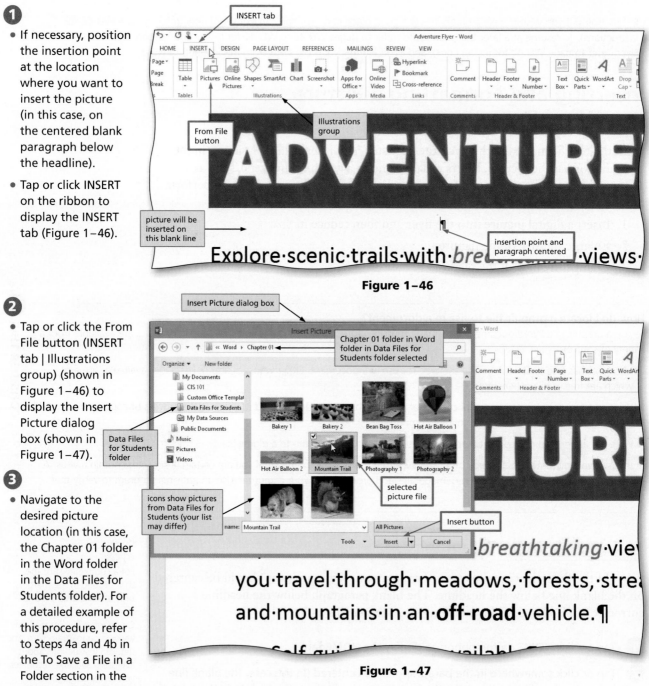

Figure 1–46

2

- Tap or click the From File button (INSERT tab | Illustrations group) (shown in Figure 1–46) to display the Insert Picture dialog box (shown in Figure 1–47).

3

- Navigate to the desired picture location (in this case, the Chapter 01 folder in the Word folder in the Data Files for Students folder). For a detailed example of this procedure, refer to Steps 4a and 4b in the To Save a File in a Folder section in the Office and Windows chapter at the beginning of this book.

- Tap or click Mountain Trail to select the file (Figure 1–47).

Figure 1–47

4

- Tap or click the Insert button (Insert Picture dialog box) to insert the picture at the location of the insertion point in the document (Figure 1–48).

Q&A What are the symbols around the picture?
A selected graphic appears surrounded by a **selection rectangle**, which has small squares and circles, called **sizing handles**, at each corner and middle location.

What is the purpose of the Layout Options button?
When you tap or click the Layout Options button, Word provides options for changing how the graphic is positioned with text in the document.

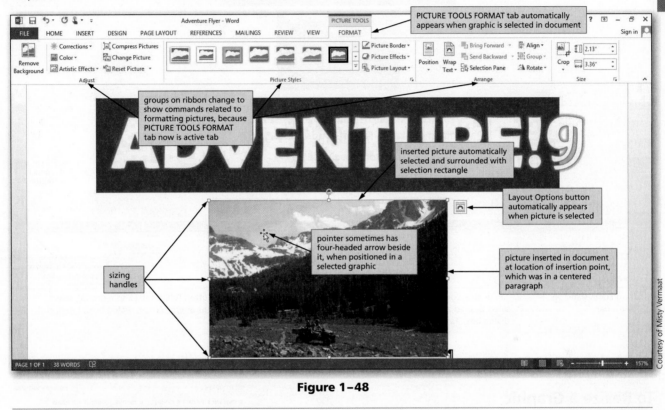

Figure 1–48

How do you know where to position a graphic on a flyer?
The content, size, shape, position, and format of a graphic should capture the interest of passersby, enticing them to stop and read the flyer. Often, the graphic is the center of attention and visually the largest element on a flyer. If you use colors in the graphical image, be sure they are part of the document's color scheme.

CONSIDER THIS

1 ENTER TEXT | 2 FORMAT TEXT | 3 INSERT PICTURE | **4 FORMAT PICTURE**
5 ENHANCE PAGE | 6 CORRECT & REVISE | 7 PRINT OR READ

To Zoom the Document

In the steps on the following pages, you will work with the picture just inserted. The next task is to adjust the zoom percentage. *Why? Currently, you can see only a small amount of text with the picture. Seeing more of the document at once helps you determine the appropriate size for the picture.* The following step zooms the document.

1

Experiment

- If you are using a mouse, repeatedly click the Zoom Out and Zoom In buttons on the status bar and watch the size of the document change in the document window.
- If you are using a touch screen, repeatedly pinch (move two fingers together) and stretch (move two fingers apart) and watch the size of the document change in the document window.

• Pinch and stretch or click the Zoom Out or Zoom In button as many times as necessary until the Zoom button on the status bar displays 80% on its face (Figure 1–49).

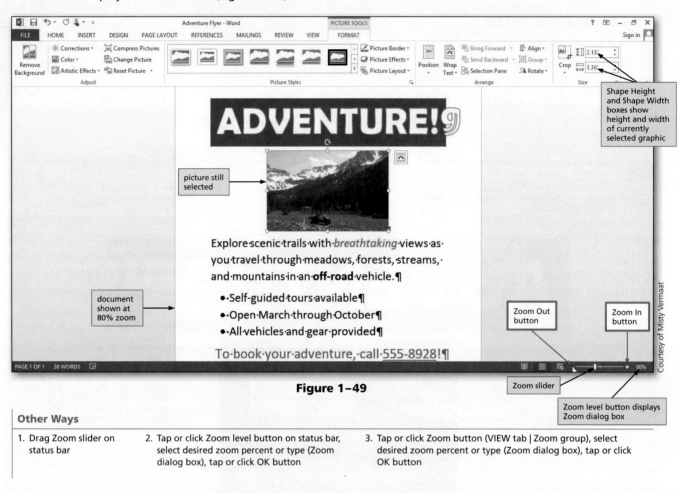

Figure 1–49

Other Ways

1. Drag Zoom slider on status bar

2. Tap or click Zoom level button on status bar, select desired zoom percent or type (Zoom dialog box), tap or click OK button

3. Tap or click Zoom button (VIEW tab | Zoom group), select desired zoom percent or type (Zoom dialog box), tap or click OK button

To Resize a Graphic

Resizing includes both increasing and reducing the size of a graphic. The next step is to resize the picture so that it is larger in the flyer. *Why? You want the graphic as large as possible on a single page flyer to draw the attention of passersby.* The following steps resize a selected graphic.

1

• Be sure the graphic still is selected.

Q&A What if my graphic (picture) is not selected?
To select a graphic, tap or click it.

• If you are using a mouse, point to the lower-left corner sizing handle on the picture so that the pointer shape changes to a two-headed arrow (Figure 1–50).

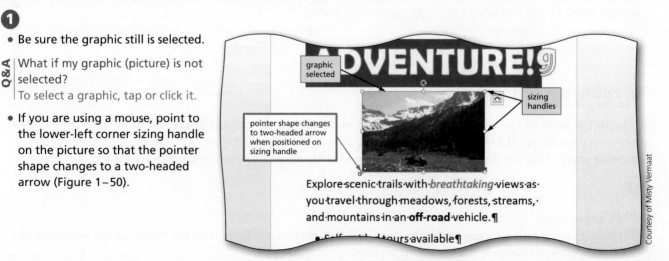

Figure 1–50

2

- Drag the sizing handle diagonally outward until the lower-left corner of the picture is positioned approximately as shown in Figure 1–51. Do not lift your finger or release the mouse button at this point.

3

- Release your finger or the mouse button to resize the graphic, which in this case, should have a height of about 3.26" and a width of about 5.04".

Q&A

How can I see the height and width measurements?
Look in the Size group on the PICTURE TOOLS FORMAT tab to see the height and width measurements of the currently selected graphic (shown in Figure 1–49).

What if the graphic is the wrong size?
Repeat Steps 1, 2, and 3, or enter the desired height and width values in the Shape Height and Shape Width boxes (PICTURE TOOLS FORMAT tab | Size group).

What if I want to return a graphic to its original size and start again?
With the graphic selected, tap or click the Size Dialog Box Launcher (PICTURE TOOLS FORMAT tab | Size group), tap or click the Size tab (Layout dialog box), tap or click the Reset button, and then tap or click the OK button.

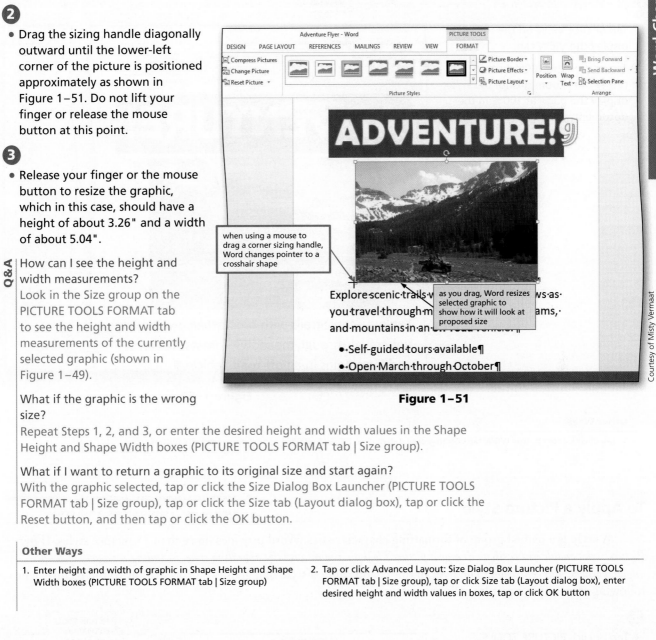

when using a mouse to drag a corner sizing handle, Word changes pointer to a crosshair shape

as you drag, Word resizes selected graphic to show how it will look at proposed size

Courtesy of Misty Vermaat

Figure 1–51

Other Ways

1. Enter height and width of graphic in Shape Height and Shape Width boxes (PICTURE TOOLS FORMAT tab | Size group)

2. Tap or click Advanced Layout: Size Dialog Box Launcher (PICTURE TOOLS FORMAT tab | Size group), tap or click Size tab (Layout dialog box), enter desired height and width values in boxes, tap or click OK button

---

To Zoom 100%

1 ENTER TEXT | 2 FORMAT TEXT | 3 INSERT PICTURE | **4 FORMAT PICTURE**
5 ENHANCE PAGE | 6 CORRECT & REVISE | 7 PRINT OR READ

In the next series of steps, you will format the picture. Earlier in this chapter, you changed the zoom to 80% so that you could see more of the page while resizing the graphic. The step on the next page zooms the screen to 100%. **Why?** *You want the contents of the image to be enlarged a bit, while still seeing some of the text in the document.*

1

- Tap or click VIEW on the ribbon to display the VIEW tab.

- Tap or click the 100% button (VIEW tab | Zoom group) to display the page at 100% in the document window (Figure 1–52).

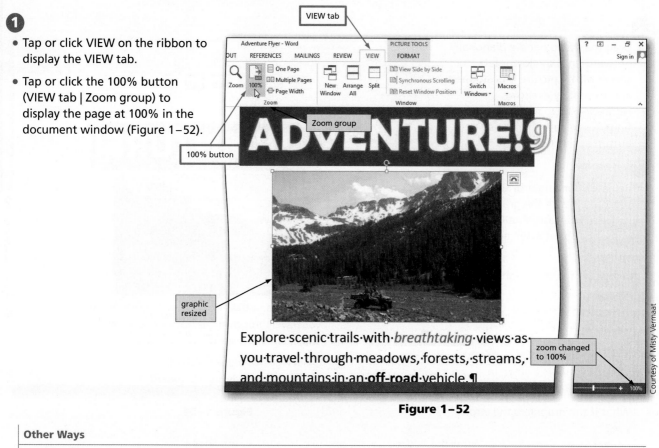

Figure 1–52

Other Ways

1. Tap or click Zoom button (VIEW tab | Zoom group), tap or click 100% (Zoom dialog box), tap or click OK button

To Apply a Picture Style

1 ENTER TEXT | 2 FORMAT TEXT | 3 INSERT PICTURE | 4 FORMAT PICTURE
5 ENHANCE PAGE | 6 CORRECT & REVISE | 7 PRINT OR READ

A **style** is a named group of formatting characteristics. Word provides more than 25 picture styles. *Why? Picture styles enable you easily to change a picture's look to a more visually appealing style, including a variety of shapes, angles, borders, and reflections.* The flyer in this chapter uses a style that applies a drop shadow to the picture. The following steps apply a picture style to a picture.

1

- Tap or click PICTURE TOOLS FORMAT on the ribbon to display the PICTURE TOOLS FORMAT tab.

- Be sure the graphic still is selected (Figure 1–53).

Q&A What if my graphic (picture) is not selected?
To select a graphic, tap or click it.

What is the white circle attached to top of the selected graphic?
It is called a rotate handle. When you drag a graphic's **rotate handle**, the graphic moves in either a clockwise or counterclockwise direction.

Figure 1–53

2

- Tap or click the More button in the Picture Styles gallery (PICTURE TOOLS FORMAT tab | Picture Styles group) (shown in Figure 1–53) to expand the gallery.

- If you are using a mouse, point to 'Drop Shadow Rectangle' in the Picture Styles gallery to display a live preview of that style applied to the picture in the document (Figure 1–54).

🔍 **Experiment**

- If you are using a mouse, point to various picture styles in the Picture Styles gallery and watch the style of the picture change in the document window.

3

- Tap or click 'Drop Shadow Rectangle' in the Picture Styles gallery (fourth style in first row) to apply the style to the selected picture.

Figure 1–54

Other Ways

1. Press and hold or right-click picture, tap or click 'Picture Quick Styles' on mini toolbar, select desired style

To Apply Picture Effects

1 ENTER TEXT | 2 FORMAT TEXT | 3 INSERT PICTURE | 4 FORMAT PICTURE
5 ENHANCE PAGE | 6 CORRECT & REVISE | 7 PRINT OR READ

Word provides a variety of picture effects, such as shadows, reflections, glow, soft edges, bevel, and 3-D rotation. The difference between the effects and the styles is that each effect has several options, providing you with more control over the exact look of the image.

In this flyer, the picture has a slight green glow effect and beveled edges. The following steps apply picture effects to the selected picture. *Why? Picture effects enable you to further customize the a picture.*

1

- With the picture still selected, tap or click the Picture Effects button (PICTURE TOOLS FORMAT tab | Picture Styles group) to display the Picture Effects menu.

- Tap or point to Glow on the Picture Effects menu to display the Glow gallery.

- If you are using a mouse, point to 'Turquoise, 5 pt glow, Accent color 6' in the Glow Variations area (rightmost glow in first row) to display a live preview of the selected glow effect applied to the picture in the document window (Figure 1–55).

🔍 **Experiment**

- If you are using a mouse, point to various glow effects in the Glow gallery and watch the picture change in the document window

Figure 1–55

2

- Tap or click 'Turquoise, 5 pt glow, Accent color 6' in the Glow gallery to apply the selected picture effect.

Q&A

What if I wanted to discard formatting applied to a picture?

You would tap or click the Reset Picture button (PICTURE TOOLS FORMAT tab | Adjust group). To reset formatting and size, you would tap or click the Reset Picture arrow (PICTURE TOOLS FORMAT tab | Adjust group) and then tap or click 'Reset Picture & Size' on the Reset Picture menu.

3

- Tap or click the Picture Effects button (PICTURE TOOLS FORMAT tab | Picture Styles group) to display the Picture Effects menu again.

- Tap or point to Bevel on the Picture Effects menu to display the Bevel gallery.

- If you are using a mouse, point to Angle in the Bevel area (first effect in second row) to display a live preview of the selected bevel effect applied to the picture in the document window (Figure 1–56).

🔍 **Experiment**

- If you are using a mouse, point to various bevel effects in the Bevel gallery and watch the picture change in the document window.

4

- Tap or click Angle in the Bevel gallery to apply the selected picture effect.

Figure 1–56

Courtesy of Misty Vermaat

Other Ways

1. Tap 'Show Context Menu' button on mini toolbar or right-click picture, tap or click Format Object or Format Picture on shortcut menu, tap or click Effects button (Format Picture task pane), select desired options, tap or click Close button

2. Tap or click Format Shape Dialog Box Launcher (PICTURE TOOLS FORMAT tab | Picture Styles group), tap or click Effects button (Format Picture task pane), select desired options, tap or click Close button

---

BTW

Word Help

At any time while using Word, you can find answers to questions and display information about various topics through Word Help. Used properly, this form of assistance can increase your productivity and reduce your frustrations by minimizing the time you spend learning how to use Word. For instruction about Word Help and exercises that will help you gain confidence in using it, read the Office and Windows chapter at the beginning of this book.

Enhancing the Page

With the text and graphics entered and formatted, the next step is to look at the page as a whole and determine if it looks finished in its current state. As you review the page, answer these questions:

- Does it need a page border to frame its contents, or would a page border make it look too busy?

- Is the spacing between paragraphs and graphics on the page adequate? Do any sections of text or graphics look as if they are positioned too closely to the items above or below them?

- Does the flyer have too much space at the top or bottom? Should the contents be centered vertically?

You determine that a graphical, color-coordinated border would enhance the flyer. You also notice that the flyer would look better proportioned if it had a little more space above and below the picture. You also want to ensure that the contents are centered vertically. The following pages make these enhancements to the flyer.

To Add a Page Border

In Word, you can add a border around the perimeter of an entire page. The flyer in this chapter has a light green border. *Why? This border color complements the color of the flyer contents.* The following steps add a page border.

1
- Tap or click DESIGN on the ribbon to display the DESIGN tab.
- Tap or click the 'Borders and Shading' button (DESIGN tab | Page Background group) to display the Borders and Shading dialog box (Figure 1–57).

Figure 1–57

2
- Tap or click the second border style in the Style list (Borders and Shading dialog box) to select the style.
- Tap or click the Color arrow to display a Color palette (Figure 1–58).

Figure 1–58

3

- Tap or click 'Lime, Accent 2, Lighter 80%' (sixth color in second row) in the Color palette to select the color for the page border.

- Tap or click the Width arrow to display the Width list and then tap or click 4 ½ pt to select the thickness of the page border (Figure 1–59).

4

- Tap or click the OK button to add the border to the page (shown in Figure 1–60).

Q&A What if I wanted to remove the border?
You would tap or click None in the Setting list in the Borders and Shading dialog box.

Figure 1–59

To Zoom One Page

1 ENTER TEXT | 2 FORMAT TEXT | 3 INSERT PICTURE | 4 FORMAT PICTURE
5 ENHANCE PAGE | 6 CORRECT & REVISE | 7 PRINT OR READ

The next steps zoom one page so that you can see the entire page on the screen at once.

1 Tap or click VIEW on the ribbon to display the VIEW tab.

2 Tap or click the One Page button (VIEW tab | Zoom group) to display the entire page in the document window as large as possible.

To Change Spacing before and after Paragraphs

1 ENTER TEXT | 2 FORMAT TEXT | 3 INSERT PICTURE | 4 FORMAT PICTURE
5 ENHANCE PAGE | 6 CORRECT & REVISE | 7 PRINT OR READ

The default spacing above (before) a paragraph in Word is 0 points and below (after) is 8 points. In the flyer, you want to increase the spacing below the paragraph containing the headline and above the signature line. *Why? The flyer spacing will look more balanced with spacing increased above and below these paragraphs.* The following steps change the spacing above and below a paragraph.

1

- Position the insertion point in the paragraph to be adjusted, in this case, the paragraph containing the headline.

Q&A What happened to the PICTURE TOOLS FORMAT tab?

When you tap or click outside of a graphic or press a key to scroll through a document, Word deselects the graphic and removes the PICTURE TOOLS FORMAT tab from the screen. That is, this tab appears only when a graphic is selected.

- Tap or click PAGE LAYOUT on the ribbon to display the PAGE LAYOUT tab.

- If you are using a touch screen, tap the Spacing After box (PAGE LAYOUT tab | Paragraph group) and then type 12 to change the spacing below the paragraph; if you are using a mouse, click the Spacing After up arrow (PAGE LAYOUT tab | Paragraph group) so that 12 pt is displayed in the Spacing After box to increase the space below the current paragraph (Figure 1–60).

Figure 1–60

2

- Position the insertion point in the paragraph to be adjusted, in this case, the paragraph containing the signature line.

- If you are using a touch screen, tap the Spacing Before box (PAGE LAYOUT tab | Paragraph group) and then type 12 to change the spacing above the paragraph; if you are using a mouse, click the Spacing Before up arrow (PAGE LAYOUT tab | Paragraph group) as many times as necessary so that 12 pt is displayed in the Spacing Before box to increase the space above the current paragraph (Figure 1–61).

- If the text flows to two pages, reduce the spacing above and below paragraphs as necessary.

Figure 1–61

Other Ways

1. Tap 'Show Context Menu' button on mini toolbar or right-click paragraph, tap or click Paragraph on shortcut menu, tap or click Indents and Spacing tab (Paragraph dialog box), enter spacing before and after values, tap or click OK button

2. Tap or click Paragraph Settings Dialog Box Launcher (HOME tab or PAGE LAYOUT tab | Paragraph group), tap or click Indents and Spacing tab (Paragraph dialog box), enter spacing before and after values, tap or click OK button

---

To Center Page Contents Vertically

1 ENTER TEXT | 2 FORMAT TEXT | 3 INSERT PICTURE | 4 FORMAT PICTURE

5 ENHANCE PAGE | **6 CORRECT & REVISE** | 7 PRINT OR READ

In Word, you can center the page contents vertically. *Why? This places the same amount of space at the top and bottom of the page.* The following steps center page contents vertically.

1

- If necessary, tap or click PAGE LAYOUT on the ribbon to display the PAGE LAYOUT tab.

- Tap or click the Page Setup Dialog Box Launcher (PAGE LAYOUT tab | Page Setup group) to display the Page Setup dialog box.

- Tap or click the Layout tab (Page Setup dialog box) to display the Layout sheet (Figure 1–62).

Figure 1–62

2

• Tap or click the Vertical alignment arrow (Page Setup dialog box) to display the list of alignment options and then tap or click Center in the list (Figure 1–63).

3

• Tap or click the OK button to center the page contents vertically on the screen (shown in Figure 1–1 on page WD 3).

Q&A

What if I wanted to change the alignment back?
You would select the Top vertical alignment from the Vertical alignment list in the Layout sheet (Page Setup dialog box).

Figure 1–63

To Save an Existing Document with the Same File Name

You have made several modifications to the document since you last saved it. Thus, you should save it again. The following step saves the document again. For an example of the step listed below, refer to the Office and Windows chapter at the beginning of this book.

1 Tap or click the Save button on the Quick Access Toolbar to overwrite the previously saved file.

Document Properties

Word helps you organize and identify your files by using **document properties**, which are the details about a file such as the project author, title, and subject. For example, a class name or document topic can describe the file's purpose or content.

Why would you want to assign document properties to a document?
Document properties are valuable for a variety of reasons:

• Users can save time locating a particular file because they can view a file's document properties without opening the document.

• By creating consistent properties for files having similar content, users can better organize their documents.

• Some organizations require Word users to add document properties so that other employees can view details about these files.

The more common document properties are standard and automatically updated properties. **Standard properties** are associated with all Microsoft Office files and include author, title, and subject. **Automatically updated properties** include file system properties, such as the date you create or change a file, and statistics, such as the file size.

To Change Document Properties

To change document properties, you would follow these steps.

1. Tap or click FILE on the ribbon to open the Backstage view and then, if necessary, tap or click the Info tab in the Backstage view to display the Info gallery.

2. If the property you wish to change is displayed in the Properties list in the right pane of the Info gallery, try to tap or click to the right of the property. If a text box appears to the right of the property, type the text for the property in the text box, and then tap or click the Back button in the upper-left corner of the Backstage view to return to the Word window. Skip the remaining steps.

3. If the property you wish to change is not displayed in the Properties list in the right pane of the Info gallery or you cannot change it in the Info gallery, tap or click the Properties button in the right pane to display the Properties menu, and then tap or click 'Show Document Panel' on the Properties menu to close the Backstage view and display the Document Information Panel in the Word document window.

Q&A | Why are some of the document properties in my Document Information Panel already filled in?
The person who installed Office 2013 on your computer or network may have set or customized the properties.

4. Type the desired text in the appropriate property text boxes.

Q&A | What if the property I want to change is not displayed in the Document Information Panel?
Tap or click the Document Properties button in the Document Information Panel and then tap or click Advanced Properties on the menu to display the Properties dialog box. If necessary, tap or click the Summary tab (Properties dialog box) to display the Summary sheet, fill in the appropriate text boxes, and then tap or click the OK button.

5. Tap or click the 'Close the Document Information Panel' button at the right edge of the Document Information Panel so that the panel no longer appears in the Word document window.

To Sign Out of a Microsoft Account

If you are signed in to a Microsoft account and are using a public computer or otherwise wish to sign out of your Microsoft account, you should sign out of the account from the Account gallery in the Backstage view before exiting Word. Signing out of the account is the safest way to make sure that nobody else can access SkyDrive files or settings stored in your Microsoft account. The following steps sign out of a Microsoft account from Word. For a detailed example of the procedure summarized below, refer to the Office and Windows chapter at the beginning of this book.

1 If you wish to sign out of your Microsoft account, tap or click FILE on the ribbon to open the Backstage view and then tap or click the Account tab to display the Account gallery.

2 Tap or click the Sign out link, which displays the Remove Account dialog box. If a Can't remove Windows accounts dialog box appears instead of the Remove Account dialog box, tap or click the OK button and skip the remaining steps.

Q&A | Why does a Can't remove Windows accounts dialog box appear?
If you signed in to Windows using your Microsoft account, then you also must sign out from Windows, rather than signing out from within the Word. When you are finished using Windows, be sure to sign out at that time.

3 Tap or click the Yes button (Remove Account dialog box) to sign out of your Microsoft account on this computer.

Q&A | Should I sign out of Windows after signing out of my Microsoft account?
When you are finished using the computer, you should sign out of your account for maximum security.

4 Tap or click the Back button in the upper-left corner of the Backstage view to return to the document.

BTW
Q&As
For a complete list of the Q&As found in many of the step-by-step sequences in this book, visit the Q&A resource on the Student Companion Site located on www.cengagebrain.com. For detailed instructions about accessing available resources, visit www.cengage.com/ct/studentdownload or contact your instructor for information about accessing the required files.

To Exit Word

Although you still need to make some edits to this document, you want to exit Word and resume working on the project at a later time. Thus, the following steps exit Word. For a detailed example of the procedure summarized below, refer to the Office and Windows chapter at the beginning of this book.

1a If you have one Word document open, tap or click the Close button on the right side of the title bar to close the open document and exit Word.

1b If you have multiple Word documents open, press and hold or right-click the Word app button on the taskbar and then tap or click 'Close all windows' on the shortcut menu to close all open documents and exit Word.

Q&A | Could I press and hold or repeatedly click the Close button to close all open documents and exit Word?
Yes.

2 If a Microsoft Word dialog box appears, tap or click the Save button to save any changes made to the document since the last save.

Break Point: If you wish to take a break, this is a good place to do so. To resume at a later time, continue following the steps from this location forward.

Correcting Errors and Revising a Document

After creating a document, you may need to change it. For example, the document may contain an error, or new circumstances may require you to add text to the document.

Types of Changes Made to Documents

The types of changes made to documents normally fall into one of the three following categories: additions, deletions, or modifications.

Additions Additional words, sentences, or paragraphs may be required in a document. Additions occur when you omit text from a document and want to insert it later. For example, you may want to add your email address to the flyer.

Deletions Sometimes, text in a document is incorrect or no longer is needed. For example, you may discover that the tours no longer provide gear. In this case, you would delete the words, and gear, from the flyer.

Modifications If an error is made in a document or changes take place that affect the document, you might have to revise a word(s) in the text. For example, the tours may start in April instead of March.

To Run Word

Once you have created and saved a document, you may need to retrieve it from your storage medium. For example, you might want to revise the document or print it. The following steps, which assume Windows 8 is running, use the Start screen or the Search box to run Word based on a typical installation. You may need to ask your instructor how to run Word on your computer. For a detailed example of the procedure summarized below, refer to the Office and Windows chapter.

BTW
Certification
The Microsoft Office Specialist (MOS) program provides an opportunity for you to obtain a valuable industry credential — proof that you have the Word 2013 skills required by employers. For more information, visit the Certification resource on the Student Companion Site located on www.cengagebrain.com. For detailed instructions about accessing available resources, visit www.cengage.com/ct/studentdownload or contact your instructor for information about accessing the required files.

1 Scroll the Start screen for a Word 2013 tile. If your Start screen contains a Word 2013 tile, tap or click it to run Word and then proceed to Step 5; if the Start screen does not contain the Word 2013 tile, proceed to the next step to search for the Word app.

2 Swipe in from the right edge of the screen or point to the upper-right corner of the screen to display the Charms bar and then tap or click the Search charm on the Charms bar to display the Search menu.

3 Type **Word** as the search text in the Search box and watch the search results appear in the Apps list.

4 Tap or click Word 2013 in the search results to run Word.

5 Tap or click the Blank document thumbnail on the Word start screen to create a blank document and display it in the Word window.

6 If the Word window is not maximized, tap or click the Maximize button on its title bar to maximize the window.

To Open a Document from Word

Earlier in this chapter you saved your flyer using the file name, Adventure Flyer. The following steps open the Adventure Flyer file from the Word folder in the CIS 101 folder. For a detailed example of the procedure summarized below, refer to the Office and Windows chapter at the beginning of this book.

1 Tap or click FILE on the ribbon to open the Backstage view and then tap or click the Open tab in the Backstage view to display the Open gallery.

2 If the file you wish to open is displayed in the Recent Documents list, tap or click the file name to open the file and display the opened document in the Word window; then, skip the remaining steps. If the file you wish to open is not displayed in the Recent Documents list, proceed to the next step to locate the file.

3 Tap or click Computer, SkyDrive, or another location in the left pane, tap or click the Browse button, and then navigate to the location of the file to be opened (in this case the Word folder in the CIS 101 folder).

4 Tap or click Adventure Flyer to select the file to be opened.

5 Tap or click the Open button (Open dialog box) to open the selected file and display the opened document in the Word window.

To Zoom the Document

While modifying the document, you prefer the document at 100% so that it is easier to read. Thus, the following step changes the zoom back to 100%.

1 Tap or click VIEW on the ribbon to display the VIEW tab.

2 Tap or click the 100% button (VIEW tab | Zoom group) to display the page at 100% in the document window.

BTW
Quick Reference
For a table that lists how to complete the tasks covered in this book using touch gestures, the mouse, ribbon, shortcut menu, and keyboard, see the Quick Reference Summary at the back of this book, or visit the Quick Reference resource on the Student Companion Site located on www.cengagebrain.com. For detailed instructions about accessing available resources, visit www.cengage.com/ct/studentdownload or contact your instructor for information about accessing the required files.

To Insert Text in an Existing Document

Word inserts text to the left of the insertion point. The text to the right of the insertion point moves to the right and downward to fit the new text. The following steps insert the word, today, to the left of the word, with, in the flyer. *Why? These steps illustrate the process of inserting text.*

1

- Scroll through the document and then tap or click to the left of the location of text to be inserted (in this case, the w in with) to position the insertion point where text should be inserted (Figure 1–64).

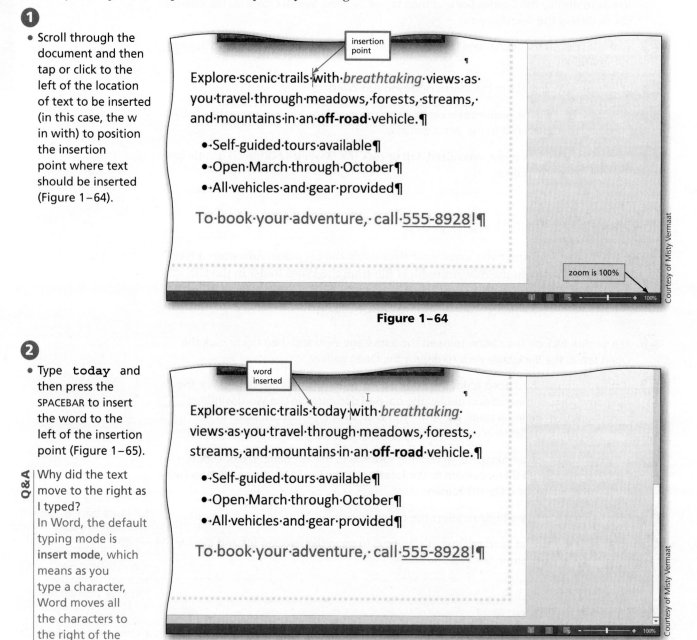

Figure 1–64

2

- Type **today** and then press the SPACEBAR to insert the word to the left of the insertion point (Figure 1–65).

Q&A Why did the text move to the right as I typed?
In Word, the default typing mode is **insert mode**, which means as you type a character, Word moves all the characters to the right of the typed character one position to the right.

Figure 1–65

Courtesy of Misty Vermaat

To Delete Text

It is not unusual to type incorrect characters or words in a document. As discussed earlier in this chapter, you can tap or click the Undo button on the Quick Access Toolbar to undo a command or action immediately — this includes typing. Word also provides other methods of correcting typing errors.

To delete an incorrect character in a document, simply tap or click next to the incorrect character and then press the BACKSPACE key to erase to the left of the insertion point, or press the DELETE key to erase to the right of the insertion point.

To delete a word or phrase, you first must select the word or phrase. The following steps select the word, today, which was just added in the previous steps and then delete the selection. *Why? These steps illustrate the process of selecting a word and then deleting selected text.*

1
- Double-tap or double-click the word to be selected (in this case, today) to select the word (Figure 1–66).

2
- If you are using a touch screen, tap the selected text to display the mini toolbar and then tap the Cut button on the mini toolbar to delete the selected text; if you are using a keyboard, with the text selected, press the DELETE key to delete the selected text.

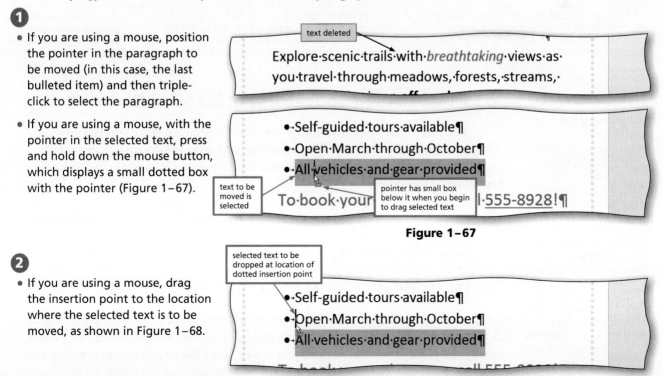

mini toolbar appears because text is selected

text to be deleted is selected

pointer

Explore·scenic·trails·today·with·*breathtaking*· views·as·you·travel·through·meadows,·forests,· streams,·and·mountains·in·an·off-road·vehicle.¶

- •Self-guided·tours·available¶
- •Open·March·through·October¶
- •All·vehicles·and·gear·provided¶

Figure 1–66

Other Ways

1. Press and hold or right-click selected item, tap Cut on mini toolbar or click Cut on shortcut menu
2. Select item, press BACKSPACE to delete to left of insertion point or press DELETE to delete to right of insertion point
3. Select item, press CTRL+X

To Move Text

1 ENTER TEXT | 2 FORMAT TEXT | 3 INSERT PICTURE | 4 FORMAT PICTURE
5 ENHANCE PAGE | 6 CORRECT & REVISE | **7 PRINT OR READ**

An efficient way to move text a short distance is drag-and-drop editing. With **drag-and-drop editing**, you select the item to be moved, drag the selected item to the new location, and then drop, or insert, it in the new location. Another technique for moving text is the cut-and-paste technique, which is discussed in the next chapter.

The following steps use drag-and-drop editing to move text. *Why? While proofreading the flyer, you realize that the body copy would read better if the last two bulleted paragraphs were reversed.*

1
- If you are using a mouse, position the pointer in the paragraph to be moved (in this case, the last bulleted item) and then triple-click to select the paragraph.

- If you are using a mouse, with the pointer in the selected text, press and hold down the mouse button, which displays a small dotted box with the pointer (Figure 1–67).

text deleted

Explore·scenic·trails·with·*breathtaking*·views·as· you·travel·through·meadows,·forests,·streams,·

- •Self-guided·tours·available¶
- •Open·March·through·October¶
- •All·vehicles·and·gear·provided¶

text to be moved is selected

pointer has small box below it when you begin to drag selected text

To·book·your   l-555-8928!¶

Figure 1–67

2
- If you are using a mouse, drag the insertion point to the location where the selected text is to be moved, as shown in Figure 1–68.

selected text to be dropped at location of dotted insertion point

- •Self-guided·tours·available¶
- •Open·March·through·October¶
- •All·vehicles·and·gear·provided¶

Figure 1–68

3

- If you are using a mouse, release the mouse button to move the selected text to the location of the dotted insertion point (Figure 1–69).

Q&A
What if I accidentally drag text to the wrong location?
Tap or click the Undo button on the Quick Access Toolbar and try again.

Can I use drag-and-drop editing to move any selected item?
Yes, you can select words, sentences, phrases, and graphics and then use drag-and-drop editing to move them.

What is the purpose of the Paste Options button?
If you are using a mouse and click the Paste Options button, a menu appears that allows you to change the format of the item that was moved. The next chapter discusses the Paste Options menu.

- Tap or click anywhere in the document window to remove the selection from the bulleted item.

Figure 1–69

Courtesy of Misty Vermaat

Q&A
What if I am using a touch screen?
If you have a stylus, you can follow Steps 1 through 3 using the stylus. If you are using your finger, you will need to use the cut-and-paste technique: tap to position the insertion point in the text to be moved and then drag the selection handles as necessary to select the text that you want to move; tap the selection to display the mini toolbar and then tap the Cut button on the mini toolbar to remove the text; tap to position the insertion point at the location where you want to move the text; display the HOME tab and then tap the Paste button on the HOME tab to place the text at the location of the insertion point. The next chapter discusses this procedure in more depth.

Other Ways

1. Tap or click Cut button (HOME tab | Clipboard group), tap or click where text or object is to be pasted, tap or click Paste button (HOME tab | Clipboard group)
2. Press and hold or right-click selected text, tap or click Cut on mini toolbar or shortcut menu, press and hold or right-click where text or object is to be pasted, tap Paste on mini toolbar or click Keep Source Formatting on shortcut menu
3. Press CTRL+X, position insertion point where text or object is to be pasted, press CTRL+V

BTW
Conserving Ink and Toner
If you want to conserve ink or toner, you can instruct Word to print draft quality documents by tapping or clicking FILE on the ribbon to open the Backstage view, tapping or clicking Options in the Backstage view, tapping or clicking Advanced in the left pane (Word Options dialog box), sliding or scrolling to the Print area in the right pane, placing a check mark in the 'Use draft quality' check box, and then tapping or clicking the OK button. Then, use the Backstage view to print the document as usual.

To Save an Existing Document with the Same File Name

You have made several modifications to the document since you last saved it. Thus, you should save it again. The following step saves the document again. For an example of the step listed below, refer to the Office and Windows chapter at the beginning of this book.

1 Tap or click the Save button on the Quick Access Toolbar to overwrite the previously saved file.

Printing or Reading a Document

After creating a document, you may want to print it or read it on-screen. Printing a document enables you to distribute it to others in a form that can be read or viewed but typically not edited. It is a good practice to save a document before printing it, in the event you experience difficulties printing. Some users prefer reading a document on-screen instead of on paper.

What is the best method for distributing a document?

The traditional method of distributing a document uses a printer to produce a hard copy. A **hard copy** or **printout** is information that exists on a physical medium such as paper. Hard copies can be useful for the following reasons:

- Some people prefer proofreading a hard copy of a document rather than viewing it on the screen to check for errors and readability.

- Hard copies can serve as a backup reference if your storage medium is lost or becomes corrupted and you need to recreate the document.

Instead of distributing a hard copy of a document, users can distribute the document as an electronic image that mirrors the original document's appearance. The electronic image of the document can be sent as an email attachment, posted on a website, or copied to a portable storage medium such as a USB flash drive. Two popular electronic image formats, sometimes called fixed formats, are PDF by Adobe Systems and XPS by Microsoft. In Word, you can create electronic image files through the Save As dialog box and the Export, Share, and Print tabs in the Backstage view. Electronic images of documents, such as PDF and XPS, can be useful for the following reasons:

- Users can view electronic images of documents without the software that created the original document (e.g., Word). Specifically, to view a PDF file, you use a program called Adobe Reader, which can be downloaded free from Adobe's website. Similarly, to view an XPS file, you use a program called XPS Viewer, which is included in the latest versions of Windows and Internet Explorer.

- Sending electronic documents saves paper and printer supplies. Society encourages users to contribute to **green computing**, which involves reducing the electricity consumed and environmental waste generated when using computers, mobile devices, and related technologies.

To Print a Document

1 ENTER TEXT | 2 FORMAT TEXT | 3 INSERT PICTURE | 4 FORMAT PICTURE
5 ENHANCE PAGE | 6 CORRECT & REVISE | 7 PRINT OR READ

With the completed document saved, you may want to print it. *Why? Because this flyer is being posted, you will print a hard copy on a printer.* The following steps print a hard copy of the contents of the saved Adventure Flyer document.

1

- Tap or click FILE on the ribbon to open the Backstage view.

- Tap or click the Print tab in the Backstage view to display the Print gallery (Figure 1–70).

Q&A

How can I print multiple copies of my document?
Increase the number in the Copies box in the Print gallery.

What if I decide not to print the document at this time?
Tap or click the Back button in the upper-left corner of the Backstage view to return to the document window.

2

- Verify that the printer listed on the Printer Status button will print a hard copy of the document. If necessary, click the Printer Status button to display a list of available printer options and then click the desired printer to change the currently selected printer.

Figure 1–70

Courtesy of Misty Vermaat

3

- Tap or click the Print button in the Print gallery to print the document on the currently selected printer.

- When the printer stops, retrieve the hard copy (Figure 1–71).

Q&A

Do I have to wait until my document is complete to print it?
No, you can follow these steps to print a document at any time while you are creating it.

What if I want to print an electronic image of a document instead of a hard copy?
You would click the Printer Status button in the Print gallery and then select the desired electronic image option, such as Microsoft XPS Document Writer, which would create an XPS file.

What if one or more of my borders do not print?
Tap or click the Page Borders button (DESIGN tab | Page Background group), tap or click the Options button (Borders and Shading dialog box), tap or click the Measure from arrow and click Text, change the four text boxes to 15 pt, and then tap or click the OK button in each dialog box. Try printing the document again. If the borders still do not print, adjust the boxes in the dialog box to a number smaller than 15 point.

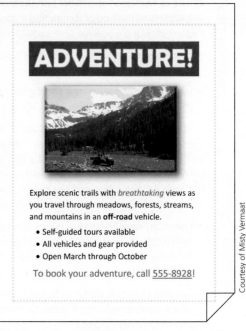

Explore scenic trails with *breathtaking* views as you travel through meadows, forests, streams, and mountains in an **off-road** vehicle.

- Self-guided tours available
- All vehicles and gear provided
- Open March through October

To book your adventure, call 555-8928!

Courtesy of Misty Vermaat

Figure 1–71

To Switch to Read Mode

1 ENTER TEXT | 2 FORMAT TEXT | 3 INSERT PICTURE | 4 FORMAT PICTURE
5 ENHANCE PAGE | 6 CORRECT & REVISE | **7 PRINT OR READ**

The next steps switch from Print Layout view to Read mode. **Why?** *If you are not composing a document, you can switch to* **Read mode,** *which hides the ribbon and other writing tools so that more content fits on the screen. Read mode is intended to make it easier to read a document.* The following step switches to Read mode.

1

- Tap or click the Read Mode button on the status bar to switch to Read mode (Figure 1–72).

Experiment

- Tap or click the arrows to advance forward and then move backward through the document.

Q&A

Besides reading, what can I do in Read mode?
You can zoom, copy text, highlight text, search, add comments, and more.

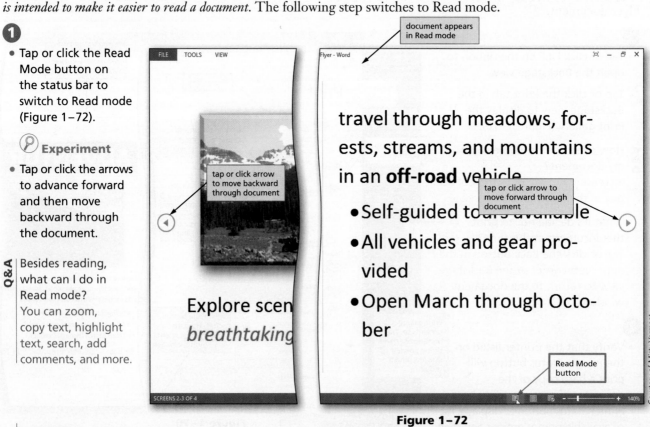

Figure 1–72

Other Ways

1. Tap or click Read Mode button (VIEW tab | Views group)   2. Tap or click VIEW on the ribbon, tap or click Edit Document

To Switch to Print Layout View

The next steps switch back to Print Layout view. *Why? If you want to show the document on a mock sheet of paper in the document window, along with the ribbon and other writing tools, you should switch to Print Layout view.* The following step switches to Print Layout view.

1

- Tap or click the Print Layout button on the status bar to switch to Print Layout view (Figure 1–73).

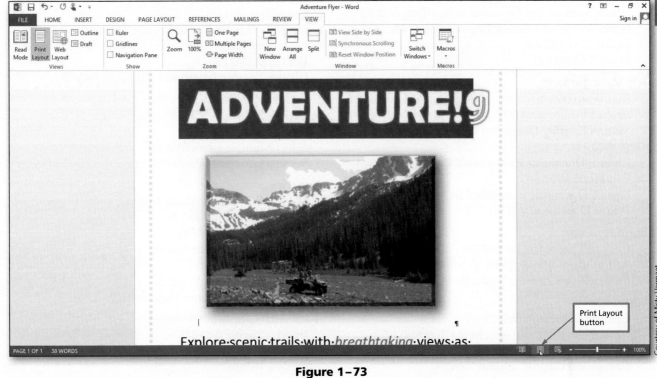

Figure 1–73

Other Ways

1. Tap or click Print Layout button (VIEW tab | Views group)

To Exit Word

This project now is complete. The following steps exit Word. For a detailed example of the procedure summarized below, refer to the Office and Windows chapter at the beginning of this book.

1a If you have one Word document open, tap or click the Close button on the right side of the title bar to close the open document and exit Word.

1b If you have multiple Word documents open, press and hold or right-click the Word app button on the taskbar and then tap or click 'Close all windows' on the shortcut menu to close all open documents and exit Word.

2 If a Microsoft Word dialog box appears, tap or click the Save button to save any changes made to the document since the last save.

BTW
Printing Document Properties
To print document properties, tap or click FILE on the ribbon to open the Backstage view, tap or click the Print tab in the Backstage view to display the Print gallery, tap or click the first button in the Settings area to display a list of options specifying what you can print, tap or click Document Info in the list to specify you want to print the document properties instead of the actual document, and then tap or click the Print button in the Print gallery to print the document properties on the currently selected printer.

Chapter Summary

In this chapter, you have learned how to enter text in a document, format text, insert and format a picture, add a page border, adjust paragraph and page spacing, and print and read a document. The items listed below include all the new Word skills you have learned in this chapter, with the tasks grouped by activity.

Enter and Edit Text
Type Text (WD 5)
Insert a Blank Line (WD 7)
Wordwrap Text as You Type (WD 9)
Check Spelling and Grammar as You Type (WD 10)
Insert Text in an Existing Document (WD 48)
Delete Text (WD 48)
Move Text (WD 49)

File Management
Run Word (WD 4)
Save a Document (WD 12)
Save an Existing Document with the Same File Name (WD 33)
Change Document Properties (WD 44)
Exit Word (WD 46)
Open a Document from Word (WD 47)
Print a Document (WD 51)

Format a Page
Change Theme Colors (WD 31)
Add a Page Border (WD 41)
Center Page Contents Vertically (WD 43)

Format Text
Center a Paragraph (WD 15)
Change the Font Size of Selected Text (WD 17)
Change the Font of Selected Text (WD 18)
Change the Case of Selected Text (WD 19)
Apply a Text Effect to Selected Text (WD 20)

Shade a Paragraph (WD 21)
Bullet a List of Paragraphs (WD 23)
Undo and Redo an Action (WD 24)
Italicize Text (WD 25)
Color Text (WD 26)
Use the Mini Toolbar to Format Text (WD 27)
Underline Text (WD 29)
Bold Text (WD 29)
Change Spacing before and after Paragraphs (WD 42)

Select Text
Select a Line (WD 16)
Select Multiple Lines (WD 22)
Select a Group of Words (WD 28)

Word Settings
Display Formatting Marks (WD 6)
Zoom Page Width (WD 7)
Zoom One Page (WD 30)
Zoom the Document (WD 35)
Zoom 100% (WD 37)
Switch to Read Mode (WD 52)
Switch to Print Layout View (WD 53)

Work with Graphics (Pictures)
Insert a Picture (WD 34)
Resize a Graphic (WD 36)
Apply a Picture Style (WD 38)
Apply Picture Effects (WD 39)

CONSIDER THIS: PLAN AHEAD

What decisions will you need to make when creating your next flyer?
Use these guidelines as you complete the assignments in this chapter and create your own flyers outside of this class.

1. Choose the text for the headline, body copy, and signature line — using as few words as possible to make a point.

2. Format various elements of the text.

    a) Select appropriate font sizes for text in the headline, body copy, and signature line.

    b) Select appropriate fonts for text in the headline, body copy, and signature line.

    c) Adjust paragraph alignment, as appropriate.

    d) Highlight key paragraphs with bullets.

    e) Emphasize important words.

    f) Use color to convey meaning and add appeal.

3. Find an eye-catching graphic(s) that conveys the overall message and meaning of the flyer.

4. Establish where to position and how to format the graphical image(s) so that the image grabs the attention of passersby and draws them into reading the flyer.

5. Determine whether the flyer needs enhancements such as a graphical, color-coordinated border or spacing adjustments to improve readability or overall appearance.

6. Correct errors and revise the document as necessary.

    a) Post the flyer on a wall and make sure all text and images are legible from a distance.

    b) Ask someone else to read the flyer and give you suggestions for improvements.

7. Determine the best method for distributing the document such as printing, sending via email, or posting on the web.

How should you submit solutions to questions in the assignments identified with a ✳ symbol?
Every assignment in this book contains one or more questions identified with a ✳ symbol. These questions require you to think beyond the assigned document. Present your solutions to the questions in the format required by your instructor. Possible formats may include one or more of these options: write the answer; create a document that contains the answer; present your answer to the class; discuss your answer in a group; record the answer as audio or video using a webcam, smartphone, or portable media player; or post answers on a blog, wiki, or website.

Apply Your Knowledge

Reinforce the skills and apply the concepts you learned in this chapter.

Modifying Text and Formatting a Document

Note: To complete this assignment, you will be required to use the Data Files for Students. Visit www.cengage.com/ct/studentdownload for detailed instructions or contact your instructor for information about accessing the required files.

Instructions: Run Word. Open the document, Apply 1-1 County Park Flyer Unformatted, from the Data Files for Students. The document you open is an unformatted flyer. You are to modify text, format paragraphs and characters, and insert a picture in the flyer to create the flyer shown in Figure 1–74.

Perform the following tasks:

1. Delete the word, below, in the sentence below the headline.

2. Insert the word, Valley, between the words, Green County, in the second to last line of the flyer.

3. Change the period to an exclamation point in the last line so that the text reads: Thank You!

4. If requested by your instructor, change the phone number in the flyer to your phone number.

5. Center the headline and the last two paragraphs of the flyer.

6. Select the third, fourth, and fifth paragraphs in the flyer and add bullets to the selected paragraphs.

7. Change the theme colors to the Red Orange color scheme.

8. Change the font and font size of the headline to 48-point Franklin Gothic Heavy, or a similar font. Change the case of the headline text to uppercase letters. Apply the text effect called Fill - Black, Text 1, Outline - Background 1, Hard Shadow - Background 1 to the headline. Change the font color of the headline text to Dark Red, Accent 6.

headline →

PLEASE DO NOT FEED THE WILDLIFE!

Follow these guidelines to keep our wildlife healthy and our environment clean.

bulleted list →

- Do **not** feed the wildlife.
- Never leave food unattended.
- Discard *all* trash in provided containers.

Questions? Call Green Valley County Park at 329-555-1020.

Thank You!

Courtesy of Misty Vermaat

Figure 1–74

Continued >

Apply Your Knowledge *continued*

9. Change the font size of the sentence below the headline, the bulleted list, and the last line of flyer to 26 point.

10. Use the mini toolbar to change the font size of the sentence below the bulleted list to 18 point.

11. Select the words, Follow these guidelines, in the paragraph below the headline and underline them.

12. Bold the word, not, in the first bulleted paragraph. Change the font color of this same word to Dark Red, Accent 6.

13. Italicize the word, all, in the second bulleted item. Undo this change and then redo the change.

14. Switch the last two bulleted paragraphs. That is, select the 'Never leave food unattended' bullet and move it so that it is the second bulleted paragraph.

15. Bold the text, Thank You!, in the last line of the flyer. Shade this same paragraph Dark Red, Accent 6, Darker 25%. If the font color does not automatically change to a lighter color, change its color to White, Background 1.

16. Change the zoom so that the entire page is visible in the document window.

17. Insert the picture of the squirrel eating the sucker centered on the blank line below the headline. The picture is called Squirrel and is available on the Data Files for Students. Apply the Soft Edge Oval picture style to the inserted picture.

18. Change the spacing before the first bulleted paragraph to 12 point and the spacing after the last bulleted paragraph to 24 point.

19. The entire flyer should fit on a single page. If it flows to two pages, resize the picture or decrease spacing before and after paragraphs until the entire flyer text fits on a single page.

20. Change the zoom to text width, then page width, then 100% and notice the differences.

21. If requested by your instructor, enter the text, Green Valley, as the keywords in the document properties. Change the other document properties, as specified by your instructor.

22. Click FILE on the ribbon and then click Save As. Save the document using the file name, Apply 1-1 County Park Flyer Formatted.

23. Print the document. Switch to Read Mode and browse pages through the document. Switch to Print Layout view.

24. Submit the revised document, shown in Figure 1–74, in the format specified by your instructor.

25. Exit Word.

26. ✳ If this flyer were announcing the park reopening instead of including a warning, which color scheme would you apply and why?

Extend Your Knowledge

Extend the skills you learned in this chapter and experiment with new skills. You may need to use Help to complete the assignment.

Modifying Text and Picture Formats and Adding Page Borders

Note: To complete this assignment, you will be required to use the Data Files for Students. Visit www.cengage.com/ct/studentdownload for detailed instructions or contact your instructor for information about accessing the required files.

Instructions: Run Word. Open the document, Extend 1-1 Baseball Tryouts Flyer Draft, from the Data Files for Students. You will enhance the look of the flyer shown in Figure 1–75.
Hint: Remember, if you make a mistake while formatting the picture, you can reset it by using the Reset Picture button or Reset Picture arrow (PICTURE TOOLS FORMAT tab | Adjust group).

Perform the following tasks:

1. Use Help to learn about the following: remove bullets, grow font, shrink font, art page borders, decorative underline(s), picture bullets, picture border shading, picture border color, shadow picture effects, and color saturation and tone.

2. Remove the bullet from the last line of the flyer.

3. Select the text, August 30, and use the 'Increase Font Size' button (HOME tab | Font group) to increase its font size.

4. Add an art page border to the flyer. If the border is not in color, add color to it.

5. Change the solid underline below the word, Travel, to a decorative underline. Change the color of the underline.

6. Change the style of the bullets to picture bullet(s). Adjust the hanging indent, if necessary, to align the text in bulleted list.

7. Change the color of the picture border. Add the Perspective Right 3-D Rotation picture effect to the picture.

8. Change the color saturation and color tone of the picture.

9. If requested by your instructor, change the name of the field (High Crop) to your last name.

10. Save the revised document with the file name, Extend 1-1 Baseball Tryouts Flyer Final, and then submit it in the format specified by your instructor.

11. ☀ In this assignment you added an art page border to the flyer. Which border did you select and why?

Figure 1–75

Analyze, Correct, Improve

Analyze a document, correct all errors, and improve it.

Correcting Spelling and Grammar Errors and Adding Color

Note: To complete this assignment, you will be required to use the Data Files for Students. Visit www.cengage.com/ct/studentdownload for detailed instructions or contact your instructor for information about accessing the required files.

Instructions: Run Word. Open the document, Analyze 1-1 Beauty Salon Flyer Draft, from the Data Files for Students. The document is a flyer that contains spelling and grammar errors, as shown in Figure 1–76 on the next page. It also could include color to make it more visually appealing.

Continued >

Analyze, Correct, Improve *continued*

1. Correct You are to correct each spelling (red wavy underline) and grammar (green and blue wavy underlines) error by pressing and holding or right-clicking the flagged text and then clicking the appropriate correction on the shortcut menu.

If your screen does not display the wavy underlines, tap or click FILE on the ribbon and then tap or click Options in the Backstage view. When the Word Options dialog box is displayed, tap or click Proofing in the left pane, be sure the 'Hide spelling errors in this document only' and 'Hide grammar errors in this document only' check boxes do not contain check marks, and then tap or click the OK button. If your screen still does not display the wavy underlines, redisplay the Word Options dialog box, tap or click Proofing, and then tap or click the Recheck Document button.

2. Improve Enhance the flyer by (a) adding a shading color to the first and last lines (paragraphs) on the flyer, (b) changing the color of the text in the first line and last line of the flyer, and (c) adding a color glow effect to the three pictures in the flyer.

If requested by your instructor, change the street name in the flyer to your first name. Save the revised document with the file name, Extend 1-1 Beauty Salon Flyer Final, and then submit it in the format specified by your instructor.

3. ☀ In this assignment, you selected color to add to the flyer. Which color(s) did you select and why?

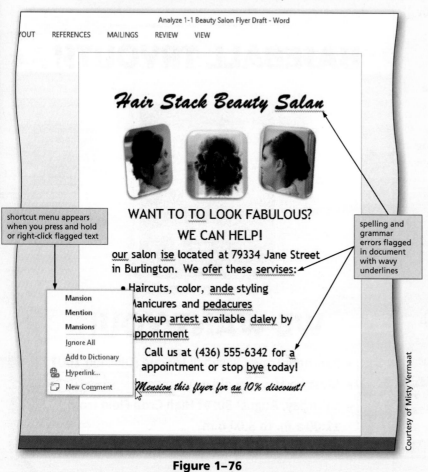

Figure 1–76

Courtesy of Misty Vermaat

In the Labs

Design and/or create a document using the guidelines, concepts, and skills presented in this chapter. Labs 1 and 2, which increase in difficulty, require you to create solutions based on what you learned in the chapter; Lab 3 requires you to create a solution, which uses cloud and web technologies, by learning and investigating on your own from general guidance.

Lab 1: Creating a Flyer with a Picture

Problem: Your friend asked you to prepare a flyer that advertises the puppy she has for sale. First, you prepare the unformatted flyer shown in Figure 1–77a, and then you format it so that it looks like Figure 1–77b on page WD 60. *Hint:* Remember, if you make a mistake while formatting the flyer, you can use the Undo button on the Quick Access Toolbar to undo your last action.

Note: To complete this assignment, you will be required to use the Data Files for Students. Visit www.cengage.com/ct/studentdownload for detailed instructions or contact your instructor for information about accessing the required files.

Instructions: Perform the following tasks:
1. Run Word. Display formatting marks on the screen.
2. Type the flyer text, unformatted, as shown in Figure 1–77a, inserting a blank line between the headline and the body copy. If Word flags any misspelled words as you type, check their spelling and correct them.
3. Save the document using the file name, Lab 1-1 Puppy for Sale Flyer.
4. Center the headline and the signature line.
5. Change the theme colors to Aspect.
6. Change the font size of the headline to 72 point and the font to Gil Sans Ultra Bold Condensed, or a similar font. Apply the text effect called Fill - Dark Purple, Accent 1, Outline - Background, Hard Shadow - Accent 1.
7. Change the font size of body copy between the headline and the signature line to 22 point.
8. Change the font size of the signature line to 20 point.
9. Change the font of the body copy and signature line to Comic Sans MS.
10. Bullet the three lines (paragraphs) of text above the signature line.
11. Change the color of the words, purebred American Cocker Spaniel, to Dark Green, Accent 4, Darker 50%.
12. Italicize the word, and, in the third bulleted paragraph.
13. Bold the text in the signature line. Shade this paragraph containing the signature line in Dark Purple, Accent 5, Lighter 80%.
14. Underline the phone number in the signature line.
15. Change the zoom so that the entire page is visible in the document window.
16. Insert the picture centered on a blank line below the headline. The picture is called Puppy and is available on the Data Files for Students.
17. Apply the Rotated, White picture style to the inserted picture. Apply the glow effect called Dark Purple, 5 pt glow, Accent color 5 to the picture.

Puppy for Sale

blank line →

Own this six-month-old male, potty-trained, purebred American Cocker Spaniel puppy.

Fun, smart, cuddly, and playful

Needs a loving home

Knows these commands: sit, down, stay, heel, and leave it

If interested, call Vivian at (356) 555-7733.

(a) Unformatted Text
Figure 1–77 (Continued)

Continued >

In the Labs *continued*

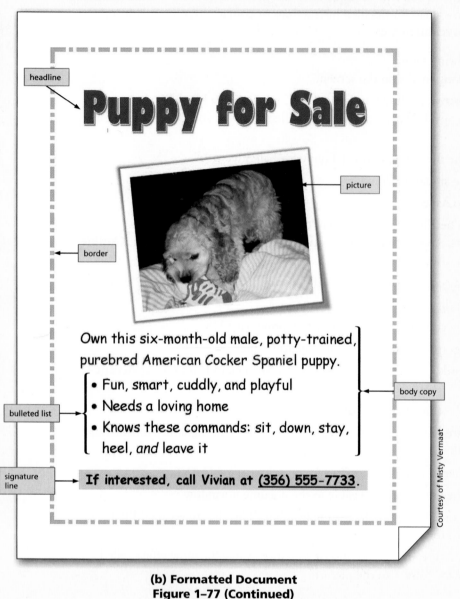

(b) Formatted Document
Figure 1–77 (Continued)

18. Change the spacing after the paragraph containing the headline to 0 pt. Change the spacing above (before) the signature line to 18 pt. The entire flyer should fit on a single page. If it flows to two pages, resize the picture or decrease spacing before and after paragraphs until the entire flyer text fits on a single page.

19. Add a 6-pt Dark Green, Accent 4, Lighter 60% page border, as shown in Figure 1–77b.

20. If requested by your instructor, change the contact name in the flyer to your first name.

21. Save the flyer again with the same file name. Submit the document, shown in Figure 1–77b, in the format specified by your instructor.

22. ✷ Why do you think this flyer used shades of purple and green?

Lab 2: **Creating a Flyer with a Resized Pictures**

Problem: Your boss at Junior's Wedding Bakery has asked you to prepare a flyer that promotes its business. You prepare the flyer shown in Figure 1–78. *Hint:* Remember, if you make a mistake while formatting the flyer, you can use the Undo button on the Quick Access Toolbar to undo your last action.

Note: To complete this assignment, you will be required to use the Data Files for Students. Visit www.cengage.com/ct/studentdownload for detailed instructions or contact your instructor for information about accessing the required files.

Instructions: Perform the following tasks:

1. Run Word. Type the flyer text, unformatted. If Word flags any misspelled words as you type, check their spelling and correct them.

2. Save the document using the file name, Lab 1-2 Wedding Bakery Flyer.

3. Change the theme colors to the Marquee color scheme.

4. Add bullets to the three paragraphs shown in the figure. Center all paragraphs, except the paragraphs containing the bulleted list.

5. Change the font size of the headline to 36 point and the font to Franklin Gothic Heavy, or a similar font. Apply the text effect called Fill - Orange, Accent 3, Sharp Bevel.

6. Change the font size of body copy between the headline and signature line to 20 point, except for line above the bulleted list, which is 24 point.

7. Change the font size of the signature line to 22 point. Bold the text in the signature line. Change the font color of the text in the signature line to Orange, Accent 3.

8. Italicize the word, personalize.

9. Bold the text above the bulleted list.

10. Underline the text, Junior's Wedding Bakery.

11. Shade the line above the bulleted list to the Orange, Accent 3 color. If the font color does not automatically change to a lighter color, change it to White, Background 1.

12. Change the zoom so that the entire page is visible in the document window.

13. Insert the first picture on a blank line below the headline and the second picture on a blank line below the bulleted list. The pictures are called Bakery 1 and Bakery 2, respectively, and are available on the Data Files for Students.

14. Resize the top picture so that it is approximately 2.8" × 5.39". Apply the Soft Edge Oval picture style to the top inserted picture. Apply the Offset Right Shadow picture effect to the top picture. Resize the bottom picture so that it is approximately 1.5" × 4.05". Apply the Simple Frame, Black picture style to the bottom inserted picture.

15. Change the spacing after the paragraph containing the bakery name to 0 pt and the spacing after the last bulleted paragraph to 12 pt. The entire flyer should fit on a single page. If it flows to two pages, resize the picture or decrease spacing before and after paragraphs until the entire flyer text fits on a single page.

16. Add the page border shown in Figure 1–78, using the color Gold, Accent 5.

17. Center the page contents vertically.

18. If requested by your instructor, change the bakery name to your last name.

19. Save the flyer again with the same file name. Submit the document, shown in Figure 1–78, in the format specified by your instructor.

20. ✷ Why do you think this flyer used shades of orange and yellow?

Figure 1–78

Lab 3: Expand Your World: Cloud and Web Technologies
Using the Word Web App to Create a Flyer with a Picture

Problem: You have a side business where you build bean bag toss boards. You would like to create a flyer that promotes this business. You will use the Word Web App to prepare a flyer. The text for the unformatted flyer is shown in Figure 1–79.

Note: To complete this assignment, you will be required to use the Data Files for Students. Visit www.cengage.com/ct/studentdownload for detailed instructions or contact your instructor for information about accessing the required files.

Instructions: Perform the following tasks:

1. Run a browser. Search for the text, Word Web App, using a search engine. Visit several websites to learn about the Word Web App. Navigate to the Office Web Apps website. You will need to sign in to your SkyDrive account.

2. Use the Create button to begin creating a Word document using the Word Web App. Name the document Lab 1-3 Bean Bag Toss Flyer.

3. Notice the differences between the Word Web App and the Word desktop app you used to create the project in this chapter.

4. Enter the text in the flyer, shown in Figure 1–79, checking spelling as you type.

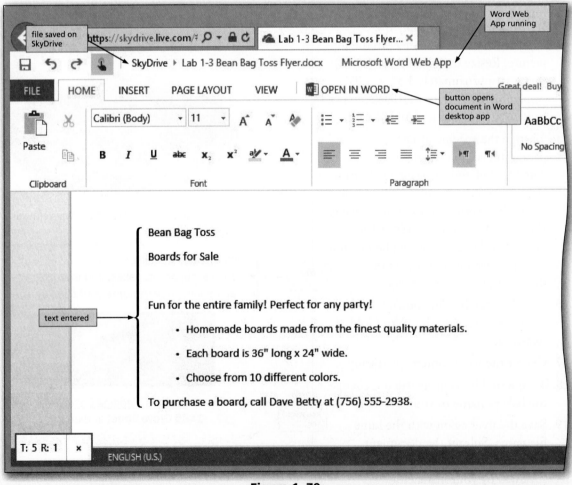

Figure 1–79

5. Insert the picture called Bean Bag Toss, which is located on the Data Files for Students.

6. Use the features available in the Word Web App, along with the concepts and techniques presented in this chapter, to format this flyer. Be sure to change the font and font size of text, center a paragraph(s), italicize text, color text, underline text, and apply a picture style. Adjust spacing above and below paragraphs as necessary. Resize the picture, if necessary.

7. If requested by your instructor, replace the contact name in the flyer with your name.

8. Save the document again. Tap or click the button to open the document in the Word desktop app. If necessary, sign in to your Microsoft account when prompted. Notice how the document appears in the Word desktop app.

9. Using either the Word Web App or Word desktop app, submit the document in the format requested by your instructor. Exit the Word Web App (FILE tab | Exit). Sign out of your SkyDrive account. Sign out of the Microsoft account in Word.

10. ✷ What is the Word Web App? Which features that are covered in this chapter are not available in the Word Web App? Do you prefer using the Word Web App or the Word desktop app? Why?

✷ Consider This: Your Turn

Apply your creative thinking and problem solving skills to design and implement a solution.

Note: To complete these assignments, you may be required to use the Data Files for Students. Visit www.cengage.com/ct/studentdownload for detailed instructions or contact your instructor for information about accessing the required files.

1: Design and Create a Photography Club Flyer
Personal

Part 1:   As secretary of your school's Photography Club, you are responsible for creating and distributing flyers announcing the club. The flyer should contain two digital pictures appropriately resized; the Data Files for Students contains two pictures called Photography 1 and Photography 2, or you can use your own digital pictures if they are appropriate for the topic of the flyer. The flyer should contain the headline, Photography Club, and this signature line: Questions? Call Emily at (883) 555-0901. The body copy consists of the following text, in any order: Do you love photography? This is the club for you! All skill levels are welcome. Meetings every Tuesday at 5:00 p.m. in the Student Center (room 232). Bring your camera. We look forward to seeing you at our next meeting!

Use the concepts and techniques presented in this chapter to create and format this flyer. Be sure to check spelling and grammar. Submit your assignment and answers to the critical thinking questions in the format specified by your instructor.

Part 2:   ✷ You made several decisions while creating the flyer in this assignment: where to place text, how to format the text (i.e., font, font size, paragraph alignment, bulleted paragraphs, underlines, italics, bold, color, etc.), which graphics to use, where to position the graphics, how to format the graphics, and which page enhancements to add (i.e., borders and spacing). What was the rationale behind each of these decisions? When you proofread the document, what further revisions did you make and why? How would you recommend distributing this flyer?

2: Design and Create a Hot Air Balloon Rides Flyer
Professional

Part 1:   As a part-time employee at Galaxy Recreations, your boss has asked you to create and distribute flyers announcing hot air balloon rides. The flyer should contain two digital pictures appropriately resized; the Data Files for Students contains two pictures called Hot Air Balloon 1

Continued >

Consider This: Your Turn *continued*

and Hot Air Balloon 2, or you can use your own digital pictures if they are appropriate for the topic of the flyer. The flyer should contain the headline, Hot Air Balloon Rides, and this signature line: For reservations, call (485) 555-2295. The body copy consists of the following text, in any order: Amazing sights from incredible heights! The experience of a lifetime. Fun for the whole family. No pets. Bring your camera. Open seven days a week from 10:00 a.m. to 4:00 p.m. Book your private tour with Galaxy Recreations today!

Use the concepts and techniques presented in this chapter to create and format this flyer. Be sure to check spelling and grammar. Submit your assignment in the format specified by your instructor.

Part 2: ✸ You made several decisions while creating the flyer in this assignment: where to place text, how to format the text (i.e., font, font size, paragraph alignment, bulleted paragraphs, underlines, italics, bold, color, etc.), which graphics to use, where to position the graphics, how to format the graphics, and which page enhancements to add (i.e., borders and spacing). What was the rationale behind each of these decisions? When you proofread the document, what further revisions did you make and why? How would you recommend distributing this flyer?

3: Design and Create a Water Park Flyer

Research and Collaboration

Part 1: As a part-time employee at a local water park, your boss has asked you and two other employees to create and distribute flyers for the upcoming water park season. Form a three-member team to compose and create this flyer. Research a local water park: its location, hours, prices, rules, specials, etc. As a group, determine the text for the flyer's headline, body copy, and signature line. Your team also will need to obtain at least two digital pictures appropriate for the content of this flyer. You could take the pictures with a digital camera or search for public-domain images on the web.

Use the concepts and techniques presented in this chapter to create and format this flyer. Be sure to check spelling and grammar. Submit your team assignment in the format specified by your instructor.

Part 2: ✸ You made several decisions while creating the flyer in this assignment: text to use, where to place text, how to format the text (i.e., font, font size, paragraph alignment, bulleted paragraphs, underlines, italics, bold, color, etc.), which graphics to use, where to position the graphics, how to format the graphics, and which page enhancements to add (i.e., borders and spacing). What was the rationale behind each of these decisions? When you proofread the document, what further revisions did you make and why? What research methods did you use to create the flyer? Where did you obtain your pictures? How would you recommend distributing this flyer?

Learn Online

Reinforce what you learned in this chapter with games, exercises, training, and many other online activities and resources.

Student Companion Site Reinforcement activities and resources are available at no additional cost on www.cengagebrain.com. Visit www.cengage.com/ct/studentdownload for detailed instructions about accessing the resources available at the Student Companion Site.

SAM Put your skills into practice with SAM Projects! If you have a SAM account, go to www.cengage.com/sam2013 to access SAM assignments for this chapter.

1 Creating and Editing a Presentation with Pictures

Microsoft product screenshots used with permission from Microsoft Corporation.

Objectives

You will have mastered the material in this chapter when you can:

- Select and change a document theme and variant
- Create a title slide and a text slide with a multilevel bulleted list
- Add new slides and change slide layouts
- Insert photos and illustrations into slides with and without content placeholders
- Move and resize photos and illustrations

- Change font size and color
- Bold and italicize text
- Duplicate a slide
- Arrange slides
- Select slide transitions
- View a presentation in Slide Show view
- Print a presentation

1 | Creating and Editing a Presentation with Pictures

Introduction

A PowerPoint **presentation,** also called a **slide show,** can help you deliver a dynamic, professional-looking message to an audience. PowerPoint allows you to produce slides to use in an academic, business, or other environment. The collection of slides in a presentation is called a **deck**, resembling a deck of cards that are stacked on top of each other. A common use of slide decks is to enhance an oral presentation. A speaker might desire to convey information, such as urging students to volunteer at a fund-raising event, explaining changes in employee compensation packages, or describing a new laboratory procedure. The PowerPoint slides should reinforce the speaker's message and help the audience retain the information presented. Custom slides can fit your specific needs and contain diagrams, charts, tables, pictures, shapes, video, sound, and animation effects to make your presentation more effective. An accompanying handout gives audience members reference notes and review material for your presentation.

Project — Presentation with a Bulleted List, Photos, and an Illustration

In this chapter's project, you will follow proper design guidelines and learn to use PowerPoint to create, save, and print the slides shown in Figures 1–1a through 1–1e. The objective is to produce a presentation, titled Keeping Hydrated, to help athletes understand the need to drink water before, during, and after a workout. This slide show has a variety of pictures and visual elements to add interest and give facts about proper hydration. Some of the text has formatting and color enhancements. Transitions help one slide flow gracefully into the next during a slide show. In addition, you will print a handout of your slides to distribute to audience members.

(a) Slide 1 (Title Slide with Photo)

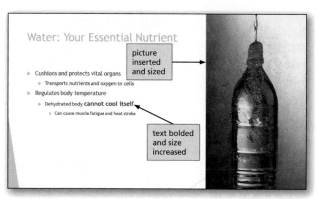

(b) Slide 2 (Multilevel Bulleted List with Photo)

(c) Slide 3 (Title and Illustration)

(d) Slide 4 (Comparison Layout and Photos)

(e) Slide 5 (Closing Slide)

Figure 1–1

For an introduction to Windows and instruction about how to perform basic Windows tasks, read the Office and Windows chapter at the beginning of this book, where you can learn how to resize windows, change screen resolution, create folders, move and rename files, use Windows Help, and much more.

Roadmap

In this chapter, you will learn how to create the slides shown in Figure 1–1 on the previous page. The following roadmap identifies general activities you will perform as you progress through this chapter:

1. INSERT the four PRESENTATION SLIDES, using various layouts.
2. ENTER the TEXT for the slides.
3. FORMAT the TEXT on each slide.
4. INSERT GRAPHICAL ELEMENTS, including photos and an illustration.
5. SIZE AND POSITION the graphical elements.
6. ENHANCE the SLIDE SHOW by adding a closing slide and transition.
7. DISPLAY AND PRINT the SLIDES and a handout.

At the beginning of step instructions throughout the chapter, you will see an abbreviated form of this roadmap. The abbreviated roadmap uses colors to indicate chapter progress: gray means the chapter is beyond that activity; blue means the task being shown is covered in that activity, and black means that activity is yet to be covered. For example, the following abbreviated roadmap indicates the chapter would be showing a task in the 5 Size & Position activity.

1 INSERT PRESENTATION SLIDES | 2 ENTER TEXT | 3 FORMAT TEXT | 4 INSERT GRAPHICAL ELEMENTS

5 SIZE & POSITION | 6 ENHANCE SLIDE SHOW | 7 DISPLAY & PRINT SLIDES

Use the abbreviated roadmap as a progress guide while you read or step through the instructions in this chapter.

To Run PowerPoint

One of the few differences between Windows 7 and Windows 8 occurs in the steps to run PowerPoint. If you are using Windows 7, click the Start button, type **PowerPoint** in the 'Search programs and files' box, click PowerPoint 2013, and then, if necessary, maximize the PowerPoint window. For detailed steps to run PowerPoint in Windows 7, refer to the Office and Windows chapter at the beginning of this book. For a summary of the steps, refer to the Quick Reference located at the back of this book.

If you are using a computer to step through the project in this chapter and you want your screens to match the figures in this book, you should change your screen's resolution to 1366 × 768. For information about how to change a computer's resolution, refer to the Office and Windows chapter at the beginning of this book.

The following steps, which assume Windows 8 is running, use the Start screen or the search box to run PowerPoint based on a typical installation. You may need to ask your instructor how to run PowerPoint on your computer. For a detailed example of the procedure summarized below, refer to the Office and Windows chapter.

1 Scroll the Start screen for a PowerPoint 2013 tile. If your Start screen contains a PowerPoint 2013 tile, tap or click it to run PowerPoint and then proceed to Step 5; if the Start screen does not contain the PowerPoint 2013 tile, proceed to the next step to search for the PowerPoint app.

2 Swipe in from the right edge of the screen or point to the upper-right corner of the screen to display the Charms bar and then tap or click the Search charm on the Charms bar to display the Search menu.

3 Type **PowerPoint** as the search text in the Search box and watch the search results appear in the Apps list.

4 Tap or click PowerPoint 2013 in the search results to run PowerPoint.

5 If the PowerPoint window is not maximized, tap or click the Maximize button on its title bar to maximize the window.

Choosing a Document Theme and Variant

You easily can give the slides in a presentation a professional and integrated appearance by using a theme. A document **theme** is a specific design with coordinating colors, fonts, and special effects such as shadows and reflections. Several themes are available when you run PowerPoint, each with a specific name. Using one of the formatted themes makes creating a professional-looking presentation easier and quicker than using the Blank Presentation template, where you would need to make all design decisions.

Each theme has a set of four alternate designs, called **variants.** Each variant has the same overall composition, but the colors, fonts, and design elements differ. Once you select a theme, you then can select a variation that best fits your overall design needs. If you later decide that another theme or variant would better fit the presentation's general theme, you can change these elements while you are developing slides.

To Choose a Document Theme and Variant

1 INSERT PRESENTATION SLIDES | 2 ENTER TEXT | 3 FORMAT TEXT | 4 INSERT GRAPHICAL ELEMENTS

5 SIZE & POSITION | 6 ENHANCE SLIDE SHOW | 7 DISPLAY & PRINT SLIDES

When you begin creating a new PowerPoint presentation, you need to select a theme. You either can start with no design elements by using the Blank Presentation, or you select one of the available professionally designed themes. The following steps apply the Ion theme and then change the variant. *Why? The title slide will have text and a photo, so you want to select a theme, like Ion, with an uncluttered background. The presentation discusses the importance of drinking water while exercising, and blue is the color commonly associated with water in lakes and oceans. The default Ion theme is predominantly green and white, but one of its variants is blue and is an appropriate choice to relate to the water concept.*

1

- Press and hold or point to the Ion theme on the New screen (Figure 1–2).

Q&A Why are my theme images, called thumbnails, displaying in a different order?

PowerPoint places the themes you have used recently in the first rows. You may need to scroll down to locate the Ion theme.

Figure 1–2

2

- Tap or click the Ion theme to display a theme preview dialog box with a thumbnail view of the theme and its variants (Figure 1–3).

Q&A Can I see previews of other themes?
Yes. Tap or click the right or left arrows on the sides of the theme preview dialog box.

Figure 1–3

3

- Tap or click the upper-right (blue) variant to view previews of that style applied to the thumbnail.

Q&A Can I see previews of the Ion theme and blue variant applied to layouts other than the title slide?
Yes. Tap or click the right or left arrows beside the words, More Images, below the thumbnail. Three other layouts will be displayed: Title and Content, Two Content, and Photo.

- Tap or click the Create button to apply the Ion theme and blue variant to the presentation and to display Slide 1 (Figure 1–4).

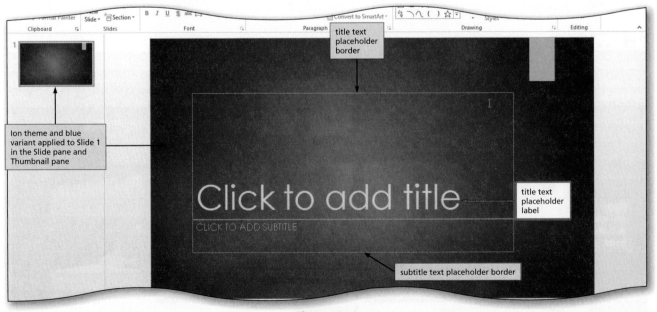

Figure 1–4

Creating a Title Slide

When you open a new presentation, the default **Title Slide** layout appears. The purpose of this layout is to introduce the presentation to the audience. PowerPoint includes other standard layouts for each of the themes. The slide layouts are set up in **landscape orientation**, where the slide width is greater than its height. In landscape orientation, the slide size is preset to 10 inches wide and 7.5 inches high when printed on a standard sheet of paper measuring 11 inches wide and 8.5 inches high.

Placeholders are boxes with dotted or hatch-marked borders that are displayed when you create a new slide. Most layouts have both a title text placeholder and at least one content placeholder. Depending on the particular slide layout selected, title and subtitle placeholders are displayed for the slide title and subtitle; a content text placeholder is displayed for text, art, or a table, chart, picture, graphic, or movie. The title slide has two text placeholders where you can type the main heading, or title, of a new slide and the subtitle.

With the exception of the Blank slide layout, PowerPoint assumes every new slide has a title. To make creating a presentation easier, any text you type after a new slide appears becomes title text in the title text placeholder. The following steps create the title slide for this presentation.

Choose the words for the slide.

All presentations should follow the 7 × 7 rule, which states that each slide should have a maximum of seven lines, and each line should have a maximum of seven words. PowerPoint designers must choose their words carefully and, in turn, help viewers read the slides easily.

Avoid line wraps. Your audience's eyes want to stop at the end of a line. Thus, you must plan your words carefully or adjust the font size so that each point displays on only one line.

To Enter the Presentation Title

1 INSERT PRESENTATION SLIDES | 2 ENTER TEXT | 3 FORMAT TEXT | 4 INSERT GRAPHICAL ELEMENTS
5 SIZE & POSITION | 6 ENHANCE SLIDE SHOW | 7 DISPLAY & PRINT SLIDES

The presentation title for Project 1 is Healthy Hydration. *Why? The presentation discusses the importance of drinking water while exercising, and blue is the color associated with water.* The following step creates the slide show's title.

1

• Tap or click the label, 'Tap to add title', or, 'Click to add title', located inside the title text placeholder to select the placeholder (Figure 1–5).

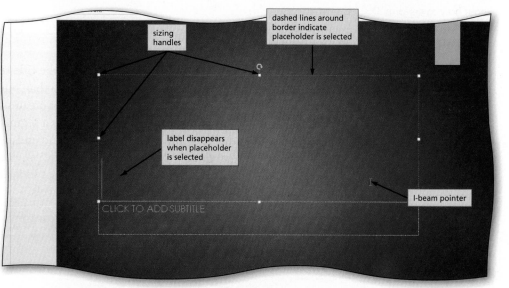

Figure 1–5

2

• Type **Healthy Hydration** in the title text placeholder. Do not press the ENTER key (Figure 1–6).

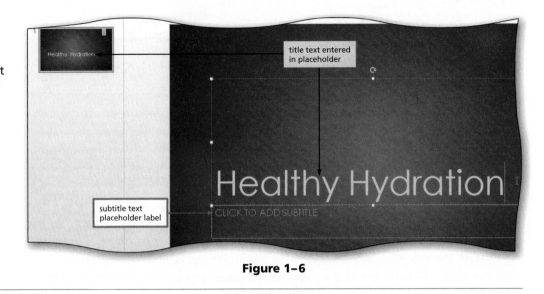

Figure 1–6

BTW

Q&As
For a complete list of the Q&As found in many of the step-by-step sequences in this book, visit the Q&A resource on the Student Companion Site located on www.cengagebrain.com. For detailed instructions about accessing available resources, visit www.cengage.com/ct/ studentdownload or see the inside back cover of this book.

For an introduction to Office and instruction about how to perform basic tasks in Office apps, read the Office and Windows chapter at the beginning of this book, where you can learn how to run an application, use the ribbon, save a file, open a file, exit an application, use Help, and much more.

Correcting a Mistake When Typing

If you type the wrong letter, press the BACKSPACE key to erase all the characters back to and including the one that is incorrect. If you mistakenly press the ENTER key after typing the title and the insertion point is on the new line, simply press the BACKSPACE key to return the insertion point to the right of the letter in the word, Water.

When you install PowerPoint, the default setting allows you to reverse up to the last 20 changes by tapping or clicking the Undo button on the Quick Access Toolbar. The ScreenTip that appears when you point to the Undo button changes to indicate the type of change just made. For example, if you type text in the title text placeholder and then point to the Undo button, the ScreenTip that appears is Undo Typing. For clarity, when referencing the Undo button in this project, the name displaying in the ScreenTip is referenced. You can reapply a change that you reversed with the Undo button by tapping or clicking the Redo button on the Quick Access Toolbar. Tapping or clicking the Redo button reverses the last undo action. The ScreenTip name reflects the type of reversal last performed.

Paragraphs

Text in the subtitle text placeholder supports the title text. It can appear on one or more lines in the placeholder. To create more than one subtitle line, you press the ENTER key after typing some words. PowerPoint creates a new line, which is the second paragraph in the placeholder. A **paragraph** is a segment of text with the same format that begins when you press the ENTER key and ends when you press the ENTER key again. This new paragraph is the same level as the previous paragraph. A **level** is a position within a structure, such as an outline, that indicates the magnitude of importance. PowerPoint allows for five paragraph levels.

How do you use the touch keyboard with a touch screen?

To display the on-screen touch keyboard, tap the Touch Keyboard button on the Windows taskbar. When finished using the touch keyboard, tap the X button on the touch keyboard to close the keyboard.

To Enter the Presentation Subtitle Paragraph

1 INSERT PRESENTATION SLIDES | 2 ENTER TEXT | 3 FORMAT TEXT | 4 INSERT GRAPHICAL ELEMENTS
5 SIZE & POSITION | 6 ENHANCE SLIDE SHOW | 7 DISPLAY & PRINT SLIDES

The first subtitle paragraph links to the title. *Why? The subtitle gives additional detail that the presentation will focus on water consumption while exercising.* The following steps enter the presentation subtitle.

1

- Tap or click the label, 'Tap to add subtitle', or, 'Click to add subtitle', located inside the subtitle text placeholder to select the placeholder (Figure 1–7).

Figure 1–7

2

- Type **Drinking Water While Exercising** but do not press the ENTER key (Figure 1–8).

Q&A Why does the text display with capital letters despite the fact I am typing uppercase and lowercase letters? The Ion theme uses the All Caps effect for the subtitle text. This effect converts lowercase letters to uppercase letters.

Figure 1–8

To Zoom a Slide

You will be modifying the text and other slide components as you create the presentation, so you can enlarge the slide on the screen. *Why? Zooming the slide can help you see slide elements more clearly so that you can position them precisely where desired.* The following step changes the zoom to 80 percent.

1

Experiment

- Repeatedly tap or click the Zoom In and Zoom Out buttons on the status bar and watch the size of the slide change in the Slide pane.

- Tap or click the Zoom In or Zoom Out button as many times as necessary until the Zoom button on the status bar displays 80% on its face (Figure 1–9).

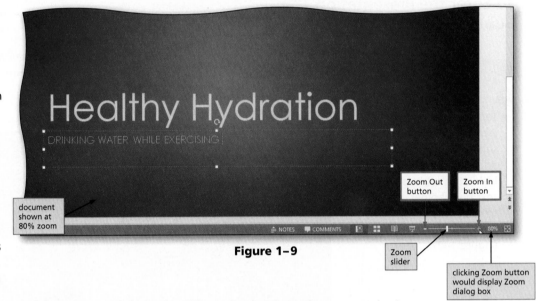

Figure 1–9

Q&A If I change the zoom percentage, will the slide display differently when I run the presentation?
No. Changing the zoom helps you develop the slide content and does not affect the slide show.

Other Ways

1. Drag Zoom slider on status bar	2. Tap or click Zoom level button on status bar, select desired zoom percent or type (Zoom dialog box), tap or click OK button	3. Tap or click Zoom button (VIEW tab | Zoom group), select desired zoom percent or type (Zoom dialog box), tap or click OK button	4. For touch screens: Pinch two fingers together in Slide pane (zoom out) or stretch two fingers apart (zoom in)

Formatting Characters in a Presentation

Recall that each document theme determines the color scheme, font set, and layout of a presentation. You can use a specific document theme and then change the characters' formats any time before, during, or after you type the text.

Fonts and Font Styles

Characters that appear on the screen are a specific shape and size. Examples of how you can modify the appearance, or **format**, of these typed characters on the screen and in print include changing the font, style, size, and color. The **font**, or typeface, defines the appearance and shape of the letters, numbers, punctuation marks, and symbols. **Style** indicates how the characters are formatted. PowerPoint's text font styles include regular, italic, bold, and bold italic. **Size** specifies the height of the characters and is gauged by a measurement system that uses points. A **point** is 1/72 of an inch in height. Thus, a character with a font size of 36 is 36/72 (or 1/2) of an inch in height. **Color** defines the hue of the characters.

BTW
BTWs
For a complete list of the BTWs found in the margins of this book, visit the BTW resource on the Student Companion Site located on www.cengagebrain.com. For detailed instructions about accessing available resources, visit www.cengage.com/ct/studentdownload or see the inside back cover of this book.

This presentation uses the Ion document theme, which has particular font styles and font sizes. The Ion document theme default title text font is named Century Gothic. It has no special effects, and its size is 54 point. The Ion default subtitle text font also is Century Gothic with a font size of 18 point.

To Select a Paragraph

1 INSERT PRESENTATION SLIDES | 2 ENTER TEXT | 3 FORMAT TEXT | 4 INSERT GRAPHICAL ELEMENTS
5 SIZE & POSITION | 6 ENHANCE SLIDE SHOW | 7 DISPLAY & PRINT SLIDES

You can use many techniques to format characters. When you want to apply the same formats to multiple words or paragraphs, it is helpful to select these words. *Why? It is efficient to select the desired text and then make the desired changes to all the characters simultaneously.* The first formatting change you will make will apply to the title slide subtitle. The following step selects this paragraph.

1

- If you are using a touch screen, tap to position the insertion point in the text to select, and then drag the selection handles as necessary to select the entire paragraph; if you are using a mouse, triple-click the paragraph, Drinking Water While Exercising, in the subtitle text placeholder to select the paragraph (Figure 1–10).

Figure 1–10

Q&A What is the selection handle?

When working on a touch screen, a **selection handle** (small circle) appears below the insertion point. Using a fingertip, you drag the selection handle to select text.

Other Ways

1. Position pointer to left of first paragraph and drag to end of line

To Italicize Text

1 INSERT PRESENTATION SLIDES | 2 ENTER TEXT | 3 FORMAT TEXT | 4 INSERT GRAPHICAL ELEMENTS
5 SIZE & POSITION | 6 ENHANCE SLIDE SHOW | 7 DISPLAY & PRINT SLIDES

Different font styles often are used on slides. *Why? These style changes make the words more appealing to the reader and emphasize particular text.* **Italicized** text has a slanted appearance. Used sparingly, it draws the readers' eyes to these characters. The following step adds emphasis to the line of the subtitle text by changing regular text to italic text.

1

- With the subtitle text still selected, tap or click the Italic button on the mini toolbar to italicize that text on the slide (Figure 1–11).

Q&A If I change my mind and decide not to italicize the text, how can I remove this style?

Tap or click the Italic button a second time, immediately tap or click the Undo button on the Quick Access Toolbar, or press CTRL+Z.

Figure 1–11

Other Ways

1. Tap 'Show Context Menu' button on mini toolbar or right-click selected text, tap or click Font on shortcut menu, tap or click Font tab (Font dialog box), tap or click Italic in Font style list, tap or click OK button

2. Select text, tap or click Italic button (HOME tab | Font group)

3. Tap or click Font dialog box launcher (HOME tab | Font group), tap or click Font tab (Font dialog box), tap or click Italic in Font style list, tap or click OK button

4. Select text, press CTRL+I

To Increase Font Size

1 INSERT PRESENTATION SLIDES | 2 ENTER TEXT | 3 FORMAT TEXT | 4 INSERT GRAPHICAL ELEMENTS
5 SIZE & POSITION | 6 ENHANCE SLIDE SHOW | 7 DISPLAY & PRINT SLIDES

Why? *To add emphasis, you increase the font size for the subtitle text.* The Increase Font Size button on the mini toolbar increases the font size in preset increments. The following step uses this button to increase the font size.

1

• Tap or click the 'Increase Font Size' button on the mini toolbar three times to increase the font size of the selected text from 20 to 32 point (Figure 1–12).

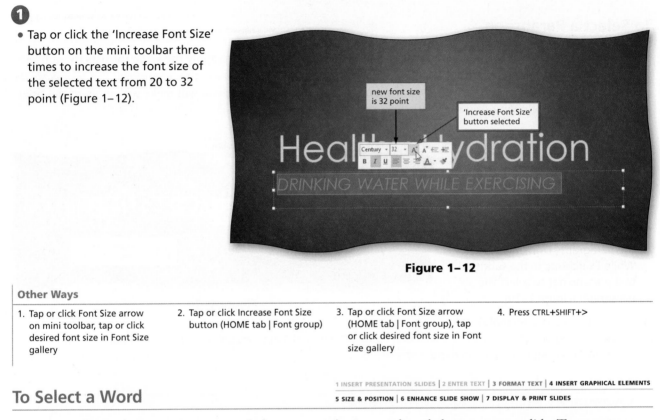

Figure 1–12

Other Ways

1. Tap or click Font Size arrow on mini toolbar, tap or click desired font size in Font Size gallery	2. Tap or click Increase Font Size button (HOME tab | Font group)	3. Tap or click Font Size arrow (HOME tab | Font group), tap or click desired font size in Font size gallery	4. Press CTRL+SHIFT+>

To Select a Word

1 INSERT PRESENTATION SLIDES | 2 ENTER TEXT | 3 FORMAT TEXT | 4 INSERT GRAPHICAL ELEMENTS
5 SIZE & POSITION | 6 ENHANCE SLIDE SHOW | 7 DISPLAY & PRINT SLIDES

PowerPoint designers use many techniques to emphasize words and characters on a slide. To accentuate the word, Water, on your slide, you want to increase the font size and change the font color to dark blue for the word, WATER, in the subtitle text. To make these changes, you should begin by selecting the word, WATER. *Why?* *You could perform these actions separately, but it is more efficient to select the word and then change the font attributes.* The following steps select a word.

1

• Position the pointer somewhere in the word to be selected (in this case, in the word, WATER) (Figure 1–13).

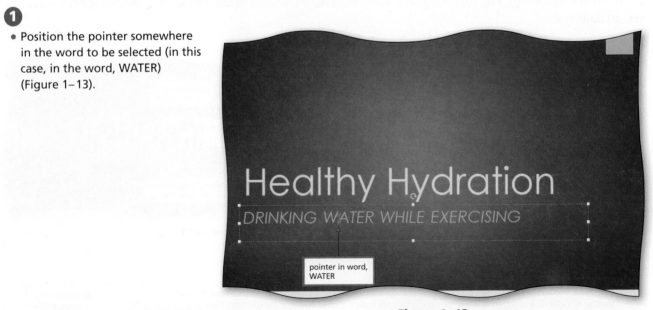

Figure 1–13

2

- Double-tap or double-click the word to select it (Figure 1–14).

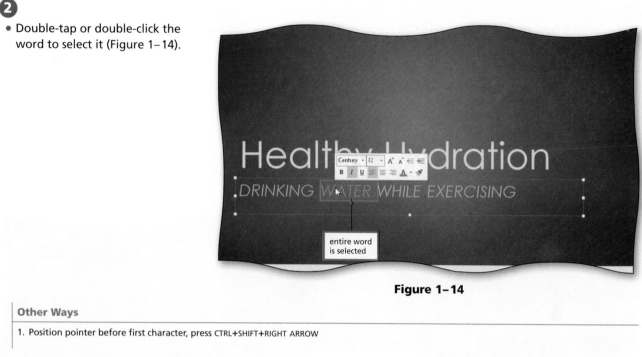

Figure 1–14

Other Ways

1. Position pointer before first character, press CTRL+SHIFT+RIGHT ARROW

To Change the Text Color

1 INSERT PRESENTATION SLIDES | 2 ENTER TEXT | 3 FORMAT TEXT | 4 INSERT GRAPHICAL ELEMENTS
5 SIZE & POSITION | 6 ENHANCE SLIDE SHOW | 7 DISPLAY & PRINT SLIDES

PowerPoint allows you to use one or more text colors in a presentation. You decide to change the color of the word you selected, WATER. **Why?** *The color, blue, is associated with water, and you want to add more emphasis, subtly, to that word in your subtitle slide text.* The following steps add emphasis to this word by changing the font color from green to blue.

1

- With the word, WATER, selected, tap or click the Font Color arrow on the mini toolbar to display the Font Color gallery, which includes Theme Colors and Standard Colors (Figure 1–15).

Q&A If the mini toolbar disappears from the screen, how can I display it once again?
Press and hold or right-click the text, and the mini toolbar should appear.

Experiment

- If you are using a mouse, point to various colors in the gallery and watch the word's font color change.

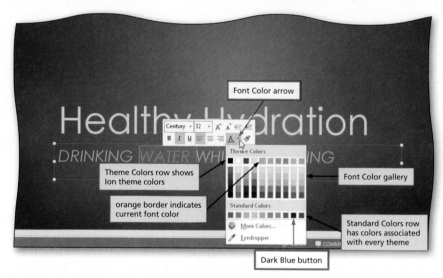

Figure 1–15

2

- Tap or click Dark Blue in the Standard Colors row on the mini toolbar (second color from right) to change the font color to Dark Blue (Figure 1–16).

Q&A

Why did I select the color Dark Blue?
Dark Blue is one of the 10 standard colors associated with every document theme, and it is a universal color representing the natural resource of water. The color will emphasize the fact that the presentation focuses on water.

What is the difference between the colors shown in the Theme Colors area and the Standard Colors?
The 10 colors in the top row of the Theme Colors area are two text, two background, and six accent colors in the Ion theme; the five colors in each column under the top row display different transparencies. The Standard Colors are available in every document theme.

Figure 1–16

3

- Tap or click outside the selected area to deselect the word.

Other Ways

1. Tap 'Show Context Menu' button on mini toolbar or right-click selected text, tap or click Font on shortcut menu, tap or click Font Color button, tap or click Dark Blue in Standard Colors row

2. Tap or click Font Color arrow (HOME tab | Font group), tap or click Dark Blue in Standard Colors row

BTW
Organizing Files and Folders
You should organize and store files in folders so that you easily can find the files later. For example, if you are taking an introductory computer class called CIS 101, a good practice would be to save all PowerPoint files in a PowerPoint folder in a CIS 101 folder. For a discussion of folders and detailed examples of creating folders, refer to the Office and Windows chapter at the beginning of this book.

To Save a Presentation with a New File Name

You have performed many tasks while creating this presentation and do not want to risk losing work completed thus far. Accordingly, you should save the presentation on your hard disk, SkyDrive, or a location that is most appropriate to your situation.

The following steps assume you already have created folders for storing your files, for example a CIS 101 folder (for your class) that contains a PowerPoint folder (for your assignments). Thus, these steps save the presentation in the PowerPoint folder in the CIS 101 folder on your desired save location. For a detailed example of the procedure for saving a file in a folder or saving a file on SkyDrive, refer to the Office and Windows chapter at the beginning of this book.

1 Tap or click the Save button on the Quick Access Toolbar, which depending on settings, will display either the Save As gallery in the Backstage view or the Save As dialog box.

2 To save on a hard disk or other storage media on your computer, proceed to Step 2a. To save on SkyDrive, proceed to Step 2b.

2a If your screen opens the Backstage view and you want to save on storage media on your computer, tap or click Computer in the left pane, if necessary, to display options in the right pane related to saving on your computer. If your screen already displays the Save As dialog box, proceed to Step 3.

2b If your screen opens the Backstage view and you want to save on SkyDrive, tap or click SkyDrive in the left pane to display SkyDrive saving options or a Sign In button. If your screen displays a Sign In button, tap or click it and then sign in to SkyDrive.

3 Tap or click the Browse button in the right pane to display the Save As dialog box associated with the selected save location (i.e., Computer or SkyDrive).

4 Type **Keeping Hydrated** in the File name box to change the file name. Do not press the ENTER key after typing the file name because you do not want to close the dialog box at this time.

5 Navigate to the desired save location (in this case, the PowerPoint folder in the CIS 101 folder [or your class folder] on your computer or SkyDrive).

6 Tap or click the Save button (Save As dialog box) to save the presentation in the selected folder on the selected save location with the entered file name.

BTW
The Ribbon and Screen Resolution
PowerPoint may change how the groups and buttons within the groups appear on the ribbon, depending on the computer's screen resolution. Thus, your ribbon may look different from the ones in this book if you are using a screen resolution other than 1366 × 768.

Adding a New Slide to a Presentation

With the text for the title slide for the presentation created, the next step is to add the first text slide immediately after the title slide. Usually, when you create a presentation, you add slides with text, pictures, graphics, or charts. Some placeholders allow you to double-tap or double-click the placeholder and then access other objects, such as videos, charts, diagrams, and organization charts. You can change the layout for a slide at any time during the creation of a presentation.

To Add a New Text Slide with a Bulleted List

1 INSERT PRESENTATION SLIDES | 2 ENTER TEXT | 3 FORMAT TEXT | **4 INSERT GRAPHICAL ELEMENTS**
5 SIZE & POSITION | 6 ENHANCE SLIDE SHOW | 7 DISPLAY & PRINT SLIDES

When you add a new slide, PowerPoint uses the Title and Content slide layout. This layout provides a title placeholder and a content area for text, art, charts, and other graphics. A vertical scroll bar appears in the Slide pane when you add the second slide. *Why? The scroll bar allows you to move from slide to slide easily.* A small image of this slide also appears in the Thumbnail pane. The step on the next page adds a new slide with the Title and Content slide layout.

1

• Tap or click the New Slide button (HOME tab | Slides group) to insert a new slide with the Title and Content layout (Figure 1–17).

Q&A

Why does the bullet character display a green triangle?
The Ion document theme determines the bullet characters. Each paragraph level has an associated bullet character.

I clicked the New Slide arrow instead of the New Slide button. What should I do?
Tap or click the Title and Content slide thumbnail in the Ion layout gallery.

How do I know which slide number I am viewing?
The left edge of the status bar shows the current slide number followed by the total number of slides in the document. In addition, the slide number is displayed to the left of the slide thumbnail.

What are those six icons grouped in the middle of the Slide pane?
You can tap or click one of the icons to insert a specific type of content: table, chart, SmartArt graphic, pictures, online pictures, or video.

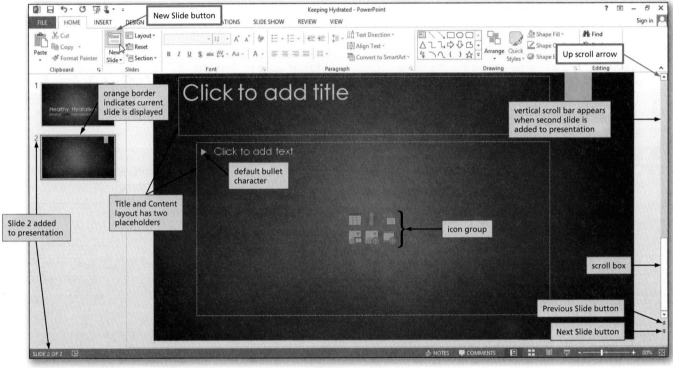

Figure 1–17

Other Ways

1. Press CTRL+M

Creating a Text Slide with a Multilevel Bulleted List

The information in the Slide 2 text placeholder is presented in a bulleted list with three levels. A **bulleted list** is a list of paragraphs, each of which may be preceded by a bullet character, such as a dot, arrow, or checkmark. Some themes, such as the Ion theme, do not display a bullet character at the start of a paragraph by default. A slide that consists of more than one level of bulleted text is called a **multilevel bulleted list slide**. In a multilevel bulleted list, a lower-level paragraph is a subset of a higher-level paragraph. It usually contains information that supports the topic in the paragraph immediately above it.

As you can see in Figure 1–1b on page PPT 3, two of the Slide 2 paragraphs appear at the same level, called the first level: Cushions and protects vital organs, and Regulates body temperature. Beginning with the second level, each paragraph indents to the right of the preceding level and is pushed down to a lower level. For example, if you increase the indent of a first-level paragraph, it becomes a second-level paragraph. The second, fourth, and fifth paragraphs on Slide 2 are second-level paragraphs. The last paragraph, Can cause muscle fatigue and heat stroke, is a third-level paragraph.

Creating a text slide with a multilevel bulleted list requires several steps. Initially, you enter a slide title in the title text placeholder. Next, you select the content text placeholder. Then, you type the text for the multilevel bulleted list, increasing and decreasing the indents as needed. The next several sections add a slide with a multilevel bulleted list.

BTW

Touch Screen Differences
The Office and Windows interfaces may vary if you are using a touch screen. For this reason, you might notice that the function or appearance of your touch screen differs slightly from this chapter's presentation.

To Enter a Slide Title

1 INSERT PRESENTATION SLIDES | 2 ENTER TEXT | 3 FORMAT TEXT | 4 INSERT GRAPHICAL ELEMENTS
5 SIZE & POSITION | 6 ENHANCE SLIDE SHOW | 7 DISPLAY & PRINT SLIDES

PowerPoint assumes every new slide has a title. *Why? The audience members read the title and then can begin to focus their attention on the information being presented on that slide.* The title for Slide 2 is Water: Your Essential Nutrient. The following step enters this title.

1
• Tap or click the label, 'Tap to add title', or, 'Click to add title', to select it and then type `Water: Your Essential Nutrient` in the title text placeholder. Do not press the ENTER key (Figure 1–18).

Figure 1–18

To Select a Text Placeholder

Why? *Before you can type text into a content placeholder, you first must select it.* The following step selects the text placeholder on Slide 2.

1

- Tap or click the label, 'Tap to add text', or 'Click to add text', to select the content placeholder (Figure 1–19).

Q&A Why does my pointer have a different shape?
If you move the pointer away from the bullet, it will change shape.

Figure 1–19

Other Ways

1. Press CTRL+ENTER

To Type a Multilevel Bulleted List

The content placeholder provides an area for the text characters. When you tap or click inside a placeholder, you then can type or paste text. As discussed previously, a bulleted list is a list of paragraphs, each of which is preceded by a bullet. A paragraph is a segment of text ended by pressing the ENTER key. The theme determines the bullets for each level. *Why?* *The bullet variations are determined by the specific paragraph levels, and they generally vary in size, shape, and color.*

The content text placeholder is selected, so the next step is to type the multilevel bulleted list that consists of six paragraphs, as shown in Figure 1–1b on page PPT 3. Creating a lower-level paragraph is called **demoting** text; creating a higher-level paragraph is called **promoting** text. The following steps create a multilevel bulleted list consisting of three levels.

1

- Type `Cushions and protects vital organs` and then press the ENTER key (Figure 1–20).

Figure 1–20

2

- Tap or click the 'Increase List Level' button (HOME tab | Paragraph group) to indent the second paragraph below the first and create a second-level paragraph (Figure 1–21).

Q&A Why does the bullet for this paragraph have a different size? A different bullet is assigned to each paragraph level.

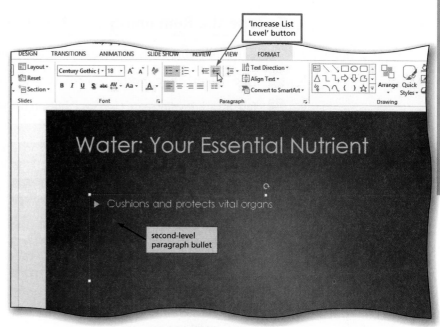

Figure 1–21

3

- Type **Transports nutrients and oxygen to cells** and then press the ENTER key (Figure 1–22).

Figure 1–22

4

- Tap or click the 'Decrease List Level' button (HOME tab | Paragraph group) so that the second-level paragraph becomes a first-level paragraph (Figure 1–23).

Q&A Can I delete bullets on a slide? Yes. If you do not want bullets to display in a particular paragraph, tap or click the Bullets button (HOME tab | Paragraph group) or press and hold or right-click the paragraph and then tap or click the Bullets button on the shortcut menu.

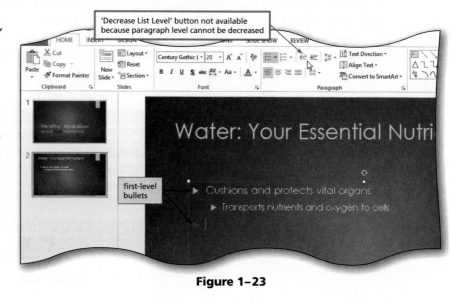

Figure 1–23

Other Ways

1. Press TAB to promote paragraph; press SHIFT+TAB to demote paragraph

To Type the Remaining Text for Slide 2

The following steps complete the text for Slide 2.

1 Type `Regulates body temperature` and then press the ENTER key.

2 Tap or click the 'Increase List Level' button (HOME tab | Paragraph group) to demote the paragraph to the second level.

3 Type `Dehydrated body cannot cool itself` and then press the ENTER key to add a new paragraph at the same level as the previous paragraph.

4 Tap or click the 'Increase List Level' button (HOME tab | Paragraph group) to demote the paragraph to the third level.

5 Type `Can cause muscle fatigue and heat stroke` but do not press the ENTER key (Figure 1–24).

Q&A ◁ I pressed the ENTER key in error, and now a new bullet appears after the last entry on this slide. How can I remove this extra bullet?

Press the BACKSPACE key twice.

remaining text for slide

Figure 1–24

To Select a Group of Words

1 INSERT PRESENTATION SLIDES | 2 ENTER TEXT | 3 FORMAT TEXT | 4 INSERT GRAPHICAL ELEMENTS
5 SIZE & POSITION | 6 ENHANCE SLIDE SHOW | 7 DISPLAY & PRINT SLIDES

PowerPoint designers use many techniques to emphasize words and characters on a slide. To highlight your slide show's concept of the dangers of not drinking water while exercising, you want to bold and increase the font size of the words, cannot cool itself, in the body text. The following steps select three words. *Why? You could perform these actions separately, but it is more efficient to select the words and then change the font attributes.*

1

• Position the pointer immediately to the left of the first character of the text to be selected (in this case, the c in the word, cannot) (Figure 1–25).

pointer

words to select

Figure 1–25

• Drag the pointer through the last character of the text to be selected (in this case, the f in the word, itself) (Figure 1–26).

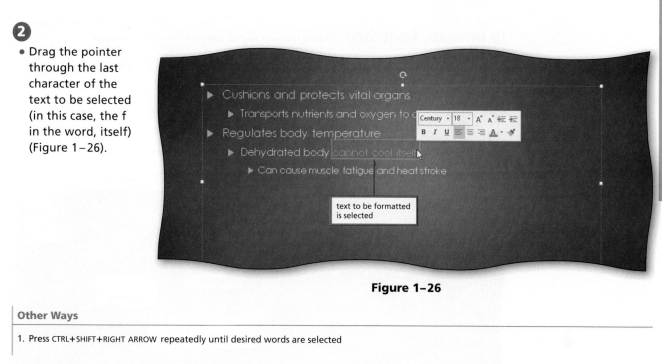

Figure 1–26

Other Ways

1. Press CTRL+SHIFT+RIGHT ARROW repeatedly until desired words are selected

To Bold Text

1 INSERT PRESENTATION SLIDES | 2 ENTER TEXT | 3 FORMAT TEXT | 4 INSERT GRAPHICAL ELEMENTS
5 SIZE & POSITION | 6 ENHANCE SLIDE SHOW | 7 DISPLAY & PRINT SLIDES

Why? *Bold characters display somewhat thicker and darker than those that display in a regular font style.* Tapping or clicking the Bold button on the mini toolbar is an efficient method of bolding text. To add more emphasis to the fact that the body needs water for cooling purposes, you want to bold the words, cannot cool itself. The following step bolds this text.

1

• With the words, cannot cool itself, selected, tap or click the Bold button on the mini toolbar to bold the three words (Figure 1–27).

Figure 1–27

Other Ways

1. Tap 'Show Context Menu' button on mini toolbar or right-click selected text, tap or click Font on shortcut menu, tap or click Font tab (Font dialog box), tap or click Bold in Font style list, tap or click OK button

2. Select text, tap or click Bold button (HOME tab | Font group)

3. Tap or click Font dialog box launcher (HOME tab | Font group), tap or click Font tab (Font dialog box), tap or click Bold in Font style list, tap or click OK button

4. Select text, press CTRL+B

To Increase Font Size

Why? *To add emphasis, you increase the font size for the words, cannot cool itself. The following steps increase the font size from 18 to 20 point.*

1 With the words, cannot cool itself, still selected, tap or click the 'Increase Font Size' button on the mini toolbar once (Figure 1–28).

2 Tap or click outside the selected area to deselect the three words.

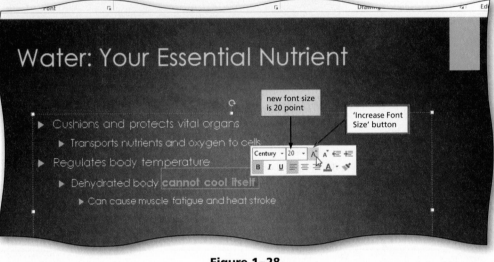

Figure 1–28

Adding New Slides, Changing Slide Layouts, and Changing the Theme

BTW

Customizing a Slide Layout

PowerPoint provides a wide variety of slide layouts for each theme, but you can customize the layouts to make your deck unique. Display the VIEW tab, tap or click Slide Master (VIEW tab | Master Views group), select the thumbnail below the slide master in the left pane that you would like to customize, and then make the desired modifications.

Slide 3 in Figure 1–1c on page PPT 3 contains an illustration of a character drinking water and does not contain a bulleted list. When you add a new slide, PowerPoint applies the Title and Content layout. This layout, along with the Title Slide layout for Slide 1, are the default styles. A **layout** specifies the arrangement of placeholders on a slide. These placeholders are arranged in various configurations and can contain text, such as the slide title or a bulleted list, or they can contain content, such as SmartArt graphics, photos, charts, tables, and shapes. The placement of the text, in relationship to content, depends on the slide layout. You can specify a particular slide layout when you add a new slide to a presentation or after you have created the slide.

Using the **layout gallery**, you can choose a slide layout. The nine layouts in this gallery have a variety of placeholders to define text and content positioning and formatting. Three layouts are for text: Title Slide, Section Header, and Title Only. Five are for text and content: Title and Content, Two Content, Comparison, Content with Caption, and Picture with Caption. The Blank layout has no placeholders. If none of these standard layouts meets your design needs, you can create a **custom layout**. A custom layout specifies the number, size, and location of placeholders, background content, and optional slide and placeholder-level properties.

When you change the layout of a slide, PowerPoint retains the text and objects and repositions them into the appropriate placeholders. Using slide layouts eliminates the need to resize objects and the font size because PowerPoint automatically sizes the objects and text to fit the placeholders. At any time when creating the slide content, you can change the theme and variant to give the presentation a different look and feel.

To Add a Slide with the Title Only Layout

The following steps add Slide 3 to the presentation with the Title Only slide layout style. *Why? The only text on the slide is the title, and the majority of the slide content is the illustration.*

1

- If necessary, tap or click HOME on the ribbon to display the HOME tab.

- Tap or click the New Slide arrow (HOME tab | Slides group) to display the Ion layout gallery (Figure 1–29).

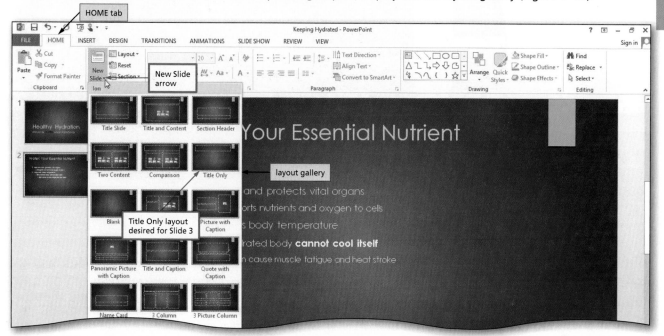

Figure 1–29

2

- Tap or click Title Only to add a new slide and apply that layout to Slide 3.

- If necessary, swipe up or click the Up scroll arrow several times until the title text placeholder is visible (Figure 1–30).

Figure 1–30

To Enter a Slide Title

The only text on Slide 3 is the title. The following step enters the title text for this slide.

1 Type **Begin Workout with Plenty of Water** as the title text but do not press the ENTER key (Figure 1–31).

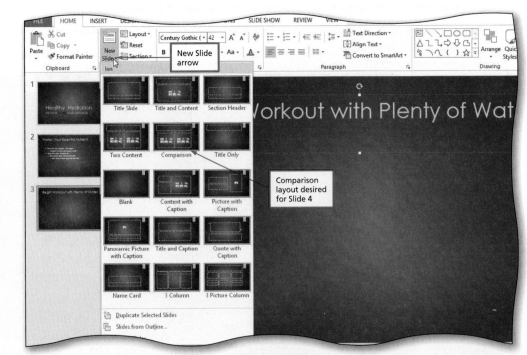

Figure 1–31

To Add a New Slide and Enter a Slide Title and Headings

1 INSERT PRESENTATION SLIDES | 2 ENTER TEXT | 3 FORMAT TEXT | **4 INSERT GRAPHICAL ELEMENTS**
5 SIZE & POSITION | 6 ENHANCE SLIDE SHOW | 7 DISPLAY & PRINT SLIDES

The text on Slide 4 in Figure 1–1d on page PPT 3 consists of a title and two headings. The appropriate layout for this slide is named Comparison. *Why? The Comparison layout has two headings and two text placeholders adjacent to each other, so an audience member easily can compare and contrast the items shown side by side.* The following steps add Slide 4 to the presentation with the Comparison layout and then enter the title and heading text for this slide.

1
• Tap or click the New Slide arrow in the Slides group to display the Ion layout gallery (Figure 1–32).

Figure 1–32

2

- Tap or click Comparison to add Slide 4 and apply that layout (Figure 1–33).

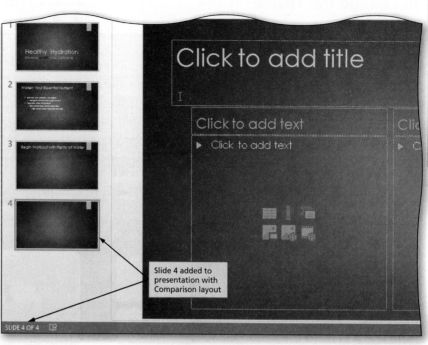

Figure 1–33

3

- Type **Keep Replenishing Fluid Levels** in the title text placeholder.

- Tap or click the left heading placeholder with the label, 'Tap to add text', or 'Click to add text', to select this placeholder (Figure 1–34).

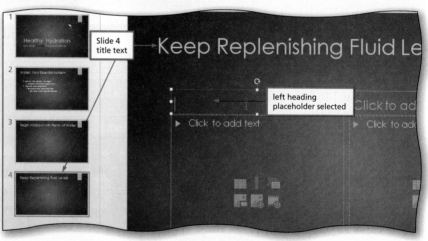

Figure 1–34

4

- Type **While Exercising:** and then press the ENTER key.

- Type **10 oz. every 20 minutes** but do not press the ENTER key.

- Select the right heading placeholder and then type **After Exercising:** and press the ENTER key.

- Type **8 oz. within 30 minutes** but do not press the ENTER key (Figure 1–35).

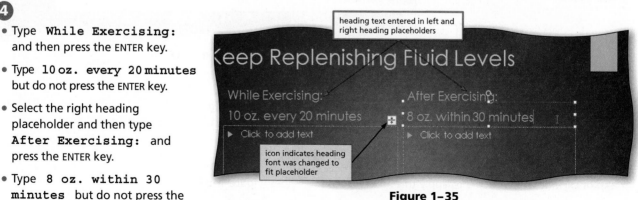

Figure 1–35

Q&A | What is the white box with the arrow between the placeholders?
The text is too large to fit in the placeholder using the default font and paragraph attributes, so PowerPoint adjusts the text so it displays properly. That icon informs you that the font was altered.

To Change the Theme

A theme provides consistency in design and color throughout the entire presentation by setting the color scheme, font set, and layout of a presentation. This collection of formatting choices includes a set of colors (the Theme Colors group), a set of heading and content text fonts (the Theme Fonts group), and a set of lines and fill effects (the Theme Effects group). These groups allow you to choose and change the appearance of all the slides or individual slides in your presentation. *Why? At any time while creating the slide deck, you may decide to switch the theme so that the slides have a totally different appearance.* The following steps change the theme for this presentation from Ion to Facet.

1

• Tap or click DESIGN on the ribbon to display the DESIGN tab (Figure 1–36).

Figure 1–36

2

• Tap or click the More button (DESIGN tab | Themes group) to expand the gallery, which shows more theme gallery options (Figure 1–37).

 Experiment

• If you are using a mouse, point to various document themes in the Themes gallery and watch the colors and fonts change on the title slide.

Figure 1–37

Q&A Are the themes displayed in a specific order?
They are listed in alphabetical order in two groups: Facet to Wisp beginning in the first row and Banded to Wood Type beginning in the second row. If you are using a mouse and point to a theme, a ScreenTip with the theme's name appears on the screen.

3

• Tap or click the Facet theme to apply this theme to all four slides (Figure 1–38).

Q&A The Facet theme is visible in the first row of the gallery, so why did I click the More button to expand the gallery?
While it is not necessary to view all the thumbnails, it sometimes is helpful to see all possible themes when deciding which one best fits the presentation.

If I decide at some future time that this design does not fit the theme of my presentation, can I apply a different design?
Yes. You can repeat these steps at any time while creating your presentation.

Figure 1–38

To Change the Variant

When you began creating this presentation, you selected the Ion theme and then chose a blue variant. You can change the color variation at any time for any theme. *Why? The new Facet theme has a default green color, but you want to emphasize the blue color associated with water, just like you initially did when you chose the blue variant for the Ion theme.* The following steps change the variant from green to blue.

1

- If you are using a mouse, point to the blue variation (DESIGN tab | Variants group) to see a preview of the blue variation on Slide 4 (Figure 1–39).

Experiment

- If you are using a mouse, point to the pink and black variants and watch the colors change on the slide.

Figure 1–39

2

- Tap or click the blue variant to apply this color to all four slides (Figure 1–40).

Q&A If I decide at some future time that this color variation does not fit the theme of my presentation, can I apply a different variant?

Yes. You can repeat these steps at any time while creating your presentation.

Figure 1–40

To Save an Existing Presentation with the Same File Name

You have made several modifications to the presentation since you last saved it. Thus, you should save it again. The following step saves the presentation again. For an example of the step listed below, refer to the Office and Windows chapter at the beginning of this book.

1 Tap or click the Save button on the Quick Access Toolbar to overwrite the previously saved file.

Break Point: If you wish to take a break, this is a good place to do so. You can exit PowerPoint now (refer to page PPT 55 for instructions). To resume at a later time, run PowerPoint (refer to page PPT 4 for instructions), open the file called Keeping Hydrated, and continue following the steps from this location forward.

BTW

Welcome Back!

If you are designing a slide in your deck other than Slide 1 and then save and close the document, PowerPoint's new Welcome back! feature allows you to continue where you left off at the last save when you open the document. You may need to adjust the zoom if you are working at a different level than the default setting.

PowerPoint Views

The PowerPoint window display varies depending on the view. A **view** is the mode in which the presentation appears on the screen. You will use some views when you are developing slides and others when you are delivering your presentation. When creating a presentation, you most likely will use Normal, Slide Sorter, Notes Page, and Outline views. When presenting your slides to an audience, you most likely will use Slide Sorter, Presenter, and Reading views.

The default view is **Normal view**, which is composed of three areas that allow you to work on various aspects of a presentation simultaneously. The large area in the middle, called the **Slide pane**, displays the slide you currently are developing and allows you to enter text, tables, charts, graphics, pictures, video, and other elements. As you create the slides, miniature views of the individual slides, called thumbnails, are displayed in the **Thumbnail pane**. You can rearrange the thumbnails in this pane. The **Notes pane**, by default, is hidden at the bottom of the window. If you want to type notes to yourself or remarks to share with your audience, you can click the Notes button in the status bar to open the Notes pane. After you have created at least two slides, a scroll bar containing **scroll arrows** and **scroll boxes** will appear on the right edge of the window.

To Move to Another Slide in Normal View

Why? *When creating or editing a presentation in Normal view (the view you are currently using), you often want to display a slide other than the current one.* Before continuing with developing this project, you want to display the title slide. If you are using a touch screen, you can tap the desired slide in the Thumbnail pane; if you are using a mouse, you can click the desired slide in the Thumbnail pane or drag the scroll box on the vertical scroll bar. When you drag the scroll box, the **slide indicator** shows the number and title of the slide you are about to display. Releasing shows the slide. The following steps move from Slide 4 to Slide 1 using the scroll box in the Slide pane.

1

- Position the pointer on the scroll box.

- Press and hold down the mouse button so that Slide: 4 of 4 Keep Replenishing Fluid Levels appears in the slide indicator (Figure 1–41).

Figure 1–41

2

- Drag the scroll box up the vertical scroll bar until Slide: 1 of 4 Healthy Hydration appears in the slide indicator (Figure 1–42).

Figure 1–42

3

- Release so that Slide 1 appears in the Slide pane and the Slide 1 thumbnail has an orange border in the Thumbnail pane (Figure 1–43).

Figure 1–43

Other Ways

1. Click Next Slide button or Previous Slide button to move forward or back one slide
2. Tap or click slide in Thumbnail pane
3. Press PAGE DOWN or PAGE UP to move forward or back one slide

Inserting Photos and Illustrations into Slides

BTW
Microsoft Clip Organizer
Previous versions of Microsoft Office stored photos, illustrations, animations, videos, and other media in the Clip Organizer. Office 2013, however, has replaced this feature with the Insert Media dialog box, which allows you to search for and insert files from the Office.com Clip Art collection, Bing, Flickr, SkyDrive, Facebook, and other online sources.

A **clip** is a single media file, such as a photo, illustration, sound, or video. Adding a clip can help increase the visual and audio appeal of many slides and can offer a quick way to add professional-looking graphics and multimedia to a presentation without creating these files yourself. This material is contained in the **Office.com Clip Art** collection of drawings, photos, sounds, and other media files shared among Microsoft Office applications.

You also can add your own clips to slides. These images may include scanned photos, illustrations, and artwork from storage media, such as USB flash drives, hard disks, and memory cards. If you have a Microsoft account, you can add photos from other websites, including Flickr and SkyDrive.

You can add images from Office.com to your presentation in two ways. One way is by selecting one of the slide layouts that includes a content placeholder with an Online Pictures button. A second method is by tapping or clicking the Online Pictures button in the Images area on the INSERT tab. Tapping or clicking the Online Pictures button opens the Insert Pictures dialog box. The **Insert Pictures dialog box** allows you to search for clip art by using descriptive keywords. Clips have one or more keywords associated with various entities, activities, labels, and emotions.

If you have an active connection to the Internet, clips from the Microsoft Office.com website will display automatically as the result of your search. Microsoft constantly revises the content of Office.com, so you may not be able to locate the pictures used in this chapter. Contact your instructor if you need the photos and illustration used in the following steps.

How can you design a title slide that holds your audience's attention?

Develop a slide that reflects the content of your presentation but does so in a thought-provoking way. A title, at the very least, should prepare your audience for the material they are about to see and hear. Look for ways to focus attention on your theme and the method in which you plan to present this theme. A unique photograph or graphic can help generate interest. You may decide to introduce your topic with a startling fact, a rhetorical question, or a quotation. The device you choose depends upon your audience, the occasion, and the presentation's purpose.

CONSIDER THIS

To Insert a Picture from Office.com into the Title Slide

1 INSERT PRESENTATION SLIDES | 2 ENTER TEXT | 3 FORMAT TEXT | **4 INSERT GRAPHICAL ELEMENTS**
5 SIZE & POSITION | 6 ENHANCE SLIDE SHOW | 7 DISPLAY & PRINT SLIDES

Slide 1 uses the Title Slide layout, which has two placeholders for text but none for graphical content. You desire to place a graphic on Slide 1. *Why? It is likely that your viewers will see an image on this slide before they read any text, so you want to include a photo to create interest in the presentation and introduce your audience to the topic. For this presentation,* you will locate a photo of a person holding a water bottle and then insert this photo in this slide. Later in this chapter, you will resize and position the photo in an appropriate location. The following steps add a photo to Slide 1.

1

- Tap or click INSERT on the ribbon to display the INSERT tab.

- Tap or click the Online Pictures button (INSERT tab | Images group) to display the Insert Pictures dialog box.

- With the insertion point in the Office.com Clip Art area, type **water bottle** in the search box (Figure 1–44).

Figure 1–44

2

- Tap or click the Search button (the magnifying glass) or press the ENTER key so that Office.com will search for and display all clips having the keywords, water bottle.

Q&A Why does the x button display when I begin typing the search terms?
Clicking the x button deletes all letters in the box.

3

- If necessary, slide or scroll down the list to display the photo shown in Figure 1–45.

- Tap or click the photo to select it (Figure 1–45).

Q&A What if the water bottle image displayed in Figure1 –45 is not shown in my Office.com Clip Art dialog box?
Select a similar photo. Microsoft updates the files in the Office.com Clip art collection, so the images change constantly.

What are the words and numbers in the lower-left corner of the dialog box?
The words are the keywords associated with this photo, and the figures are the number of pixels associated with the width and height of the clip.

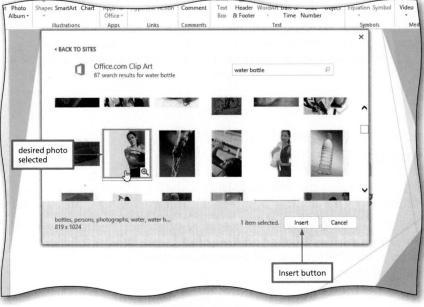

Figure 1–45

4

- Tap or click the Insert button to download the photo and insert it into the slide (Figure 1–46).

Q&A Can I double-tap or double-click the photo instead of selecting it and then tap or click the Insert button?
Yes. Either method downloads and inserts the photo.

Why is this photo displayed in this location on the slide?
The slide layout does not have a content placeholder, so PowerPoint inserts the file in the center of the slide.

Figure 1–46

To Insert a Picture from Office.com into a Slide without a Content Placeholder

The next step is to add a water bottle photo to Slide 2. This slide has a bulleted list in the text placeholder, so the icon group does not display in the center of the placeholder. Later in this chapter, you will resize the inserted photo. The following steps add one photo to Slide 2.

1 Tap or click the Slide 2 thumbnail in the Thumbnail pane to display Slide 2.

2 Tap or click INSERT on the ribbon to display the INSERT tab and then tap or click the Online Pictures button (INSERT tab | Images group) to display the Insert Pictures dialog box.

3 Type `water bottle` in the Office.com Clip Art search box and then tap or click the Search button.

4 If necessary, slide or scroll down the list to display the water bottle photo shown in Figure 1–47, tap or click the photo to select it, and then tap or click the Insert button to download and insert the photo into Slide 2 (Figure 1–47).

Q&A Why is my photo a different size from the one shown in Figure1–1b on page PPT 3? The clip was inserted into the slide and not into a content placeholder. You will resize the photo later in this chapter.

desired photo inserted into Slide 2

Figure 1–47

To Insert an Illustration from Office.com into a Slide without a Content Placeholder

Next, you will add an illustration to Slide 3. You will not insert this file into a content placeholder, so it will display in the center of the slide. Later in this chapter, you will resize this illustration. You locate and download illustrations in the same manner you used to locate and download photos. The following steps add an illustration to Slide 3.

1 Tap or click the Slide 3 thumbnail in the Thumbnail pane.

2 Display the INSERT tab, tap or click the Online Pictures button, type `drinking water` as the search text, and then tap or click the Search button.

3 If necessary, slide or scroll down the list to display the picture of a character drinking water shown in Figure 1–48 and then insert it into Slide 3 (Figure 1–48).

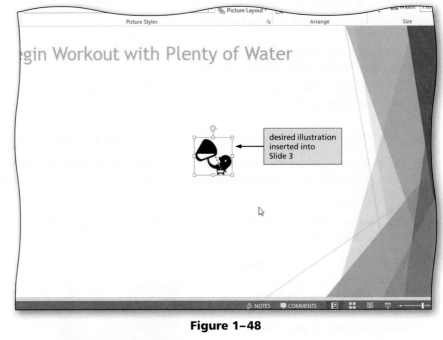

Figure 1–48

To Insert a Picture from Office.com into a Content Placeholder

1 INSERT PRESENTATION SLIDES | 2 ENTER TEXT | 3 FORMAT TEXT | 4 INSERT GRAPHICAL ELEMENTS
5 SIZE & POSITION | 6 ENHANCE SLIDE SHOW | 7 DISPLAY & PRINT SLIDES

Slide 4 uses the Comparison layout, which has a content placeholder below each of the two headings. You desire to insert photos into both content placeholders. ***Why?*** *You want to reinforce the concept that people should drink water during and after workouts.* The following steps insert photos of a female into the left content placeholder and a male into the right content placeholder on Slide 4.

• Tap or click the Slide 4 thumbnail in the Thumbnail pane to display Slide 4 (Figure 1–49).

Figure 1–49

2

- Tap or click the Online Pictures icon in the left content placeholder to select that placeholder and to open the Insert Pictures dialog box.

- Tap or click the search box, type **women bottled water** as the search text, and then press the ENTER key.

- If necessary, slide or scroll down the list to display the photo shown in Figure 1–50.

- Select the photo and then double-tap or double-click to download and insert it into the left content placeholder (Figure 1–50).

Figure 1–50

3

- Tap or click the Online Pictures icon in the right content placeholder to select that placeholder and to open the Insert Pictures dialog box.

- Tap or click the search box, type **men exercises hydration** as the search text, and press or tap the ENTER key.

- If necessary, slide or scroll down the list to display the photo shown in Figure 1–51.

- Insert the photo into the right content placeholder (Figure 1–51).

Figure 1–51

Break Point: If you wish to take a break, this is a good place to do so. You can save your presentation and then exit PowerPoint now. To resume at a later time, run PowerPoint, open the file called Keeping Hydrated, and continue following the steps from this location forward.

Resizing Photos and Illustrations

Sometimes it is necessary to change the size of photos and illustrations. **Resizing** includes enlarging or reducing the size of a graphic. You can resize these images using a variety of techniques. One method involves changing the size of a picture by specifying exact dimensions in a dialog box. Another method involves sliding or dragging one of the graphic's sizing handles to the desired location. A selected graphic appears surrounded by a **selection rectangle**, which has small squares and circles, called **sizing handles** or move handles, at each corner and middle location.

BTW
PowerPoint Help
At any time while using PowerPoint, you can find answers to questions and display information about various topics through PowerPoint Help. Used properly, this form of assistance can increase your productivity and reduce your frustrations by minimizing the time you spend learning how to use PowerPoint. For instruction about PowerPoint Help and exercises that will help you gain confidence in using it, read the Office and Windows chapter at the beginning of this book.

To Proportionally Resize Pictures

Why? On Slides 1, 2, and 3, the photo and illustration sizes are either too small or too large to display aesthetically on the slides. The photo and illustration on Slides 1 and 3 are too small, and the photo on Slide 2 is too large. The photo on Slide 1 is of a person, so it generally is important to maintain the proportions. To change the size of a photo and keep the width and height in proportion to each other, drag the corner sizing handles to view how the image will look on the slide. Using these corner handles maintains the graphic's original proportions. If, however, the proportions do not need to be maintained, as with the water bottle on Slide 2, drag the square sizing handles to alter the proportions so that the graphic's height and width become larger or smaller. The following steps proportionally increase the size of the Slide 1 photo using a corner sizing handle.

1

- Click the Slide 1 thumbnail in the Thumbnail pane to display Slide 1.

- Tap or click the photo to select it and display the selection rectangle.

- Point to the upper-right corner sizing handle on the illustration so that the pointer changes to a two-headed arrow (Figure 1–52).

Q&A I am using a touch screen and do not see a two-headed arrow when I press and hold the upper-right sizing handle. Why?
Touch screens may not display pointers; you can just press and slide sizing handles to resize.

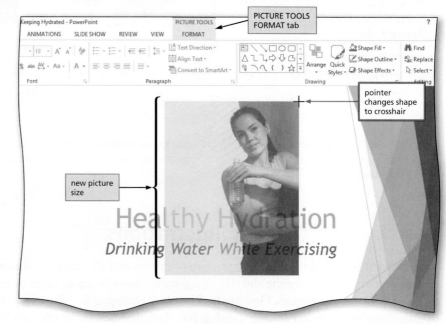

Figure 1–52

2

- Drag the sizing handle diagonally toward the upper-right corner of the slide until the upper-right sizing handle or the crosshair is positioned approximately as shown in Figure 1–53.

Q&A What if the illustration is not the same size as the one shown in Figure 1–53?
Repeat Steps 1 and 2.

Figure 1–53

③

- Release to resize the illustration.

- Tap or click outside the illustration to deselect it (Figure 1–54).

Q&A What happened to the PICTURE TOOLS FORMAT tab?
When you tap or click outside the illustration, PowerPoint deselects the illustration and removes the PICTURE TOOLS FORMAT tab from the screen.

Figure 1–54

To Nonproportionally Resize the Photograph on Slide 2

1 INSERT PRESENTATION SLIDES | 2 ENTER TEXT | 3 FORMAT TEXT | 4 INSERT GRAPHICAL ELEMENTS
5 SIZE & POSITION | **6 ENHANCE SLIDE SHOW** | 7 DISPLAY & PRINT SLIDES

Why? *The height of the water bottle photo in Slide 2 extends from the top to the bottom of the slide. The width, however, will cover some of the text when the photo is positioned on the right side of the slide.* The width of this photo can be decreased slightly without negatively distorting the original image. You can decrease the width of a photo by sliding or dragging one of the square sizing handles on the sides of the image. The following steps resize the width of the water bottle photo using a sizing handle along the side of the image.

❶

- Display Slide 2 and then tap or click the water bottle photo to select it and display the selection rectangle.

- Tap or click the Zoom Out button as many times as necessary until the Zoom level is 60%.

- Press or point to the sizing handle on the left side of the photo so that the pointer changes to a two-headed arrow (Figure 1–55).

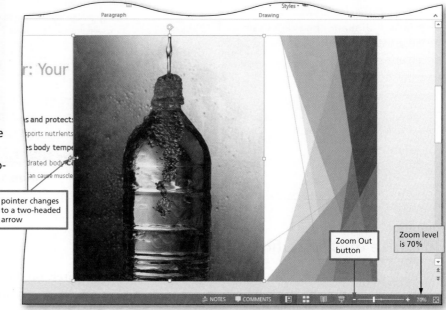

Figure 1–55

2

- Drag the sizing handle toward the right side of the slide until the sizing handle or crosshair is positioned approximately as shown in Figure 1–56.

Q&A What if the illustration is not the same size as the one shown in Figure 1–56?
Repeat Steps 1 and 2.

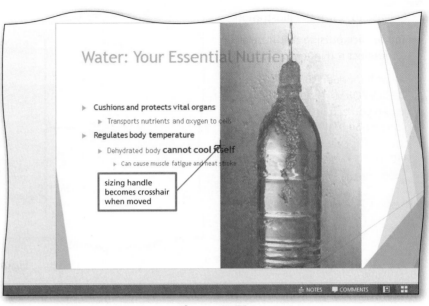

Figure 1–56

3

- Release to resize the photo.
- Tap or click outside the photo to deselect it (Figure 1–57).

Q&A What if I want to return the photo to its original size and start again?
With the photo selected, tap or click the Reset Picture arrow (PICTURE TOOLS FORMAT tab | Adjust group) and then click Reset Picture & Size in the Reset Picture gallery.

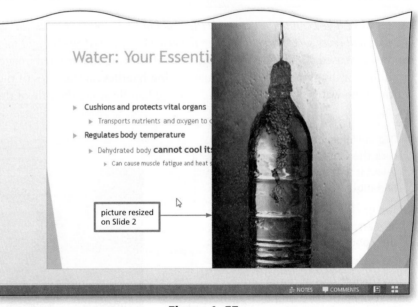

Figure 1–57

To Resize the Illustration on Slide 3

The illustration on Slide 3 can be reduced slightly to fit entirely on the slide. You resize an illustration in the same manner that you resize a photo. You want to maintain the proportions of the character and water in this illustration, so you will drag one of the corner sizing handles. The following steps resize this illustration using a corner sizing handle.

1 Display Slide 3 and then tap or click the character drinking water illustration to select it.

2 Drag the lower-left corner sizing handle on the illustration diagonally outward until the illustration is resized approximately as shown in Figure 1–58.

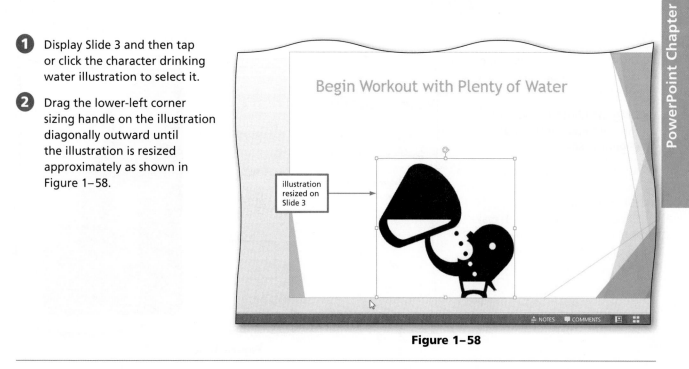

Figure 1–58

To Move Pictures

1 INSERT PRESENTATION SLIDES | 2 ENTER TEXT | 3 FORMAT TEXT | 4 INSERT GRAPHICAL ELEMENTS
5 SIZE & POSITION | 6 ENHANCE SLIDE SHOW | 7 DISPLAY & PRINT SLIDES

Why? *After you insert a photo or an illustration on a slide, you might want to reposition it. The female athlete photo on Slide 1 could be moved to the left side of the slide, the water bottle on Slide 2 could be moved to the right side of the slide, and the illustration on Slide 3 could be positioned in the center of the slide.* PowerPoint displays **Smart Guides** automatically when a photo, illustration, shape, or other object is close to lining up with another slide element. For example, a Smart Guide will display to help you align the right or left edge of a picture in relation to a text placeholder or to another picture. The following steps move the photos on Slides 1 and 2 and center the illustration on Slide 3.

1

- If necessary, tap or click the character illustration on Slide 3 to select it.

- Drag the illustration upward until the horizontal Smart Guide is displayed under the title text placeholder and the vertical Smart Guide is displayed through the center of the slide, as shown in Figure 1–59, and then release.

- If necessary, select the photo and then use the ARROW keys to position it precisely as shown in Figure 1–59.

Q&A The illustration still is not located exactly where I want it to display. What can I do to align the image? Press the CTRL key while you press the ARROW keys. This key combination moves the illustration in smaller increments than when you press only an ARROW key.

Figure 1–59

2

- Display Slide 2 and then tap or click the water bottle photo to select it.

- Drag the photo to align with the right edge of the slide (Figure 1–60).

Q&A
My water bottle photo is covering some of the title text on the slide. What should I do?
Either resize the photo to make it narrower or move the photo to the right so that it is hanging slightly off the side of the slide.

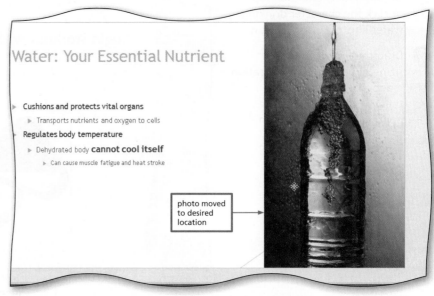

Figure 1–60

3

- Display Slide 1 and then tap or click the athlete photo to select it.

- Drag the photo to the left and either upward or downward until the horizontal center Smart Guide is displayed, as shown in Figure 1–61, and then release.

4

- Tap or click outside the photo to deselect it.

Figure 1–61

Q&A
The athlete photo is too wide and is covering some of the text on the slide. What should I do?
Changing the width of a photo showing a person generally is not advisable because the altered proportions make the person appear tall and thin or short and overweight. In this case, move the photo to the left so that it is hanging slightly off the side of the slide, as shown in Figure1–61.

Ending a Slide Show with a Closing Slide

All the text for the slides in the Healthy Hydration slide show has been entered. This presentation thus far consists of a title slide, one text slide with a multilevel bulleted list, a third slide for a photo, and a fourth slide with a Comparison layout. A closing slide that resembles the title slide is the final slide to create.

CONSIDER THIS

What factors should you consider when developing a closing slide for the presentation?
After the last slide appears during a slide show, the default PowerPoint setting is to end the presentation with a **black slide**. This black slide appears only when the slide show is running and concludes the slide show, so your audience never sees the PowerPoint window. It is a good idea, however, to end your presentation with a final closing slide to display at the end of the presentation. This slide ends the presentation gracefully and should be an exact copy, or a very similar copy, of your title slide. The audience will recognize that the presentation is drawing to a close when this slide appears. It can remain on the screen when the audience asks questions, approaches the speaker for further information, or exits the room.

To Duplicate a Slide

Why? *When two slides contain similar information and have the same format, duplicating one slide and then making minor modifications to the new slide saves time and increases consistency.*

Slide 5 will have the same layout and design as Slide 1. The most expedient method of creating this slide is to copy Slide 1 and then make minor modifications to the new slide. The following steps duplicate the title slide.

1

• With Slide 1 selected, tap or click the New Slide arrow (HOME tab | Slides group) to display the Facet layout gallery (Figure 1–62).

Figure 1–62

2

• Tap or click 'Duplicate Selected Slides' in the Facet layout gallery to create a new Slide 2, which is a duplicate of Slide 1 (Figure 1–63).

Figure 1–63

Break Point: If you wish to take a break, this is a good place to do so. Be sure to save the Keeping Hydrated file again and then you can exit PowerPoint. To resume at a later time, run PowerPoint, open the file called Keeping Hydrated, and continue following the steps from this location forward.

To Arrange a Slide

The new Slide 2 was inserted directly below Slide 1 because Slide 1 was the selected slide. This duplicate slide needs to display at the end of the presentation directly after the final title and content slide. ***Why?*** *It is a closing slide that reinforces the concept presented in Slide 1 and indicates to your audiences that your presentation is ending.*

Changing slide order is an easy process and is best performed in the Thumbnail pane. When you tap or click the thumbnail and begin to drag it to a new location, the remaining thumbnails realign to show the new sequence. When you release, the slide drops into the desired location. Hence, this process of sliding or dragging and then dropping the thumbnail in a new location is called **drag and drop**. You can use the drag-and-drop method to move any selected item, including text and graphics. The following step moves the new Slide 2 to the end of the presentation so that it becomes a closing slide.

1

- With Slide 2 selected, drag the Slide 2 slide thumbnail below the last slide in the Thumbnail pane (Figure 1–64).

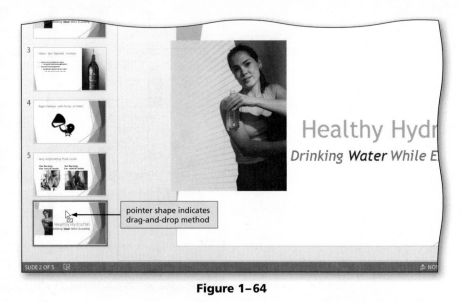

pointer shape indicates drag-and-drop method

Figure 1–64

Other Ways

1. Tap or click Slide Sorter button on status bar, drag thumbnail to new location	2. Tap or click Slide Sorter button (VIEW tab | Presentation Views group), tap or click slide thumbnail, drag thumbnail to new location

Making Changes to Slide Text Content

After creating slides in a presentation, you may find that you want to make changes to the text. Changes may be required because a slide contains an error, the scope of the presentation shifts, or the style is inconsistent. This section explains the types of changes that commonly occur when creating a presentation.

You generally make three types of changes to text in a presentation: additions, replacements, and deletions.

- Additions are necessary when you omit text from a slide and need to add it later. You may need to insert text in the form of a sentence, word, or single character. For example, you may want to add the presenter's middle name on the title slide.

- Replacements are needed when you want to revise the text in a presentation. For example, you may want to substitute the word, *their*, for the word, *there*.

- Deletions are required when text on a slide is incorrect or no longer is relevant to the presentation. For example, a slide may look cluttered. Therefore, you may want to remove one of the bulleted paragraphs to add more space.

Editing text in PowerPoint basically is the same as editing text in a word processing program. The following sections illustrate the most common changes made to text in a presentation.

Replacing Text in an Existing Slide

When you need to correct a word or phrase, you can replace the text by selecting the text to be replaced and then typing the new text. As soon as you press any key on the keyboard, the selected text is deleted and the new text is displayed.

PowerPoint inserts text to the left of the insertion point. The text to the right of the insertion point moves to the right (and shifts downward if necessary) to accommodate the added text.

Deleting Text

You can delete text using one of many methods. One is to use the BACKSPACE key to remove text just typed. The second is to position the insertion point to the left of the text you want to delete and then press the DELETE key. The third method is to drag through the text you want to delete and then tap or click the Cut button on the mini toolbar, press DELETE or BACKSPACE key, or press CTRL + X. Use the third method when deleting large sections of text.

To Delete Text in a Placeholder

1 INSERT PRESENTATION SLIDES | 2 ENTER TEXT | **3 FORMAT TEXT** | 4 INSERT GRAPHICAL ELEMENTS
5 SIZE & POSITION | 6 ENHANCE SLIDE SHOW | **7 DISPLAY & PRINT SLIDES**

Why? *To keep the ending slide clean and simple, you want to delete a few words in the slide title and subtitle text.* The following steps change Healthy Hydration to Be Healthy and then change Drinking Water While Exercising to Drink Water.

1

- With Slide 5 selected, position the pointer immediately to the right of the last character of the text to be selected in the title text placeholder (in this case, the n in the word, Hydration).

- Drag the pointer through the first character of the text to be selected (in this case, the space after the word, Healthy) (Figure 1–65).

Q&A I am having difficulty selecting the required text. Can I drag from left to right or right to left?
Yes. You may need several attempts to select the correct characters.

Could I also have selected the word, Hydration, by double-tapping or double-clicking it?
Yes. Either method works to select a word.

Figure 1–65

2

- Tap or click the Cut button (HOME tab | Clipboard group) to delete the selected text and space.

- Position the pointer to the left of the word, Healthy, and then type **Be** and press the SPACEBAR as the first word in the title text placeholder (Figure 1–66).

- If requested by your instructor, add your mother's first name after the word, Healthy, in the title text placeholder.

Figure 1–66

3

- Position the pointer immediately to the right of the last character of the text to be selected in the subtitle text placeholder (in this case, the g in the word, Exercising).

- Drag the pointer to the left through the last character of the text to be selected (in this case, the space after the word, Water) (Figure 1–67).

Figure 1–67

4

- Tap or click the Cut button.

- Select the letters, ing, in the word, Drinking.

- Tap or click the Cut button (Figure 1–68).

Figure 1–68

Other Ways

1. Tap 'Show Context Menu' button on mini toolbar or right-click selected text, tap or click Cut on shortcut menu

2. Select text, press DELETE or BACKSPACE key

3. Select text, press CTRL+X

Adding a Transition

PowerPoint includes a wide variety of visual and sound effects that can be applied to text or content. A **slide transition** is a special effect used to progress from one slide to the next in a slide show. You can control the speed of the transition effect and add a sound.

To Add a Transition between Slides

1 INSERT PRESENTATION SLIDES | 2 ENTER TEXT | 3 FORMAT TEXT | 4 INSERT GRAPHICAL ELEMENTS

5 SIZE & POSITION | 6 ENHANCE SLIDE SHOW | 7 DISPLAY & PRINT SLIDES

Why? *Transitions add interest when you advance the slides in a presentation and make a slide show presentation look professional.* In this presentation, you apply the Switch transition in the Exciting category to all slides and change the transition speed from 1.25 seconds to 2 seconds. The following steps apply this transition to the presentation.

1

- Tap or click the TRANSITIONS tab on the ribbon and then point to the More button (TRANSITIONS tab | Transition to This Slide group) in the Transition to This Slide gallery (Figure 1–69).

Figure 1–69

Q&A Is a transition applied now?

No. None, the first slide icon in the Transition to This Slide group, is selected, which indicates no transition has been applied.

2

- Tap or click the More button to expand the Transitions gallery.

- Point to the Switch transition in the Exciting category in the Transitions gallery (Figure 1–70).

Figure 1–70

3

- Tap or click Switch in the Exciting category in the Transitions gallery to apply this transition to the closing slide.

◁│ Why does a star appear next to Slide 5 in the Thumbnail pane?
Q&A│ The star indicates that a transition animation effect is applied to that slide.

- Tap or click the Duration up arrow (TRANSITIONS tab | Timing group) seven times to change the transition speed from 01.25 seconds to 03.00 seconds (Figure 1–71).

◁│ Why did the time change from the default 2.00 to 1.25?
Q&A│ Each transition has a default duration time. The default Switch transition time is 01.25 seconds.

Figure 1–71

4

- Tap or click the Preview Transitions button (TRANSITIONS tab | Preview area) to view the transition and the new transition time (Figure 1–72).

Q&A Can I adjust the duration time I just set?

Yes. Tap or click the Duration up or down arrows or type a speed in the Duration box and preview the transition until you find the time that best fits your presentation.

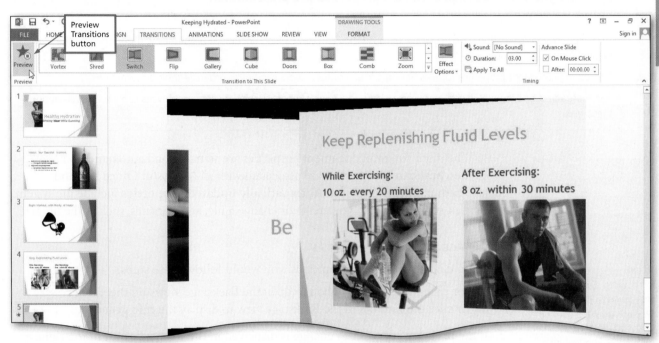

Figure 1–72

5

- Tap or click the 'Apply To All' button (TRANSITIONS tab | Timing group) to apply the Switch transition and the increased transition time to Slides 1 through 4 in the presentation (Figure 1–73).

Q&A What if I want to apply a different transition and duration to each slide in the presentation?

Repeat Steps 2 and 3 for each slide individually.

Figure 1–73

Document Properties

PowerPoint helps you organize and identify your files by using **document properties**, which are the details about a file such as the project author, title, and subject. For example, a class name or presentation topic can describe the file's purpose or content.

CONSIDER THIS

Why would you want to assign document properties to a presentation?

Document properties are valuable for a variety of reasons:

• Users can save time locating a particular file because they can view a file's document properties without opening the presentation.

• By creating consistent properties for files having similar content, users can better organize their presentations.

• Some organizations require PowerPoint users to add document properties so that other employees can view details about these files.

The more common document properties are standard and automatically updated properties. **Standard properties** are associated with all Microsoft Office files and include author, title, and subject. **Automatically updated properties** include file system properties, such as the date you create or change a file, and statistics, such as the file size.

To Change Document Properties

BTW

Printing Document Properties
PowerPoint 2013 does not allow you to print document properties. This feature, however, is available in other Office 2013 apps, including Word and Excel.

To change document properties, you would follow these steps.

1. Tap or click FILE on the ribbon to open the Backstage view and then, if necessary, tap or click the Info tab in the Backstage view to display the Info gallery.

2. If the property you wish to change is displayed in the Properties list in the right pane of the Info gallery, try to tap or click to the right of the property. If a box appears to the right of the property, type the text for the property in the box, and then tap or click the Back button in the upper-left corner of the Backstage view to return to the PowerPoint window. Skip the remaining steps.

3. If the property you wish to change is not displayed in the Properties list in the right pane of the Info gallery or you cannot change it in the Info gallery, tap or click the Properties button in the right pane to display the Properties menu, and then tap or click 'Show Document Panel' on the Properties menu to close the Backstage view and display the Document Information Panel in the PowerPoint presentation window.

Q&A | Why are some of the document properties in my Document Information Panel already filled in?
The person who installed Office 2013 on your computer or network may have set or customized the properties.

4. Type the desired text in the appropriate property boxes.

Q&A | What if the property I want to change is not displayed in the Document Information Panel?
Tap or click the Document Properties button in the Document Information Panel and then tap or click Advanced Properties on the menu to display the Properties dialog box. If necessary, tap or click the Summary tab (Properties dialog box) to display the Summary sheet, fill in the appropriate boxes, and then tap or click the OK button.

5. Tap or click the 'Close the Document Information Panel' button at the right edge of the Document Information Panel so that the panel no longer appears in the PowerPoint presentation window.

Viewing the Presentation in Slide Show View

The Start From Beginning button, located in the Quick Access Toolbar, allows you to show a presentation using a computer. As the name implies, the first slide to be displayed always will be Slide 1. You also can run a presentation starting with the slide currently displaying when you tap or click the Slide Show button on the status bar. In either case, PowerPoint displays the slides on the full screen without any of the PowerPoint window objects, such as the ribbon. The full-screen slide hides the toolbars, menus, and other PowerPoint window elements.

To Start Slide Show View

1 INSERT PRESENTATION SLIDES | 2 ENTER TEXT | 3 FORMAT TEXT | 4 INSERT GRAPHICAL ELEMENTS

5 SIZE & POSITION | 6 ENHANCE SLIDE SHOW | 7 DISPLAY & PRINT SLIDES

Why? *You run a presentation in for your audience so they can see the slides in their entirety and view any transitions or other effects added to the slides.* When making a presentation, you use **Slide Show view.** You can start Slide Show view from Normal view or Slide Sorter view. Slide Show view begins when you tap or click the Start From Beginning button or the Slide Show button. The following steps start Slide Show view starting with Slide 1.

1

- If you are using a touch screen, proceed to Step 2. If you are using a mouse, point to the Start From Beginning button (Figure 1–74).

Q&A What would have displayed if I had tapped or clicked the Slide Show button instead of the Start From Beginning button?
When you tap or click the Slide Show button to start the presentation, PowerPoint begins the show with the currently displayed slide, which in this case is Slide 5. Only Slide 5 would display during the slide show.

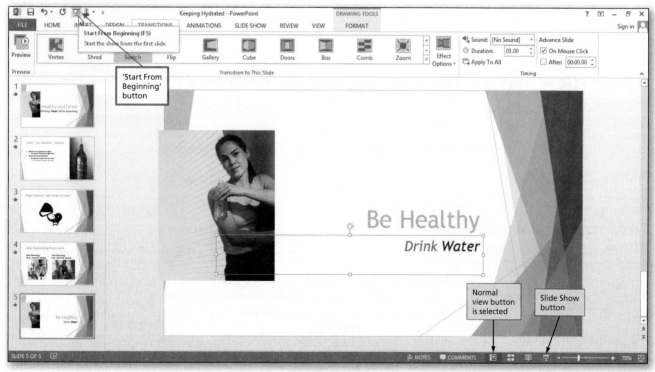

Figure 1–74

2

● Tap or click the Start From Beginning button to display the title slide (Figure 1–75).

Where is the PowerPoint window?

When you run a slide show, the PowerPoint window is hidden. It will reappear once you end your slide show.

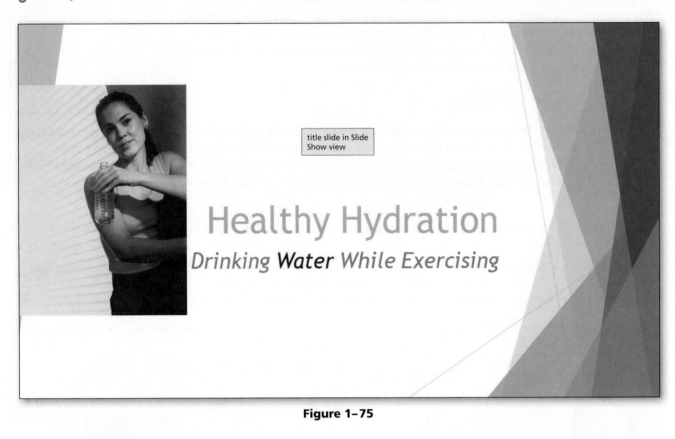

title slide in Slide Show view

Healthy Hydration
*Drinking **Water** While Exercising*

Figure 1–75

Other Ways

1. Display Slide 1, tap or click Slide Show button on status bar

2. Tap or click Start From Beginning button (SLIDE SHOW tab | Start Slide Show group)

3. Press F5

To Move Manually through Slides in a Slide Show

1 INSERT PRESENTATION SLIDES | 2 ENTER TEXT | 3 FORMAT TEXT | 4 INSERT GRAPHICAL ELEMENTS
5 SIZE & POSITION | 6 ENHANCE SLIDE SHOW | **7 DISPLAY & PRINT SLIDES**

After you begin Slide Show view, you can move forward or backward through the slides. PowerPoint allows you to advance through the slides manually or automatically. During a slide show, each slide in the presentation shows on the screen, one slide at a time. Each time you tap or click, the next slide appears. The following steps move manually through the slides. *Why? You can control the length of time each slide is displayed and change the preset order if you need to review a slide already shown or jump ahead to another slide designed to display later in the presentation.*

1

- Swipe forward on or click each slide until Slide 5 (Be Healthy) is displayed (Figure 1–76).

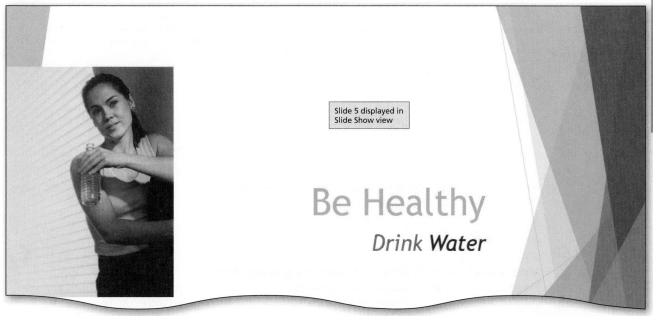

Figure 1–76

2

- Swipe forward on or click Slide 5 so that the black slide appears with a message announcing the end of the slide show (Figure 1–77).

Q&A I see a small toolbar in the lower-left corner of my slide. What is this toolbar?
The Slide Show toolbar appears when you begin running a slide show and then tap a slide or move the pointer. The buttons on this toolbar allow you to navigate to the next slide, the previous slide, to mark up the current slide, or to change the current display.

Figure 1–77

3

- Swipe forward on or click the black slide to return to Normal view in the PowerPoint window.

Other Ways

1. Press PAGE DOWN to advance one slide at a time, or press PAGE UP to go back one slide at a time

2. Press RIGHT ARROW or DOWN ARROW to advance one slide at a time, or press LEFT ARROW or UP ARROW to go back one slide at a time

3. If Slide Show toolbar is displayed, tap or click Next Slide or Previous Slide button on toolbar

Printing a Presentation

After creating a presentation, you may want to print it. Printing a presentation enables you to distribute it to others in a form that can be read or viewed but typically not edited. It is a good practice to save a presentation before printing it, in the event you experience difficulties printing.

CONSIDER THIS

What is the best method for distributing a presentation?

The traditional method of distributing a presentation uses a printer to produce a hard copy. A **hard copy** or **printout** is information that exists on a physical medium such as paper. Hard copies can be useful for the following reasons:

- Some people prefer proofreading a hard copy of a presentation rather than viewing it on the screen to check for errors and readability.

- Hard copies can serve as a backup reference if your storage medium is lost or becomes corrupted and you need to recreate the presentation.

Instead of distributing a hard copy of a presentation, users can distribute the presentation as an electronic image that mirrors the original presentation's appearance. The electronic image of the presentation can be sent as an email attachment, posted on a website, or copied to a portable storage medium such as a USB flash drive. Two popular electronic image formats, sometimes called fixed formats, are PDF by Adobe Systems and XPS by Microsoft. In PowerPoint, you can create electronic image files through the Save As dialog box and the Export, Share, and Print tabs in the Backstage view. Electronic images of presentations, such as PDF and XPS, can be useful for the following reasons:

- Users can view electronic images of presentations without the software that created the original presentation (e.g., PowerPoint). Specifically, to view a PDF file, you use a program called Adobe Reader, which can be downloaded free from Adobe's website. Similarly, to view an XPS file, you use a program called XPS Viewer, which is included in the latest versions of Windows and Internet Explorer.

- Sending electronic presentations saves paper and printer supplies. Society encourages users to contribute to **green computing**, which involves reducing the electricity consumed and environmental waste generated when using computers, mobile devices, and related technologies.

To Print a Presentation

1 INSERT PRESENTATION SLIDES | 2 ENTER TEXT | 3 FORMAT TEXT | 4 INSERT GRAPHICAL ELEMENTS |
5 SIZE & POSITION | 6 ENHANCE SLIDE SHOW | **7 DISPLAY & PRINT SLIDES**

With the completed presentation saved, you may want to print it. *Why? You could distribute a handout of the slides to your audience members, or you might want to keep a printed copy as a backup in the event you experience technical difficulties before or during your speech. You, therefore, will print a hard copy on a printer.* The following steps print a hard copy of the contents of the saved Keeping Hydrated presentation.

1

- Tap or click FILE on the ribbon to open the Backstage view.

- Tap or click the Print tab in the Backstage view to display the Print gallery (Figure 1–78).

Q&A How do I preview Slides 2 through 5?
Tap or click the Next Page button in the Print gallery to scroll forward through pages in the document; similarly, tap or click the Previous Page button to scroll backward through pages.

How can I print multiple copies of my presentation?
Increase the number in the Copies box in the Print gallery.

What if I decide not to print the presentation at this time?
Tap or click the Back button in the upper-left corner of the Backstage view to return to the presentation window.

2

- Verify that the printer listed on the Printer Status button will print a hard copy of the presentation. If necessary, click the Printer Status button to display a list of available printer options and then click the desired printer to change the currently selected printer.

Q&A The selected printer is a black-and-white laser printer, so the preview is grayscale and shows varying shades of gray. If I change the currently selected printer to a color printer, will the preview display in color?
Yes, the preview will match the printer output.

BTW
Conserving Ink and Toner
If you want to conserve ink or toner, you can instruct PowerPoint to print draft quality documents by tapping or clicking FILE on the ribbon to open the Backstage view, tapping or clicking Options in the Backstage view to display the PowerPoint Options dialog box, tapping or clicking Advanced in the left pane (PowerPoint Options dialog box), sliding or scrolling to the Print area in the right pane, not placing a check mark in the High quality check box, and then tapping or clicking the OK button. Then, use the Backstage view to print the document as usual.

Figure 1–78

3

- Tap or click the Print button in the Print gallery to print the presentation on the currently selected printer.

- When the printer stops, retrieve the hard copy (Figure 1–79).

Q&A Do I have to wait until my presentation is complete to print it?
No, you can follow these steps to print a presentation at any time while you are creating it.

What if I want to print an electronic image of a presentation instead of a hard copy?
You would click the Printer Status button in the Print gallery and then select the desired electronic image option, such as Microsoft XPS Document Writer, which would create an XPS file.

(a) Slide 1

(b) Slide 2

(c) Slide 3

(d) Slide 4

(e) Slide 5

Figure 1–79 (Handouts printed using a black-and-white printer)

Other Ways

1. Press CTRL+P, press ENTER

To Sign Out of a Microsoft Account

If you are signed in to a Microsoft account and are using a public computer or otherwise wish to sign out of your Microsoft account, you should sign out of the account from the Accounts gallery in the Backstage view before exiting PowerPoint. Signing out of the account is the safest way to make sure that nobody else can access SkyDrive files or settings stored in your Microsoft account. The following steps sign out of a Microsoft account from PowerPoint. For a detailed example of the procedure summarized below, refer to the Office and Windows chapter at the beginning of this book.

1 If you wish to sign out of your Microsoft account, tap or click FILE on the ribbon to open the Backstage view and then tap or click the Account tab to display the Account gallery.

2 Tap or click the Sign out link, which displays the Remove Account dialog box. If a Can't remove Windows accounts dialog box appears instead of the Remove Account dialog box, click the OK button and skip the remaining steps.

◄ Q&A Why does a Can't remove Windows accounts dialog box appear?
If you signed in to Windows using your Microsoft account, then you also must sign out from Windows, rather than signing out from within PowerPoint. When you are finished using Windows, be sure to sign out at that time.

3 Tap or click the Yes button (Remove Account dialog box) to sign out of your Microsoft account on this computer.

◄ Q&A Should I sign out of Windows after signing out of my Microsoft account?
When you are finished using the computer, you should sign out of your account for maximum security.

4 Tap or click the Back button in the upper-left corner of the Backstage view to return to the presentation.

To Exit PowerPoint

This project now is complete. The following steps exit PowerPoint. For a detailed example of the procedure summarized below, refer to the Office and Windows chapter at the beginning of this book.

1a If you have one PowerPoint presentation open, tap or click the Close button on the right side of the title bar to close the open document and exit PowerPoint.

1b If you have multiple PowerPoint presentations open, press and hold or right-click the PowerPoint app button on the taskbar and then tap or click 'Close all windows' on the shortcut menu, or press ALT+F4 to close all open presentations and exit PowerPoint.

◄ Q&A Could I press and hold or repeatedly click the Close button to close all open documents and exit PowerPoint?
Yes.

2 If a Microsoft PowerPoint dialog box appears, tap or click the Save button to save any changes made to the presentation since the last save.

BTW

Certification
The Microsoft Office Specialist (MOS) program provides an opportunity for you to obtain a valuable industry credential — proof that you have the PowerPoint 2013 skills required by employers. For more information, visit the Certification resource on the Student Companion Site located on www.cengagebrain.com. For detailed instructions about accessing available resources, visit www.cengage.com/ct/studentdownload or see the inside back cover of this book.

BTW

Quick Reference
For a table that lists how to complete the tasks covered in this book using touch gestures, the mouse, ribbon, shortcut menu, and keyboard, see the Quick Reference Summary at the back of this book, or visit the Quick Reference resource on the Student Companion Site located on www.cengagebrain.com. For detailed instructions about accessing available resources, visit www.cengage.com/ct/studentdownload or see the inside back cover of this book.

Chapter Summary

In this chapter you have learned how to apply and change a document theme and variant, create a title slide and text slides with a bulleted list, insert photos and an illustration and then resize and move them on a slide, format and edit text, add a slide transition, view the presentation in Slide Show view, and print slides as handouts. The items listed below include all the new PowerPoint skills you have learned in this chapter, with the tasks grouped by activity.

Enter and Edit Text
Enter the Presentation Title (PPT 7)
Enter the Presentation Subtitle Paragraph (PPT 9)
Zoom a Slide (PPT 10)
Add a New Text Slide with a Bulleted List (PPT 15)
Enter a Slide Title (PPT 17)
Type a Multilevel Bulleted List (PPT 18)
Add a Slide with the Title Only Layout (PPT 23)
Add a New Slide and Enter a Slide Title and Headings (PPT 24)
Move to Another Slide in Normal View (PPT 29)
Duplicate a Slide (PPT 41)
Arrange a Slide (PPT 42)
Delete Text in a Placeholder (PPT 43)

Format a Slide
Choose a Document Theme and Variant (PPT 5)
Change the Theme (PPT 26)
Change the Variant (PPT 27)

Format Text
Italicize Text (PPT 11)
Increase Font Size (PPT 12, 22)

Change the Text Color (PPT 13)
Bold Text (PPT 21)

Enhance Slides with Pictures and a Transition
Insert a Picture from Office.com into the Title Slide (PPT 31)
Insert a Picture from Office.com into a Content Placeholder (PPT 34)
Proportionally Resize Pictures (PPT 36)
Move Pictures (PPT 39)
Add a Transition between Slides (PPT 45)

Run and Print a Slide Show
Change Document Properties (PPT 48)
Start Slide Show View (PPT 49)
Move Manually through Slides in a Slide Show (PPT 50)
Print a Presentation (PPT 52)

Select Text and Slide Elements
Select a Paragraph (PPT 11)
Select a Word (PPT 12)
Select a Text Placeholder (PPT 18)
Select a Group of Words (PPT 20)

CONSIDER THIS

What decisions will you need to make when creating your next presentation?
Use these guidelines as you complete the assignments in this chapter and create your own slide show decks outside of this class.

1. Determine the content you want to include on your slides.

2. Determine which theme and variant are appropriate.

3. Identify the slide layouts that best communicate your message.

4. Format various text elements to emphasize important points.

   a) Select appropriate font sizes.

   b) Emphasize important words with bold or italic type and color.

5. Locate graphical elements, such as photos and illustrations, that reinforce your message.

   a) Size and position them aesthetically on slides.

6. Determine a storage location for the presentation.

7. Determine the best method for distributing the presentation.

Apply Your Knowledge

Reinforce the skills and apply the concepts you learned in this chapter.

Modifying Character Formats and Paragraph Levels and Moving an Illustration

Note: To complete this assignment, you will be required to use the Data Files for Students. Visit www.cengage.com/ct/studentdownload for detailed instructions or contact your instructor for information about accessing the required files.

Instructions: Run PowerPoint. Open the presentation, Apply 1-1 Effective Writing, from the Data Files for Students.

The two slides in the presentation discuss steps to follow when writing a persuasive essay. The document you open is an unformatted presentation. You are to modify the document theme, indent the paragraphs, resize and move the photo, and format the text so the slides look like Figure 1–80 on this page and the next page.

Perform the following tasks:

1. Change the document theme to Ion.

2. On the title slide, use your name in place of Student Name and bold and italicize your name.

3. If requested by your instructor, change your first name to your grandmother's first name on the title slide.

4. Increase the title text font size to 60 point. Size and position the photo using the Smart Guides to align the image with the bottom of the title placeholder, as shown in Figure 1–80a.

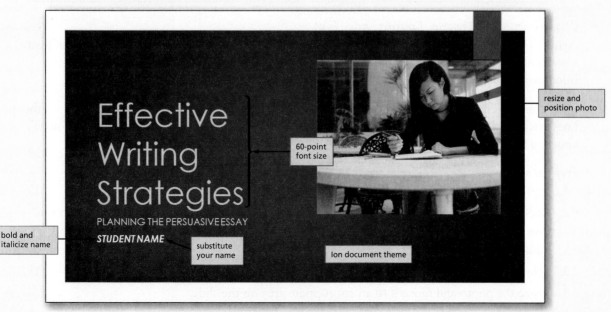

(a) Slide 1 (Title Slide with a Picture)
Figure 1–80

Continued >

Apply Your Knowledge *continued*

5. On Slide 2, increase the indent of the third and fourth paragraphs to second-level paragraphs. Then combine paragraphs six and seven (To change readers' minds? and To confirm opinions?) to read, To change readers' minds or confirm opinions?, as shown in Figure 1–80b. Increase the indent of this paragraph to second level.

6. Save the presentation using the file name, Apply 1-1 Effective Writing Strategies.

7. Submit the revised document in the format specified by your instructor.

8. ✳ In Step 5 you combined two paragraphs. How did this action improve the slide content?

(b) Slide 2 (Multilevel Bulleted List)
Figure 1–80 (Continued)

Extend Your Knowledge

Extend the skills you learned in this chapter and experiment with new skills. You may need to use Help to complete the assignment.

Changing Slide Theme, Layout, and Text
Note:　To complete this assignment, you will be required to use the Data Files for Students. Visit www.cengage.com/ct/studentdownload for detailed instructions or contact your instructor for information about accessing the required files.

Instructions:　Run PowerPoint. Open the presentation that you are going to prepare for your brother's horseback riding business, Extend 1-1 Horseback Riding, from the Data Files for Students. You will choose a theme, format slides, and create a closing slide.

Perform the following tasks:

1. Apply an appropriate document theme.

2. On Slide 1 (Figure 1–81), use your name in place of Student Name. Format the text on this slide using techniques you learned in this chapter, such as changing the font size and color and bolding and italicizing words.

3. Delete the bullets in the subtitle text.

4. Resize the photo and move it to an appropriate area on the slide.

5. On Slide 2, add bullets to the paragraphs in the Beginners and Advanced boxes, and then change the look of the default bullets.

6. On Slide 3, create paragraphs and adjust the paragraph levels to create a bulleted list. Edit the text so that the slide meets the 7 × 7 rule, which states that each line should have a maximum of seven words, and each slide should have a maximum of seven lines.

7. Create an appropriate closing slide using the title slide as a guide. Change the title text to, See you at the Trails!

8. The slides contain a variety of pictures downloaded from Office.com. Size and move them when necessary.

9. Apply an appropriate transition to all slides.

10. Save the presentation using the file name, Extend 1-1 Horseback Riding Lessons.

11. Submit the revised document in the format specified by your instructor.

12. If requested by your instructor, replace the word, you, with your mother's first name on the closing slide.

13. ☀ In this assignment, you changed the bullet style on Slide 2. Which bullet style did you select and why?

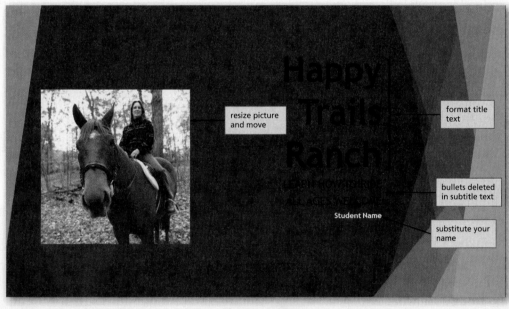

Figure 1–81

Analyze, Correct, Improve

Analyze a presentation, correct all errors, and improve it.

Correcting Formatting and List Levels

Note: To complete this assignment, you will be required to use the Data Files for Students. Visit www.cengage.com/ct/studentdownload for detailed instructions or contact your instructor for information about accessing the required files.

Instructions: Run PowerPoint. Open the presentation, Analyze 1-1 Math Tutor, from the Data Files for Students. As a part-time job while attending college, you decide to tutor students who are struggling with math. You decide to create a presentation promoting your service and begin with this document. Modify the slides by making the indicated corrections and improvements.

Continued >

Analyze, Correct, Improve *continued*

1. Correct

a. Change the document theme from Office Theme Dark, shown in Figure 1–82, to Organic with the rightmost color variant.

b. If requested by your instructor, change the Southtown Library Room number, 201, to your birth year on Slide 2.

c. Correct the spelling errors on Slides 2 and 3.

d. Use your name in place of Student Name on Slide 1.

2. Improve

a. Adjust the size of the picture on Slide 1 and move it to the left of the subtitle text.

b. Move Slide 2 to the end of the presentation so that it becomes the new Slide 3.

c. On Slide 2, increase the font size of the Slide 2 title text, A Math Tutor Is Your Answer, to 54 point. Increase the size of the picture and move it to fill the white space on the right of the bulleted list. Align the picture using the right and bottom Smart Guides.

d. On Slide 3, increase the font size of the title text, Schedule, to 60 point. Decrease the indent level for both bulleted lists to first level. Adjust the size of the picture and move it to the upper-right corner of the slide so that the upper edge of the image is aligned with the top edge of the title text placeholder.

e. Apply the same transition and duration to all slides.

f. Save the presentation using the file name, Analyze 1-1 – Math Tutor Info.

g. Submit the revised document in the format specified by your instructor.

3. ✳ Which errors existed in the starting file? How did decreasing the indent level of the bulleted lists on Slide 3 and increasing the title text on Slides 2 and 3 enhance the presentation? When you adjusted the pictures, how did you determine their final sizes?

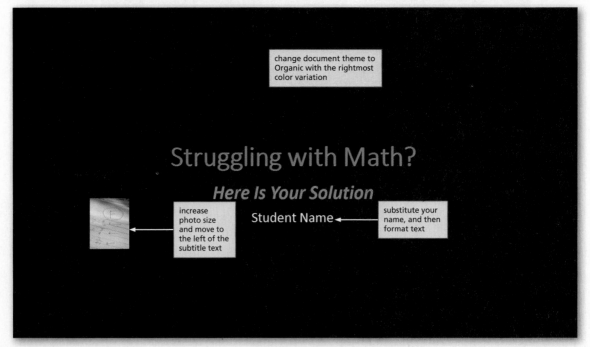

Figure 1–82

In the Labs

Design and/or create a presentation using the guidelines, concepts, and skills presented in this chapter. Labs 1 and 2, which increase in difficulty, require you to create solutions based on what you learned in the chapter; Lab 3 requires you to create a solution, which uses cloud and web technologies, by learning and investigating on your own from general guidance.

Lab 1: Creating a Presentation with Bulleted Lists, a Closing Slide, and Pictures

Problem: You are majoring in accounting and work part-time at a tax-filing service. Your clients have asked you numerous times what documents they should keep at home to support their tax returns. You decide to put together a presentation that would offer some basic guidelines about how to organize personal documents. You develop the outline shown in Figure 1–83 and then prepare the PowerPoint presentation shown in Figures 1–84a through 1–84e on pages PPT 62–64.

Files or Piles
 Document Storage and Retention at Home

Store and Retain
  In Home Office Safe
   Tax records for six years
   Pay stubs until W2 arrives
   Credit card statements
   Canceled checks
   Utility bills
  In Bank Safe Deposit Box
   Wills, deeds, and titles
   Birth and death certificates
   Passports
   Military records

Keep Indefinitely
  Personal health records
  Medical history
  Retirement benefit statements

General Rules
  Shred documents showing personal information
  Organize and store chronologically
  Keep list of important documents
   State their location
   Share with relative or friend

Figure 1–83

Continued >

In the Labs *continued*

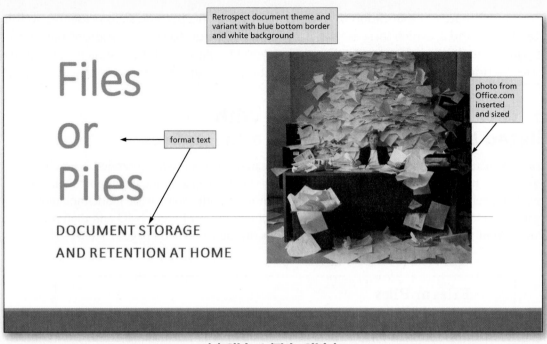

(a) Slide 1 (Title Slide)

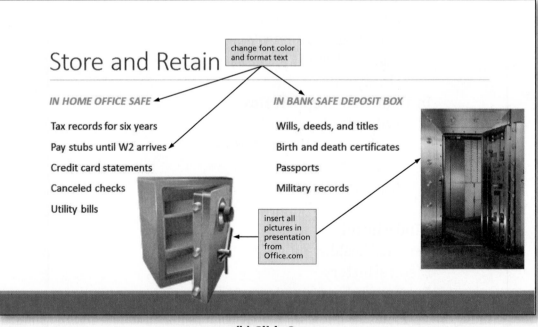

(b) Slide 2

Figure 1–84

(c) Slide 3

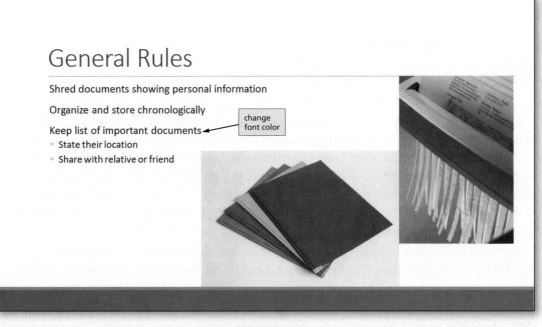

(d) Slide 4

Figure 1–84 (Continued)

Continued >

In the Labs *continued*

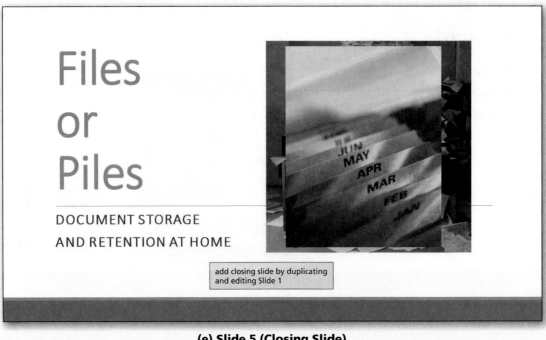

(e) Slide 5 (Closing Slide)

Figure 1–84 (Continued)

Instructions: Perform the following tasks:

1. Create a new presentation using the Retrospect document theme and select the variant with the blue bottom border and white background.

2. Using the typed outline illustrated in Figure 1–83 on page PPT 61, create the title slide shown in Figure 1–84a. Press the ENTER key to place each word on a separate line and divide the title into three lines, as shown in the figure. Increase the font size of the title text to 88 point and bold this text. Change the font color to Green (the sixth color from left in the Standard Colors row). Increase the font size of the subtitle text, DOCUMENT STORAGE AND RETENTION AT HOME, to 28 point and bold this text. Press the ENTER key to divide the subtitle into two lines, as shown in the figure. Find and insert the picture from the Office.com Clip Art collection. Size the picture and use the Smart Guides to position it as shown in the figure.

3. Using the typed outline in Figure 1–83, create the three text slides with lists and find and insert the pictures from the Office.com Clip Art collection. Size the pictures and use the Smart Guides to position these images, as shown in Figures 1–84b, 1–84c, and 1–84d. You may want to zoom the slides to help you align these graphic elements.

4. On Slide 2, change the font color in the left and right heading placeholders to Green and bold and italicize this text.

5. On Slides 2, 3 and 4, change the font color of the lists to Dark Blue (second color from right in the Standard Colors row).

6. Create a closing slide by duplicating Slide 1 and adding the photo using the Smart Guides to center it on top of the existing photo.

7. If requested by your instructor, use your father's first name in place of the word, Piles, and replace the word, or, with the word, for, on Slide 5.

8. Apply the Shred transition in the Exciting category to all slides. Change the duration to 4.5 seconds.

9. Tap or click the Start From Beginning button to start the show from the first slide. Then swipe or click to display each slide.

10. Save the presentation using the file name, Lab 1-1 Document Storage at Home.

11. Submit the document in the format specified by your instructor.

12. ✳ What is the significance of placing the neat file folders photo on top of the messy desk photo on the closing slide? Why did you change the font color on Slides 2, 3, and 4 to Dark Blue?

Lab 2: Creating a Presentation with Bulleted Lists and Pictures

Problem: The number of reported West Nile Virus (WNV) cases across the continental United States has been growing steadily. After a discussion in your biology class, your instructor assigned everyone in the class to research WNV and to outline the facts that were discussed. You use your class notes to create the outline shown in Figure 1–85 and then create the presentation shown in Figures 1–86a through 1–86d on pages PPT 66–68.

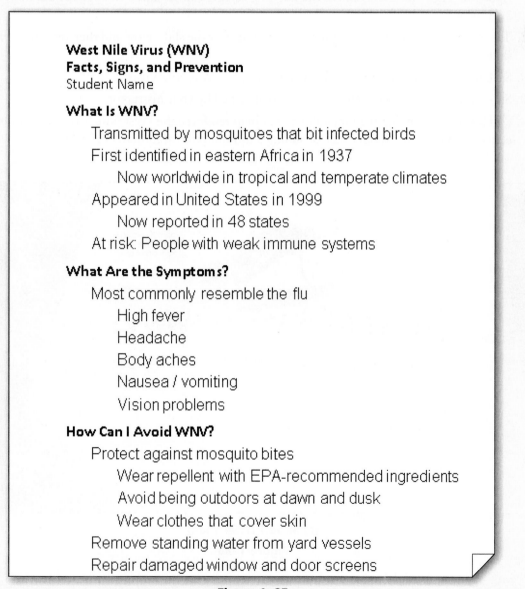

West Nile Virus (WNV)
Facts, Signs, and Prevention
Student Name

What Is WNV?
 Transmitted by mosquitoes that bit infected birds
 First identified in eastern Africa in 1937
  Now worldwide in tropical and temperate climates
 Appeared in United States in 1999
  Now reported in 48 states
 At risk: People with weak immune systems

What Are the Symptoms?
 Most commonly resemble the flu
  High fever
  Headache
  Body aches
  Nausea / vomiting
  Vision problems

How Can I Avoid WNV?
 Protect against mosquito bites
  Wear repellent with EPA-recommended ingredients
  Avoid being outdoors at dawn and dusk
  Wear clothes that cover skin
 Remove standing water from yard vessels
 Repair damaged window and door screens

Figure 1–85

Continued >

In the Labs *continued*

Instructions: Perform the following tasks:

1. Create a new presentation using the Facet document theme.

2. Using the outline illustrated in Figure 1–85 on the previous page, create the title slide shown in Figure 1–86a, using your name in place of Student Name.

3. If requested by your instructor, substitute the name of your hometown in place of your last name.

4. On Slide 1, bold the text, West Nile Virus (WNV). Decrease the font size of the text, Facts, Signs, and Prevention, to 44 point. Change the font color of all the title text to Red, Accent 5 (second color from right in the Theme Colors row).

5. Using the outline in Figure 1–85, create the three text slides with bulleted lists shown in Figures 1–86b, 1–86c, and 1–86d. Change the color of the title text on these three text slides to Red, Accent 5.

6. Add the pictures shown in Figures 1–86a through 1–86d from Office.com. Zoom the slide and then resize the pictures when necessary.

7. Apply the Page Curl transition in the Exciting category to all slides. Change the duration to 2.25 seconds.

8. Tap or click the Start From Beginning button to start the slide show and then display each slide.

9. Save the presentation using the file name, Lab 1–2 West Nile Virus.

10. Submit the revised document in the format specified by your instructor.

11. ✹ How does changing the font color to red help reinforce the West Nile Virus prevention concept? What is the significance of adding a mosquito illustration to every slide?

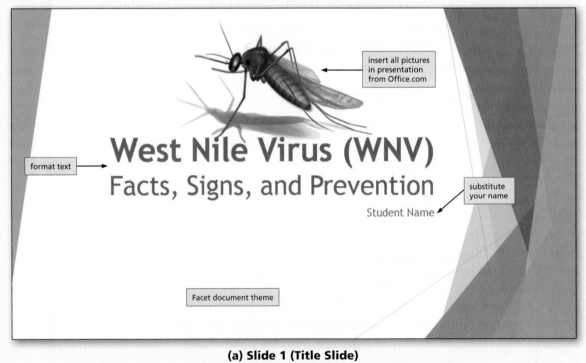

(a) Slide 1 (Title Slide)

Figure 1–86

(b) Slide 2

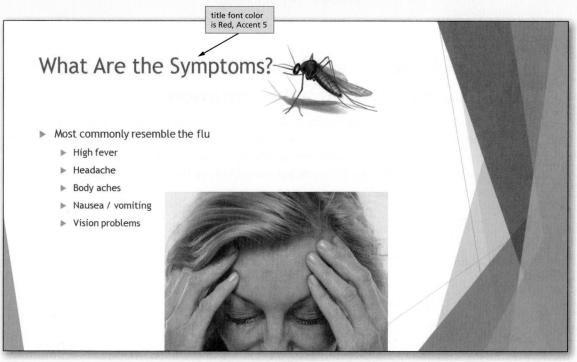

(c) Slide 3

Figure 1–86 (Continued)

Continued >

In the Labs *continued*

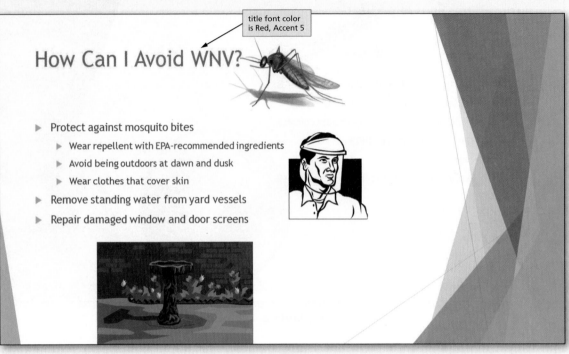

(d) Slide 4

Figure 1–86 (Continued)

Lab 3: Expand Your World: Cloud and Web Technologies
Modifying and Exporting a Presentation

Problem: Your local library is planning events to celebrate Hispanic Heritage Month, and you are part of a committee to publicize the event. You want to share the title slide of your preliminary PowerPoint presentation with fellow committee members, so you have decided to store the file on SkyDrive. You are going to modify the slide you have created thus far shown in Figure 1–87 and save it to SkyDrive.

Note: To complete this assignment, you will be required to use the Data Files for Students. Visit www.cengage.com/ct/studentdownload for detailed instructions or contact your instructor for information about accessing the required files.

Instructions:
1. Open the Lab 1–3 Hispanic Heritage file.
2. Insert another picture on the title slide in the area indicated in Figure 1–87.
3. If requested to do so by your instructor, change the city to the town where you were born.
4. Save the presentation using the file name, Lab 1–3 Heritage Month.
5. Export the file to your SkyDrive in the Chapter 01 folder in the PowerPoint folder.
6. Submit the assignment in the format specified by your instructor.
7. ✹ When would you save one of your files for school or your job to SkyDrive? Do you think using SkyDrive enhances collaboration efforts? Why?

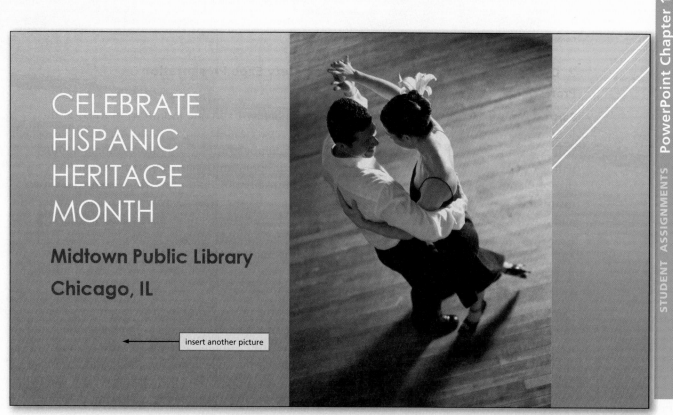

Figure 1–87   Slide 1 (Title Slide)

✳ Consider This: Your Turn

Apply your creative thinking and problem-solving skills to design and implement a solution.

1. Design and Create a Presentation about Mars Exploration

Personal

Part 1:   Your astronomy class is studying the solar system, and you have been assigned the topic of the Mars Curiosity rover and its exploration of that planet. You have learned that the rover was launched from Cape Canaveral, Florida, on November 26, 2011, and landed in the Gale Crater on Mars on August 6, 2012. The mission was scheduled to last two years and had the major goal of assessing whether Mars was or is capable of supporting life. The Curiosity rover is the size of a car and has a MastCam equipped with two camera systems to take photos of the landscape as it maneuvers around the rocky surface. The rover also can scoop up samples of the Martian soil, fire a laser at rocks as far away as nine feet (2.7 meters), and make weather station readings. Use the concepts and techniques you learned in the chapter to create a PowerPoint presentation with a suitable theme, a title slide, and three text slides with bulleted lists. Add pictures from Office.com and apply a transition. Submit your assignment in the format specified by your instructor.

Part 2:   ✳ You made several decisions while creating the presentation in this assignment: what theme to use, where to place text, how to format the text (font, font size, paragraph alignment, bulleted paragraphs, italics, bold, color). You also decided which graphical images to use, where to position the graphical images, if a closing slide would be useful, and which transition would be most effective. What was the rationale behind each of these decisions? When you proofed the document, what further revisions did you make and why? Where would you recommend showing this slide show?

Continued >

Consider This: Your Turn *continued*

2. Design and Create a Fire Department Safety Expo Presentation
Professional

Part 1: Your local fire department is sponsoring a Safety Expo one month from today at the local hardware store. The chief has asked you to prepare a slide show promoting the event, which will be held from noon to 5 p.m. A wide variety of demonstrations and informational booths will be present. They include: firefighters from your community's fire department, who will discuss home emergency planning, proper car seat installation, and fire extinguisher use; a local insurance agent, who will distribute tote bags filled with materials regarding adequate home and rental insurance coverage and also a nine-volt battery for a smoke alarm; and a children's workshop, where participants under 10 years of age can build a picture frame. Use the concepts and techniques presented in this chapter to develop and format this slide show with at least four slides with bulleted lists. Add pictures from Office.com and apply a transition. Submit your assignment in the format specified by your instructor.

Part 2: ✺ You made several decisions while creating the presentation in this assignment: what theme to use, where to place text, how to format the text (font, font size, paragraph alignment, bulleted paragraphs, italics, bold, color). You also decided which graphical images to use, where to position the graphical images, if a closing slide would be useful, and which transition would be most effective. What was the rationale behind each of these decisions? When you proofed the document, what further revisions did you make and why? Where would you recommend showing this slide show?

3. Design and Create a Presentation about Commemorative Postage Stamps
Research and Collaboration

Part 1: Stamp collecting is one of the world's more popular indoor hobbies. Collectors often seek postage stamps pertaining to a particular interest, such as birds, flowers, famous people, or ships. Have each member of your team gather information on these topics: stamp collecting equipment, popular commemorative stamps issued, current commemorative stamps for sale at your local post office, and rare stamps. After coordinating these facts, use the concepts and techniques presented in this chapter to prepare a presentation with a minimum of four slides that explore the subject of stamp collection. Select a suitable theme and include a title slide, bulleted lists, and a closing slide. Add pictures from Office.com and apply a transition. Submit your assignment in the format specified by your instructor.

Part 2: ✺ You made several decisions while creating the presentation in this assignment: what theme to use, where to place text, how to format the text (font, font size, paragraph alignment, bulleted paragraphs, italics, bold, color). You also decided which graphical images to use, where to position the graphical images, if a closing slide would be useful, and which transition would be most effective. What was the rationale behind each of these decisions? When you proofed the document, what further revisions did you make and why? Where would you recommend showing this slide show?

Learn Online

Reinforce what you learned in this chapter with games, exercises, training, and many other online activities and resources.

Student Companion Site   Reinforcement activities and resources are available at no additional cost on www.cengagebrain.com. Visit www.cengage.com/ct/studentdownload for detailed instructions about accessing the resources available at the Student Companion Site.

SAM   Put your skills into practice with SAM! If you have a SAM account, go to www.cengage.com/sam2013 to access SAM assignments for this chapter.

1 Creating a Worksheet and a Chart

Microsoft product screenshots used with permission from Microsoft Corporation.

Objectives

You will have mastered the material in this chapter when you can:

- Describe the Excel worksheet
- Enter text and numbers
- Use the Sum button to sum a range of cells
- Enter a simple function
- Copy the contents of a cell to a range of cells using the fill handle
- Apply cell styles
- Format cells in a worksheet

- Create a 3-D pie chart
- Change a worksheet name and worksheet tab color
- Change document properties
- Preview and print a worksheet
- Use the AutoCalculate area to display statistics
- Correct errors on a worksheet

1 | Creating a Worksheet and a Chart

Introduction

Almost any organization collects vast amounts of data. Often, data is consolidated into a summary so that people in the organization better understand the meaning of the data. An Excel worksheet allows data to be summarized and charted easily. A chart conveys a visual representation of data. In this chapter, you will create a worksheet that includes a chart. The data in the worksheet and chart includes data for a personal budget worksheet that contains monthly estimates on budget amounts.

Project — Worksheet and a Chart

The project in this chapter follows proper design guidelines and uses Excel to create the worksheet and chart shown in Figure 1–1a and Figure 1–1b. The worksheet contains budget data for Bob Gleamin. He wants to estimate what his personal budget will look like for the year, so he has gathered together the information on how much he pays for various expenses and has a list of his current incomes. Now, he wants an easy-to-read worksheet using this information to see how much he will be ahead or behind each month to aid him in planning his budget. In addition, a 3-D pie chart is required that shows the estimated expenses portion for each of the 12 months.

Figure 1–1 (a) Personal Budget Worksheet

Figure 1–1 (b) Pie Chart Showing Monthly Expenses by Category

The first step in creating an effective worksheet is to make sure you understand what is required. The person or persons requesting the worksheet should supply their requirements in a requirements document. A requirements document includes a needs statement, a source of data, a summary of calculations, and any other special requirements for the worksheet, such as charting and web support. Figure 1–2 shows the requirements document for the new workbook to be created in this chapter.

Worksheet Title	Personal Budget Worksheet
Needs	A yearly projection of Bob Gleamin's personal budget
Source of data	The data supplied by Bob Gleamin includes monthly estimates, including income and expenses
Calculations	The following calculations must be made: 1. For each month, a total for incomes and expenses 2. For each budget item, a total for the item 3. A total for all incomes and expenses 4. Net = income – expenses

Figure 1–2

Roadmap

In this chapter, you will learn how to perform basic workbook tasks using Excel. The following roadmap identifies general activities you will perform as you progress through this chapter:

Descriptive, Overview Roadmap

1. ENTER TEXT in a blank worksheet.
2. CALCULATE SUMS AND USE FORMULAS in the worksheet.
3. SAVE the WORKBOOK using the file name, Bob Gleamin Budget.
4. FORMAT TEXT in the worksheet.
5. INSERT a pie CHART into the worksheet.
6. Assign a NAME to the worksheet TAB.
7. PREVIEW AND PRINT the WORKSHEET.

At the beginning of step instructions throughout the chapter, you will see an abbreviated form of this roadmap. The abbreviated roadmap uses colors to indicate chapter progress: gray means the chapter is beyond that activity, blue means the task being shown is covered in that activity, and black means that activity is yet to be covered. For example, the following abbreviated roadmap indicates the chapter would be showing a task in the Save Workbook activity.

1 ENTER TEXT | 2 CALCULATE SUMS & USE FORMULAS | 3 SAVE WORKBOOK | 4 FORMAT TEXT
5 INSERT CHART | 6 NAME TAB | 7 PREVIEW & PRINT WORKSHEET

CONSIDER THIS

The key to developing a useful worksheet is careful planning. Careful planning can reduce your effort significantly and result in a worksheet that is accurate, easy to read, flexible, and useful. When analyzing a problem and designing a worksheet solution, what steps should you follow?

- Define the problem, including need, source of data, calculations, charting, and web or special requirements.
- Design the worksheet.
- Enter the data and formulas.
- Test the worksheet.

For an introduction to Windows and instruction about how to perform basic Windows tasks, read the Office and Windows chapter at the beginning of this book, where you can learn how to resize windows, change screen resolution, create folders, move and rename files, use Windows Help, and much more.

After carefully reviewing the requirements document (Figure 1–2 on the previous page) and making the necessary decisions, the next step is to design a solution or draw a sketch of the worksheet based on the requirements, including titles, column and row headings, the location of data values, and the 3-D pie chart, as shown in Figure 1–3. The dollar signs and commas that you see in the sketch of the worksheet indicate formatted numeric values.

With a good understanding of the requirements document, an understanding of the necessary decisions, and a sketch of the worksheet, the next step is to use Excel to create the worksheet and chart.

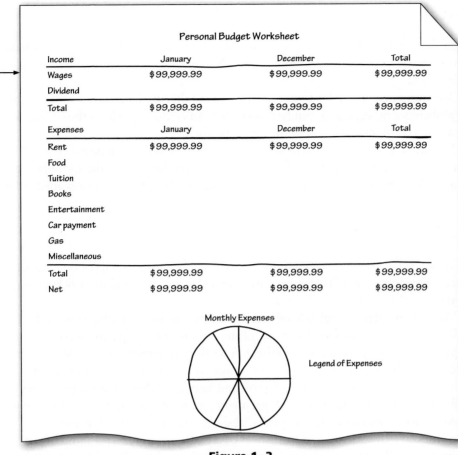

sketch of worksheet and chart

Personal Budget Worksheet

Income	January	December	Total
Wages	$99,999.99	$99,999.99	$99,999.99
Dividend			
Total	$99,999.99	$99,999.99	$99,999.99
Expenses	January	December	Total
Rent	$99,999.99	$99,999.99	$99,999.99
Food			
Tuition			
Books			
Entertainment			
Car payment			
Gas			
Miscellaneous			
Total	$99,999.99	$99,999.99	$99,999.99
Net	$99,999.99	$99,999.99	$99,999.99

Monthly Expenses

Legend of Expenses

Figure 1–3

To Run Excel and Create a Blank Workbook

If you are using a computer to step through the project in this chapter and you want your screens to match the figures in this book, you should change your screen's resolution to 1366 × 768. For information about how to change a computer's resolution, refer to the Office and Windows chapter at the beginning of this book.

The following steps, which assume Windows is running, use the Start screen or the Search box to run Excel based on a typical installation. You may need to ask your instructor how to run Excel on your computer. For a detailed example of the procedure summarized below, refer to the Office and Windows chapter.

1 Scroll the Start screen for an Excel 2013 tile. If your Start screen contains an Excel 2013 tile, tap or click it to run Excel and then proceed to Step 5; if the Start screen does not contain the Excel 2013 tile, proceed to the next step to search for the Excel app.

2 Swipe in from the right edge of the screen or point to the upper-right corner of the screen to display the Charms bar and then tap or click the Search charm on the Charms bar to display the Search menu.

3 Type **Excel** as the search text in the Search box and watch the search results appear in the Apps list.

4 Tap or click Excel 2013 in the search results to run Excel.

5 Tap or click the Blank workbook thumbnail on the Excel start screen to create a blank workbook and display it in the Excel window.

6 If the Excel window is not maximized, tap or click the Maximize button on its title bar to maximize the window.

One of the few differences between Windows 7 and Windows 8 occurs in the steps to run Excel. If you are using Windows 7, click the Start button, type **Excel** in the 'Search programs and files' text box, click Excel 2013, and then, if necessary, maximize the Excel window. For detailed steps to run Excel in Windows 7, refer to the Office and Windows chapter at the beginning of this book. For a summary of the steps, refer to the Quick Reference located at the back of this book.

BTW
BTWs
For a complete list of the BTWs found in the margins of this book, visit the BTW resource on the Student Companion Site located on www.cengagebrain.com. For detailed instructions about accessing available resources, visit www.cengage.com/ct/studentdownload or contact your instructor for information about accessing the required files.

If you are using your finger on a touch screen and are having difficulty completing the steps in this chapter, consider using a stylus. Many people find it easier to be precise with a stylus than with a finger. In addition, with a stylus you see the pointer. If you still are having trouble completing the steps with a stylus, try using a mouse.

For an introduction to Office and instruction about how to perform basic tasks in Office apps, read the Office and Windows chapter at the beginning of this book, where you can learn how to run an application, use the ribbon, save a file, open a file, exit an application, use Help, and much more.

BTW

Touch Screen Differences
The Office and Windows interfaces may vary if you are using a touch screen. For this reason, you might notice that the function or appearance of your touch screen differs slightly from this chapter's presentation.

BTW

Q&As
For a complete list of the Q&As found in many of the step-by-step sequences in this book, visit the Q&A resource on the Student Companion Site located on www.cengagebrain .com. For detailed instructions about accessing available resources, visit www.cengage .com/ct/studentdownload or contact your instructor for information about accessing the required files.

Selecting a Cell

To enter data into a cell, you first must select it. The easiest way to **select** a cell (make it active) is to tap it or use the mouse to move the block plus sign pointer to the cell and then click.

An alternative method is to use the arrow keys that are located just to the right of the alphanumeric keys on a standard keyboard. An arrow key selects the cell adjacent to the active cell in the direction of the arrow on the key.

You know a cell is selected, or active, when a heavy border surrounds the cell and the active cell reference appears in the Name box on the left side of the formula bar. Excel also changes the active cell's column heading and row heading to a shaded color.

Entering Text

In Excel, any set of characters containing a letter, hyphen (as in a telephone number), or space is considered text. **Text** is used to place titles, such as worksheet titles, column titles, and row titles, on the worksheet.

Worksheet titles and subtitles should be as brief and meaningful as possible. A worksheet title could include the name of the organization, department, or a description of the content of the worksheet. A worksheet subtitle, if included, could include a more detailed description of the content of the worksheet. Examples of worksheet titles are December 2014 Payroll and Year 2015 Projected Budget, and examples of subtitles are Marketing Department and Rent and Utilities, respectively.

As shown in Figure 1–4, data in a worksheet often is identified by row and column titles so that the user of a worksheet easily can identify the meaning of the data. Rows typically contain information that is similar to items in a list. Columns typically contain descriptive information about items in rows or contain information that helps to group the data in the worksheet. Examples of row titles are Income and Total, and examples of column titles are Wages and Gas.

Figure 1–4

To Enter the Worksheet Titles

As shown in Figure 1–4, the worksheet title, Personal Budget Worksheet, identifies the purpose for which the worksheet is being created in Chapter 1. The worksheet subtitle, Monthly Estimates, identifies the type of data contained in the worksheet. *Why? A title and subtitle help the reader to understand clearly what the worksheet contains.*

The following steps enter the worksheet titles in cells A1 and A2. Later in this chapter, the worksheet titles will be formatted so that they appear as shown in Figure 1–4.

- If necessary, tap or click cell A1 to make cell A1 the active cell (Figure 1–5).

Figure 1–5

- Type **Personal Budget Worksheet** in cell A1 and then point to the Enter box in the formula bar to prepare to enter text in the active cell (Figure 1–6).

Q&A Why did the appearance of the formula bar change? Excel displays the title in the formula bar and in cell A1. When you begin typing a cell entry, Excel displays two additional boxes in the formula bar: the Cancel box and the Enter box. Tapping or clicking the **Enter box** completes an entry. Tapping or clicking the **Cancel box** cancels an entry.

Figure 1–6

3

- Tap or click the Enter box to complete the entry and enter the worksheet title (Figure 1–7).

Q&A Why does the entered text appear in three cells?
When the text is longer than the width of a cell, Excel displays the overflow characters in adjacent cells to the right as long as those adjacent cells contain no data. If the adjacent cells contain data, Excel hides the overflow characters. Excel displays the overflow characters in the formula bar whenever that cell is the active cell.

Figure 1–7

4

- Tap or click cell A2 to select it.

- Type **Monthly Estimates** as the cell entry.

- Tap or click the Enter box to complete the entry and enter the worksheet subtitle (Figure 1–8).

Q&A What happens when I tap or click the Enter box?
When you complete an entry by tapping or clicking the Enter box, the insertion point disappears and the cell in which the text is entered remains the active cell.

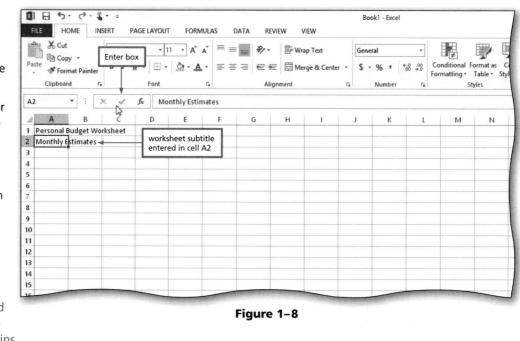

Figure 1–8

Other Ways

1. To complete entry, tap or click any cell other than active cell

2. To complete entry, press ENTER

3. To complete entry, press HOME, PAGE UP, PAGE DOWN, or END

4. To complete entry, press UP ARROW, DOWN ARROW, LEFT ARROW, or RIGHT ARROW

AutoCorrect

The **AutoCorrect feature** of Excel works behind the scenes, correcting common mistakes when you complete a text entry in a cell. AutoCorrect makes three types of corrections for you:

1. Corrects two initial uppercase letters by changing the second letter to lowercase.

2. Capitalizes the first letter in the names of days.

3. Replaces commonly misspelled words with their correct spelling. For example, it will change the misspelled word *recieve* to *receive* when you complete the entry. AutoCorrect will correct the spelling of hundreds of commonly misspelled words automatically.

BTW

The Ribbon and Screen Resolution
Excel may change how the groups and buttons within the groups appear on the ribbon, depending on the computer's screen resolution. Thus, your ribbon may look different from the ones in this book if you are using a screen resolution other than 1366 × 768.

To Enter Column Titles

1 ENTER TEXT | 2 CALCULATE SUMS & USE FORMULAS | 3 SAVE WORKBOOK | 4 FORMAT TEXT
5 INSERT CHART | 6 NAME TAB | 7 PREVIEW & PRINT WORKSHEET

The column titles in row 3 shown in Figure 1–4 (Income, January, February, March, April, May, June, July, August, September, October, November, December, and Total) identify the numbers in each column in the first part of the worksheet. The column titles in row 8 (Expenses, January, February, March, April, May, June, July, August, September, October, November, December, and Total) identify the numbers in each column in the second part of the worksheet. In the case of the Personal Budget Worksheet data, the month names identify the estimates for the budget for each month using the income or expense type, depending on which part you are reviewing.

To enter the column titles in row 3, select the appropriate cell and then enter the text. The following steps enter the column titles in row 3. **Why?** *Data entered in columns should be identified using column titles to identify what the column contains.*

1

- Tap or click cell A3 to make it the active cell.

- Type **Income** to begin entry of a column title in the active cell (Figure 1–9).

Q&A
What is the vertical line in cell A1?
The text in cell A1 is followed by the insertion point. The **insertion point** is a blinking vertical line that indicates where the next typed character will appear.

Figure 1–9

2

- If you are using a touch screen, tap cell B3; if you are using a mouse, press the RIGHT ARROW key to enter a column title and make the cell to the right the active cell (Figure 1–10).

Why is the RIGHT ARROW key used to complete the entry in the cell?

If the next entry you want to enter is in an adjacent cell, use the arrow keys to complete the entry in a cell. When you press an arrow key to complete an entry, the adjacent cell in the direction of the arrow (up, down, left, or right) becomes the active cell. If the next entry is in a nonadjacent cell, complete the current entry by tapping or clicking the next cell in which you plan to enter data. You also can tap or click the Enter box or press the ENTER key and then tap or click the appropriate cell for the next entry.

Figure 1–10

3

- Repeat Steps 1 and 2 to enter the remaining column titles; that is, enter **January** in cell B3, **February** in cell C3, **March** in cell D3, **April** in cell E3, **May** in cell F3, **June** in cell G3, **July** in cell H3, **August** in cell I3, **September** in cell J3, **October** in cell K3, **November** in cell L3, **December** in cell M3, and **Total** in cell N3 (complete the last entry in cell N3 by tapping or clicking the Enter box in the formula bar).

- Tap or click cell A8 to select it.

- Repeat Steps 1 and 2 to enter the remaining column titles; that is, enter **Expenses** in cell A8, **January** in cell B8, **February** in cell C8, **March** in cell D8, **April** in cell E8, **May** in cell F8, **June** in cell G8, **July** in cell H8, **August** in cell I8, **September** in cell J8, **October** in cell K8, **November** in cell L8, **December** in cell M8, and **Total** in cell N8 (complete the last entry in cell N8 by tapping or clicking the Enter box in the formula bar) (Figure 1–11).

Figure 1–11

To Enter Row Titles

The next step in developing the worksheet for this project is to enter the row titles in column A. For the Personal Budget Worksheet data, the list of income types and expense types make up the row titles. It is likely that in the future, Bob Gleamin may add more income or expense items. Each income or expense item, therefore, should be placed in its own row. The row titles in column A for income (Wages, Dividends, and Total), expenses (Rent, Food, Tuition, Books, Entertainment, Car Payment, Gas, Miscellaneous, and Total), and net income (Net) identify the numbers in each row.

This process for entering row titles is similar to the process for entering column titles. The following steps enter the row titles in the worksheet.

- Tap or click cell A4 to select it.

- Type **Wages** and then tap cell A5 or press the DOWN ARROW key to enter a row title (Figure 1–12).

Figure 1–12

2

- Repeat Step 1 to enter the remaining row titles in column A; that is, enter **Dividends** in cell A5, **Total** in cell A6, **Rent** in cell A9, **Food** in cell A10, **Tuition** in cell A11, **Books** in cell A12, **Entertainment** in cell A13, **Car Payment** in cell A14, **Gas** in cell A15, **Miscellaneous** in cell A16, **Total** in cell A17, and **Net** in cell A19 (Figure 1–13).

Figure 1–13

Q&A
Why is the text left-aligned in the cells?
When you enter text, Excel automatically left-aligns the text in the cell. Excel treats any combination of numbers, spaces, and nonnumeric characters as text. For example, Excel recognizes the following entries as text: 401AX21, 921–231, 619 321, 883XTY
You can change the text alignment in a cell by realigning it. Other alignment techniques are discussed later in this chapter.

Entering Numbers

In Excel, you can enter numbers into cells to represent amounts. A **number** can contain only the following characters:

0 1 2 3 4 5 6 7 8 9 + − ( ) , / . $ % E e

If a cell entry contains any other keyboard character (including spaces), Excel interprets the entry as text and treats it accordingly. The use of special characters is explained when they are used in this book.

To Enter Numbers

1 ENTER TEXT | 2 CALCULATE SUMS & USE FORMULAS | 3 SAVE WORKBOOK | 4 FORMAT TEXT
5 INSERT CHART | 6 NAME TAB | 7 PREVIEW & PRINT WORKSHEET

The Personal Budget Worksheet numbers used in Chapter 1 are summarized in Table 1–1. These numbers, which represent yearly income and expenses amounts, must be entered in rows 4–5 and 9–16.

Table 1–1 Personal Budget Worksheet												
Income	**January**	**February**	**March**	**April**	**May**	**June**	**July**	**August**	**September**	**October**	**November**	**Decembe**
Wages	1000.29	1000.29	1000.29	1000.29	1000.29	1000.29	1000.29	1000.29	1000.29	1000.29	1000.29	1000.29
Dividends	4000.75	0	0	0	0	0	0	0	4000.75	0	0	0

Expenses	**January**	**February**	**March**	**April**	**May**	**June**	**July**	**August**	**September**	**October**	**November**	**Decembe**
Rent	400.89	400.89	400.89	400.89	400.89	400.89	400.89	400.89	400.89	400.89	400.89	400.89
Food	300	300	300	300	300	300	300	300	300	300	300	300
Tuition	1500	0	0	0	0	0	0	1500	0	0	0	0
Books	500	0	0	0	0	0	0	500	0	0	0	0
Entertainment	100	100	100	100	100	100	100	100	100	100	100	100
Car Payment	154.79	154.79	154.79	154.79	154.79	154.79	154.79	154.79	154.79	154.79	154.79	154.79
Gas	100	100	100	100	150	150	150	100	100	100	100	100
Miscellaneous	100	100	100	100	100	100	100	100	100	100	100	100

The following steps enter the numbers in Table 1–1 one row at a time.

1

- Tap or click cell B4 to select it.

- Type 1000.29 and then if you are using a touch screen, tap cell C4. If you are using a mouse, press the RIGHT ARROW key to enter the data in the selected cell and make the cell to the right (cell C4) the active cell (Figure 1–14).

Figure 1–14

Q&A

Do I need to enter dollar signs, commas, or trailing zeros for the amounts?

You are not required to type dollar signs, commas, or trailing zeros. When you enter a dollar value that has cents, however, you must add the decimal point and the numbers representing the cents. Later in this chapter, the numbers will be formatted to use dollar signs, commas, and trailing zeros to improve the appearance and readability of the numbers.

2

- Enter   **1000.29**   in cells C4, D4, E4, F4, G4, H4, I4, J4, K4, L4, and M4 to complete the first row of numbers in the worksheet (Figure 1–15).

Q&A | Why are the numbers right-aligned?

When you enter numeric data in a cell, Excel recognizes the values as numbers and right-aligns the values in order to properly vertically align decimal and integer values. For example, values entered below those entered in this step automatically will be right-aligned so that the decimals of the values properly align.

Figure 1–15

3

- Tap or click cell B5 to select it and complete the entry in the previously selected cell.

- Enter the remaining personal budget numbers provided in Table 1–1 on page EX 12 for each of the nine remaining budget items in rows 5 and 9–16 to finish entering numbers in the worksheet (Figure 1–16).

Q&A | Why did tapping or clicking cell B5 complete the entry in cell M4?

Selecting another cell completes the entry in the previously selected cell in the same way as pressing the ENTER key, pressing an arrow key, or tapping or clicking the Enter box in the formula bar. In the next set of steps, the entry of the number in cell B5 will be completed by selecting another cell.

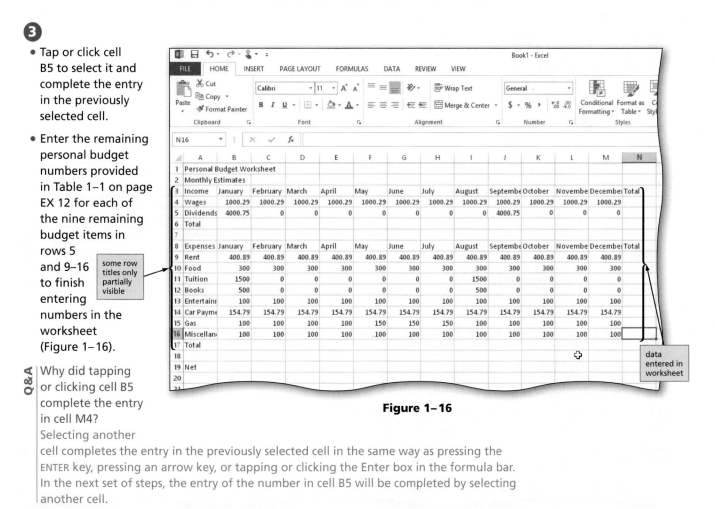

Figure 1–16

Calculating a Sum

The next step in creating the worksheet is to perform any necessary calculations, such as calculating the column and row totals. When you use functions, Excel performs the calculations for you, which helps to prevent errors and allows you to work more efficiently.

To Sum a Column of Numbers

1 ENTER TEXT | 2 CALCULATE SUMS & USE FORMULAS | 3 SAVE WORKBOOK | 4 FORMAT TEXT
5 INSERT CHART | 6 NAME TAB | 7 PREVIEW & PRINT WORKSHEET

As stated in the requirements document in Figure 1–2 on page EX 3, totals are required for each month and each budget item. The first calculation is to determine the total income for the Wages and Dividends in the month of January in column B. To calculate this value in cell B6, Excel must add, or sum, the numbers in cells B4 and B5. The **SUM function** adds all the numbers in a range of cells. *Why? Excel's SUM function provides a convenient means to accomplish this task.*

A **range** is a series of two or more adjacent cells in a column or row or a rectangular group of cells. For example, the group of adjacent cells B4 and B5 is called a range. Many Excel operations, such as summing numbers, are performed on a range of cells.

After the total income for a month in column B is determined, the totals for the remaining months for income, the totals for the expenses, and the totals for budget item will be determined. The following steps sum the numbers in column B.

1
- Tap or click cell B6 to make it the active cell and complete the entry in the previously selected cell.
- Tap or click the Sum button (HOME tab | Editing group) to display a formula in the formula bar and in the active cell (Figure 1–17).

Q&A

What if my screen displays a Sum menu?
If you are using a touch screen, you may not have a separate Sum button and Sum arrow. In this case, select the desired option on the Sum menu.

How does Excel know which cells to sum?
When you enter the SUM function using the Sum button on the ribbon, Excel automatically selects what it considers to be your choice of the range to sum. When proposing the range to sum, Excel first looks for a range of cells with numbers above the active cell and then to the left. If Excel proposes the wrong range, you can correct it by dragging through the correct range before pressing the ENTER key. You also can enter the correct range by typing the beginning cell reference, a colon (:), and the ending cell reference.

Figure 1–17

● Tap or click the Enter box in the formula bar to enter a sum in the active cell.

Q&A

◀ What is the purpose of the Sum arrow?

If you tap or click the Sum arrow on the right side of the Sum button (HOME tab | Editing group) (shown in Figure 1–17), Excel displays a list of often-used functions from which you can choose. The list includes functions that allow you to determine the average, the number of items in the selected range, the maximum value, or the minimum value of a range of numbers.

❸

● Repeat Steps 1 and 2 to enter the SUM function in cell B17 (Figure 1–18).

Figure 1–18

Other Ways

1. Tap or click Insert Function button in formula bar, select SUM in Select a function list, tap or click OK button (Insert Function dialog box),

tap or click OK button (Function Arguments dialog box)

2. Tap or click Sum arrow (HOME tab | Editing group), tap or click More Functions in list, tap

or click SUM (Insert Function dialog box), tap or click OK button, select range (Function Arguments dialog box), tap or click OK button

3. Type **=s** in cell, select SUM in list, select range, tap or click Enter box

4. Press ALT+EQUAL SIGN (=) twice

Using the Fill Handle to Copy a Cell to Adjacent Cells

Excel also must calculate the totals for income during each month in cells C6:M6. Table 1–2 on the next page illustrates the similarities between the entry in cell B6 and the entries required to sum the totals in cells C6, D6, E6, F6, G6, H6, I6, J6, K6, L6, and M6.

To place the SUM functions in range C6:M6, you could follow the same steps shown previously in Figure 1–17 and Figure 1–18. A second, more efficient method, however, is to copy the SUM function from cell B6 to the range C6:M6. The cell being copied is called the **source area** or **copy area**. The range of cells receiving the copy is called the **destination area** or **paste area**.

Table 1–2 Sum Function Entries in Row 6

Cell	SUM Function Entries	Result
B6	=SUM(B4:B5)	Sums cells B4 and B5
C6	=SUM(C4:C5)	Sums cells C4 and C5
D6	=SUM(D4:D5)	Sums cells D4 and D5
E6	=SUM(E4:E5)	Sums cells E4 and E5
F6	=SUM(F4:F5)	Sums cells F4 and F5
G6	=SUM(G4:G5)	Sums cells G4 and G5
H6	=SUM(H4:H5)	Sums cells H4 and H5
I6	=SUM(I4:I5)	Sums cells I4 and I5
J6	=SUM(J4:J5)	Sums cells J4 and J5
K6	=SUM(K4:K5)	Sums cells K4 and K5
L6	=SUM(L4:L5)	Sums cells L4 and L5
M6	=SUM(M4:M5)	Sums cells M4 and M5

Although the SUM function entries in Table 1–2 are similar, they are not exact copies. The range in each SUM function entry uses cell references that are one column to the right of the previous column. When you copy formulas that include cell references, Excel automatically adjusts them for each new position, resulting in the SUM function entries illustrated in Table 1–2. Each adjusted cell reference is called a **relative reference**.

To Copy a Cell to Adjacent Cells in a Row

1 ENTER TEXT | 2 CALCULATE SUMS & USE FORMULAS | 3 SAVE WORKBOOK | 4 FORMAT TEXT
5 INSERT CHART | 6 NAME TAB | 7 PREVIEW & PRINT WORKSHEET

The easiest way to copy the SUM formula from cell B6 to cells C6:M6 is to use the fill handle. *Why? Using the fill handle means that Excel creates the formulas for you.* The **fill handle** is the small black square located in the lower-right corner of the heavy border around the active cell. The following steps use the fill handle to copy cell B6 to the adjacent cells C6:M6.

1

- With cell B6 active, if you are using a touch screen, press and hold cell B6 to display the mini toolbar, then tap AutoFill on the mini toolbar; if you are using a mouse, point to the fill handle to activate it (Figure 1–19).

Q&A
Why is my fill handle not a black square? If you are using a touch screen, the fill handle appears as a black and white rectangle with a blue down arrow in it.

Figure 1–19

2

- Drag the fill handle to select the destination area, range C6:M6, to display a shaded border around the source area and the destination area (Figure 1–20). Do not lift your finger from the screen or release the mouse button.

Figure 1–20

3

- Lift your finger from the screen or release the mouse button to copy the SUM function from the active cell to the destination area and calculate the sums (Figure 1–21).

Q&A What is the purpose of the 'Auto Fill Options' button? When you copy one range to another, Excel displays an 'Auto Fill Options' button (Figure 1–21). The 'Auto Fill Options' button allows you to choose whether you want to copy the values from the source area to the destination area with formatting, do so without formatting, or copy only the format. To view the available fill options, tap or click the 'Auto Fill Options' button. The 'Auto Fill Options' button disappears when you begin another activity in Excel, such as typing data in another cell or applying formatting to a cell or range of cells.

Figure 1–21

4

• Repeat Steps 1–3 to copy the SUM function from cell B17 to the range C17:M17 (Figure 1–22).

Figure 1–22

Other Ways

1. Select source area, tap or click Copy button (HOME tab | Clipboard group), select destination area, tap or click Paste button (HOME tab | Clipboard group)

2. Press and hold or right-click source area, tap or click Copy on shortcut menu; press and hold or right-click destination area, tap or click Paste on shortcut menu

To Determine Multiple Totals at the Same Time

1 ENTER TEXT | 2 CALCULATE SUMS & USE FORMULAS | 3 SAVE WORKBOOK | 4 FORMAT TEXT
5 INSERT CHART | 6 NAME TAB | 7 PREVIEW & PRINT WORKSHEET

The next step in building the worksheet is to determine the budget item totals for each budget item and total income and expenses in column N. To calculate these totals, you can use the SUM function much as it was used to total the budget items for each month in rows 6 and 17.

In this example, however, Excel will determine totals for all of the rows at the same time. *Why? By determining multiple totals at the same time, the number of steps to add totals is reduced.* The following steps sum multiple totals at once.

1

• Tap or click cell N4 to make it the active cell (Figure 1–23).

Figure 1–23

2

- If you are using a touch screen, drag the lower-right selection handle down to cell N6; if you are using a mouse, with the pointer in cell N4 and in the shape of a block plus sign, drag the pointer down to cell N6 to highlight the range with a transparent view (Figure 1– 24).

Figure 1–24

3

- Tap or click the Sum button (HOME tab | Editing group) to calculate and display the sums of the corresponding rows (Figure 1– 25).

Q&A How does Excel create unique totals for each row?

If each cell in a selected range is next to a row of numbers, Excel assigns the SUM function to each cell when you tap or click the Sum button.

Figure 1–25

4

- Repeat Steps 1–3 to select cells N9 to N17 and calculate and display the sums of the corresponding rows (Figure 1–26).

Figure 1–26

1 ENTER TEXT | 2 CALCULATE SUMS & USE FORMULAS | 3 SAVE WORKBOOK | 4 FORMAT TEXT
5 INSERT CHART | 6 NAME TAB | 7 PREVIEW & PRINT WORKSHEET

To Enter a Formula Using the Keyboard

The formulas needed in the worksheet are noted in the requirements document as follows:

Net (row 19) = Income – Expenses

The net for each month, which appears in row 19, is equal to the income total in row 6 minus the expense total in row 17. The following steps enter the initial net formula in cell B19 using the keyboard. *Why? Sometimes a predefined function does not fit your needs; therefore, you enter a formula of your own.*

1

- Select cell B19 to deselect the selected range.

- Type `=b6-b17` in the cell to display the formula in the formula bar and in the current cell and to display colored borders around the cells referenced in the formula (Figure 1–27).

Q&A

What occurs on the worksheet as I enter the formula?

The **equal sign (=)** preceding b6–b17 in the formula alerts Excel that you are entering a

Figure 1–27

formula or function and not text. Because the most common error when entering a formula is to reference the wrong cell in a formula, Excel colors the borders of the cells referenced in the formula. The coloring helps in the reviewing process to ensure the cell references are correct. The **minus sign (–)** following b6 in the formula is the arithmetic operator that directs Excel to perform the subtraction operation.

2

- Tap or click cell C19 to complete the arithmetic operation indicated by the formula, to display the result in the worksheet, and to select the cell to the right (Figure 1–28).

	A	B	C	D	E	F	G	H	I	J	K	L	M	N	O	P
1	Personal Budget Worksheet															
2	Monthly Estimates															
3	Income	January	February	March	April	May	June	July	August	September	October	November	December	Total		
4	Wages	1000.29	1000.29	1000.29	1000.29	1000.29	1000.29	1000.29	1000.29	1000.29	1000.29	1000.29	1000.29	12003.48		
5	Dividends	4000.75	0	0	0	0	0	0	0	4000.75	0	0	0	8001.5		
6	Total	5001.04	1000.29	1000.29	1000.29	1000.29	1000.29	1000.29	1000.29	5001.04	1000.29	1000.29	1000.29	20004.98		
7																
8	Expenses	January	February	March	April	May	June	July	August	September	October	November	December	Total		
9	Rent	400.89	400.89	400.89	400.89	400.89	400.89	400.89	400.89	400.89	400.89	400.89	400.89	4810.68		
10	Food	300	300	300	300	300	300	300	300	300	300	300	300	3600		
11	Tuition	1500	0	0	0	0	0	0	1500	0	0	0	0	3000		
12	Books	500	0	0	0	0	0	0	500	0	0	0	0	1000		
13	Entertainr	100	100	100	100	100	100	100	100	100	100	100	100	1200		
14	Car Payme	154.79	154.79	154.79	154.79	154.79	154.79	154.79	154.79	154.79	154.79	154.79	154.79	1857.48		
15	Gas	100	100	100	100	150	150	150	100	100	100	100	100	1350		
16	Miscellan	100	100	100	100	100	100	100	100	100	100	100	100	1200		
17	Total	3155.68	1155.68	1155.68	1155.68	1205.68	1205.68	1205.68	3155.68	1155.68	1155.68	1155.68	1155.68	18018.16		
18																
19	Net	1845.36														
20																

cell C19 selected

sum displayed

Figure 1–28

To Copy a Cell to Adjacent Cells in a Row

The easiest way to copy the SUM formula from cell B19 to cells C19, D19, E19, F19, G19, H19, I19, J19, K19, L19, M19, and N19 is to use the fill handle. The following steps use the fill handle to copy the formula in cell B19 to the adjacent cells C19:N19.

1 Select cell B19.

2 Drag the fill handle to select the destination area, range C19:N19, to display a shaded border around the source area and the destination area. Do not lift your finger or release the mouse button.

3 Lift your finger or release the mouse button to copy the simple formula function from the active cell to the destination area and calculate the results.

To Save a Workbook with a New File Name

You have performed many tasks while creating this workbook and do not want to risk losing work completed thus far. Accordingly, you should save the workbook on your hard disk, SkyDrive, or a location that is most appropriate to your situation.

The following steps assume you already have created folders for storing your files, for example, a CIS 101 folder (for your class) that contains an Excel folder (for your assignments). Thus, these steps save the workbook in the Excel folder in the CIS 101 folder on your desired save location. For a detailed example of the procedure for saving a file in a folder or saving a file on SkyDrive, refer to the Office and Windows chapter at the beginning of this book.

1 Tap or click the Save button on the Quick Access Toolbar, which depending on settings, will display either the Save As gallery in the Backstage view or the Save As dialog box.

2 To save on a hard disk or other storage media on your computer, proceed to Step 2a. To save on SkyDrive, proceed to Step 2b.

2a If your screen opens the Backstage view and you want to save on storage media on your computer, tap or click Computer in the left pane, if necessary, to display options in the right pane related to saving on your computer. If your screen already displays the Save As dialog box, proceed to Step 3.

2b If your screen opens the Backstage view and you want to save on SkyDrive, tap or click SkyDrive in the left pane to display SkyDrive saving options or a Sign In button. If your screen displays a Sign In button, tap or click it and then sign in to SkyDrive.

3 Tap or click the Browse button in the right pane to display the Save As dialog box associated with the selected save location (i.e., Computer or SkyDrive).

4 Type `Bob Gleamin Budget` in the File name box to change the file name. Do not press the ENTER key after typing the file name because you do not want to close the dialog box at this time.

5 Navigate to the desired save location (in this case, the Excel folder in the CIS 101 folder [or your class folder] on your computer or SkyDrive).

6 Tap or click the Save button (Save As dialog box) to save the workbook in the selected folder on the selected save location with the entered file name.

Break Point: If you wish to take a break, this is a good place to do so. You can exit Excel. To resume at a later time, run Excel, open the file called Bob Gleamin Budget, and continue following the steps from this location forward.

Formatting the Worksheet

The text, numeric entries, and functions for the worksheet now are complete. The next step is to format the worksheet. You **format** a worksheet to emphasize certain entries and make the worksheet easier to read and understand.

Figure 1–29a shows the worksheet before formatting. Figure 1–29b shows the worksheet after formatting. As you can see from the two figures, a worksheet that is formatted not only is easier to read but also looks more professional.

CONSIDER THIS

The key to formatting a worksheet is to consider the ways you can enhance the worksheet so that it appears professional. When formatting a worksheet, what steps should you consider?

• Identify how to format various elements of the worksheet.

• Increase the font size of cells.

• Change the font color of cells.

• Center the worksheet titles, subtitles, and column headings.

• Modify column widths to best fit text in cells.

• Change the font style of cells.

To change the unformatted worksheet in Figure 1–29a so that it appears like the formatted worksheet in Figure 1–29b, the following tasks must be completed:

1. Change the font, change the font style to bold, increase the font size, and change the font color of the worksheet titles in cells A1 and A2.

2. Center the worksheet titles in cells A1 and A2 across columns A through N.

(a) Unformatted Worksheet

(b) Formatted Worksheet

Figure 1–29

3. Format the body of the worksheet. The body of the worksheet, range A3:N19, includes the column titles, row titles, and numbers. Formatting the body of the worksheet changes the numbers to use a dollars-and-cents format, with dollar signs in rows 4 and 9 and the total rows (row 6 and 17); changes the styles of some rows; adds underlining that emphasizes portions of the worksheet; and modifies the column widths to fit the text in the columns and make the text and numbers readable.

The remainder of this section explains the process required to format the worksheet. Although the formatting procedures are explained in the order described above, you should be aware that you could make these format changes in any order. Modifying the column widths, however, usually is done last because other formatting changes may affect the size of data in the cells in the column.

Font Style, Size, and Color

The characters that Excel displays on the screen are a specific font, style, size, and color. The **font**, or font face, defines the appearance and shape of the letters, numbers, and special characters. Examples of fonts include Calibri, Cambria, Times New Roman, Arial, and Courier. **Font style** indicates how the characters are emphasized. Common font styles include regular, bold, underline, and italic. The **font size** specifies the size of the characters on the screen. Font size is gauged by a measurement system called points. A single point is about 1/72 of one inch in height. Thus, a character with a **point size** of 10 is about 10/72 of one inch in height. The **font color** defines the color of the characters. Excel can display characters in a wide variety of colors.

When Excel first runs, the preset font for the entire workbook is Calibri, with a font size, font style, and font color of 11–point regular black. Excel allows you to change the font characteristics in a single cell, a range of cells, the entire worksheet, or the entire workbook.

BTW

Organizing Files and Folders
You should organize and store files in folders so that you easily can find the files later. For example, if you are taking an introductory computer class called CIS 101, a good practice would be to save all Excel files in a Excel folder in a CIS 101 folder. For a discussion of folders and detailed examples of creating folders, refer to the Office and Windows chapter at the beginning of this book.

To Change a Cell Style

Excel includes the capability of changing several characteristics of a cell, such as the font, font size, and font color, all at once by assigning a predefined cell style to a cell. *Why? Using the predefined styles that Excel includes provides a consistent appearance to common portions of your worksheets, such as worksheet titles, worksheet subtitles, column headings, and total rows.* The following steps assign the Title cell style to the worksheet title in cell A1.

1

- Tap or click cell A1 to make cell A1 the active cell.

- Tap or click the Cell Styles button (HOME tab | Styles group) to display the Cell Styles gallery (Figure 1– 30).

Figure 1–30

2

- If you are using a mouse, point to the Title cell style in the Titles and Headings area of the Cell Styles gallery to see a live preview of the cell style in the active cell (Figure 1– 31).

Q&A Can I use live preview on a touch screen?
Live preview is not available on a touch screen.

Experiment

- If you are using a mouse, point to several other cell styles in the Cell Styles gallery to see a live preview of other cell styles in cell A1.

Figure 1–31

3

- Tap or click the Title cell style to apply the cell style to the active cell (Figure 1– 32).

Q&A Why do several items in the Font group on the ribbon change?
The changes to the Font box and Font Size box indicate the font changes applied to the active cell, cell A1, as a result of applying the Title cell style.

Figure 1–32

---

1 ENTER TEXT | 2 CALCULATE SUMS & USE FORMULAS | 3 SAVE WORKBOOK | 4 FORMAT TEXT

5 INSERT CHART | 6 NAME TAB | 7 PREVIEW & PRINT WORKSHEET

To Change the Font

Why? *Different fonts often are used in a worksheet to make it more appealing to the reader and to relate or distinguish data in the worksheet.* The following steps change the worksheet subtitle's font to Cambria.

1

- Tap or click cell A2 to make it the active cell.

- Tap or click the Font arrow (HOME tab | Font group) to display the Font gallery. If necessary, scroll to display Cambria.

- If you are using a mouse, point to Cambria in the Font gallery to see a live preview of the selected font in the active cell (Figure 1–33).

 Experiment

- If you are using a mouse, point to several other fonts in the Font gallery to see a live preview of other fonts in the selected cell.

Figure 1–33

2

- Tap or click Cambria in the Font gallery to change the font of the worksheet subtitle to Cambria (Figure 1–34).

Figure 1–34

Other Ways

1. Tap or click Font Settings Dialog Box Launcher, tap or click Font tab (Format Cells dialog box), tap or click desired font in Font list, tap or click OK button

2. If you are using a mouse, click Font box arrow on mini toolbar, click desired font in Font gallery

3. Tap 'Show Context Menu' button on mini toolbar or right-click selected cell, tap or click Format Cells on shortcut menu, tap or click Font tab (Format Cells dialog box), tap or click desired font, tap or click OK button

To Bold a Cell

1 ENTER TEXT | 2 CALCULATE SUMS & USE FORMULAS | 3 SAVE WORKBOOK | 4 FORMAT TEXT
5 INSERT CHART | 6 NAME TAB | 7 PREVIEW & PRINT WORKSHEET

Bold text has a darker appearance than normal text. *Why? You bold an entry in a cell to emphasize it or make it stand out from the rest of the worksheet.* The following steps bold the worksheet title and subtitle.

1

- Tap or click cell A1 to make it active and then tap or click the Bold button (HOME tab | Font group) to change the font style of the active cell to bold (Figure 1–35).

Q&A

What if a cell already includes a bold style?

If the active cell already is bold, then Excel displays the Bold button with a transparent green background.

How do I remove the bold style from a cell?

Tapping or clicking the Bold button (HOME tab | Font group) a second time removes the bold style.

Figure 1–35

2

- Repeat Step 1 to bold cell A2.

Other Ways

1. Tap or click Font Settings Dialog Box Launcher, tap or click Font tab (Format Cells dialog box), tap or click Bold in Font style list, tap or click OK button

2. If you are using a mouse, click Bold button on mini toolbar

3. Tap 'Show Context Menu' button on mini toolbar or right-click selected cell, tap or click Format Cells on shortcut menu, tap or click Font tab (Format Cells dialog box), tap or click Bold, tap or click OK button

4. Press CTRL+B

To Increase the Font Size of a Cell Entry

Increasing the font size is the next step in formatting the worksheet subtitle. *Why? You increase the font size of a cell so that the entry stands out and is easier to read.* The following steps increase the font size of the worksheet subtitle in cell A2.

1

- With cell A2 selected, tap or click the Font Size arrow (HOME tab | Font group) to display the Font Size gallery.

- If you are using a mouse, point to 14 in the Font Size gallery to see a live preview of the active cell with the selected font size (Figure 1–36).

Experiment

- If you are using a mouse, point to several other font sizes in the Font Size list to see a live preview of other font sizes in the selected cell.

Figure 1–36

2

- Tap or click 14 in the Font Size gallery to change the font size in the active cell (Figure 1–37).

Q&A Can I assign a font size that is not in the Font Size gallery?
Yes. An alternative to tapping or clicking a font size in the Font Size gallery is to tap or click the Font Size box (HOME tab | Font group), type the font size, and then press the ENTER key. This procedure allows you to assign a font size not available in the Font Size gallery to a selected cell entry.

Figure 1–37

Other Ways

1. Tap or click 'Increase Font Size' button (HOME tab | Font group) or 'Decrease Font Size' button (HOME tab | Font group)

2. Tap or click Font Settings Dialog Box Launcher, tap or click Font tab (Format Cells dialog box), tap or click desired size in Size list, tap or click OK button

3. Tap or click Font Size arrow on mini toolbar, tap or click desired font size in Font Size gallery

4. Tap 'Show Context Menu' button on mini toolbar or right-click selected cell, tap or click Format Cells on shortcut menu, tap or click Font tab (Format Cells dialog box), select font size in Size box, tap or click OK button

To Change the Font Color of a Cell Entry

The next step is to change the color of the font in cells A1 and A2 to blue. *Why? Changing the font color of cell entries can help the text stand out more.* The following steps change the font color of a cell entry.

1

- Tap or click cell A1 and then tap or click the Font Color arrow (HOME tab | Font group) to display the Font Color gallery.

- If you are using a mouse, point to 'Blue, Accent 1' (column 5, row 1) in the Theme Colors area of the Font Color gallery to see a live preview of the font color in the active cell (Figure 1–38).

Experiment

- If you are using a mouse, point to several other colors in the Font Color gallery to see a live preview of other font colors in the active cell.

Figure 1–38

Q&A Which colors does Excel make available in the Font Color gallery?

You can choose from more than 60 different font colors in the Font Color gallery. Your Font Color gallery may have more or fewer colors, depending on color settings of your operating system. The Theme Colors area contains colors that are included in the current workbook's theme.

2

- Tap or click 'Blue, Accent 1' (column 5, row 1) in the Font Color gallery to change the font color of the worksheet title in the active cell (Figure 1–39).

Q&A Why does the Font Color button change after I select the new font color?

When you choose a color on the Font Color gallery, Excel changes the Font Color button (HOME tab | Font group) to the chosen color. Thus, to change the font color of the cell entry in another cell to the same color, you need only to select the cell and then tap or click the Font Color button (HOME tab | Font group).

Figure 1–39

3

- Repeat Steps 1 and 2 to apply Blue, Accent 1 (column 5, row 1) to cell A2.

Other Ways

1. Tap or click Font Settings Dialog Box Launcher, tap or click Font tab (Format Cells dialog box), tap or click desired color in Color list, tap or click OK button

2. Tap or click Font Color arrow on mini toolbar, tap or click desired font color in the Font Color gallery

3. Tap 'Show Context Menu' button on mini toolbar or right-click selected cell, tap or click Format Cells on shortcut menu, tap or click Font tab (Format Cells dialog box), select color in Font Color gallery, tap or click OK button

To Center Cell Entries across Columns by Merging Cells

The final step in formatting the worksheet title and subtitle is to center them across columns A through N. *Why? Centering a title across the columns used in the body of the worksheet improves the worksheet's appearance.* To do this, the 14 cells in the range A1:N1 are combined, or merged, into a single cell that is the width of the columns in the body of the worksheet. The 14 cells in the range A2:N2 are merged in a similar manner. **Merging** cells involves creating a single cell by combining two or more selected cells. The following steps center the worksheet title and subtitle across columns by merging cells.

1

- Select cell A1 and then if you are using a touch screen, drag the selection handles as necessary to cell N1; if you are using a mouse, drag to cell N1 to highlight the range to be merged and centered (Figure 1–40).

Q&A What if a cell in the range B1:N1 contains data?
For the 'Merge & Center' button (HOME tab | Alignment group) to work properly, all the cells except the leftmost cell in the selected range must be empty.

Figure 1–40

2

- Tap or click the 'Merge & Center' button (HOME tab | Alignment group) to merge cells A1 through N1 and center the contents of the leftmost cell across the selected columns (Figure 1–41).

Q&A What if my screen displays a Merge & Center menu?
If you are using a touch screen, you may not have a separate 'Merge & Center' button and 'Merge & Center' arrow. In this case, select the desired option on the Merge & Center menu.

What happened to cells B1 through N1?
After the merge, cells B1 through N1 no longer exist. The new cell A1 now extends across columns A through N.

Figure 1–41

❸

- Repeat Steps 1 and 2 to merge and center the worksheet subtitle across cells A2 through N2 (Figure 1–42).

Q&A
Are cells B1 through N1 and B2 through N2 lost forever?
No. The opposite of merging cells is **splitting** a merged cell.

Figure 1–42

After you have merged multiple cells to create one merged cell, you can unmerge, or split, the merged cell to display the original cells on the worksheet. You split a merged cell by selecting it and tapping or clicking the 'Merge & Center' button. For example, if you tap or click the 'Merge & Center' button a second time in Step 2, it will split the merged cell A1 into cells A1, B1, C1, D1, E1, F1, G1, H1, I1, J1, K1, L1, M1, and N1.

Other Ways

1. If you are using a mouse, right-click selection, click 'Merge & Center' button on mini toolbar
2. Tap 'Show Context Menu' button on mini toolbar or right-click selected cell, tap or click Format Cells on shortcut menu, tap or click Alignment tab (Format Cells dialog box), select 'Center Across Selection' in Horizontal list, tap or click OK button

---

To Format Rows Using Cell Styles

1 ENTER TEXT | 2 CALCULATE SUMS & USE FORMULAS | 3 SAVE WORKBOOK | 4 FORMAT TEXT
5 INSERT CHART | 6 NAME TAB | 7 PREVIEW & PRINT WORKSHEET

The next step to format the worksheet is to format the rows. *Why? Row titles and the total row should be formatted so that anyone who views the worksheet can distinguish quickly the column titles and total row from the data in the body of the worksheet. Data rows can be formatted to make them easier to read, as well.* The following steps format the column titles and total row using cell styles in the default worksheet theme.

❶

- Tap or click cell A3 and then drag to cell N3 to select the range.
- Tap or click the Cell Styles button (HOME tab | Styles group) to display the Cell Styles gallery.
- If you are using a mouse, point to the Heading 1 cell style in the Titles and Headings area of the Cell Styles gallery to see a live preview of the cell style in the selected range (Figure 1–43).

🔑 Experiment

- If you are using a mouse, point to other cell styles in the Titles and Headings area of the Cell Styles gallery to see a live preview of other cell styles in the selected range, A3:N3.

Figure 1–43

2

- Tap or click the Heading 1 cell style to apply the cell style to the selected range.

- Tap or click the Center button (HOME tab | Alignment group) to center the column headings in the selected range.

- Tap or click cell A8 and then drag the pointer to cell N8 to select the range (Figure 1–44).

Figure 1–44

3

- Use Steps 1 and 2 to center the column headings and format the range A8:N8 with the Heading 1 cell style format (Figure 1–45).

Figure 1–45

4

- Use Steps 1 and 2 to format the range A6:N6 and A17:N17 with the Total cell style format.

- Use Steps 1 and 2 to format the range A19:N19 with the Accent 1 cell style format.

- Use Steps 1 and 2 to format the range A4:N4, A9:N9, A11:N11, A13:N13, A15:N15 with the 20% - Accent 1 cell style format.

- Use Steps 1 and 2 to format the range A5:N5, A10:N10, A12:N12, A14:N14, A16:N16 with the 40% - Accent 1 cell style format (Figure 1–46).

Figure 1–46

To Format Numbers in the Worksheet

1 ENTER TEXT | 2 CALCULATE SUMS & USE FORMULAS | 3 SAVE WORKBOOK | 4 FORMAT TEXT
5 INSERT CHART | 6 NAME TAB | 7 PREVIEW & PRINT WORKSHEET

Why? As previously noted, the numbers in the first row and last row of each section should be formatted to use a dollar-and-cents format, while the others use a comma format. Excel allows you to format numbers in a variety of ways, and these methods are discussed in other chapters in this book. The following steps use buttons on the ribbon to format the numbers in the worksheet.

1

- Select the range B4:N4.

- Tap or click the 'Accounting Number Format' button (HOME tab | Number group) to apply the accounting number format to the cells in the selected range.

Q&A What if my screen displays an Accounting Number Format menu?
If you are using a touch screen, you may not have a separate 'Accounting Number Format' button and 'Accounting Number Format' arrow. In this case, select the desired option on the Accounting Number Format menu.

Figure 1–47

- Select the range B5:N5 (Figure 1–47).

Q&A What effect does the accounting number format have on the selected cells?
The accounting number format causes the cells to be displayed with two decimal places so that decimal places in cells below the selected cells align vertically. Cell widths are adjusted automatically to accommodate the new formatting.

2

- Tap or click the Comma Style button (HOME tab | Number group) to apply the comma style format to the selected range.

- Select the range B6:N6 to make it the active range (Figure 1–48).

Q&A What effect does the comma style format have on the selected cells?

The comma style format causes the cells to be displayed with two decimal places and commas as thousands separators.

Figure 1–48

3

- Tap or click the 'Accounting Number Format' button (HOME tab | Number group) to apply the accounting number format to the cells in the selected range.

- Select cell A7.

4

- Use Steps 1–3 to format the ranges B9:N9, B17:N17, and B19:N19 with the accounting number format.

- Use Steps 1–3 to format the range B10:N16 with the comma style format (Figure 1–49).

Figure 1–49

Other Ways

1. Tap or click 'Accounting Number Format' or Comma Style button on mini toolbar

2. Tap 'Show Context Menu' button on mini toolbar or right-click selected cell, tap or click Format Cells on shortcut menu, tap or click Number tab (Format Cells dialog box), select Accounting in Category list or select Number and tap or click 'Use 1000 Separator', tap or click OK button

To Adjust the Column Width

The last step in formatting the worksheet is to adjust the width of the columns so that all the titles can be seen clearly. *Why? To make a worksheet easy to read, the column widths should be adjusted appropriately.* Excel includes several methods for adjusting cell widths and row heights, and these methods are discussed later in this book. The following steps adjust the width of columns A through N so that the contents of the columns are seen clearly.

- If you are using a mouse, point to the boundary on the right side of the column A heading above row 1 to change the pointer to a split double arrow (Figure 1–50).

Figure 1–50

2

- If you are using a mouse, double-click the boundary to adjust the width of the column to the width of the largest item in the column (Figure 1–51).

Q&A What if none of the items in column A extends through the entire width of the column?
If all of the items in column A were shorter in length than the width of the column when you double-tap or double-click the right side of the column A heading, then Excel still would adjust the column width to the largest item in the column. That is, Excel would reduce the width of the column to the largest item.

Figure 1–51

❸

• Repeat Steps 1 and 2 to adjust the column width of columns B through N (Figure 1–52).

	A	B	C	D	E	F	G	H	I	J	K	L	M	N
1						Personal Budget Worksheet								
2							Monthly Estimates							
3	Income	January	February	March	April	May	June	July	August	September	October	November	December	Total
4	Wages	$1,000.29	$ 1,000.29	$1,000.29	$1,000.29	$1,000.29	$1,000.29	$1,000.29	$ 1,000.29	$ 1,000.29	$ 1,000.29	$ 1,000.29	$ 1,000.29	$12,003.48
5	Dividends	4,000.75	-	-	-	-	-	-	-	4,000.75	-	-	-	8,001.50
6	Total	$5,001.04	$ 1,000.29	$1,000.29	$1,000.29	$1,000.29	$1,000.29	$1,000.29	$ 1,000.29	$ 5,001.04	$ 1,000.29	$ 1,000.29	$ 1,000.29	$20,004.98
7														
8	Expenses	January	February	March	April	May	June	July	August	September	October	November	December	Total
9	Rent	$ 400.89	$ 400.89	$ 400.89	$ 400.89	$ 400.89	$ 400.89	$ 400.89	$ 400.89	$ 400.89	$ 400.89	$ 400.89	$ 400.89	$ 4,810.68
10	Food	300.00	300.00	300.00	300.00	300.00	300.00	300.00	300.00	300.00	300.00	300.00	300.00	3,600.00
11	Tuition	1,500.00	-	-	-	-	-	-	1,500.00	-	-	-	-	3,000.00
12	Books	500.00	-	-	-	-	-	-	500.00	-	-	-	-	1,000.00
13	Entertainment	100.00	100.00	100.00	100.00	100.00	100.00	100.00	100.00	100.00	100.00	100.00	100.00	1,200.00
14	Car Payment	154.79	154.79	154.79	154.79	154.79	154.79	154.79	154.79	154.79	154.79	154.79	154.79	1,857.48
15	Gas	100.00	100.00	100.00	100.00	150.00	150.00	150.00	100.00	100.00	100.00	100.00	100.00	1,350.00
16	Miscellaneous	100.00	100.00	100.00	100.00	100.00	100.00	100.00	100.00	100.00	100.00	100.00	100.00	1,200.00
17	Total	$3,155.68	$ 1,155.68	$1,155.68	$1,155.68	$1,205.68	$1,205.68	$1,205.68	$ 3,155.68	$ 1,155.68	$ 1,155.68	$ 1,155.68	$ 1,155.68	$18,018.16
18														
19	Net	$1,845.36	$ (155.39)	$ (155.39)	$ (155.39)	$ (205.39)	$ (205.39)	$ (205.39)	$(2,155.39)	$ 3,845.36	$ (155.39)	$ (155.39)	$ (155.39)	$ 1,986.82
20														
21														
22														

Figure 1–52

To Use the Name Box to Select a Cell

1 ENTER TEXT | 2 CALCULATE TOTALS | 3 SAVE WORKBOOK | 4 FORMAT TEXT
5 INSERT CHART | 6 NAME TAB | 7 PREVIEW & PRINT WORKSHEET

The next step is to chart the monthly expenses. To create the chart, you first must select the cell in the upper-left corner of the range to chart (cell A3). Rather than tapping or clicking cell A3 to select it, the next section describes how to use the Name box to select the cell. The Name box is located on the left side of the formula bar. ***Why?*** *To select any cell, tap or click the Name box and enter the cell reference of the cell you want to select.* The following steps select cell A3 using the Name box.

❶

• Tap or click the Name box in the formula bar and then type   a3 as the cell you want to select (Figure 1–53).

Q&A

Why is cell A7 still selected?
The current cell will remain selected until you press the ENTER key.

Figure 1–53

2

- Press the ENTER key to change the active cell in the Name box and make cell A3 the active cell (Figure 1–54).

Figure 1–54

Other Ways to Select Cells

As you will see in later chapters, in addition to using the Name box to select any cell in a worksheet, you also can use it to assign names to a cell or range of cells. Excel supports several additional ways to select a cell, as summarized in Table 1–3.

Table 1–3 Selecting Cells in Excel	
Key, Box, or Command	**Function**
ALT+PAGE DOWN	Selects the cell one worksheet window to the right and moves the worksheet window accordingly.
ALT+PAGE UP	Selects the cell one worksheet window to the left and moves the worksheet window accordingly.
ARROW	Selects the adjacent cell in the direction of the arrow on the key.
CTRL+ARROW	Selects the border cell of the worksheet in combination with the arrow keys and moves the worksheet window accordingly. For example, to select the rightmost cell in the row that contains the active cell, press CTRL+RIGHT ARROW. You also can press the END key, release it, and then press the appropriate arrow key to accomplish the same task.
CTRL+HOME	Selects cell A1 or the cell one column and one row below and to the right of frozen titles and moves the worksheet window accordingly.
Find command on Find and Select menu or SHIFT+F5	Finds and selects a cell that contains specific contents that you enter in the Find and Replace dialog box. If necessary, Excel moves the worksheet window to display the cell. You also can press CTRL+F to display the Find dialog box.
Go To command on Find and Select menu or F5	Selects the cell that corresponds to the cell reference you enter in the Go To dialog box and moves the worksheet window accordingly. You also can press CTRL+G to display the Go To dialog box.
HOME	Selects the cell at the beginning of the row that contains the active cell and moves the worksheet window accordingly.
Name box	Selects the cell in the workbook that corresponds to the cell reference you enter in the Name box.
PAGE DOWN	Selects the cell down one worksheet window from the active cell and moves the worksheet window accordingly.
PAGE UP	Selects the cell up one worksheet window from the active cell and moves the worksheet window accordingly.

Adding a Pie Chart to the Worksheet

Excel includes 10 chart types from which you can choose, including column, line, pie, bar, area, X Y (scatter), stock, surface, bubble, and radar. The type of chart you choose depends on the type of data that you have, how much data you have, and the message you want to convey.

A line chart often is used to illustrate changes in data over time. Pie charts show the contribution of each piece of data to the whole, or total, of the data. Area charts, like line charts, illustrate changes over time, but often are used to compare more than one set of data, and the area below the lines is filled in with a different color for each set of data. An X Y (scatter) chart is used much like a line chart, but each piece of data is represented by a dot and is not connected with a line. A stock chart provides a number of methods commonly used in the financial industry to show stock market data. A surface chart compares data from three columns and/or rows in a three-dimensional manner. A bubble chart is much like an X Y (scatter) chart, but a third set of data results indicates how large each individual dot, or bubble, is on the chart. A radar chart can compare several sets of data in a manner that resembles a radar screen, with each set of data represented by a different color. A column or cylinder chart is a good way to compare values side by side. A pie chart can go even further in comparing values across categories by showing each pie piece in comparison with the others.

As outlined in the requirements document in Figure 1–2 on page EX 3, the worksheet should include a pie chart to represent graphically the yearly expenses totals for the expenses budget items for Bob Gleamin's budget. The pie chart shown in Figure 1–55 is on its own sheet in the workbook. The pie chart resides on a separate sheet, called a **chart sheet**, which contains only the chart.

BTW

Excel Help

At any time while using Excel, you can find answers to questions and display information about various topics through Excel Help. Used properly, this form of assistance can increase your productivity and reduce your frustrations by minimizing the time you spend learning how to use Excel. For instruction about Excel Help and exercises that will help you gain confidence in using it, read the Office and Windows chapter at the beginning of this book.

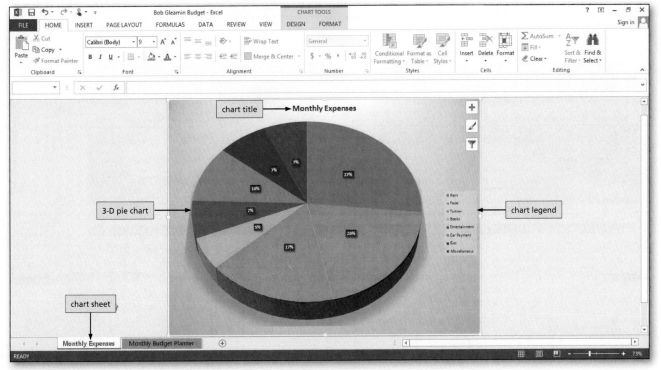

Figure 1–55

In this worksheet, the ranges to chart are the nonadjacent ranges A9:A16 (category names) and N9:N16 (yearly expense totals). The expense titles in the range A9:A16 will identify the slices of the pie chart; these entries are called **category names**. The range N9:N16 contains the data that determines the size of the slices in the pie; these entries are called the **data series**. Because eight budget items are being charted, the 3-D pie chart contains eight slices.

To Add a 3-D Pie Chart

1 ENTER TEXT | 2 CALCULATE SUMS & USE FORMULAS | 3 SAVE WORKBOOK | 4 FORMAT TEXT
5 INSERT CHART | 6 NAME TAB | 7 PREVIEW & PRINT WORKSHEET

Why? *When you want to see how each part relates to the whole, you use a pie chart.* The following steps draw the 3-D pie chart.

1

- Select the range A9:A16 to identify the range of the category names for the 3-D pie chart.
- While holding down the CTRL key, select the range N9:N16.
- Tap or click INSERT on the ribbon to display the INSERT tab.
- Tap or click the 'Insert Pie or Doughnut Chart' button (INSERT tab | Charts group) to display the Insert Pie or Doughnut Chart gallery (Figure 1–56).

Q&A Why does the ribbon display extra tabs?
Excel displays additional tabs that provide options for use when you are working with certain objects, such as charts.

Figure 1–56

2

- Tap or click 3-D Pie in the Insert Pie or Doughnut Chart gallery to insert the chart in the worksheet (Figure 1–57).

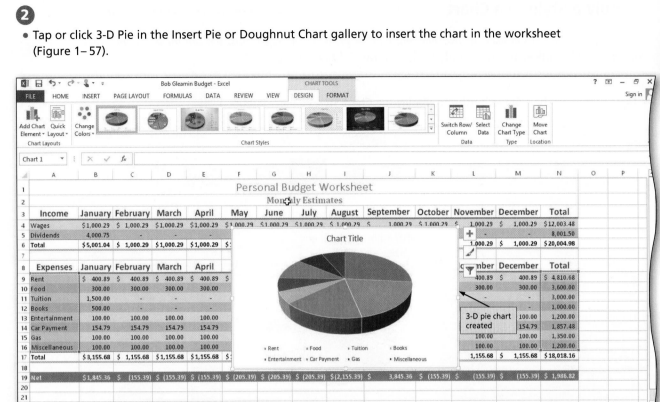

Figure 1–57

3

- Tap or click the chart title to select it.

- Type **Monthly Expenses** and then press the ENTER key to change the title.

- Deselect the chart title (Figure 1–58).

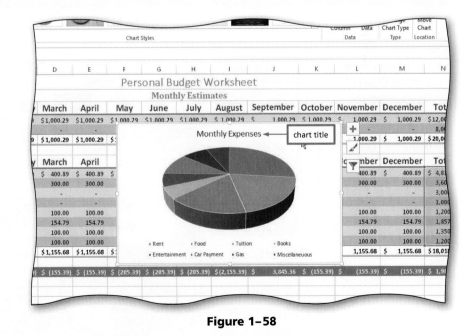

Figure 1–58

To Apply a Style to a Chart

Why? If you want to make it clear how much of the pie each slice represents, you can use a style to include a percentage. The following steps apply Style 3 to the 3-D pie chart.

1

● Tap or click the Chart Styles button to display the Chart Styles gallery (Figure 1–59).

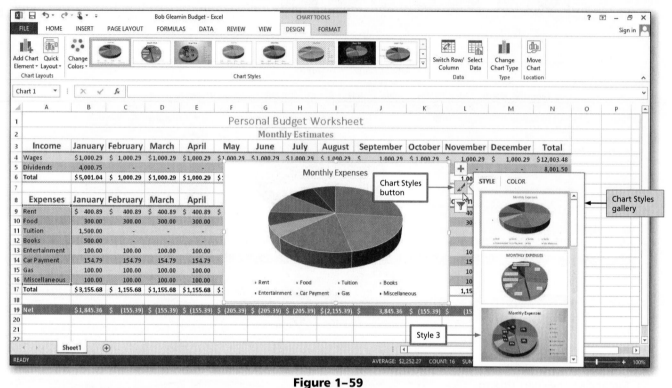

Figure 1–59

2

● Tap or click Style 3 in the Chart Styles gallery to change the chart style to Style 3 (Figure 1–60).

3

● Tap or click the Chart Styles button to close the Chart Styles gallery.

Figure 1–60

Changing the Sheet Tab Names

The sheet tabs at the bottom of the window allow you to view any worksheet in the workbook. You tap or click the sheet tab of the worksheet you want to view in the Excel window. By default, Excel presets the names of the worksheets to Sheet1, Sheet2, and so on. The worksheet names become increasingly important as you move toward more sophisticated workbooks, especially workbooks in which you reference cells between worksheets.

BTW

Exploding a Pie Chart
If you want to draw attention to a particular slice in a pie chart, you can offset the slice so that it stands out from the rest. A pie chart with one or more slices offset is referred to as an exploded pie chart. To offset a slice, tap or click the slice two times to select it (do not double-tap or double-click) and then drag the slice outward.

To Move a Chart to a New Sheet

1 ENTER TEXT | 2 CALCULATE SUMS & USE FORMULAS | 3 SAVE WORKBOOK | 4 FORMAT TEXT
5 INSERT CHART | 6 NAME TAB | 7 PREVIEW & PRINT WORKSHEET

Why? *By moving a chart to its own sheet, the size will increase, which allows better viewing.* The following steps move the 3-D pie chart to a chart sheet named, Monthly Expenses.

1
- Tap or click the Move Chart button (CHART TOOLS DESIGN tab | Location group) to display the Move Chart dialog box (Figure 1–61).

Figure 1–61

2

- Tap or click New sheet to select it (Move Chart dialog box) and then type `Monthly Expenses` in the New sheet text box to enter a sheet tab name for the worksheet that will contain the chart.

- Tap or click the OK button (Move Chart dialog box) to move the chart to a new chart sheet with a new sheet tab name, Monthly Expenses in this case (Figure 1–62).

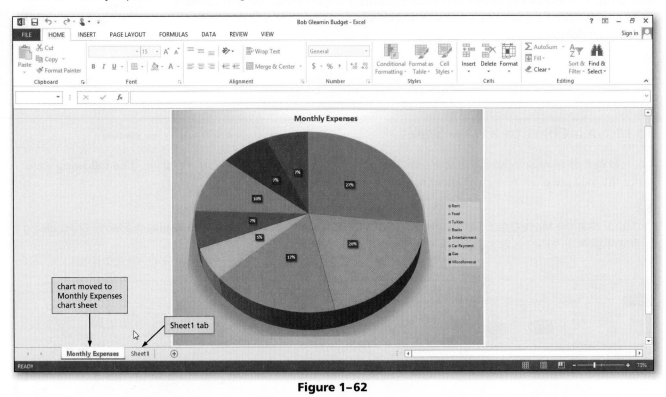

Figure 1–62

To Change the Worksheet Tab Name

1 ENTER TEXT | 2 CALCULATE SUMS & USE FORMULAS | 3 SAVE WORKBOOK | 4 FORMAT TEXT
5 INSERT CHART | 6 NAME TAB | 7 PREVIEW & PRINT WORKSHEET

You decide to change the name of the Sheet1 worksheet tab to Monthly Budget Planner. *Why? Use simple, meaningful names for each worksheet tab. Worksheet tab names often match the worksheet title. If a worksheet includes multiple titles in multiple sections of the worksheet, use a sheet tab name that encompasses the meaning of all of the sections.*

The following steps rename the worksheet tab.

1

- Double-tap or double-click the sheet tab labeled Sheet1 in the lower-left corner of the window.

- Type `Monthly Budget Planner` as the worksheet tab name and then press the ENTER key to display the new worksheet tab name on the sheet tab (Figure 1–63).

Q&A What is the maximum length for a sheet tab name?
Worksheet tab names can be up to 31 characters (including spaces) in length. Longer worksheet names, however, mean that fewer sheet tabs will show. If you have multiple sheets, you will be able to scroll through sheet tabs.

	100.00	100.00	100.00				100.00	100.00				1,350.00
16 Miscellaneuous	100.00	100.00	100.00	100.00	100.00	100.00	100.00	100.00	100.00	100.00	100.00	100.00	1,200.00
17 Total	$3,155.68	$ 1,155.68	$1,155.68	$1,155.68	$1,205.68	$1,205.68	$1,205.68	$ 3,155.68	$	1,155.68	$ 1,155.68	$	1,155.68	$18,018.16
18												
19 Net	$1,845.36	$ (155 | | 155.39)	$ (205.39)	$ (205.39)	$ (205.39)	$(2,155.39)	$	3,845.36	$ (155.39)	$	(155.39)	$ 1,986.82
20												
21												
22												

Monthly Expenses | **Monthly Budget Planner**

Figure 1–63

2

- Press and hold or right-click the sheet tab labeled, Monthly Budget Planner, in the lower-left corner of the window to display a shortcut menu.

- Tap or point to Tab Color on the shortcut menu to display the Tab Color gallery (Figure 1–64).

Figure 1–64

3

- Tap or click the color of your shirt in the Theme Colors area to change the color of the tab (Figure 1–65).

- If necessary, tap or click HOME on the ribbon to display the HOME tab.

Figure 1–65

Document Properties

Excel helps you organize and identify your files by using **document properties**, which are the details about a file such as the project author, title, and subject. For example, a class name or workbook topic can describe the file's purpose or content.

CONSIDER THIS

Why would you want to assign document properties to a workbook?

Document properties are valuable for a variety of reasons:

• Users can save time locating a particular file because they can view a file's document properties without opening the workbook.

• By creating consistent properties for files having similar content, users can better organize their workbooks.

• Some organizations require Excel users to add document properties so that other employees can view details about these files.

The more common document properties are standard and automatically updated properties. **Standard properties** are associated with all Microsoft Office files and include author, title, and subject. **Automatically updated properties** include file system properties, such as the date you create or change a file, and statistics, such as the file size.

To Change Document Properties

To change document properties, you would follow these steps.

1. Tap or click FILE on the ribbon to open the Backstage view and then, if necessary, tap or click the Info tab in the Backstage view to display the Info gallery.

2. If the property you wish to change is displayed in the Properties list in the right pane of the Info gallery, try to tap or click to the right of the property. If a text box appears to the right of the property, type the text for the property in the text box and then tap or click the Back button in the upper-left corner of the Backstage view to return to the Excel window. Skip the remaining steps.

3. If the property you wish to change is not displayed in the Properties list in the right pane of the Info gallery or you cannot change it in the Info gallery, tap or click the Properties button in the right pane to display the Properties menu, and then tap or click 'Show Document Panel' on the Properties menu to close the Backstage view and display the Document Information Panel in the Excel workbook window.

Q&A

Why are some of the document properties in my Document Information Panel already filled in?

The person who installed Office 2013 on your computer or network may have set or customized the properties.

4. Type the desired text in the appropriate property text boxes.

Q&A What if the property I want to change is not displayed in the Document Information Panel?
Tap or click the Document Properties button in the Document Information Panel and then tap or click Advanced Properties on the menu to display the Properties dialog box. If necessary, tap or click the Summary tab (Properties dialog box) to display the Summary sheet, fill in the appropriate text boxes, and then tap or click the OK button.

5. Tap or click the 'Close the Document Information Panel' button at the right edge of the Document Information Panel so that the panel no longer appears in the Excel workbook window.

To Save an Existing Workbook with the Same File Name

You have made several modifications to the workbook since you last saved it. Thus, you should save it again. The following step saves the workbook again. For an example of the step listed below, refer to the Office and Windows chapter at the beginning of this book.

1 Tap or click the Save button on the Quick Access Toolbar to overwrite the previously saved file.

Printing a Worksheet

After creating a worksheet, you may want to print it. Printing a worksheet enables you to distribute the worksheet to others in a form that can be read or viewed but typically not edited. It is a good practice to save a workbook before printing a worksheet, in the event you experience difficulties printing.

CONSIDER THIS

What is the best method for distributing a workbook?
The traditional method of distributing a workbook uses a printer to produce a hard copy. A **hard copy** or **printout** is information that exists on a physical medium such as paper. Hard copies can be useful for the following reasons:

- Some people prefer proofreading a hard copy of a workbook rather than viewing it on the screen to check for errors and readability.

- Hard copies can serve as a backup reference if your storage medium is lost or becomes corrupted and you need to recreate the workbook.

Instead of distributing a hard copy of a workbook, users can distribute the workbook as an electronic image that mirrors the original workbook's appearance. The electronic image of the workbook can be sent as an email attachment, posted on a website, or copied to a portable storage medium such as a USB flash drive. Two popular electronic image formats, sometimes called fixed formats, are PDF by Adobe Systems and XPS by Microsoft. In Excel, you can create electronic image files through the Save As dialog box and the Export, Share, and Print tabs in the Backstage view. Electronic images of workbooks, such as PDF and XPS, can be useful for the following reasons:

- Users can view electronic images of workbooks without the software that created the original workbook (e.g., Excel). Specifically, to view a PDF file, you use a program called Adobe Reader, which can be downloaded free from Adobe's website. Similarly, to view an XPS file, you use a program called XPS Viewer, which is included in the latest versions of Windows and Internet Explorer.

- Sending electronic workbooks saves paper and printer supplies. Society encourages users to contribute to **green computing**, which involves reducing the electricity consumed and environmental waste generated when using computers, mobile devices, and related technologies.

To Preview and Print a Worksheet in Landscape Orientation

Pages printed in portrait orientation have the short (8½") edge at the top of the printout; the printed page is taller than it is wide. Landscape orientation prints the long (11") edge at the top of the paper; the printed page is wider than it is tall. With the completed workbook saved, you may want to print it. *Why? Because the worksheet is included in a report, you will print a hard copy on a printer.* The following steps print a hard copy of the contents of the worksheet.

1

- Tap or click FILE on the ribbon to open the Backstage view.

- Tap or click the Print tab in the Backstage view to display the Print gallery (Figure 1–66).

Q&A How can I print multiple copies of my worksheet?
Increase the number in the Copies box in the Print gallery.

What if I decide not to print the worksheet at this time?
Tap or click the Back button in the upper-left corner of the Backstage view to return to the workbook window.

Figure 1–66

2

- Verify that the printer listed on the Printer Status button will print a hard copy of the workbook. If necessary, tap or click the Printer Status button to display a list of available printer options and then tap or click the desired printer to change the currently selected printer.

3

- Tap or click the Portrait Orientation button in the Settings area and then select Landscape Orientation to change the orientation of the page to landscape.

- Tap or click the No Scaling button and then select 'Fit Sheet on One Page' to print the entire worksheet on one page (Figure 1–67).

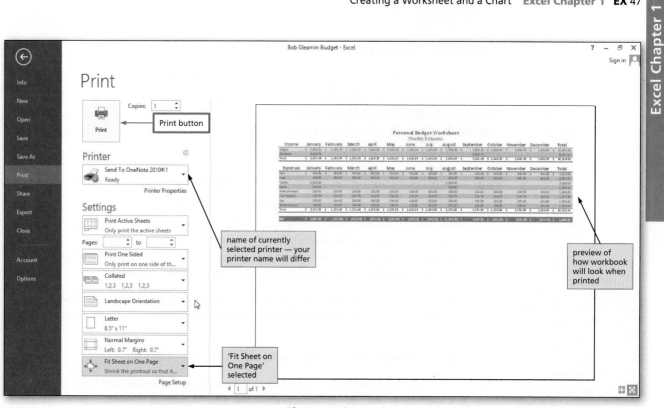

Figure 1–67

4

- Tap or click the Print button in the Print gallery to print the worksheet in landscape orientation on the currently selected printer.

- When the printer stops, retrieve the hard copy (Figure 1–68).

Q&A

Do I have to wait until my worksheet is complete to print it?

No, you can follow these steps to print a document at any time while you are creating it.

Personal Budget Worksheet
Monthly Estimates

Income	January	February	March	April	May	June	July	August	September	October	November	December	Total
Wages	$1,000.29	$ 1,000.29	$1,000.29	$1,000.29	$1,000.29	$1,000.29	$1,000.29	$ 1,000.29	$ 1,000.29	$1,000.29	$ 1,000.29	$ 1,000.29	$ 12,003.48
Dividends	4,000.75	-	-	-	-	-	-	-	4,000.75	-	-	-	8,001.50
Total	**$ 5,001.04**	**$ 1,000.29**	**$1,000.29**	**$1,000.29**	**$1,000.29**	**$1,000.29**	**$1,000.29**	**$ 1,000.29**	**$ 5,001.04**	**$1,000.29**	**$ 1,000.29**	**$ 1,000.29**	**$ 20,004.98**

Expenses	January	February	March	April	May	June	July	August	September	October	November	December	Total
Rent	$ 400.89	$ 400.89	$ 400.89	$ 400.89	$ 400.89	$ 400.89	$ 400.89	$ 400.89	$ 400.89	$ 400.89	$ 400.89	$ 400.89	$ 4,810.68
Food	300.00	300.00	300.00	300.00	300.00	300.00	300.00	300.00	300.00	300.00	300.00	300.00	3,600.00
Tuition	1,500.00	-	-	-	-	-	-	1,500.00	-	-	-	-	3,000.00
Books	500.00	-	-	-	-	-	-	500.00	-	-	-	-	1,000.00
Entertainment	100.00	100.00	100.00	100.00	100.00	100.00	100.00	100.00	100.00	100.00	100.00	100.00	1,200.00
Car Payment	154.79	154.79	154.79	154.79	154.79	154.79	154.79	154.79	154.79	154.79	154.79	154.79	1,857.48
Gas	100.00	100.00	100.00	100.00	150.00	150.00	150.00	100.00	100.00	100.00	100.00	100.00	1,350.00
Miscellaneous	100.00	100.00	100.00	100.00	100.00	100.00	100.00	100.00	100.00	100.00	100.00	100.00	1,200.00
Total	**$ 3,155.68**	**$ 1,155.68**	**$1,155.68**	**$1,155.68**	**$1,205.68**	**$1,205.68**	**$1,205.68**	**$ 3,155.68**	**$ 1,155.68**	**$1,155.68**	**$ 1,155.68**	**$ 1,155.68**	**$ 18,018.16**

| Net | $1,845.36 | $ (155.39) | $ (155.39) | $ (155.39) | $ (205.39) | $ (205.39) | $ (205.39) | $(2,155.39) | $ 3,845.36 | $ (155.39) | $ (155.39) | $ (155.39) | $ 1,986.82 |

Figure 1–68

Other Ways

1. Press CTRL+P, press ENTER

To Open a Document from Excel

Earlier in this chapter you saved your workbook using the file name, Bob Gleamin Budget. The following steps open the Bob Gleamin Budget file from the Excel folder in the CIS 101 folder. For a detailed example of the procedure summarized below, refer to the Office and Windows chapter at the beginning of this book.

1 Tap or click FILE on the ribbon to open the Backstage view and then tap or click the Open tab in the Backstage view to display the Open gallery.

2 If the file you wish to open is displayed in the Recent Workbooks list, tap or click the file name to open the file and display the opened workbook in the Excel window; then skip the remaining steps. If the file you wish to open is not displayed in the Recent Workbooks list, proceed to the next step to locate the file.

3 Tap or click Computer, SkyDrive, or another location in the left pane and then navigate to the location of the file to be opened (in this case, the Excel folder in the CIS 101 folder).

4 Tap or click Bob Gleamin Budget to select the file to be opened.

5 Tap or click the Open button (Open dialog box) to open the selected file and display the opened workbook in the Excel window.

BTW
Printing Document Properties
To print document properties, tap or click FILE on the ribbon to open the Backstage view, tap or click the Print tab in the Backstage view to display the Print gallery, tap or click the first button in the Settings area to display a list of options specifying what you can print, tap or click Document Info in the list to specify you want to print the document properties instead of the actual document, and then tap or click the Print button in the Print gallery to print the document properties on the currently selected printer.

AutoCalculate

You easily can obtain a total, an average, or other information about the numbers in a range by using the **AutoCalculate area** on the status bar. First, select the range of cells containing the numbers you want to check. Next, press and hold or right-click the AutoCalculate area to display the Customize Status Bar shortcut menu (Figure 1–69). The check marks indicate that the calculations are included in the status bar; more than one may be selected. The functions of the AutoCalculate commands on the Customize Status Bar shortcut menu are described in Table 1–4.

Table 1–4 Commonly Used Status Bar Commands	
Command	**Function**
Average	AutoCalculate area displays the average of the numbers in the selected range
Count	AutoCalculate area displays the number of nonblank cells in the selected range
Numerical Count	AutoCalculate area displays the number of cells containing numbers in the selected range
Minimum	AutoCalculate area displays the lowest value in the selected range
Maximum	AutoCalculate area displays the highest value in the selected range
Sum	AutoCalculate area displays the sum of the numbers in the selected range

To Use the AutoCalculate Area to Determine a Maximum

1 ENTER TEXT | 2 CALCULATE SUMS & USE FORMULAS | 3 SAVE WORKBOOK | 4 FORMAT TEXT
5 INSERT CHART | 6 NAME TAB | **7 PREVIEW & PRINT WORKSHEET**

The following steps display the largest total for the months in the budget. *Why? Sometimes, you want to see a quick analysis, which can be shown in the AutoCalculate area on the status bar.*

1

- Select the range B19:M19. Press and hold or right-click the status bar to display the Customize Status Bar shortcut menu (Figure 1–69).

Q&A

What is displayed on the Customize Status Bar shortcut menu?

This shortcut menu includes several commands that allow you to control the items displayed on the Customize Status Bar shortcut menu. The AutoCalculate area includes six commands as well as the result of the associated calculation on the right side of the menu.

Figure 1–69

2

- Tap or click Maximum on the shortcut menu to display the Maximum value in the range B19:M19 in the AutoCalculate area of the status bar.

- Tap or click anywhere on the worksheet to cause the shortcut menu to disappear (Figure 1–70).

3

- Press and hold or right-click the AutoCalculate area and then tap or click Maximum on the shortcut menu to cause the Maximum value to no longer appear in the AutoCalculate area.

- Tap or click anywhere in the worksheet to cause the shortcut menu to disappear.

Figure 1–70

Correcting Errors

You can correct errors on a worksheet using one of several methods. The method you choose will depend on the extent of the error and whether you notice it while entering the data or after you have entered the incorrect data into the cell.

Correcting Errors while Entering Data into a Cell

If you notice an error while you are entering data into a cell, press the BACKSPACE key to erase the incorrect character(s) and then enter the correct character(s). If the error is a major one, tap or click the Cancel box in the formula bar or press the ESC key to erase the entire entry and then reenter the data from the beginning.

Correcting Errors after Entering Data into a Cell

If you find an error in the worksheet after entering the data, you can correct the error in one of two ways:

1. If the entry is short, select the cell, retype the entry correctly, and then tap or click the Enter box or press the ENTER key. The new entry will replace the old entry.

2. If the entry in the cell is long and the errors are minor, using Edit mode may be a better choice than retyping the cell entry. Use Edit mode as described below.

   a. Double-tap or double-click the cell containing the error to switch Excel to Edit mode. In **Edit mode**, Excel displays the active cell entry in the formula bar and a flashing insertion point in the active cell. With Excel in Edit mode, you can edit the contents directly in the cell — a procedure called **in-cell editing** (Figure 1– 71).

Figure 1–71

   b. Make changes using in-cell editing, as indicated below.

      (1) To insert new characters between two characters, place the insertion point between the two characters and begin typing. Excel inserts the new characters to the left of the insertion point.

      (2) To delete a character in the cell, move the insertion point to the left of the character you want to delete and then press the DELETE key, or place the insertion point to the right of the character you want to delete and then press the BACKSPACE key. You also can drag to select the character or adjacent characters you want to delete and then press the DELETE key or CTRL+X, or tap or click the Cut button (HOME tab | Clipboard group).

      (3) When you are finished editing an entry, tap or click the Enter box or press the ENTER key.

When Excel enters Edit mode, the keyboard usually is in Insert mode. In **Insert mode**, as you type a character, Excel inserts the character and moves all characters to the right of the typed character one position to the right. You can change to Overtype mode by pressing the INSERT key. In **Overtype mode**, Excel overtypes, or replaces, the character to the right of the insertion point. The INSERT key toggles the keyboard between Insert mode and Overtype mode.

While in Edit mode, you may have reason to move the insertion point to various points in the cell, select portions of the data in the cell, or switch from inserting characters to overtyping characters. Table 1– 5 summarizes the more common tasks performed during in-cell editing.

Table 1–5 Summary of In-Cell Editing Tasks

	Task	Touch / Mouse	Keyboard
1.	Move the insertion point to the beginning of data in a cell.	Point to the left of the first character and tap or click.	Press HOME
2.	Move the insertion point to the end of data in a cell.	Point to the right of the last character and tap or click.	Press END
3.	Move the insertion point anywhere in a cell.	Point to the appropriate position and tap or click the character.	Press RIGHT ARROW or LEFT ARROW
4.	Highlight one or more adjacent characters.	Drag through adjacent characters.	Press SHIFT+RIGHT ARROW or SHIFT+LEFT ARROW
5.	Select all data in a cell.	Double-tap or double-click the cell with the insertion point in the cell if the data in the cell contains no spaces.	
6.	Delete selected characters.	Tap or click the Cut button (HOME tab | Clipboard group).	Press DELETE
7.	Delete characters to the left of the insertion point.		Press BACKSPACE
8.	Delete characters to the right of the insertion point.		Press DELETE
9.	Toggle between Insert and Overtype modes.		Press INSERT

Undoing the Last Cell Entry

Excel provides the Undo button on the Quick Access Toolbar (Figure 1–72), which allows you to erase recent cell entries. Thus, if you enter incorrect data in a cell and notice it immediately, tap or click the Undo button and Excel changes the cell entry to what it was prior to the incorrect data entry.

Figure 1–72

Excel remembers the last 100 actions you have completed. Thus, you can undo up to 100 previous actions by tapping or clicking the Undo arrow to display the Undo list and then tapping or clicking the action to be undone (Figure 1–72). You can drag through several actions in the Undo list to undo all of them at once. If no actions are available for Excel to undo, then the Undo button is unavailable; its dimmed appearance indicates that it is unavailable.

The Redo button, next to the Undo button on the Quick Access Toolbar, allows you to repeat previous actions; that is, if you accidentally undo an action, you can use the Redo button to redo it.

Clearing a Cell or Range of Cells

If you enter data into the wrong cell or range of cells, you can erase, or clear, the data using one of the first four methods listed below. The fifth method clears the formatting from the selected cells. To clear a cell or range of cells, you would perform the following steps:

TO CLEAR CELL ENTRIES USING THE FILL HANDLE

1. Select the cell or range of cells and then point to the fill handle so that the pointer changes to a crosshair.
2. Drag the fill handle back into the selected cell or range until a shadow covers the cell or cells you want to erase.

TO CLEAR CELL ENTRIES USING THE SHORTCUT MENU

1. Select the cell or range of cells to be cleared.
2. Press and hold or right-click the selection.
3. Tap or click Clear Contents on the shortcut menu.

TO CLEAR CELL ENTRIES USING THE DELETE KEY

1. Select the cell or range of cells to be cleared.
2. Press the DELETE key.

TO CLEAR CELL ENTRIES AND FORMATTING USING THE CLEAR BUTTON

1. Select the cell or range of cells to be cleared.
2. Tap or click the Clear button (HOME tab | Editing group).
3. Tap or click Clear Contents on the menu.

TO CLEAR FORMATTING USING THE CELL STYLES BUTTON

1. Select the cell or range of cells from which you want to remove the formatting.
2. Tap or click the Cell Styles button (HOME tab | Styles group) and point to Normal.
3. Tap or click Normal in the Cell Styles gallery.

The Clear All command on the Clear menu is the only command that clears both the cell entry and the cell formatting. As you are clearing cell entries, always remember that you should *never press the SPACEBAR to clear a cell*. Pressing the SPACEBAR enters a blank character. A blank character is text and is different from an empty cell, even though the cell may appear empty.

Clearing the Entire Worksheet

If the required worksheet edits are extremely extensive or if the requirements drastically change, you may want to clear the entire worksheet and start over. To clear the worksheet or delete an embedded chart, you would use the following steps.

TO CLEAR THE ENTIRE WORKSHEET

1. Tap or click the Select All button on the worksheet.
2. Tap or click the Clear button (HOME tab | Editing group) and then tap or click Clear All on the menu to delete both the entries and formats.

BTW

Certification
The Microsoft Office Specialist (MOS) program provides an opportunity for you to obtain a valuable industry credential — proof that you have the Excel 2013 skills required by employers. For more information, visit the Certification resource on the Student Companion Site located on www.cengagebrain.com. For detailed instructions about accessing available resources, visit www.cengage.com/ct/studentdownload or contact your instructor for information about accessing the required files.

The Select All button selects the entire worksheet. Instead of tapping or clicking the Select All button, you can press CTRL+A. To clear an unsaved workbook, tap or click the Close Window button on the workbook's title bar or tap or click the Close button in the Backstage view. Tap or click the No button if the Microsoft Excel dialog box asks if you want to save changes. To start a new, blank workbook, tap or click the New button in the Backstage view.

To Sign Out of a Microsoft Account

If you are signed in to a Microsoft account and are using a public computer or otherwise wish to sign out of your Microsoft account, you should sign out of the account from the Account gallery in the Backstage view before exiting Excel. Signing out of the account is the safest way to make sure that nobody else can access SkyDrive files or settings stored in your Microsoft account. The following steps sign out of a Microsoft account from Excel. For a detailed example of the procedure summarized below, refer to the Office and Windows chapter at the beginning of this book.

1 If you wish to sign out of your Microsoft account, tap or click FILE on the ribbon to open the Backstage view and then tap or click the Account tab to display the Account gallery.

2 Tap or click the Sign out link, which displays the Remove Account dialog box. If a Can't remove Windows accounts dialog box appears instead of the Remove Account dialog box, click the OK button and skip the remaining steps.

Q&A Why does a Can't remove Windows accounts dialog box appear?
If you signed in to Windows using your Microsoft account, then you also must sign out from Windows, rather than signing out from within Excel. When you are finished using Windows, be sure to sign out at that time.

3 Tap or click the Yes button (Remove Account dialog box) to sign out of your Microsoft account on this computer.

Q&A Should I sign out of Windows after signing out of my Microsoft account?
When you are finished using the computer, you should sign out of your account for maximum security.

4 Tap or click the Back button in the upper-left corner of the Backstage view to return to the worksheet.

To Exit Excel

This project now is complete. The following steps exit Excel. For a detailed example of the procedure summarized below, refer to the Office and Windows chapter at the beginning of this book.

 1a If you have one Excel workbook open, tap or click the Close button on the right side of the title bar to close the open workbook and exit Excel.

1b If you have multiple Excel workbooks open, press and hold or right-click the Excel app button on the taskbar and then tap or click 'Close all windows' on the shortcut menu, or press ALT+F4 to close all open workbooks and exit Excel.

Q&A Could I press and hold or repeatedly click the Close button to close all open documents and exit Excel?
Yes.

 2 If a Microsoft Excel dialog box appears, tap or click the Save button to save any changes made to the workbook since the last save.

BTW
Quick Reference
For a table that lists how to complete the tasks covered in this book using touch gestures, the mouse, ribbon, shortcut menu, and keyboard, see the Quick Reference Summary at the back of this book, or visit the Quick Reference resource on the Student Companion Site located on www.cengagebrain.com. For detailed instructions about accessing available resources, visit www.cengage.com/ct/studentdownload or contact your instructor for information about accessing the required files.

Chapter Summary

In this chapter you have learned how to enter text and numbers to create a worksheet, select a range, use the Sum button, format cells, insert a chart, and preview and print a worksheet. The items listed below include all the new Excel skills you have learned in this chapter, with the tasks grouped by activity.

Clear Cells
Clear Cell Entries Using the Fill Handle (EX 52)
Clear Cell Entries Using the Shortcut Menu (EX 52)
Clear Cell Entries Using the DELETE Key
(EX 52)
Clear Cell Entries and Formatting Using the Clear
Button (EX 52)
Clear Cell Formatting Using the Cell Styles
Button (EX 52)
Clear the Entire Worksheet (EX 52)

Display AutoCalculate Functions
Use the AutoCalculate Area to Determine a
Maximum (EX 48)

Enter Data
Enter the Worksheet Titles (EX 7)
Enter Column Titles (EX 9)
Enter Row Titles (EX 11)
Enter Numbers (EX 12)

Enter Functions and Formulas
Sum a Column of Numbers (EX 14)
Copy a Cell to Adjacent Cells in a Row (EX 16)
Determine Multiple Totals at the Same Time (EX 18)
Enter a Formula Using the Keyboard (EX 20)

File Management
Change Document Properties (EX 44)

Format a Worksheet
Change a Cell Style (EX 24)
Change the Font (EX 25)
Bold a Cell (EX 26)
Increase the Font Size of a Cell Entry (EX 27)
Change the Font Color of a Cell Entry (EX 28)
Center Cell Entries across Columns by Merging
Cells (EX 29)
Format Rows Using Cell Styles (EX 30)
Format Numbers in the Worksheet (EX 32)
Adjust the Column Width (EX 34)
Use the Name Box to Select a Cell (EX 35)

Insert a Chart
Add a 3-D Pie Chart (EX 38)
Apply a Style to a Chart (EX 40)

Manage Worksheets
Move a Chart to a New Sheet (EX 41)
Change the Worksheet Tab Name (EX 42)

Preview and Print Worksheets
Preview and Print a Worksheet in Landscape
Orientation (EX 46)

CONSIDER THIS

What decisions will you need to make when creating workbooks and charts in the future?

1. Determine the workbook structure.

   a) Determine the data you will need for your workbook.

   b) Sketch a layout of your data and your chart.

2. Create the worksheet.

   a) Enter titles, subtitles, and headings.

   b) Enter data, functions, and formulas.

3. Format the worksheet.

   a) Format the titles, subtitles, and headings using styles.

   b) Format the totals.

   c) Format the numbers.

   d) Format the text.

4. Create the chart.

   a) Determine the type of chart to use.

   b) Determine the chart title and data.

   c) Format the chart.

How should you submit solutions to questions in the assignments identified with a ✳ symbol?
Every assignment in this book contains one or more questions identified with a ✳ symbol. These questions require you to think beyond the assigned file. Present your solutions to the questions in the format required by your instructor. Possible formats may include one or more of these options: write the answer; create a document that contains the answer; present your answer to the class; discuss your answer in a group; record the answer as audio or video using a webcam, smartphone, or portable media player; or post answers on a blog, wiki, or website.

Apply Your Knowledge

Reinforce the skills and apply the concepts you learned in this chapter.

Changing the Values in a Worksheet

Note: To complete this assignment, you will be required to use the Data Files for Students. Visit www.cengage.com/ct/studentdownload for detailed instructions or contact your instructor for information about accessing the required files.

Instructions: Run Excel. Open the workbook Apply 1–1 Treagle Market (Figure 1–73a on the next page).

1. Make the changes to the worksheet described in Table 1–6 so that the worksheet appears as shown in Figure 1–73b on the next page. As you edit the values in the cells containing numeric data, watch the totals in row 8, the totals in column G, and the chart change.

2. Change the worksheet title in cell A1 to the Title cell style and then merge and center it across columns A through G. Use buttons in the Font group on the HOME tab on the ribbon to change the worksheet subtitle in cell A2 to 14-point font and then center it across columns A through G. Use the Aqua, Accent 5 color (column 9, row 1 in the Font Color gallery) for the aqua font color.

3. Apply the worksheet name, Yearly Analysis, to the sheet tab and apply the Aqua, Accent 5 theme color to the sheet tab.

4. Move the chart to a new sheet called Sales Analysis Chart. Apply the Style 2 chart style to the chart (Figure 1–73c on the next page). Change the chart title to SALES ANALYSIS.

5. Replace Treagle in cell A1 with your last name. Save the workbook using the file name, Apply 1–1 Treagle Market Sales Analysis. Submit the revised workbook as specified by your instructor.

6. Exit Excel.

7. ✳ Besides the styles used in the worksheet, what other changes could you make to enhance the worksheet?

Table 1–6 New Worksheet Data	
Cell	**Change Cell Contents To**
A2	Yearly Sales Analysis
B7	3895.23
C5	26125.75
D6	30589.14
E7	35450.82
F6	6352.78

Continued >

Apply Your Knowledge *continued*

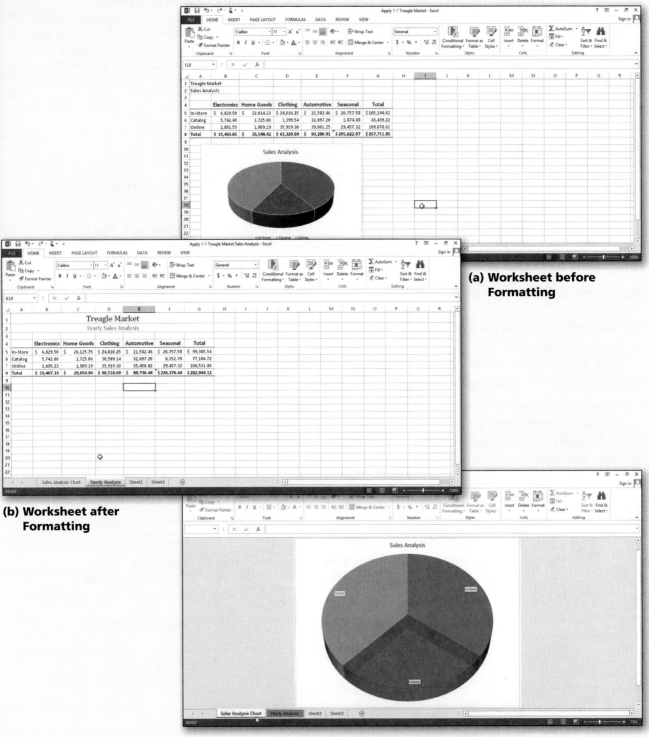

(a) Worksheet before Formatting

(b) Worksheet after Formatting

(c) 3-D Pie Chart on Separate Sheet

Figure 1–73

Extend Your Knowledge

Extend the skills you learned in this chapter and experiment with new skills. You may need to use Help to complete the assignment.

Creating Styles and Formatting a Worksheet

Note: To complete this assignment, you will be required to use the Data Files for Students. Visit www.cengage.com/ct/studentdownload for detailed instructions or contact your instructor for information about accessing the required files.

Instructions: Run Excel. Open the workbook Extend 1–1 Kaseey Vehicles (Figure 1–74). Perform the following tasks to create styles and format a worksheet using them.

1. Select cell A4. Use the New Cell Style command in the Cell Styles gallery to create a style that fills only cell A4 using the Orange, Accent 2, Lighter 40% color (row 4, column 6). Name the style, MyHeadings.

2. Select cell A5. Use the New Cell style dialog box to create a style that fills only cell A5 using the Orange, Accent 2, Lighter 80% color. Name the style, MyRows.

Figure 1–74

3. Select cell ranges B4:G4 and A5:A8. Apply the MyHeadings style to the cell ranges.

4. Select cell ranges B5:G5 and B7:G7. Apply the MyRows style to the cell ranges.

5. Apply a worksheet name to the sheet tab and apply a color of your choice to the sheet tab.

6. Change the font color for the text in cells A1 and A2 to the color of your eyes. Save the workbook using the file name, Extend 1–1 Kaseey Vehicles First Quarter. Submit the revised workbook as specified by your instructor.

7. Exit Excel.

8. ✵ What other styles would you create to improve the worksheet's appearance?

Analyze, Correct, Improve

Analyze a workbook and correct all errors and/or improve the design.

Fixing Formatting Problems and Data Errors in a Worksheet

Note: To complete this assignment, you will be required to use the Data Files for Students. Visit www.cengage.com/ct/studentdownload for detailed instructions or contact your instructor for information about accessing the required files.

Instructions: Run Excel. Open the workbook Analyze 1–1 CPJ Clothing. Correct the following formatting problems and data in the worksheet, while keeping in mind the guidelines presented in this chapter. Your worksheet should look like Figure 1–75 when it is corrected.

Figure 1–75

1. Correct

a. Correct the spelling mistake in cell A2 by changing Semiannul to Semiannual. Correct the spelling mistake in cell A5 by changing Orlndo to Orlando.

b. The SUM function in cell H7 does not sum all of the numbers in the column. Correct this error by editing the range for the SUM function in the cell.

2. Improve

a. Merge and center the worksheet title and subtitle appropriately.

b. Format the worksheet title and subtitle with appropriate cell styles. Change the font size of the subtitle to 16.

c. Apply the Green, Accent 6 color to the title and subtitle and bold them.

d. Add a title for totals row 10 and create the necessary totals in row 10.

e. Apply proper formatting to the column headers and total row, including centering the column headers.

f. Adjust the column sizes so that all data in each column is visible.

g. Create the grand total for the annual cost of goods.

h. Apply a worksheet name to the sheet tab and apply the Green, Accent 6 color to the sheet tab.

i. Change the document properties as specified by your instructor. Save the workbook using the file name, Analyze 1–1 CPJ Clothing Sales. Submit the revised workbook as specified by your instructor.

j. Change the city in cell A5 to the city you were born.

3. ✹ If you were going to create a pie chart of the expenses for each city, what data would you use?

In the Labs

Design and/or create a workbook using the guidelines, concepts, and skills presented in this chapter. Labs 1 and 2, which increase in difficulty, require you to create solutions based on what you learned in the chapter; Lab 3 requires you to create a solution, which uses cloud and web technologies, by learning and investigating on your own from general guidance.

Lab 1: Fourth Quarter Revenue Analysis Worksheet

Problem: You work as a spreadsheet specialist for Caitlyn's Candles, which has four regional shops in the state of California. Your manager has asked you to develop a fourth quarter revenue analysis similar to the one shown in Figure 1–76.

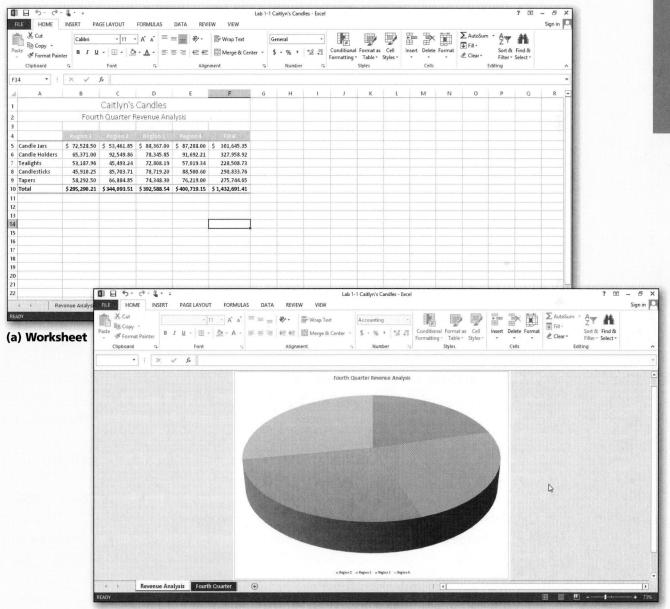

(a) Worksheet

(b) Pie Chart

Figure 1–76

Continued >

In the Labs *continued*

Instructions: Perform the following tasks.

1. Run Excel and create a new blank workbook. Enter the worksheet title, Caitlyn's Candles, in cell A1 and the worksheet subtitle, Fourth Quarter Revenue Analysis, in cell A2. Beginning in row 4, enter the region data shown in Table 1–7.

Table 1–7 Caitlyn's Candles				
	Region 1	**Region 2**	**Region 3**	**Region 4**
Candle Jars	72,528.50	53,461.85	88,367.00	87,288.00
Candle Holders	65,371.00	92,549.86	78,345.85	91,692.21
Tealights	53,187.96	45,493.24	72,808.19	57,019.34
Candlesticks	45,910.25	85,703.71	78,719.20	88,500.60
Tapers	58,292.50	66,884.85	74,348.30	76,219.00

2. Create totals for each region, product, and company grand total.

3. Format the worksheet title with the Title cell style. Center the title across columns A through F.

4. Format the worksheet subtitle to 14-point Calibri Light, and change the font color to Blue-Gray, Text 2. Center the subtitle across columns A through F.

5. Use Cell Styles to format the range A4:F4 with the Heading 2 cell style, the range B4:F4 with the 60% - Accent 4 cell style, and the range A10:F10 with the Total cell style. Center the column titles in row 4. Apply the accounting number format to the ranges B5:F5 and B10:F10. Apply the comma style format to the range B6:F9. Adjust any column widths to the widest text entry in each column.

6. Select the ranges B4:E4 and B10:E10 and then insert a 3-D pie chart. Apply the Style 4 chart style to the chart. Move the chart to a new worksheet named Revenue Analysis. Change the chart title to Fourth Quarter Revenue Analysis.

7. Rename the Sheet1 tab, Fourth Quarter, and apply the Purple color to the sheet tab. Change the document properties, as specified by your instructor.

8. Save the workbook using the file name, Lab 1-1 Caitlyn's Candles.

9. Preview and print the worksheet in landscape orientation.

10. Make the following two corrections to the Tealights: 55899.23 for Region 4 (cell E7) and 55,238.56 for Candle Jars for Region 2 (cell C5). After you enter the corrections, the total in cell F10 should equal $1,433,348.01.

11. Change the font color of the text in cells A1 and A2 to the color of the shirt you currently are wearing.

12. Preview and print the revised worksheet in landscape orientation. Close the workbook without saving the changes.

13. ✷ If you wanted to chart the item totals instead of the regions, which ranges would you use to create the chart?

14. Submit the assignment as specified by your instructor.

Lab 2: **Sales Analysis Worksheet**

Problem: As the chief accountant for CinCar Satellite, a satellite service serving seven states, you have been asked by the vice president to create a worksheet to analyze the yearly sales for each state (Figure 1–77). The packages and corresponding sales by state for the year are shown in Table 1–8 on the next page.

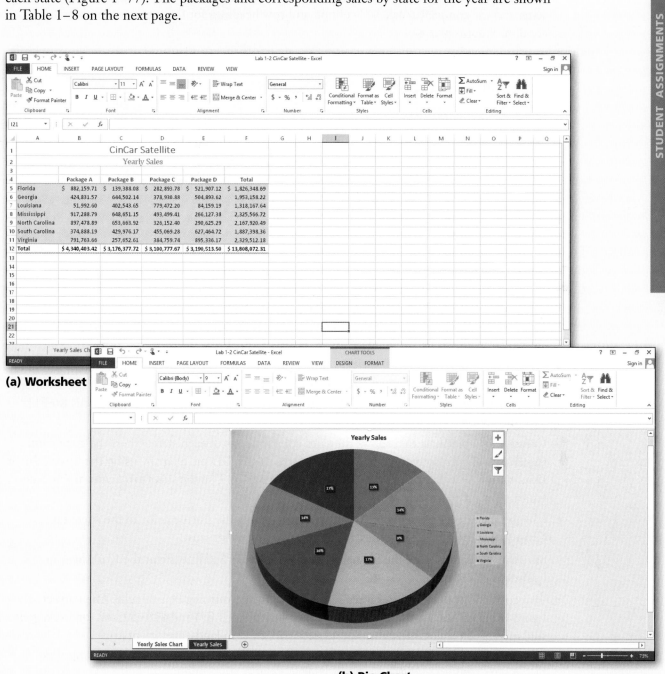

(a) Worksheet

(b) Pie Chart

Figure 1–77

Continued >

Instructions: Perform the following tasks.

1. Create the worksheet shown in Figure 1– 77a on the previous page using the data in Table 1– 8.

2. Use the SUM function to determine total revenue for the four packages, the totals for each state, and the company total. Add column and row headings for the totals row and totals column, as appropriate.

Table 1–8 CinCar Satellite				
	Package A	**Package B**	**Package C**	**Package D**
Florida	$882,159.71	$139,388.08	$282,893.78	$521,907.12
Georgia	424,831.57	644,502.14	378,930.88	504,893.62
Louisiana	51,992.60	402,543.65	779,472.20	84,159.19
Mississippi	917,288.79	648,651.15	493,499.41	266,127.38
North Carolina	897,478.89	653,663.92	326,152.40	290,625.29
South Carolina	374,888.19	429,976.17	455,069.28	627,464.72
Virginia	$791,763.66	$257,652.61	$384,759.74	$895,336.17

3. Format the worksheet title and subtitle with the Title cell style and center them across columns A through F. Use the Font group on the ribbon to format the worksheet subtitle as 14-point Cambria red. Format the title with Dark Red, bold font color. Center the titles across columns A through F.

4. Format the range B4:F4 with the Heading 3 cell style and center the text in the cells. Format the range A5:F11 with the 20% - Accent 1 cell style, and the range A12:F12 with the Total cell style. Format cells B5:F5 and B12:F12 with the accounting number format and cells B6:F11 with the comma style format.

5. Create a 3-D pie chart that shows the sales contributions of each state. Chart the state names (A5:A11) and corresponding totals (F5:F11). Insert the 3-D pie chart by using the 'Insert Pie or Doughnut Chart' button (INSERT tab | Charts group). Use the sheet tab name, Yearly Sales Chart. Apply a chart style of your choosing.

6. Change the Sheet1 tab name to Yearly Sales, and apply the Purple color to the sheet tab. Change the document properties, as specified by your instructor.

7. Save the workbook using the file name, Lab 1-2 CinCar Satellite. Print the worksheet in landscape orientation.

8. Two corrections to the figures were sent in from the accounting department. The correct sales figure is $151,992.60 for Package A sold in Louisiana (cell B7) and $183,573.67 for Package B sold in Virginia (cell C11). Print the revised worksheet in landscape orientation.

9. Use the Undo button to change the worksheet back to the original numbers in Table 1–8. Use the Redo button to change the worksheet back to the revised state.

10. Exit Excel without saving the latest changes to the workbook.

11. Change the state in cell A11 to the state in which you were born. If your state already is listed in the spreadsheet, choose a different state.

12. ☀ If you wanted to make a distinction between the rows in the table, what could you do?

13. Submit the assignment as specified by your instructor.

Lab 3: Expand Your World: Cloud and Web Technologies Online

Problem: You are tasked with creating a travel expense report for two trips you made to conferences during the past six months. You decide to download and use one of Excel's templates to create your worksheet.

Instructions Part 1: Tap or click the New tab in the Backstage view and then search for and tap or click the Travel expense report template to download it. Enter data for two trips, one to Las Vegas and one for San Diego, using the web to search for data. Save the file as Lab 1-3 Part 1 Travel Expenses. Print the worksheet. Submit the assignment as specified by your instructor.

Instructions Part 2: ☀ Which template would you use if you wanted to create a workout plan or a training plan for employees?

☀ Consider This: Your Turn

Apply your creative thinking and problem solving skills to design and implement a solution.

1: Create a Personal Budget

Personal

Part 1: To estimate your budget, you decide to create a worksheet listing your income and expenses. Create a worksheet that lists your incomes and your expenses using estimates for the next six months. Total your income and expenses. Calculate your net value using a simple formula. Use the concepts and techniques presented in this chapter to format your worksheet and create a 3-D pie chart for your net result for the six months. Submit your assignment in the format specified by your instructor.

Part 2: ☀ Now that you have looked over your results, did you neglect to include any income? How did you determine the values you used in your estimates? Did you anticipate possible changes in the near future?

2: Create a Sales Worksheet

Professional

Part 1: You are working for a popular sports restaurant that has five branches. Your boss has asked you to create a worksheet to show results for drinks, meals, games, and souvenir sales. Using estimates, create the worksheet for Sports & You. Include totals and averages. Use the concepts and techniques presented in this chapter to format the workbook. Include a chart to compare your revenues. Submit your assignment in the format specified by your instructor.

Part 2: ☀ What steps did you use to create your estimates? Based upon your knowledge of restaurants, do you think seasonal sales would be different, and if so, why?

3: Compare Car Prices

Research and Collaboration

Part 1: Working in a group, research current cars for sale. Create a worksheet that compares the type of cars and the base price for each model, as well as the costs to add various additional options. Calculate the average price for the cars and averages of the additional options. Use the concepts and techniques presented in this chapter to format the worksheet. Include a chart to compare the different car costs. Submit your assignment in the format specified by your instructor.

Part 2: ☀ Based upon the data you found, how could you chart the information to show the comparisons? Which chart would be the best to use?

Learn Online

Reinforce what you learned in this chapter with games, exercises, training, and many other online activities and resources.

Student Companion Site Reinforcement activities and resources are available at no additional cost on www.cengagebrain.com. Visit www.cengage.com/ct/studentdownload for detailed instructions about accessing the resources available at the Student Companion Site.

SAM Put your skills into practice with SAM! If you have a SAM account, go to www.cengage.com/sam2013 to access SAM assignments for this chapter.

1 Databases and Database Objects: An Introduction

Microsoft product screenshots used with permission from Microsoft Corporation.

Objectives

You will have mastered the material in this chapter when you can:

- Describe the features of the Access window
- Create a database
- Create tables in Datasheet and Design views
- Add records to a table
- Close a database
- Open a database

- Print the contents of a table
- Create and use a query
- Create and use a form
- Create and print custom reports
- Modify a report in Layout view
- Perform special database operations
- Design a database to satisfy a collection of requirements

1 | Databases and Database Objects: An Introduction

Introduction

The term **database** describes a collection of data organized in a manner that allows access, retrieval, and use of that data. Microsoft Access 2013, usually referred to as simply Access, is a database management system. A **database management system** is software that allows you to use a computer to create a database; add, change, and delete data in the database; ask and answer questions concerning the data; and create forms and reports using the data.

Project — Database Creation

Bavant Publishing Inc. is a publishing company that specializes in foreign language textbooks. Bavant sells in both the K-12 and the higher education markets. Recently, Bavant purchased a small, private publisher of Arabic, Russian, Chinese, and Japanese language textbooks. These languages are increasing in popularity with college students. All textbooks are available in hardcover and some are available as e-books. Bavant Publishing also provides ancillary materials, such as workbooks and laboratory manuals, video resources, audio resources, and companion websites.

Bavant representatives visit campuses and meet with faculty, describing the features and strengths of the textbooks and providing review materials for instructors. Bavant pays a base salary to its book reps, who can earn bonus pay based on exceeding sales goals. Customers place orders with the publisher following the organization's procedures; for example, colleges and universities place orders through their bookstores. Because institutions can cancel classes due to low enrollments, customers sometimes return unused books. At the end of an accounting period, these returns are subtracted from the current amount due.

Bavant wants to maintain records on the sales of textbooks from the newly acquired publisher separately from their other foreign language textbooks to better track profitability and market potential. Bavant organizes this data on its customers and book representatives in a database managed by Access. In this way, Bavant keeps its data current and accurate and can analyze it for trends and produce a variety of useful reports.

In a **relational database** such as those maintained by Access, a database consists of a collection of tables, each of which contains information on a specific subject. Figure 1–1 shows the database for Bavant Publishing. It consists of two tables: the Customer table (Figure 1–1a) contains information about Bavant customers, and the Book Rep table (Figure 1–1b) contains information about the book reps to whom these customers are assigned.

TABLE TOOLS   Bavant Publishin

FILE   HOME   CREATE   EXTERNAL DATA   DATABASE TOOLS   FIELDS   TABLE

caption for Customer Number field

fields

CU #	Customer Name	Street	City	State	Postal Code	Amount Paid	Current Due	Returns	BR #	Click to Add
ASU37	Applewood State University	300 University Ave.	Greer	PA	19158	$41,530.98	$38,812.66	$12,008.02	42	
BCJ21	Brodkin Junior College	4806 Park Dr.	Greer	PA	19158	$0.00	$6,081.98	$0.00	42	
CSD25	Cowpens ISD	829 Wooster Ave.	Gossett	PA	19157	$12,750.00	$13,275.00	$2,000.00	53	
CSU10	Camellia State University	725 Camellia St.	Pleasantburg	NJ	07025	$63,246.88	$69,847.76	$14,967.98	53	
DCC34	Dartt Community College	3827 Burgess Dr.	Chambers	NJ	07037	$21,345.50	$23,467.75	$4,496.80	65	
FSC12	First State College	7300 Cedar Rd.	Quaker	DE	19719	$34,557.25	$23,875.98	$7,234.99	65	
FSU23	Farnham State University	1445 Hubert St.	Gaston	DE	19723	$18,268.00	$22,024.50	$3,496.23	42	
HSD05	Hammonds County ISD	446 Lincoln Blvd.	Chesnee	NJ	07053	$18,434.75	$0.00	$0.00	53	
KCC78	Key Community College System	7523 Penn Ave.	Adelphia	PA	19159	$21,288.65	$11,367.49	$2,256.98	65	
MCC45	Mauldin Community College	72 Montrose St.	Chesnee	NJ	07053	$9,500.00	$5,000.00	$0.00	53	
MEC56	Mehitable College	202 College St.	Gaston	DE	19723	$9,111.19	$7,310.76	$574.25	42	
PLI22	PrattLast Institute	236 Ashton Ave.	Pleasantburg	NJ	07025	$17,229.45	$11,769.75	$3,450.50	53	
SCC77	Stallone Community College	1200 Franklin Blvd.	Adelphia	PA	19156	$7,525.98	$2,515.78	$0.00	53	
SEC19	Seaborn College	345 Mather Rd.	Quaker	DE	19719	$9,225.34	$10,496.89	$2,017.67	65	
TSC02	Tri-State Consortium	3400 Metro Pkwy.	Adelphia	PA	19156	$34,578.90	$9,432.56	$943.34	65	

records

BR # (Book Rep Number) is 42

Figure 1–1 (a) Customer Table

Book Rep

BR #	Last Name	First Name	Street	City	State	Postal Code	Start Date	Salary	Bonus Rate	Click to Add
42	Perez	Melina	261 Porter Dr.	Adelphia	PA	19156	5/14/2012	$31,500.00	0.20	
48	Statnik	Michael	3135 Simpson Dr.	Pleasantburg	NJ	07025	1/15/2013	$29,000.00	0.20	
53	Ch		265 Maxwell St.	Gossett	PA	19157	6/1/2013	$26,250.00	0.19	
65	Ro		1827 Maple Ave.	Adelphia	PA	19159	7/1/2014	$7,750.00	0.18	
								$0.00	0.00	

BR # (Book Rep Number) for Melina Perez is 42

Figure 1–1 (b) Book Rep Table

The rows in the tables are called **records**. A record contains information about a given person, product, or event. A row in the Customer table, for example, contains information about a specific customer, such as the customer's name, address information, and other data.

The columns in the tables are called fields. A **field** contains a specific piece of information within a record. In the Customer table, for example, the fourth field, City, contains the name of the city where the customer is located.

The first field in the Customer table is CU #, which is an abbreviation for Customer Number. Bavant Publishing assigns each customer a number; the Bavant customer numbers consist of three uppercase letters followed by a two-digit number.

The customer numbers are unique; that is, no two customers have the same number. Such a field is a **unique identifier**. A unique identifier, as its name suggests, is a way of uniquely identifying each record in the database. A given customer number will appear only in a single record in the table. Only one record exists, for example, in which the customer number is TSC02. A unique identifier also is called a **primary key**. Thus, the Customer Number field is the primary key for the Customer table.

BTW

BTWs

For a complete list of the BTWs found in the margins of this book, visit the BTW resource on the Student Companion Site located on www.cengagebrain.com. For detailed instructions about accessing available resources, visit www.cengage.com/ ct/studentdownload or contact your instructor for information about accessing the required files.

BTW
Naming Fields
Access 2013 has a number
of reserved words, words
that have a special meaning
to Access. You cannot use
these reserved words as field
names. For example, Name
is a reserved word and could
not be used in the Customer
table to describe a customer's
name. For a complete list
of reserved words in Access
2013, consult Access Help.

The next eight fields in the Customer table are Customer Name, Street, City, State, Postal Code, Amount Paid, Current Due, and Returns. The Amount Paid column contains the amount that the customer has paid Bavant Publishing year to date (YTD) prior to the current period. The Current Due column contains the amount due to Bavant for the current period. The Returns column contains the dollar value of the books or other products the customer was unable to sell and has returned to Bavant in the current period. For example, customer TSC02 is Tri-State Consortium. The address is 3400 Metro Pkwy., in Adelphia, Pennsylvania. The postal code is 19156. The customer has paid $34,578.90 for products purchased so far. The amount due for the current period is $9,432.56. The customer has returned products worth $943.34.

Bavant assigns a single book rep to work with each customer. The last column in the Customer table, BR # (an abbreviation for Book Rep Number) gives the number of the customer's book rep. The book rep number for Tri-State Consortium is 65.

The first field in the Book Rep table is also BR #, for Book Rep Number. The book rep numbers are unique, so the Book Rep Number field is the primary key of the Book Rep table.

The other fields in the Book Rep table are Last Name, First Name, Street, City, State, Postal Code, Start Date, Salary, and Bonus Rate. The Start Date field gives the date the rep began working for Bavant. The Salary field gives the salary paid to the rep thus far this year. The Bonus Rate gives the potential bonus percentage based on personal performance. The bonus rate applies when the book rep exceeds a predetermined sales goal. For example, book rep 65 is Tracy Rogers. Her address is 1827 Maple Ave., in Adelphia, Pennsylvania. The postal code is 19159. Tracy started working for Bavant on July 1, 2014. So far this year, she has been paid $7,750.00 in salary. Her bonus rate is 0.18 (18%).

The book rep number appears in both the Customer table and the Book Rep table, and relates customers and book reps. Book rep 48, Michael Statnik, recently transferred from another division of the company and has not yet been assigned any customers. His book rep number, therefore, does not appear on any row in the Customer table.

CONSIDER THIS

How would you find the name of the book rep for Tri-State Consortium?
In the Customer table, you see that the book rep number for customer Tri-State Consortium is 65. To find the name of this book rep, look for the row in the Book Rep table that contains 65 in the BR # column. After you have found it, you know that the book rep for Tri-State Consortium is Tracy Rogers.

CONSIDER THIS

How would you find all the customers assigned to Tracy Rogers?
First, look in the Book Rep table to find that her number is 65. You would then look through the Customer table for all the customers that contain 65 in the BR # column. Tracy's customers are DCC34 (Dartt Community College), FSC12 (First State College), KCC78 (Key Community College System), SEC19 (Seaborn College), and TSC02 (Tri-State Consortium).

Roadmap

In this chapter, you will learn how to create and use the database shown in Figure 1–1 on page AC 3. The following roadmap identifies general activities you will perform as you progress through this chapter:

1. CREATE the FIRST TABLE, Book Rep, using Datasheet view.
2. ADD RECORDS to the Book Rep table.
3. PRINT the CONTENTS of the Book Rep table.
4. IMPORT RECORDS into the second table, Customer.
5. MODIFY the SECOND TABLE using Design view.
6. CREATE a QUERY for the Customer table.
7. CREATE a FORM for the Customer table.
8. CREATE a REPORT for the Customer table.

At the beginning of step instructions throughout the chapter, you will see an abbreviated form of this roadmap. The abbreviated roadmap uses colors to indicate chapter progress: gray means the chapter is beyond that activity, blue means the task being shown is covered in that activity, and black means that activity is yet to be covered. For example, the following abbreviated roadmap indicates the chapter would be showing a task in the 3 PRINT CONTENTS activity.

1 CREATE FIRST TABLE | 2 ADD RECORDS | 3 PRINT CONTENTS | 4 IMPORT RECORDS | 5 MODIFY SECOND TABLE

6 CREATE QUERY | 7 CREATE FORM | 8 CREATE REPORT

Use the abbreviated roadmap as a progress guide while you read or step through the instructions in this chapter.

To Run Access

If you are using a computer to step through the project in this chapter and you want your screens to match the figures in this book, you should change your screen's resolution to 1366 × 768. For information about how to change a computer's resolution, refer to the Office and Windows chapter at the beginning of this book.

The following steps, which assume Windows is running, use the Start screen or the search box to run Access based on a typical installation. You may need to ask your instructor how to run Access on your computer. For a detailed example of the procedure summarized below, refer to the Office and Windows chapter.

1 Scroll the Start screen for an Access 2013 tile. If your Start screen contains an Access 2013 tile, tap or click it to run Access and then proceed to Step 5; if the Start screen does not contain the Access 2013 tile, proceed to the next step to search for the Access app.

2 Swipe in from the right edge of the screen or point to the upper-right corner of the screen to display the Charms bar, and then tap or click the Search charm on the Charms bar to display the Search menu.

3 Type Access as the search text in the Search box and watch the search results appear in the Apps list.

4 Tap or click Access 2013 in the search results to run Access.

5 If the Access window is not maximized, tap or click the Maximize button on its title bar to maximize the window.

For an introduction to Windows and instruction about how to perform basic Windows tasks, read the Office and Windows chapter at the beginning of this book, where you can learn how to resize windows, change screen resolution, create folders, move and rename files, use Windows Help, and much more.

For an introduction to Office and instruction about how to perform basic tasks in Office apps, read the Office and Windows chapter at the beginning of this book, where you can learn how to run an application, use the ribbon, save a file, open a file, exit an application, use Help, and much more.

Creating a Database

In Access, all the tables, reports, forms, and queries that you create are stored in a single file called a database. Thus, you first must create the database to hold the tables, reports, forms, and queries. You can use either the Blank desktop database option or a template to create a new database. If you already know the tables and fields you want in your database, you would use the Blank desktop database option. If not, you can use a template. Templates can guide you by suggesting some commonly used databases.

To Create a Database

Because you already know the tables and fields you want in the Bavant Publishing database, you would use the Blank desktop database option rather than using a template. The following steps assume you already have created folders for storing your files, for example, a CIS 101 folder (for your class) that contains an Access folder (for your assignments). Thus, these steps save the database in the Access folder in the CIS 101 folder on your desired save location. For a detailed example of the procedure for saving a file in a folder or saving a file on SkyDrive, refer to the Office and Windows chapter at the beginning of this book.

1 Tap or click the 'Blank desktop database' thumbnail to select the database type.

2 Type `Bavant Publishing` in the File Name text box to enter the new file name. Do not press the ENTER key after typing the file name because you do not want to create the database at this time.

3 Tap or click the 'Browse for a location to put your database' button to display the File New Database dialog box.

4 Navigate to the location for the database, for example, the Documents library, the My Documents folder, the folder identifying your class (CIS 101, in this case), and then to the Access folder.

5 Tap or click the OK button (File New Database dialog box) to select the location for the database and close the dialog box.

6 Tap or click the Create button to create the database on the selected drive in the selected folder with the file name, Bavant Publishing (Figure 1–2).

Q&A
The title bar for my Navigation Pane contains All Tables rather than All Access Objects, as in the figure. Is that a problem?
It is not a problem. The title bar indicates how the Navigation Pane is organized. You can carry out the steps in the text with either organization. To make your screens match the ones in the text, tap or click the Navigation Pane arrow and then tap or click Object Type.

I do not have the Search bar that appears on the figure. Is that a problem?
It is not a problem. If your Navigation Pane does not display a Search bar and you want your screens to match the ones in the text, press and hold or right-click the Navigation Pane title bar arrow to display a shortcut menu, and then tap or click Search Bar.

One of the few differences between Windows 7 and Windows 8 occurs in the steps to run Access. If you are using Windows 7, click the Start button, type `Access` in the 'Search programs and files' box, click Access 2013, and then, if necessary, maximize the Access window. For detailed steps to run Access in Windows 7, refer to the Office and Windows chapter at the beginning of this book. For a summary of the steps, refer to the Quick Reference located at the back of this book.

BTW
Organizing Files and Folders
You should organize and store files in folders so that you easily can find the files later. For example, if you are taking an introductory computer class called CIS 101, a good practice would be to save all Access files in an Access folder in a CIS 101 folder. For a discussion of folders and detailed examples of creating folders, refer to the Office and Windows chapter at the beginning of this book.

BTW
Q&As
For a complete list of the Q&As found in many of the step-by-step sequences in this book, visit the Q&A resource on the Student Companion Site located on www.cengagebrain.com. For detailed instructions about accessing available resources, visit www.cengage.com/ct/studentdownload or contact your instructor for information about accessing the required files.

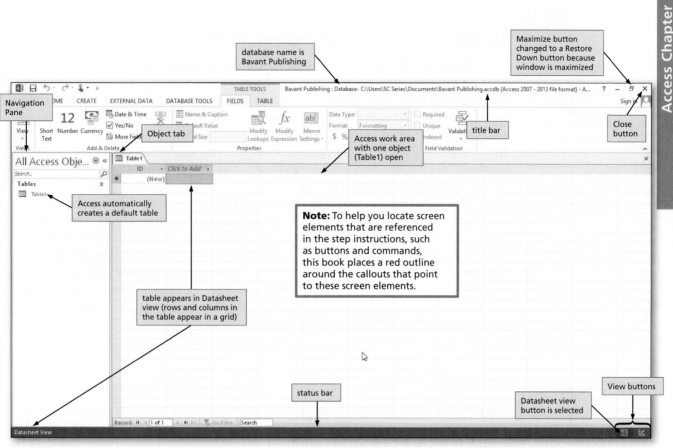

Figure 1–2

TO CREATE A DATABASE USING A TEMPLATE

Ideally, you will design your own database, create a blank database, and then create the tables you have determined that your database should contain. If you are not sure what database design you will need, you could use a template. Templates can guide you by suggesting some commonly used databases. To create a database using a template, you would use the following steps.

1. If you have another database open, close it without exiting Access by tapping or clicking FILE on the ribbon to open the Backstage view and then tapping or clicking Close.

2. If you do not see a template that you want, you can search Microsoft Office online for additional templates.

3. Tap or click the template you want to use. Be sure you have selected one that indicates it is for a desktop database.

4. Enter a file name and select a location for the database.

5. Tap or click the Create button to create the database.

The Access Window

The Access window consists of a variety of components to make your work more efficient. These include the Navigation Pane, Access work area, ribbon, shortcut menus, and Quick Access Toolbar. Some of these components are common to other Microsoft Office apps; others are unique to Access.

BTW

Naming Files
The following characters cannot be used in a file name: question mark (?), quotation mark ("), slash (/), backslash (\ ), colon (:), asterisk (*), vertical bar (|), greater than symbol (>), and less than symbol (<).

BTW

Available Templates
The templates gallery includes both desktop and web-based templates. If you are creating an Access database for your own use, select a desktop template. Web-based templates allow you to create databases that you can publish to a SharePoint server.

Navigation Pane and Access Work Area

BTW
The Ribbon and Screen Resolution
Access may change how the groups and buttons within the groups appear on the ribbon, depending on the computer's screen resolution. Thus, your ribbon may look different from the ones in this book if you are using a screen resolution other than 1366 × 768.

You work on objects such as tables, forms, and reports in the **Access work area**. In the work area in Figure 1–2 on the previous page, a single table, Table1, is open in the work area. **Object tabs** for the open objects appear at the top of the work area. If you have multiple objects open at the same time, you can select one of the open objects by tapping or clicking its tab. To the left of the work area is the Navigation Pane. The **Navigation Pane** contains a list of all the objects in the database. You use this pane to open an object. You also can customize the way objects are displayed in the Navigation Pane.

The **status bar**, located at the bottom of the Access window, presents information about the database object, the progress of current tasks, and the status of certain commands and keys; it also provides controls for viewing the object. As you type text or perform certain commands, various indicators may appear on the status bar. The left edge of the status bar in Figure 1–2 shows that the table object is open in **Datasheet view**. In Datasheet view, the table is represented as a collection of rows and columns called a **datasheet**. Toward the right edge are View buttons, which you can use to change the view that currently appears.

Determining Tables and Fields

Once you have created the database, you need to create the tables and fields that your database will contain. Before doing so, however, you need to make some decisions regarding the tables and fields.

Naming Tables and Fields

BTW
Naming Tables
Database users typically have their own guidelines for naming tables. Some use the singular version of the object being described while others use the prefix tbl with a table name. This book uses the singular version of the object (Customer, Book Rep).

In creating your database, you must name tables and fields. Before beginning the design process, you must understand the rules Access applies to table and field names. These rules are:

1. Names can be up to 64 characters in length.
2. Names can contain letters, digits, and spaces, as well as most of the punctuation symbols.
3. Names cannot contain periods (.), exclamation points (!), accent graves (`), or square brackets ([ ]).
4. Each field in a table must have a unique name.

BTW
Multiple-Word Names
There are several ways to handle multiple word names. You can omit the space (CustomerNumber) or use an underscore in place of the space (Customer_Number). Another option is to use an underscore in place of a space, but use the same case for all letters (CUSTOMER_NUMBER or customer_number).

The approach to naming tables and fields used in this text is to begin the names with an uppercase letter and to use lowercase for the other letters. In multiple-word names, each word begins with an uppercase letter, and there is a space between words (for example, Customer Number).

Determining the Primary Key

For each table, you need to determine the primary key, the unique identifier. In many cases, you will have obvious choices, such as Customer Number or Book Rep Number. If you do not have an obvious choice, you can use the primary key that Access creates automatically. It is a field called ID. It is an autonumber field, which means that Access will assign the value 1 to the first record, 2 to the second record, and so on.

Determining Data Types for the Fields

For each field in your database, you must determine the field's **data type**, that is, the type of data that can be stored in the field. Four of the most commonly used data types in Access are:

1. **Short Text** — The field can contain any characters. A maximum number of 255 characters is allowed in a field whose data type is Short Text.

2. **Number** — The field can contain only numbers. The numbers can be either positive or negative. Fields assigned this type can be used in arithmetic operations. You usually assign fields that contain numbers but will not be used for arithmetic operations (such as postal codes) a data type of Short Text.

3. **Currency** — The field can contain only monetary data. The values will appear with currency symbols, such as dollar signs, commas, and decimal points, and with two digits following the decimal point. Like numeric fields, you can use currency fields in arithmetic operations. Access assigns a size to currency fields automatically.

4. **Date & Time** — The field can store dates and/or times.

Table 1–1 shows the other data types that are available in Access.

Table 1–1 Additional Data Types	
Data Type	**Description**
Long Text	Field can store a variable amount of text or combinations of text and numbers where the total number of characters may exceed 255.
AutoNumber	Field can store a unique sequential number that Access assigns to a record. Access will increment the number by 1 as each new record is added.
Yes/No	Field can store only one of two values. The choices are Yes/No, True/False, or On/Off.
OLE Object	Field can store an OLE object, which is an object linked to or embedded in the table.
Hyperlink	Field can store text that can be used as a hyperlink address.
Attachment	Field can contain an attached file. Images, spreadsheets, documents, charts, and other elements can be attached to this field in a record in the database. You can view and edit the attached file.
Calculated	Field specified as a calculation based on other fields. The value is not actually stored.

© 2014 Cengage Learning

In the Customer table, because the Customer Number, Customer Name, Street, City, and State all can contain letters, their data types should be Short Text. The data type for Postal Code is Short Text instead of Number because you typically do not use postal codes in arithmetic operations; you do not add postal codes or find an average postal code, for example. The Amount Paid, Current Due, and Returns fields contain monetary data, so their data types should be Currency. The Book Rep Number field contains numbers, but you will not use these numbers in arithmetic operations, so its type should be Short Text.

Similarly, in the Book Rep table, the data type for the Book Rep Number, Last Name, First Name, Street, City, State, and Postal Code fields all should be Short Text. The Start Date field should be Date & Time. The Salary field contains monetary amounts, so its data type should be Currency. The Bonus Rate field contains numbers that are not dollar amounts, so its data type should be Number.

For fields whose type is Short Text, you can change the field size, that is, the maximum number of characters that can be entered in the field. If you set the field size for the State field to 2, for example, Access will not allow the user to enter more than two characters in the field. On the other hand, fields whose data type is Number often

BTW

Text Data Types
Short Text replaces the Text data type in previous editions of Access. Long Text replaces the Memo data type in previous editions.

BTW

Data Types
Different database management systems have different available data types. Even data types that are essentially the same can have different names. The Currency data type in Access, for example, is referred to as Money in SQL Server.

BTW

AutoNumber Fields
AutoNumber fields also are called AutoIncrement fields. In Design view, the New Values field property allows you to increment the field sequentially (Sequential) or randomly (Random). The default is sequential.

require you to change the field size, which is the storage space assigned to the field by Access. Table 1–2 shows the possible field sizes for Number fields.

Table 1–2 Field Sizes for Number Fields	
Field Size	**Description**
Byte	Integer value in the range of 0 to 255
Integer	Integer value in the range of -32,768 to 32,767
Long Integer	Integer value in the range of -2,147,483,648 to 2,147,483,647
Single	Numeric values with decimal places to seven significant digits — requires 4 bytes of storage
Double	Numeric values with decimal places to more accuracy than Single — requires 8 bytes of storage
Replication ID	Special identifier required for replication
Decimal	Numeric values with decimal places to more accuracy than Single or Double — requires 12 bytes of storage

© 2014 Cengage Learning

CONSIDER THIS

What is the appropriate size for the Bonus Rate field?

If the size were Byte, Integer, or Long Integer, only integers could be stored. If you try to store a value that has decimal places, such as 0.18, in fields of these sizes, the portion to the right of the decimal point would be removed, giving a result of 0. To address this problem, the bonus rate should have a size of Single, Double, or Decimal. With such small numbers involved, Single, which requires the least storage of the three, is the appropriate choice.

Creating a Table

BTW

On Screen Keyboard
To display the on-screen touch keyboard, tap the Touch Keyboard button on the Windows taskbar. When finished using the touch keyboard, tap the X button on the touch keyboard to close the keyboard.

To create a table in Access, you must define its structure. That is, you must define all the fields that make up the table and their characteristics. You also must indicate the primary key.

In Access, you can use two different views to create a table: Datasheet view and Design view. In **Datasheet view**, the data in the table is presented in rows and columns, similar to a spreadsheet. Although the main reason to use Datasheet view is to add or update records in a table, you also can use it to create a table or to later modify its structure. The other view, **Design view**, is only used to create a table or to modify the structure of a table.

As you might expect, Design view has more functionality for creating a table than Datasheet view. That is, there are certain actions that only can be performed in Design view. One such action is assigning Single as the field size for the Bonus Rate field. In this chapter, you will create the first table, the Book Rep table, in Datasheet view. Once you have created the table in Datasheet view, you will use Design view to change the field size.

Whichever view you choose to use, before creating the table, you need to know the names and data types of the fields that will make up the table. You also can decide to enter a **description** for a particular field to explain important details about the field. When you select this field, this description will appear on the status bar. You also might choose to assign a **caption** to a particular field. If you assign a caption, Access will display the value you assign, rather than the field name, in datasheets and in forms. If you do not assign a caption, Access will display the field name.

CONSIDER THIS

When would you want to use a caption?

You would use a caption whenever you want something other than the field name displayed. One common example is when the field name is relatively long and the data in the field is relatively short. In the Book Rep table, the name of the first field is Book Rep Number, but the field contains data that is only two characters long. You will change the caption for this field to BR #, which is much shorter than Book Rep Number yet still describes the field. Doing so will enable you to greatly reduce the width of the column.

The results of these decisions for the fields in the Book Rep table are shown in Table 1–3. The table also shows the data types and field sizes of the fields as well as any special properties that need to be changed. The Book Rep Number field has a caption of BR #, enabling the width of the Book Rep Number column to be reduced in the datasheet.

Table 1–3 Structure of Book Rep Table

Field Name	Data Type	Field Size	Notes
Book Rep Number	Short Text	2	Primary Key **Description:** Unique identifier of book rep **Caption:** BR #
Last Name	Short Text	15	
First Name	Short Text	15	
Street	Short Text	20	
City	Short Text	20	
State	Short Text	2	
Postal Code	Short Text	5	
Start Date	Date/Time		(This appears as Date & Time on the menu of available data types)
Salary	Currency		
Bonus Rate	Number	Single	Format: Fixed Decimal Places: 2

© 2014 Cengage Learning

If you are using your finger on a touch screen and are having difficulty completing the steps in this chapter, consider using a stylus. Many people find it easier to be precise with a stylus than with a finger. In addition, with a stylus you see the pointer. If you still are having trouble completing the steps with a stylus, try using a mouse.

How do you determine the field size?
You need to determine the maximum number of characters that can be entered in the field. In some cases, it is obvious. Field sizes of 2 for the State field and 5 for the Postal Code field are certainly the appropriate choices. In other cases, you need to determine how many characters you wish to allow. In the list shown in Table 1–3, Bavant evidently decided allowing 15 characters was sufficient for last names. This field size can be changed later if it proves to be insufficient.

What is the purpose of the Format and Decimal Places properties?
The format guarantees that bonus rates will be displayed with a fixed number of decimal places. Setting the decimal places property to 2 guarantees that the rates will be displayed with precisely two decimal places. Thus, a bonus rate of 0.2 will be displayed as 0.20.

CONSIDER THIS

CONSIDER THIS

To Modify the Primary Key

1 CREATE FIRST TABLE | 2 ADD RECORDS | 3 PRINT CONTENTS | 4 IMPORT RECORDS | 5 MODIFY SECOND TABLE
6 CREATE QUERY | 7 CREATE FORM | 8 CREATE REPORT

When you first create your database, Access automatically creates a table for you. You can immediately begin defining the fields. If, for any reason, you do not have this table or inadvertently delete it, you can create the table by tapping or clicking CREATE on the ribbon and then tapping or clicking the Table button (CREATE tab | Tables group). In either case, you are ready to define the fields.

The steps on the next page change the name, data type, and other properties of the first field to match the Book Rep Number field in Table 1–3, which is the primary key. *Why? Access has already created the first field as the primary key field, which it has named ID. Book Rep Number is a more appropriate choice.*

①

- Press and hold or right-click the column heading for the ID field to display a shortcut menu (Figure 1–3).

Q&A Why does my shortcut menu look different?
You displayed a shortcut menu for the column instead of the column heading. Be sure you press and hold or right-click the column heading.

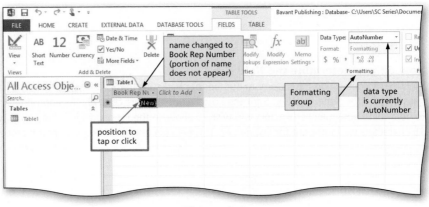

Figure 1–3

②

- Tap or click Rename Field on the shortcut menu to highlight the current name.
- Type `Book Rep Number` to assign a name to the new field.
- Tap or click the white space immediately below the field name to complete the addition of the field (Figure 1–4).

Q&A Why does the full name of the field not appear?
The default column size is not large enough for Book Rep Number to be displayed in its entirety. You will address this issue in later steps.

Figure 1–4

③

- Because the data type needs to be changed from AutoNumber to Short Text, tap or click the Data Type arrow (TABLE TOOLS FIELDS tab | Formatting group) to display a menu of available data types (Figure 1–5).

Figure 1–5

4

- Tap or click Short Text to select the data type for the field (Figure 1–6).

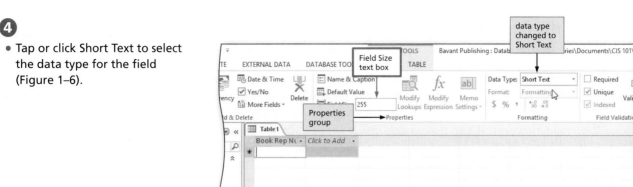

Figure 1–6

5

- Tap or click the Field Size text box (TABLE TOOLS FIELDS tab | Properties group) to select the current field size, use either the DELETE or BACKSPACE keys to erase the current field size, if necessary, and then type 2 as the new field size.

- Tap or click the Name & Caption button (TABLE TOOLS FIELDS tab | Properties group) to display the Enter Field Properties dialog box.

- Tap or click the Caption text box (Enter Field Properties dialog box), and then type BR # as the caption.

- Tap or click the Description text box, and then type Unique identifier of book rep as the description (Figure 1–7).

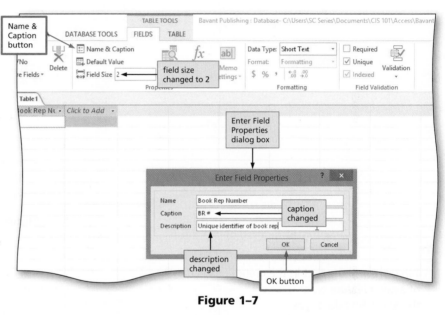

Figure 1–7

6

- Tap or click the OK button (Enter Field Properties dialog box) to change the caption and description (Figure 1–8).

Figure 1–8

To Define the Remaining Fields in a Table

To define an additional field, you tap or click the Click to Add column heading, select the data type, and then type the field name. This is different from the process you used to modify the ID field. The following steps define the remaining fields shown in Table 1–3 on page AC 11. These steps do not change the field size of the Bonus Rate field, however. *Why? You can only change the field size of a Number field in Design view. Later, you will use Design view to change this field size and change the format and number of decimal places.*

1

- Tap or click the 'Click to Add' column heading to display a menu of available data types (Figure 1–9).

Figure 1–9

2

- Tap or click Short Text in the menu of available data types to select the Short Text data type.

- Type `Last Name` to enter a field name.

- Tap or click the blank space below the field name to complete the change of the name. Tap or click the blank space a second time to select the field (Figure 1–10).

Q&A

After entering the field name, I realized that I selected the wrong data type. How can I correct it?
Tap or click the Data Type arrow, and then select the correct type.

I inadvertently clicked the blank space before entering the field name. How can I correct the name?
Press and hold or right-click the field name, tap or click Rename Field on the shortcut menu, and then type the new name.

Figure 1–10

3

- Change the field size to 15 just as you changed the field size of the Book Rep Number field.

- Using the same technique, add the remaining fields in the Book Rep table. For the First Name, Street, City, State, and Postal Code fields, use the Short Text data type, but change the field sizes to match Table 1–3 on page AC 11. For the Start Date field, change the data type to Date & Time. For the Salary field, change the data type to Currency. For the Bonus Rate field, change the data type to Number (Figure 1–11).

Figure 1–11

Q&A I have an extra row between the row containing the field names and the row that begins with the asterisk. What happened? Is this a problem? If so, how do I fix it?
You inadvertently added a record to the table by pressing a key. Even pressing the SPACEBAR would add a record. You now have an unwanted record. To fix it, press the ESC key or tap or click the Undo button to undo the action. You may need to do this more than once.

When I try to move on to specify another field, I get an error message indicating that the primary key cannot contain a null value. How do I correct this?
First, tap or click the OK button to remove the error message. Next, press the ESC key or tap or click the Undo button to undo the action. You may need to do this more than once.

Making Changes to the Structure

When creating a table, check the entries carefully to ensure they are correct. If you discover a mistake while still typing the entry, you can correct the error by repeatedly pressing the BACKSPACE key until the incorrect characters are removed. Then, type the correct characters. If you do not discover a mistake until later, you can use the following techniques to make the necessary changes to the structure:

- To undo your most recent change, tap or click the Undo button on the Quick Access Toolbar. If there is nothing that Access can undo, this button will be dim, and tapping or clicking it will have no effect.

- To delete a field, press and hold or right-click the column heading for the field (the position containing the field name), and then tap or click Delete Field on the shortcut menu.

- To change the name of a field, press and hold or right-click the column heading for the field, tap or click Rename Field on the shortcut menu, and then type the desired field name.

- To insert a field as the last field, tap or click the 'Click to Add' column heading, tap or click the appropriate data type on the menu of available data types, type the desired field name, and, if necessary, change the field size.

- To insert a field between existing fields, press and hold or right-click the column heading for the field that will follow the new field, and then tap or click Insert

BTW
Currency Symbols
To show the symbol for the Euro (€) instead of the dollar sign, change the Format property for the field whose data type is currency. To change the default symbols for currency, change the settings in Windows.

BTW
Touch Screen Differences
The Office and Windows interfaces may vary if you are using a touch screen. For this reason, you might notice that the function or appearance of your touch screen differs slightly from this chapter's presentation.

Field on the shortcut menu. Press and hold or right-click the column heading for the field, tap or click Rename Field on the shortcut menu, and then type the desired field name.

- To move a field, tap or click the column heading for the field to be moved to select the field, and then drag the field to the desired position.

As an alternative to these steps, you might want to start over. To do so, tap or click the Close button for the table, and then tap or click the No button in the Microsoft Access dialog box. Tap or click CREATE on the ribbon, and then tap or click the Table button to create a table. You then can repeat the process you used earlier to define the fields in the table.

To Save a Table

1 CREATE FIRST TABLE | 2 ADD RECORDS | 3 PRINT CONTENTS | 4 IMPORT RECORDS | 5 MODIFY SECOND TABLE
6 CREATE QUERY | 7 CREATE FORM | 8 CREATE REPORT

The Book Rep table structure is complete. The final step is to save the table within the database. As part of the process, you will give the table a name. The following steps save the table, giving it the name Book Rep. *Why? Bavant has decided that Book Rep is an appropriate name for the table.*

1

- Tap or click the Save button on the Quick Access Toolbar to display the Save As dialog box (Figure 1–12).

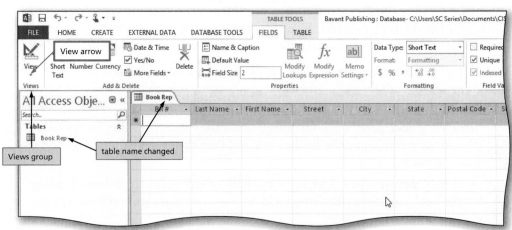

Figure 1–12

2

- Type `Book Rep` to change the name assigned to the table.

- Tap or click the OK button (Save As dialog box) to save the table (Figure 1–13).

Figure 1–13

Other Ways

1. Tap or click FILE on the ribbon, tap or click Save in the Backstage view

2. Press and hold or right-click tab for table, tap or click Save on shortcut menu

3. Press CTRL+S

To View the Table in Design View

Even when creating a table in Datasheet view, Design view can be helpful. *Why? You easily can view the fields, data types, and properties to ensure you have entered them correctly. It is also easier to determine the primary key in Design view.* The following steps display the structure of the Book Rep table in Design view so that you can verify the design is correct.

1

- Tap or click the View arrow (TABLE TOOLS FIELDS tab | Views group) to display the View menu (Figure 1–14).

Q&A

Could I just tap or click the View button rather than the arrow?

Yes. Tapping or clicking the button is equivalent to tapping or clicking the command represented by the icon currently appearing on the button. Because the icon on the button in Figure 1–14 is for Design view, tapping or clicking the button would display the table in Design view. If you are uncertain, you can always tap or click the arrow and select from the menu.

Figure 1–14

2

- Tap or click Design View on the View menu to view the table in Design view (Figure 1–15).

Figure 1–15

Other Ways

1. Tap or click Design View button on status bar

Checking the Structure in Design View

You should use Design view to carefully check the entries you have made. In Figure 1–15 on the previous page, for example, you can see that the Book Rep Number field is the primary key of the Book Rep table by the key symbol in front of the field name. If your table does not have a key symbol, you can tap or click the Primary Key button (TABLE TOOLS DESIGN tab | Tools group) to designate the field as the primary key. You also can check that the data type, description, field size, and caption are all correct.

For the other fields, you can see the field name, data type, and description without taking any special action. To see the field size and/or caption for a field, tap or click the field's **row selector**, the small box that precedes the field. Tapping or clicking the row selector for the Last Name field, for example, displays the properties for the field. You then can check to see that the field size is correct. In addition, if the field has a caption, you can check to see if that is correct. If you find any mistakes, you can make the necessary corrections on this screen. When you have finished, you would tap or click the Save button to save your changes.

To Change a Field Size in Design View

1 CREATE FIRST TABLE | 2 ADD RECORDS | 3 PRINT CONTENTS | 4 IMPORT RECORDS | 5 MODIFY SECOND TABLE
6 CREATE QUERY | 7 CREATE FORM | 8 CREATE REPORT

Most field size changes can be made in either Datasheet view or Design view. However, changing the field size for Number fields, such as the Bonus Rate field, can only be made in Design view. Because the values in the Bonus Rate field have decimal places, only Single, Double, or Decimal would be possible choices for the field size. The difference between these choices concerns the amount of accuracy. Double is more accurate than Single, for example, but requires more storage space. Because the rates are only two decimal places, Single is an acceptable choice.

The following steps change the field size of the Bonus Rate field to Single, the format to Fixed, and the number of decimal places to 2. *Why change the format and number of decimal places? To ensure that each value will appear with precisely two decimal places.*

1

- If necessary, tap or click the vertical scroll bar to display the Bonus Rate field. Tap or click the row selector for the Bonus Rate field to select the field (Figure 1–16).

Figure 1–16

2

- Tap or click the Field Size box to display the Field Size arrow.

- Tap or click the Field Size arrow to display the Field Size menu (Figure 1–17).

Figure 1–17

Q&A What would happen if I left the field size set to Long Integer?

If the field size is Long Integer, Integer, or Byte, no decimal places can be stored. For example, a value of .10 would be stored as 0. If you enter rates and the values all appear as 0, chances are you did not change the field size property.

3

- Tap or click Single to select single precision as the field size.

- Tap or click the Format box to display the Format arrow.

- Tap or click the Format arrow to open the Format menu (Figure 1–18).

Figure 1–18

4

- Tap or click Fixed to select fixed as the format.

- Tap or click the Decimal Places box to display the Decimal Places arrow.

- Tap or click the Decimal Places arrow to enter the number of decimal places.

- Tap or click 2 to assign the number of decimal places.

- Tap or click the Save button to save your changes (Figure 1–19).

Figure 1–19

Q&A Why did the Property Update Options button appear?

You changed the number of decimal places. The Property Update Options button offers a quick way of making the same change everywhere Bonus Rate appears. So far, you have not added any data or created any forms or reports that use the Bonus Rate field, so no such changes are necessary.

To Close the Table

Once you are sure that your entries are correct and you have saved your changes, you can close the table. The following step closes the table.

1 Tap or click the Close button for the Book Rep table to close the table.

Other Ways

1. Press and hold or right-click tab for table, tap or click Close on shortcut menu

---

To Add Records to a Table

1 CREATE FIRST TABLE | 2 ADD RECORDS | 3 PRINT CONTENTS | 4 IMPORT RECORDS | 5 MODIFY SECOND TABLE
6 CREATE QUERY | 7 CREATE FORM | 8 CREATE REPORT

Creating a table by building the structure and saving the table is the first step in the two-step process of using a table in a database. The second step is to add records to the table. To add records to a table, the table must be open. When making changes to tables, you work in Datasheet view.

You often add records in phases. *Why? You might not have enough time to add all the records in one session, or you might not have all the records currently available.* The following steps open the Book Rep table in Datasheet view and then add the first two records in the Book Rep table (Figure 1–20).

BR #	Last Name	First Name	Street	City	State	Postal Code	Start Date	Salary	Bonus Rate
53	Chin	Robert	265 Maxwell St.	Gossett	PA	19157	6/1/2013	$26,250.00	0.19
42	Perez	Melina	261 Porter Dr.	Adelphia	PA	19156	5/14/2012	$31,500.00	0.20

Figure 1–20

1

- Press and hold or right-click the Book Rep table in the Navigation Pane to display the shortcut menu (Figure 1–21).

Figure 1–21

2

- Tap or click Open on the shortcut menu to open the table in Datasheet view.

- Tap or click the Shutter Bar Open/Close Button to close the Navigation Pane (Figure 1–22).

Figure 1–22

3

- Tap or click the first row in the BR # field if necessary to display an insertion point, and type 53 to enter the first book rep number (Figure 1–23).

Figure 1–23

4

- Press the TAB key to move to the next field.

- Enter the last name, first name, street, city, state, and postal code by typing the following entries, pressing the TAB key after each one: `Chin` as the last name, `Robert` as the first name, `265 Maxwell St.` as the street, `Gossett` as the city, `PA` as the state, and `19157` as the postal code.

Figure 1–24

- If requested by your instructor, enter your address instead of 265 Maxwell St. as the street. If your address is longer than 20 characters, enter the first 20 characters.

- Type `6/1/2013` in the Start Date field (Figure 1–24).

5

- Press the TAB key and then type `26250` in the Salary field.

Q&A Do I need to type a dollar sign?
You do not need to type dollar signs or commas. In addition, because the digits to the right of the decimal point are both zeros, you do not need to type either the decimal point or the zeros.

Figure 1–25

- Press the TAB key to complete the entry for the Salary field.

- Type `0.19` in the Bonus Rate field, and then press the TAB key to complete the entry of the first record (Figure 1–25).

Q&A Do I need to type the leading zero for the Bonus Rate?
Typing the leading zero is not necessary. You could type .19 if you prefer. In addition, you would not have to type any final zeros. For example, if you needed to enter 0.20, you could simply type .2 as your entry.

How and when do I save the record?
As soon as you have entered or modified a record and moved to another record, Access saves the original record. This is different from other applications. The rows entered in an Excel worksheet, for example, are not saved until the entire worksheet is saved.

6

- Use the techniques shown in Steps 3 through 5 to enter the data for the second record (Figure 1–26).

Q&A Does it matter that I entered book rep 42 after I entered book rep 53? Should the book rep numbers be in order?

Figure 1–26

The order in which you enter the records is not important. When you close and later reopen the table, the records will be in book rep number order, because the Book Rep Number field is the primary key.

When I entered the Salary field and changed the data type to Currency, I noticed that the word Currency appeared twice. Why?
The second Currency is the format, which indicates how the data will be displayed. For the Currency data type, Access automatically sets the format to Currency, which is usually what you would want. You could change it to something else, if desired, by tapping or clicking the arrow and selecting the desired format.

Experiment

- Tap or click the Salary field on either of the records. Be sure the TABLE TOOLS FIELDS tab is selected. Tap or click the Format arrow, and then tap or click each of the formats in the Format box menu to see the effect on the values in the Salary field. When finished, tap or click Currency in the Format box menu.

Making Changes to the Data

As you enter data, check your entries carefully to ensure they are correct. If you make a mistake and discover it before you press the TAB key, correct it by pressing the BACKSPACE key until the incorrect characters are removed, and then type the correct characters. If you do not discover a mistake until later, you can use the following techniques to make the necessary corrections to the data:

- To undo your most recent change, tap or click the Undo button on the Quick Access Toolbar. If there is nothing that Access can undo, this button will be dimmed, and tapping or clicking it will have no effect.

- To add a record, tap or click the New (blank) record button, tap or click the position for the Book Rep Number field on the first open record, and then add the record. Do not worry about it being in the correct position in the table. Access will reposition the record based on the primary key, in this case, the Book Rep Number.

- To delete a record, tap or click the record selector, shown in Figure 1–26, for the record to be deleted. Then press the DELETE key to delete the record, and tap or click the Yes button when Access asks you to verify that you want to delete the record.

- To change the contents of one or more fields in a record, the record must be on the screen. If it is not, use any appropriate technique, such as the UP ARROW and DOWN ARROW keys or the vertical scroll bar, to move to the record. If the field you want to correct is not visible on the screen, use the horizontal scroll bar along the bottom of the screen to shift all the fields until the one you want appears. If the value in the field is currently highlighted, you can simply type the new value. If you would rather edit the existing value, you must have an insertion point in the field. You can place the insertion point by tapping or clicking in the field or by pressing the F2 key. You then can use the arrow keys, the DELETE key, and the BACKSPACE key for making the correction. You also can use the INSERT key to switch between Insert and Overtype mode. When you have made the change, press the TAB key to move to the next field.

BTW

AutoCorrect Feature
The AutoCorrect feature of Access corrects common data entry errors. AutoCorrect corrects two capital letters by changing the second letter to lowercase and capitalizes the first letter in the names of days. It also corrects more than 400 commonly misspelled words.

BTW

Other AutoCorrect Options
Using the Office AutoCorrect feature, you can create entries that will replace abbreviations with spelled-out names and phrases automatically. To specify AutoCorrect rules, tap or click FILE on the ribbon to open the Backstage view, tap or click Options, and then tap or click Proofing in the Access Options dialog box.

If you cannot determine how to correct the data, you may find that you are "stuck" on the record, in which case Access neither allows you to move to another record nor allows you to close the table until you have made the correction. If you encounter this situation, simply press the ESC key. Pressing the ESC key will remove from the screen the record you are trying to add. You then can move to any other record, close the table, or take any other action you desire.

To Close a Table

Now that you have created and saved the Book Rep table, you can close it. The following step closes the table.

1 Tap or click the Close button for the Book Rep table, shown in Figure 1–26 on the previous page, to close the table (Figure 1–27).

Figure 1–27

To Exit Access

The following steps exit Access. For a detailed example of the procedure summarized below, refer to the Office and Windows chapter at the beginning of this book.

1 Tap or click the Close button on the right side of the title bar to exit Access.

2 If a Microsoft Access dialog box appears, tap or click the Save button to save any changes made to the object since the last save.

Break Point: If you wish to take a break, this is a good place to do so. To resume later, continue following the steps from this location forward.

Starting Access and Opening a Database

Once you have created and later closed a database, you will need to open it in the future in order to use it. Opening a database requires that Access is running on your computer.

To Run Access

1 Scroll the Start screen for an Access 2013 tile. If your Start screen contains an Access 2013 tile, tap or click it to run Access. If the Start screen does not contain the Access 2013 tile, proceed to the next step to search for the Access app.

2 Swipe in from the right edge of the screen or point to the upper-right corner of the screen to display the Charms bar, and then tap or click the Search charm on the Charms bar to display the Search menu.

3 Type `Access` as the search text in the Search text box and watch the search results appear in the Apps list.

4 Tap or click Access 2013 in the search results to run Access.

To Open a Database from Access

Earlier in this chapter, you created the Bavant Publishing database in an appropriate storage location. The following steps open the database from the location you specified when you first created it (for example, the Access folder in the CIS 101 folder). For a detailed example of the procedure summarized below, refer to the Office 2013 and Windows chapter at the beginning of this book.

1 Tap or click FILE on the ribbon to open the Backstage view, if necessary.

2 If the database you want to open is displayed in the Recent list, tap or click the file name to open the database and display the opened database in the Access window; then skip to Step 7. If the database you want to open is not displayed in the Recent list or if the Recent list does not appear, tap or click 'Open Other Files' to display the Open Gallery.

3 If the database you want to open is displayed in the Recent list in the Open gallery, tap or click the file name to open the database and display the opened database in the Access window; then skip to Step 7.

4 Tap or click Computer, SkyDrive, or another location in the left pane and then navigate to the location of the database to be opened (for example, the Access folder in the CIS 101 folder).

5 Tap or click Bavant Publishing to select the database to be opened.

6 Tap or click the Open button (Open dialog box) to open the selected file and display the opened database in the Access window (Figure 1–28).

7 If a Security Warning appears, tap or click the Enable Content button.

BTW
Enabling Content
If the database is one that you created, or if it comes from a trusted source, you can enable the content. You should disable the content of a database if you suspect that your database might contain harmful content or damaging macros.

Figure 1–28

To Add Records to a Table that Contains Data

You can add records to a table that already contains data using a process almost identical to that used to add records to an empty table. The only difference is that you place the insertion point after the last record before you enter the additional data. To position the insertion point after the last record, you can use the **Navigation buttons**, which are buttons used to move within a table, found near the lower-left corner of the screen when a table is open. *Why not just tap or click the Book Rep Number (BR #) on the first open record? You could do this, but it is a good habit to use the New (blank) record button. Once a table contains more records than will fit on the screen, it is easier to tap or click the New (blank) record button.* The purpose of each Navigation button is described in Table 1–4.

Table 1–4 Navigation Buttons in Datasheet View	
Button	**Purpose**
First record	Moves to the first record in the table
Previous record	Moves to the previous record
Next record	Moves to the next record
Last record	Moves to the last record in the table
New (blank) record	Moves to the end of the table to a position for entering a new record

© 2014 Cengage Learning

The following steps add the remaining records (Figure 1–29) to the Book Rep table.

BR # ▾	Last Name ▾	First Name ▾	Street ▾	City ▾	State ▾	Postal Code ▾	Start Date ▾	Salary ▾	Bonus Rate ▾
65	Rogers	Tracy	1827 Maple Ave.	Adelphia	PA	19159	7/1/2014	$7,750.00	0.18
48	Statnik	Michael	3135 Simpson Dr.	Pleasantburg	NJ	07025	1/15/2013	$29,000.00	0.20

Figure 1–29

1

- If the Navigation Pane is closed, tap or click the Shutter Bar Open/Close Button, shown in Figure 1–27 on page AC 24, to open the Navigation Pane (Figure 1–30).

Figure 1–30

2

- Press and hold or right-click the Book Rep table in the Navigation Pane to display a shortcut menu.

- Tap or click Open on the shortcut menu to open the table in Datasheet view.

Q&A Why do the records appear in a different order than the order in which I entered them?
When you open the table, they are sorted in the order of the primary key. In this case, that means they will appear in Book Rep Number order.

- Close the Navigation Pane by tapping or clicking the Shutter Bar Open/Close Button (Figure 1–31).

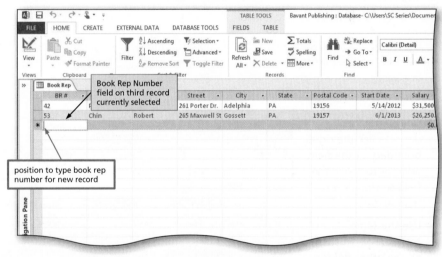

Figure 1–31

3

- Tap or click the 'New (blank) record' button to move to a position to enter a new record (Figure 1–32).

Figure 1–32

4

- Add the records shown in Figure 1–29 using the same techniques you used to add the first two records (Figure 1–33).

Figure 1–33

Other Ways

1. Tap or click New button (HOME tab | Records group)   2. Press CTRL+PLUS SIGN (+)

To Resize Columns in a Datasheet

Access assigns default column sizes, which do not always provide space to display all the data in the field. In some cases, the data might appear but the entire field name will not. You can correct this problem by **resizing** the column (changing its size) in the datasheet. In some instances, you may want to reduce the size of a column. *Why? Some fields, such as the State field, are short enough that they do not require all the space on the screen that is allotted to them.* Changing a column width changes the **layout**, or design, of a table. The following steps resize the columns in the Book Rep table and save the changes to the layout.

1

- Point to the right boundary of the field selector for the Book Rep Number (BR #) field (Figure 1–34) so that the pointer becomes a two-headed arrow.

Q&A I am using touch and I cannot see the pointer. Is this a problem?
It is not a problem. Remember that if you are using your finger on a touch screen, you will not see the pointer.

Figure 1–34

2

- Double-tap or double-click the right boundary of the field selector to resize the field so that it best fits the data.

- Use the same technique to resize all the other fields to best fit the data.

- Save the changes to the layout by tapping or clicking the Save button on the Quick Access Toolbar (Figure 1–35).

Figure 1–35

3

- Tap or click the table's Close button (shown in Figure 1–33 on the previous page) to close the table.

Q&A What if I closed the table without saving the layout changes?
You would be asked if you want to save the changes.

Other Ways

1. Press and hold or right-click field name, tap or click Field Width

What is the best method for distributing database objects?

The traditional method of distributing database objects such as tables, reports, and forms uses a printer to produce a hard copy. A **hard copy** or **printout** is information that exists on a physical medium such as paper. Hard copies can be useful for the following reasons:

- Some people prefer proofreading a hard copy of a document rather than viewing it on the screen to check for errors and readability.

- Hard copies can serve as a backup reference if your storage medium is lost or becomes corrupted and you need to recreate the document.

Instead of distributing a hard copy, users can distribute the document as an electronic image that mirrors the original document's appearance. The electronic image of the document can be emailed, posted on a website, or copied to a portable storage medium such as a USB flash drive. Two popular electronic image formats, sometimes called fixed formats, are PDF by Adobe Systems and XPS by Microsoft. In Access, you can create electronic image files through the EXTERNAL DATA tab on the ribbon. Electronic images of documents, such as PDF and XPS, can be useful for the following reasons:

- Users can view electronic images of documents without the software that created the original document (e.g., Access). Specifically, to view a PDF file, you use a program called Adobe Reader, which can be downloaded free from Adobe's website. Similarly, to view an XPS file, you use a program called XPS Viewer, which is included in the latest versions of Windows and Internet Explorer.

- Sending electronic documents saves paper and printer supplies. Society encourages users to contribute to **green computing,** which involves reducing the electricity consumed and environmental waste generated when using computers, mobile devices, and related technologies.

Previewing and Printing the Contents of a Table

When working with a database, you often will need to print a copy of the table contents. Figure 1–36 shows a printed copy of the contents of the Book Rep table. (Yours may look slightly different, depending on your printer.) Because the Book Rep table is substantially wider than the screen, it also will be wider than the normal printed page in portrait orientation. **Portrait orientation** means the printout is across the width of the page. **Landscape orientation** means the printout is across the height of the page. To print the wide database table, you might prefer to use landscape orientation. A convenient way to change to landscape orientation is to preview what the printed copy will look like by using Print Preview. This allows you to determine whether landscape orientation is necessary and, if it is, to change the orientation easily to landscape. In addition, you also can use Print Preview to determine whether any adjustments are necessary to the page margins.

BTW

Changing Printers

To change the default printer that appears in the Print dialog box, tap or click FILE on the ribbon, tap or click the Print tab in the Backstage view, tap or click Print in the Print gallery, then tap or click the Name arrow and select the desired printer.

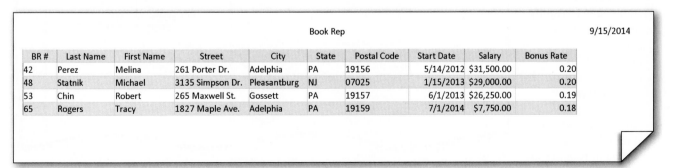

	Book Rep								9/15/2014
BR #	Last Name	First Name	Street	City	State	Postal Code	Start Date	Salary	Bonus Rate
42	Perez	Melina	261 Porter Dr.	Adelphia	PA	19156	5/14/2012	$31,500.00	0.20
48	Statnik	Michael	3135 Simpson Dr.	Pleasantburg	NJ	07025	1/15/2013	$29,000.00	0.20
53	Chin	Robert	265 Maxwell St.	Gossett	PA	19157	6/1/2013	$26,250.00	0.19
65	Rogers	Tracy	1827 Maple Ave.	Adelphia	PA	19159	7/1/2014	$7,750.00	0.18

Figure 1–36

To Preview and Print the Contents of a Table

The following steps use Print Preview to preview and then print the contents of the Book Rep table. *Why?* *By previewing the contents of the table in Print Preview, you can make any necessary adjustments to the orientation or to the margins before printing the contents.*

1

• If the Navigation Pane is closed, open the Navigation Pane by tapping or clicking the Shutter Bar Open/Close Button.

• Be sure the Book Rep table is selected.

Q&A Why do I have to be sure the Book Rep table is selected? It is the only object in the database. When the database contains only one object, you do not have to worry about selecting the object. Ensuring that the correct object is selected is a good habit to form, however, to make sure that the object you print is the one you want.

Figure 1–37

• Tap or click FILE on the ribbon to open the Backstage view.

• Tap or click the Print tab in the Backstage view to display the Print gallery (Figure 1–37).

2

• Tap or click the Print Preview button in the Print gallery to display a preview of what the table will look like when printed (Figure 1–38).

Q&A I cannot read the table. Can I magnify a portion of the table?
Yes. Point the pointer, whose shape will change to a magnifying glass, at the portion of the table that you want to magnify, and then tap or click. You can return to the original view of the table by tapping or clicking a second time.

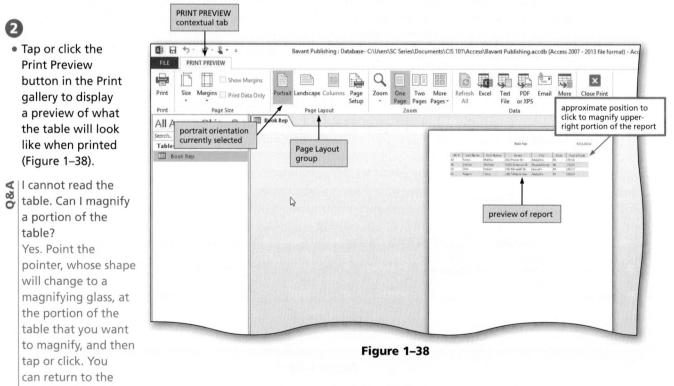

Figure 1–38

3

- Tap or click the pointer in the position shown in Figure 1–38 to magnify the upper-right section of the table (Figure 1–39).

Q&A My table was already magnified in a different area. How can I see the area shown in the figure? One way is to use the scroll bars to move to the desired portion of the table. You also can tap or click the pointer anywhere in the table to produce a screen like the one shown in Figure 1–38, and then tap or click in the location shown in the figure.

Figure 1–39

4

- Tap or click the Landscape button (PRINT PREVIEW tab | Page Layout group) to change to landscape orientation.

- Tap or click the Margins button (PRINT PREVIEW tab | Page Size group) and then click Normal if necessary to display all the fields (Figure 1–40).

Figure 1–40

5

- Tap or click the Print button (PRINT PREVIEW tab | Print group) to display the Print dialog box.

- Tap or click the OK button (Print dialog box) to print the table.

- When the printer stops, retrieve the hard copy of the Book Rep table.

- Tap or click the Close Print Preview button (PRINT PREVIEW tab | Close Preview group) to close the Print Preview window.

Q&A Do I have to select Print Preview before printing the table?
No. If you wish to print without previewing, you would select either Print or Quick Print rather than Print Preview.

Other Ways

1. Press CTRL+P, tap or click OK button in Print dialog box

Importing or Linking Data from Other Applications to Access

BTW

Importing Data in Other Formats
You can import data into a table from Excel workbooks, Access databases, XML files, ODBC databases such as SQL Server, text files, HTML documents, Outlook folders, and SharePoint lists.

BTW

Linking Versus Importing
When you link to the data in the worksheet, the data appears as a table in the Access database but it is maintained in its original form in Excel. Any changes to the Excel data are reflected when the linked table is viewed in Access. In this arrangement, Access would typically be used as a vehicle for querying and presenting the data, with actual updates being made in Excel.

If your data for a table is stored in an Excel worksheet, you can **import** the data, which means to make a copy of the data as a table in the Access database. In this case, any changes to the data made in Access would not be reflected in the Excel worksheet.

Figure 1–41, which contains the Customer data, is an example of the type of worksheet that can be imported. In this type of worksheet, the data is stored as a **list**, that is, a collection of rows and columns in which all the entries in a column represent the same type of data. In this type of list, the first row contains **column headings**, that is, descriptions of the contents of the column, rather than data. In the worksheet in Figure 1–41, for example, the entry in the first column of the first row is Customer Number. This indicates that all the other values in this column are customer numbers. The fact that the entry in the second column of the first row is Customer Name indicates that all the other values in the second column are customer names.

Figure 1–41

Does it matter how the data in the Excel workbook is formatted? If so, how can you be sure the Excel data is formatted in such a way you can import it?

The format of data in an Excel workbook is important when you want to import it into Access. To ensure the data is in an appropriate format:

1. Make sure the data is in the form of a list, a collection of rows and columns in which all the entries in a column represent the same type of data.

2. Make sure there are no blank rows within the list. If there are, remove them prior to importing or linking.

3. Make sure there are no blank columns within the list. If there are, remove them prior to importing or linking.

4. Determine whether the first row contains column headings that will make appropriate field names in the resulting table. If not, you might consider adding such a row. In general, the process is simpler if the first row in the worksheet contains appropriate column headings.

The Import process will create a table. In this table, the column headings in the first row of the worksheet become the field names. The rows of the worksheet, other than the first row, become the records in the table. In the process, each field will be assigned the data type that seems the most reasonable, given the data currently in the worksheet. When the Import process is finished, you can use Datasheet or Design view to modify these data types or to make any other changes to the structure you feel are necessary.

To Import an Excel Worksheet

1 CREATE FIRST TABLE | 2 ADD RECORDS | 3 PRINT CONTENTS | 4 IMPORT RECORDS | 5 MODIFY SECOND TABLE
6 CREATE QUERY | 7 CREATE FORM | 8 CREATE REPORT

You import a worksheet by using the Import Spreadsheet Wizard. In the process, you will indicate that the first row in the worksheet contains the column headings. **Why?** *You are indicating that Access is to use those column headings as the field names in the Access table.* In addition, you will indicate the primary key for the table. As part of the process, you could, if appropriate, choose not to include all the fields from the worksheet in the resulting table.

The following steps import the Customer worksheet.

1
- Tap or click EXTERNAL DATA on the ribbon to display the EXTERNAL DATA tab (Figure 1–42).

Figure 1–42

2
- Tap or click the Excel button (EXTERNAL DATA tab | Import & Link group) to display the Get External Data - Excel Spreadsheet dialog box.

- Tap or click the Browse button in the Get External Data - Excel Spreadsheet dialog box.

- Navigate to the location containing the workbook (for example, the Access folder in the CIS 101 folder). For a detailed example of this procedure, refer to Steps 4a – 4b in the To Save a File in a Folder section in the Office and Windows chapter at the beginning of this book.

- Tap or click the Customer Data workbook, and then tap or click the Open button to select the workbook (Figure 1–43).

Figure 1–43

3

- With the option button to import the data to a new table selected, tap or click the OK button to display the Import Spreadsheet Wizard dialog box (Figure 1–44).

Q&A What happens if I select the option button to append records to an existing table?
Instead of the records being placed in a new table, they will be added to an existing table that you specify, provided the value in the primary key field does not duplicate that on an existing record.

Figure 1–44

4

- If necessary, tap or click First Row Contains Column Headings to select it.

- Tap or click the Next button (Figure 1–45).

Q&A When would I use the Field Options on the Import Spreadsheet Wizard?
You would use these options if you wanted to change properties for one or more fields. You can change the name, the data type, and whether the field is indexed. You also can indicate that some fields should not be imported.

Figure 1–45

5

- Because the Field Options need not be specified, tap or click the Next button (Figure 1–46).

Figure 1–46

6

- Tap or click the 'Choose my own primary key' option button (Figure 1–47).

Q&A

How do I decide which option button to select?

If one of the fields is an appropriate primary key, choose your own primary key from the list of fields. If you are sure you do not want a primary key, choose No primary key. Otherwise, let Access add the primary key.

Figure 1–47

7

- Because the Customer Number field, which is the correct field, is already selected as the primary key, tap or click the Next button.

- Use the DELETE or BACKSPACE keys as necessary to erase the current entry, and then type `Customer` in the Import to Table text box.

- Tap or click the Finish button to import the data (Figure 1–48).

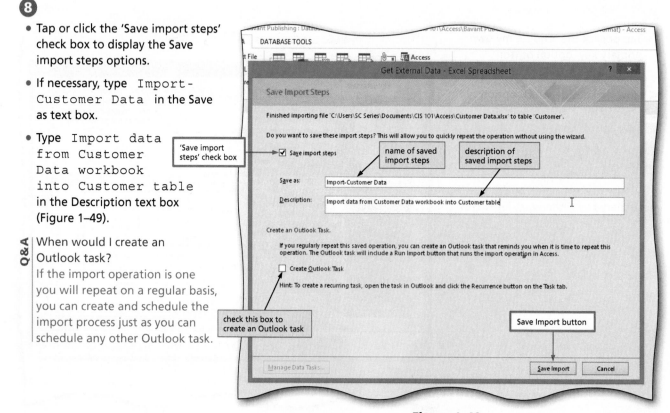

Figure 1–48

8

- Tap or click the 'Save import steps' check box to display the Save import steps options.

- If necessary, type `Import-Customer Data` in the Save as text box.

- Type `Import data from Customer Data workbook into Customer table` in the Description text box (Figure 1–49).

Q&A When would I create an Outlook task?

If the import operation is one you will repeat on a regular basis, you can create and schedule the import process just as you can schedule any other Outlook task.

Figure 1–49

9
- Tap or click the Save Import button to save the import steps (Figure 1–50).

Q&A I saved the table as Customer Data. How can I change the name?
Press and hold or right-click the table name in the Navigation Pane. Click Rename on the shortcut menu and change the table name to Customer.

Figure 1–50

Modifying the Table

The import process has created the Customer table. The table has the correct fields and records. There are some details the process cannot handle, however. These include field sizes, descriptions, and captions. You will use Design view to make the necessary changes. The information you need is shown in Table 1–5.

BTW
Creating a Table in Design View
To create a table in Design view, display the CREATE tab, and then tap or click the Table Design button (CREATE tab | Tables group). You will then see the same screen as in Figure 1–51 on the following page, except that there will be no entries. Make all the necessary entries for the fields in your table, save the table, and assign the table a name.

Table 1–5 Structure of Customer Table			
Field Name	**Data Type**	**Field Size**	**Notes**
Customer Number	Short Text	5	Primary Key **Description:** Customer Number (three uppercase letters followed by 2-digit number) **Caption:** CU #
Customer Name	Short Text	30	
Street	Short Text	20	
City	Short Text	20	
State	Short Text	2	
Postal Code	Short Text	5	
Amount Paid	Currency		
Current Due	Currency		
Returns	Currency		
Book Rep Number	Short Text	2	**Description:** Book Rep Number (number of book rep for customer) **Caption:** BR #

© 2014 Cengage Learning

To Modify a Table in Design View

1 CREATE FIRST TABLE | 2 ADD RECORDS | 3 PRINT CONTENTS | 4 IMPORT RECORDS | **5 MODIFY SECOND TABLE**
6 CREATE QUERY | 7 CREATE FORM | 8 CREATE REPORT

You will usually need to modify the design of a table created during the import process. *Why? Some properties of a table are not specified during the import process, such as descriptions, captions, and field sizes. You also might need to change a data type.* The steps on the next page make the necessary modifications to the design of the Customer table.

1

- Open the Navigation Pane, if necessary.

- Press and hold or right-click the Customer table in the Navigation Pane to display the shortcut menu, and then tap or click Design View on the shortcut menu to open the table in Design view (Figure 1–51).

Customer Number field is primary key

Customer Number field selected

Design view

Field Name		Description (Optional)
Customer Number	Short Text	
Customer Name	Short Text	
Street	Short Text	
City	Short Text	
State	Short Text	
Postal Code	Short Text	
Amount Paid	Currency	
Current Due	Currency	
Returns	Currency	
Book Rep Number	Short Text	

column to enter field names

column to enter data types

column to enter descriptions

Field Properties

Field Size	255
Format	@
Input Mask	
Caption	
Default Value	
Validation Rule	
Validation Text	
Required	Yes
Allow Zero Length	Yes
Indexed	Yes (No Duplicates)
Unicode	

Field Size box

Caption box

A field name can be up including spaces. Pres nam

Figure 1–51

2

- Tap or click the Description (Optional) box for the Customer Number field, and then type `Customer Number (three uppercase letters followed by 2-digit number)` as the description.

- With the Customer Number field selected, tap or click the Field Size box, erase the current field size, and type `5` as the new field size.

- Tap or click the Caption box, and type `CU #` as the caption (Figure 1–52).

EXTERNAL DATA   DATABASE TOOLS   DESIGN

Insert Rows
Delete Rows
Modify Lookups

Validation Rules

Tools

Property Sheet   Indexes

Show/Hide

Create Data Macros ▾   Rename/ Delete Mac

Field, Record & Table Eve

Description (Optional) box

Sign in

Close button

Field Name	Data Type	Description (Optional)
Customer Number	Short Text	Customer Number (three uppercase letters followed by 2-digit number)
Customer Name	Short Text	
Street	Short Text	
City	Short Text	
State	Short Text	
Postal Code	Short Text	
Amount Paid	Currency	
Current Due	Currency	
Returns	Currency	
Book Rep Number	Short Text	

row selector

Field Properties

General Lookup

Field Size	5
Format	@
Input Mask	
Caption	CU #
Default Value	
Validation Rule	
Validation Text	
Required	

field size changed

caption changed

ssed on a view. If he field name is l for help on

Figure 1–52

3

- Make the other changes shown in Table 1–5 on the previous page. To select a field to be changed, tap or click the field's row selector. For most fields, you only need to change the field size. For the Book Rep Number field, you also need to change the description and caption.

- Tap or click the Save button on the Quick Access Toolbar to save your changes.

- Because you know the data will satisfy the new field sizes, click the Yes button when given a message about the possibility of data loss.

Other Ways

1. Press F6 to move between upper and lower panes in Table Design window

Correcting Errors in the Structure

Whenever you create or modify a table in Design view, you should check the entries carefully to ensure they are correct. If you make a mistake and discover it before you press the TAB key, you can correct the error by repeatedly pressing the BACKSPACE key until the incorrect characters are removed. Then, type the correct characters. If you do not discover a mistake until later, you can tap or click the entry, type the correct value, and then press the ENTER key. You can use the following techniques to make changes to the structure:

- If you accidentally add an extra field to the structure, select the field by tapping or clicking the row selector (the leftmost column on the row that contains the field to be deleted). Once you have selected the field, press the DELETE key. This will remove the field from the structure.

- If you forget to include a field, select the field that will follow the one you want to add by tapping or clicking the row selector, and then press the INSERT key. The remaining fields move down one row, making room for the missing field. Make the entries for the new field in the usual manner.

- If you made the wrong field a primary key field, tap or click the correct primary key entry for the field and then tap or click the Primary Key button (TABLE TOOLS DESIGN tab | Tools group).

- To move a field, tap or click the row selector for the field to be moved to select the field, and then drag the field to the desired position.

As an alternative to these steps, you may want to start over. To do so, tap or click the Close button for the window containing the table, and then tap or click the No button in the Microsoft Access dialog box. You then can repeat the process you used earlier to define the fields in the table.

BTW
Importing Data to an Existing Table
When you create a new table in Design view, you can import data from other sources into the table using the EXTERNAL DATA tab.

To Close the Table

Now that you have completed and saved the Customer table, you can close it. The following step closes the table.

 Tap or click the Close button for the Customer table (see Figure 1–52) to close the table.

To Resize Columns in a Datasheet

You can resize the columns in the datasheet for the Customer table just as you resized the columns in the datasheet for the Book Rep table. The following steps resize the columns in the Customer table to best fit the data.

1 Open the Customer table in Datasheet view.

2 Double-tap or double-click the right boundary of the field selectors of each of the fields to resize the columns so that they best fit the data.

3 Save the changes to the layout by tapping or clicking the Save button on the Quick Access Toolbar.

4 Close the table.

BTW
Resizing Columns
To resize all columns in a datasheet to best fit simultaneously, select the column heading for the first column, hold down the SHIFT key and select the last column in the datasheet. Then, double-tap or double-click the right boundary of any field selector.

> **Break Point:** If you wish to take a break, this is a good place to do so. You can exit Access now. To resume at a later time, run Access, open the database called Bavant Publishing, and continue following the steps from this location forward.

Additional Database Objects

BTW
Tabbed Documents Versus Overlapping Windows
By default, Access 2013 displays database objects in tabbed documents instead of in overlapping windows. If your database is in overlapping windows mode, tap or click FILE on the ribbon, tap or click Options in the Backstage view, tap or click Current Database in the Access Options dialog box, and select the Display Document Tabs check box and the Tabbed Documents option button.

A database contains many types of objects. Tables are the objects you use to store and manipulate data. Access supports other important types of objects as well; each object has a specific purpose that helps maximize the benefits of a database. Through queries (questions), Access makes it possible to ask complex questions concerning the data in the database and then receive instant answers. Access also allows the user to produce attractive and useful forms for viewing and updating data. Additionally, Access includes report creation tools that make it easy to produce sophisticated reports for presenting data.

Creating Queries

Queries are simply questions, the answers to which are in the database. Access contains a powerful query feature that helps you find the answers to a wide variety of questions. Once you have examined the question you want to ask to determine the fields involved in the question, you can begin creating the query. If the query involves no special sort order, restrictions, or calculations, you can use the Simple Query Wizard.

To Use the Simple Query Wizard to Create a Query

1 CREATE FIRST TABLE | 2 ADD RECORDS | 3 PRINT CONTENTS | 4 IMPORT RECORDS | 5 MODIFY SECOND TABLE
6 CREATE QUERY | 7 CREATE FORM | 8 CREATE REPORT

The following steps use the Simple Query Wizard to create a query that Bavant Publishing might use to obtain financial information on its customers. *Why? The Simple Query Wizard is the quickest and easiest way to create a query.* This query displays the number, name, amount paid, current due, returns, and book rep number of all customers.

1

- If the Navigation Pane is closed, tap or click the Shutter Bar Open/Close Button to open the Navigation Pane.

- Be sure the Customer table is selected.

- Tap or click CREATE on the ribbon to display the CREATE tab.

- Tap or click the Query Wizard button (CREATE tab | Queries group) to display the New Query dialog box (Figure 1–53).

Figure 1–53

2

- Be sure Simple Query Wizard is selected, and then tap or click the OK button (New Query dialog box) to display the Simple Query Wizard dialog box (Figure 1–54).

Q&A What would happen if the Book Rep table were selected instead of the Customer table?
The list of available fields would contain fields from the Book Rep table rather than the Customer table.

If the list contained Book Rep table fields, how could I make it contain Customer table fields?
Tap or click the arrow in the Tables / Queries box, and then tap or click the Customer table in the list that appears.

Figure 1–54

3

- With the Customer Number field selected, tap or click the Add Field button to add the field to the query.

- With the Customer Name field selected, tap or click the Add Field button a second time to add the field.

- Tap or click the Amount Paid field, and then tap or click the Add Field button to add the field.

- In a similar fashion, add the Current Due, Returns, and Book Rep Number fields (Figure 1–55).

Figure 1–55

4

- Tap or click the Next button to move to the next screen.

- Ensure that the Detail (shows every field of every record) option button is selected (Figure 1–56).

Q&A What is the difference between Detail and Summary?
Detail shows all the records and fields. Summary only shows computations (for example, the total amount paid).

Figure 1–56

5

- Tap or click the Next button to move to the next screen.

- Confirm that the title of the query is Customer Query (Figure 1–57).

Q&A What should I do if the title is incorrect? Click the box containing the title to produce an insertion point. Erase the current title and then type Customer Query.

Figure 1–57

6

- Tap or click the Finish button to create the query (Figure 1–58).

7

- Tap or click the Close button for the Customer Query to remove the query results from the screen.

Q&A If I want to use this query in the future, do I need to save the query? Normally you would. The one exception is a query created by the wizard. The wizard automatically saves the query it creates.

CU #	Customer Name	Amount Paid	Current Due	Returns	BR #
ASU37	Applewood State University	$41,530.98	$38,812.66	$12,008.02	42
BCJ21	Brodkin Junior College	$0.00	$6,081.98	$0.00	42
CSD25	Cowpens ISD	$12,750.00	$13,275.00	$2,000.00	53
CSU10	Camellia State University	$63,246.88	$69,847.76	$14,967.98	53
DCC34	Dartt Community College	$21,345.50	$23,467.75	$4,496.80	65
FSC12	First State College	$34,557.25	$23,875.98	$7,234.99	65
FSU23	Farnham State University	$18,268.00	$22,024.50	$3,496.23	42
HSD05	Hammonds County ISD	$18,434.75	$0.00	$0.00	53
KCC78	Key Community College System	$21,288.65	$11,367.49	$2,256.98	65
MCC45	Mauldin Community College	$9,500.00	$5,000.00	$0.00	53
MEC56	Mehitable College	$9,111.19	$7,310.76	$574.25	42
PLI22	PrattLast Institute	$17,229.45	$11,769.75	$3,450.50	53
SCC77	Stallone Community College	$7,525.98	$2,515.78	$0.00	42
SEC19	Seaborn College	$9,225.34	$10,496.89	$2,017.67	65
TSC02	Tri-State Consortium	$34,578.90	$9,432.56	$943.34	65

Figure 1–58

BTW

Access Help
At any time while using Access, you can find answers to questions and display information about various topics through Access Help. Used properly, this form of assistance can increase your productivity and reduce your frustrations by minimizing the time you spend learning how to use Access. For instruction about Access Help and exercises that will help you gain confidence in using it, read the Office and Windows chapter at the beginning of this book.

Using Queries

After you have created and saved a query, Access stores it as a database object and makes it available for use in a variety of ways:

- If you want to change the design of the query, press and hold or right-click the query in the Navigation Pane and then tap or click Design View on the shortcut menu to open the query in Design view.

- To view the results of the query from Design view, tap or click the Run button to instruct Access to **run** the query, that is, to perform the necessary actions to produce and display the results in Datasheet view.

- To view the results of the query from the Navigation Pane, open it by pressing and holding or right-clicking the query and tapping or clicking Open on the shortcut menu. Access automatically runs the query and displays the results in Datasheet view.

- To print the results with the query open in either Design view or Datasheet view, tap or click FILE on the ribbon, tap or click the Print tab, and then tap or click either Print or Quick Print.

- To print the query without first opening it, be sure the query is selected in the Navigation Pane and tap or click FILE on the ribbon, tap or click the Print tab, and then tap or click either Print or Quick Print.

You can switch between views of a query using the View button (HOME tab | Views group). Tapping or clicking the arrow in the bottom of the button produces the View button menu. You then tap or click the desired view in the menu. The two query views you will use in this chapter are Datasheet view (which displays the query results) and Design view (for changing the query design). You also can tap or click the top part of the View button, in which case, you will switch to the view identified by the icon on the button. In the figure, the button contains the icon for Design view, so tapping or clicking the button would change to Design view. For the most part, the icon on the button represents the view you want, so you can usually simply tap or click the button.

BTW
Creating Queries
Although the Simple Query Wizard is a convenient way to create straightforward queries, you will find that many of the queries you create require more control than the wizard provides. In Chapter 2, you will use Design view to create customized queries.

To Use a Criterion in a Query

1 CREATE FIRST TABLE | 2 ADD RECORDS | 3 PRINT CONTENTS | 4 IMPORT RECORDS | 5 MODIFY SECOND TABLE
6 CREATE QUERY | 7 CREATE FORM | 8 CREATE REPORT

After you have determined the fields to be included in a query, you will determine whether you need to further restrict the results of the query. For example, you might want to include only those customers whose book rep number is 53. In such a case, you need to enter the number 53 as a criterion for the book rep field. *Why? A criterion is a condition that the records must satisfy in order to be included in the query results.* To do so, you will open the query in Design view, enter the criterion below the appropriate field, and then view the results of the query. The following steps enter a criterion to include only the customers of book rep 53 and then view the query results.

- Press and hold or right-click the Customer Query in the Navigation Pane to produce a shortcut menu (Figure 1–59).

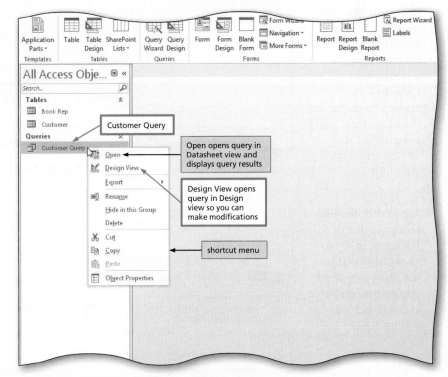

Figure 1–59

❷
- Tap or click Design View on the shortcut menu to open the query in Design view (Figure 1–60).

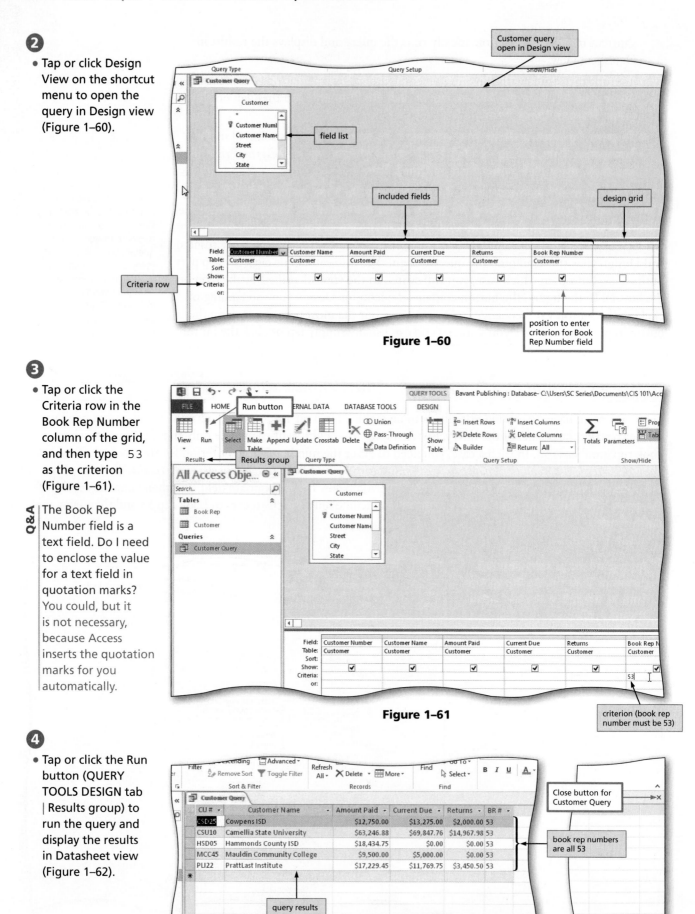

Figure 1–60

❸
- Tap or click the Criteria row in the Book Rep Number column of the grid, and then type 53 as the criterion (Figure 1–61).

Q&A

The Book Rep Number field is a text field. Do I need to enclose the value for a text field in quotation marks? You could, but it is not necessary, because Access inserts the quotation marks for you automatically.

Figure 1–61

❹
- Tap or click the Run button (QUERY TOOLS DESIGN tab | Results group) to run the query and display the results in Datasheet view (Figure 1–62).

Figure 1–62

5
- Tap or click the Close button for the Customer Query to close the query.
- When asked if you want to save your changes, tap or click the No button.

Q&A
If I saved the query, what would happen the next time I ran the query?
You would see only customers of book rep 53.

Could I save a query with another name?
Yes. To save a query with a different name, tap or click FILE on the ribbon, tap or click the Save As tab, tap or click Save Object As, tap or click the Save As button, enter a new file name in the Save As dialog box, and then tap or click the OK button (Save As dialog box).

Other Ways

1. Tap or click View button (QUERY TOOLS DESIGN tab | Results group)   2. Tap or click Datasheet View button on status bar

---

To Print the Results of a Query

The following steps print the results of a saved query.

1 With the Customer Query selected in the Navigation Pane, tap or click FILE on the ribbon to open the Backstage view.

2 Tap or click the Print tab in the Backstage view to display the Print gallery.

3 Tap or click the Quick Print button to print the query.

Creating and Using Forms

In Datasheet view, you can view many records at once. If there are many fields, however, only some of the fields in each record might be visible at a time. In **Form view**, where data is displayed in a form on the screen, you usually can see all the fields, but only for one record.

To Create a Form

1 CREATE FIRST TABLE | 2 ADD RECORDS | 3 PRINT CONTENTS | 4 IMPORT RECORDS | 5 MODIFY SECOND TABLE
6 CREATE QUERY | 7 CREATE FORM | **8 CREATE REPORT**

Like a paper form, a **form** in a database is a formatted document with fields that contain data. Forms allow you to view and maintain data. Forms also can be used to print data, but reports are more commonly used for that purpose. The simplest type of form in Access is one that includes all the fields in a table stacked one above the other. The following steps use the Form button to create a form. *Why? Using the Form button is the simplest way to create this type of form.* The steps then use the form to view records and then save the form.

1
- Select the Customer table in the Navigation Pane.
- If necessary, tap or click CREATE on the ribbon to display the CREATE tab (Figure 1–63).

Figure 1–63

2

- Tap or click the Form button (CREATE tab | Forms group) to create a simple form (Figure 1–64).

Q&A A Field list appeared on my screen. What should I do?

Tap or click the Add Existing Fields button (FORM LAYOUT TOOLS DESIGN tab | Tools group) to remove the Field list from the screen.

Figure 1–64

3

- Tap or click the Form View button on the Access status bar to display the form in Form view rather than Layout view.

Q&A What is the difference between Layout view and Form view?

Layout view allows you to make changes to the look of the form. Form view is the view you use to examine or make changes to the data.

How can I tell when I am in Layout view?

Access identifies Layout view in three ways. The left side of the status bar will contain the words Layout View; shading will appear around the outside of the selected field in the form; and the Layout View button will be selected on the right side of the status bar.

- Tap or click the Next record button three times to move to record 4 (Figure 1–65).

CU #   CSU10

Customer Name   Camellia State University

Street   725 Camellia St.

City   Pleasantburg

State   NJ

Postal Code   07025

Amount Paid $63,246.88

Current Due $69,847.76

$14,967.98

BR #   53

form appears in Form view

fourth record appears in form

Next record button

Record: 14 ◄ 4 of 15 ► ►I ►* 🔾 No Filter   Search

letters followed by 2-digit number

Figure 1–65

4

- Tap or click the Save button on the Quick Access Toolbar to display the Save As dialog box (Figure 1–66).

Q&A Do I have to tap or click the Next record button before saving?
No. The only reason you were asked to tap or click the button was so that you could experience navigation within the form.

5

- Type Customer Form as the form name, and then tap or click the OK button to save the form.

- Tap or click the Close button for the form to close the form.

Save button

Bavant Publishing : Database- C:\Users\SC Series\Documents\CIS 101\Access\Bavant Publishing.accdb (Access

FILE   HOME   CREATE   EXTERNAL DATA   DATABASE TOOLS

View | Paste | Filter | Ascending / Descending | Refresh All | New Save Delete | Totals Spelling More | Find | Replace Go To | B I U A

Views   Clipboard   Sort & Filter   Records

All Access Obje... ⊗ «
Search...
Tables ☆
  Book Rep
  Customer
Queries ☆
  Customer Query

Customer

Customer

CU #

Customer Na...   rsity

Street   725 Camellia St.

City   Pleasantburg

State   NJ

Postal Code   07025

Save As dialog box

position to enter form name

Save As   ?   ✕

Form Name:
Customer

OK   Cancel

OK button

Figure 1–66

Other Ways

1. Tap or click View button (FORM LAYOUT TOOLS DESIGN tab | Views group)

Using a Form

After you have saved a form, you can use it at any time by pressing and holding or right-clicking the form in the Navigation Pane and then tapping or clicking Open on the shortcut menu. In addition to viewing data in the form, you also can use it to enter or update data, a process that is very similar to updating data using a datasheet. If you plan to use the form to enter or revise data, you must ensure you are viewing the form in Form view.

Break Point: If you wish to take a break, this is a good place to do so. You can exit Access now. To resume at a later time, run Access, open the database called Bavant Publishing, and continue following the steps from this location forward.

Creating and Printing Reports

Bavant Publishing wants to create the Customer Financial Report shown in Figure 1–67. To create this report, you will first create a simple report containing all records. Then, you will modify the report to match the one shown in Figure 1–67.

Customer Number	Customer Name	Amount Paid	Current Due	Returns	Book Rep Number
ASU37	Applewood State University	$41,530.98	$38,812.66	$12,008.02	42
BCJ21	Brodkin Junior College	$0.00	$6,081.98	$0.00	42
CSD25	Cowpens ISD	$12,750.00	$13,275.00	$2,000.00	53
CSU10	Camellia State University	$63,246.88	$69,847.76	$14,967.98	53
DCC34	Dartt Community College	$21,345.50	$23,467.75	$4,496.80	65
FSC12	First State College	$34,557.25	$23,875.98	$7,234.99	65
FSU23	Farnham State University	$18,268.00	$22,024.50	$3,496.23	42
HSD05	Hammonds County ISD	$18,434.75	$0.00	$0.00	53
KCC78	Key Community College System	$21,288.65	$11,367.49	$2,256.98	65
MCC45	Mauldin Community College	$9,500.00	$5,000.00	$0.00	53
MEC56	Mehitable College	$9,111.19	$7,310.76	$574.25	42
PLI22	PrattLast Institute	$17,229.45	$11,769.75	$3,450.50	53
SCC77	Stallone Community College	$7,525.98	$2,515.78	$0.00	42
SEC19	Seaborn College	$9,225.34	$10,496.89	$2,017.67	65
TSC02	Tri-State Consortium	$34,578.90	$9,432.56	$943.34	65
		$318,592.87	$255,278.86	$53,446.76	

Customer Financial Report — Monday, September 15, 2014 — 2:23:09 PM

Figure 1–67

To Create a Report

1 CREATE FIRST TABLE | 2 ADD RECORDS | 3 PRINT CONTENTS | 4 IMPORT RECORDS | 5 MODIFY SECOND TABLE
6 CREATE QUERY | 7 CREATE FORM | **8 CREATE REPORT**

You will first create a report containing all fields. *Why? It is easiest to create a report with all the fields and then delete the fields you do not want.* The following steps create and save the initial report. They also modify the report title.

1

- Be sure the Customer table is selected in the Navigation Pane.

- Tap or click CREATE on the ribbon to display the CREATE tab (Figure 1–68).

Q&A Do I need to select the Customer table prior to tapping or clicking CREATE on the ribbon?

You do not need to select the table at that point. You do need to select a table prior to tapping or clicking the Report button, because Access will include all the fields in whichever table or query is currently selected.

Figure 1–68

2

- Tap or click the Report button (CREATE tab | Reports group) to create the report (Figure 1–69).

Q&A Why is the report title Customer? Access automatically assigns the name of the table or query as the title of the report. It also automatically includes the date. You can change either of these later.

Figure 1–69

3

- Tap or click the Save button on the Quick Access Toolbar to display the Save As dialog box, and then type `Customer Financial Report` as the name of the report (Figure 1–70).

Figure 1–70

4

- Tap or click the OK button (Save As dialog box) to save the report (Figure 1–71).

Q&A The name of the report changed. Why did the report title not change? The report title is assigned the same name as the report by default. Changing the name of the report does not change the report title. You can change the title at any time to anything you like.

Figure 1–71

5

- Close the report by tapping or clicking its Close button.

Using Layout View in a Report

Access has four different ways to view reports: Report view, Print Preview, Layout view, and Design view. Report view shows the report on the screen. Print Preview shows the report as it will appear when printed. Layout view is similar to Report view in that it shows the report on the screen, but also allows you to make changes to the report. Layout view is usually the easiest way to make such changes. Design view also allows you to make changes, but does not show you the actual report. Design view is most useful when the changes you need to make are especially complex. In this chapter, you will use Layout view to modify the report.

To Modify Report Column Headings and Resize Columns

1 CREATE FIRST TABLE | 2 ADD RECORDS | 3 PRINT CONTENTS | 4 IMPORT RECORDS | 5 MODIFY SECOND TABLE
6 CREATE QUERY | 7 CREATE FORM | **8 CREATE REPORT**

To make the report match the one shown in Figure 1–67 on page AC 48, you need to change the title, remove some columns, modify the column headings, and also resize the columns. The following steps use Layout view to make the necessary modifications to the report. *Why? Working in Layout view gives you all the tools you need to make the desired modifications. You can view the results of the modifications immediately.*

1

- Press and hold or right-click Customer Financial Report in the Navigation Pane, and then tap or click Layout View on the shortcut menu to open the report in Layout view.

- If a Field list appears, tap or click the Add Existing Fields button (REPORT LAYOUT TOOLS DESIGN tab | Tools group) to remove the Field list from the screen.

- Close the Navigation Pane.

- Tap or click the report title once to select it.

- Tap or click the report title a second time to produce an insertion point (Figure 1–72).

Figure 1–72

Q&A
My insertion point is in the middle of Customer. How do I produce an insertion point at the position shown in the figure?

You can use the RIGHT ARROW key to move the insertion point to the position in the figure, or you can tap or click the desired position.

2

- Press the SPACEBAR to insert a space, and then type Financial Report to complete the title.

- Tap or click the column heading for the Street field to select it.

- Hold the SHIFT key down and then tap or click the column headings for the City, State, and Postal Code fields to select multiple column headings.

Figure 1–73

Q&A What happens if I do not hold down the SHIFT key?
When you tap or click another column heading, it will be the only one that is selected. To select multiple objects, you need to hold the SHIFT key down for every object after the first selection.

I selected the wrong collection of objects. What should I do?
You can tap or click somewhere else on the report so that the objects you want are not selected, and then begin the process again. Alternatively, you can repeatedly tap or click the Undo button on the Quick Access Toolbar to undo your selections. Once you have done so, you can select the objects you want.

- Tap or click ARRANGE on the ribbon to display the REPORT LAYOUT TOOLS ARRANGE tab (Figure 1–73).

3

- Tap or click the Select Column button (REPORT LAYOUT TOOLS ARRANGE tab | Rows & Columns group) to select the entire columns corresponding to the column headings you selected in the previous step.

- Press the DELETE key to delete the selected columns.

- Tap or click the column heading for the Customer Number field twice, once to select it and the second time to produce an insertion point (Figure 1–74).

Figure 1–74

Q&A I selected the wrong field. What should I do?
Tap or click somewhere outside the various fields to deselect the one you have selected. Then, tap or click the Customer Number field twice.

4

- Use the DELETE or BACKSPACE keys as necessary to erase the current entry, and then type `Customer Number` as the new entry.

- Tap or click the heading for the Book Rep Number field twice, erase the current entry, and then type `Book Rep Number` as the new entry.

- Tap or click the Customer Number field heading to select it, point to the lower boundary of the heading for the Customer Number field so that the pointer changes to a two-headed arrow, and then drag the lower boundary to the approximate position shown in Figure 1–75 to expand the column headings.

Figure 1–75

Q&A

I did something wrong when I dragged and now my report looks strange. What should I do?
Tap or click the Undo button on the Quick Access Toolbar to undo the change. Depending on the specific action you took, you may need to tap or click it more than once.

My screen displays Book Rep Number on one line not two. Is this a problem?
No. You will adjust the column heading in a later step.

5

- Point to the right boundary of the heading for the Customer Number field so that the pointer changes to a two-headed arrow, and then drag the right boundary to the approximate position shown in Figure 1–76 to reduce the width of the column.

Figure 1–76

6

- Using the same technique, resize the other columns to the sizes shown in Figure 1–77.

Figure 1–77

To Add Totals to a Report

The report in Figure 1–67 contains totals for the Amount Paid, Current Due, and Returns columns. You can use Layout view to add these totals. The following steps use Layout view to include totals for these three columns. *Why? In Layout view you can tap or click a single button to add totals. This button sums all the values in the field.*

1

- Tap or click the Amount Paid field heading (shown in Figure 1–77) to select the field.

Q&A Do I have to tap or click the heading? Could I tap or click the field on one of the records?
You do not have to tap or click the heading. You also could tap or click the Amount Paid field on any record.

- Tap or click DESIGN on the ribbon to display the DESIGN tab.

- Tap or click the Totals button (REPORT LAYOUT TOOLS DESIGN tab | Grouping & Totals group) to display the Totals menu containing a list of available calculations (Figure 1–78).

Figure 1–78

2

- Tap or click Sum to calculate the sum of the amount of paid values.

- Using the same technique, add totals for the Current Due and Returns columns.

Q&A When I clicked the Totals button after selecting the Returns field heading, Sum was already checked. Do I still need to tap or click Sum?
No. In fact, if you do tap or click it, you will remove the check mark, which will remove the total from the column.

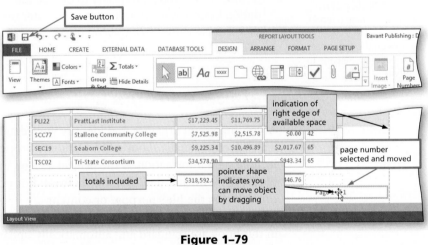

Figure 1–79

- Scroll down to the bottom of the report to verify that the totals are included. If necessary, expand the size of the total controls so they appear completely by dragging the lower boundary of the controls to the approximate position shown in Figure 1–79.

- Tap or click the page number to select it, and then drag it to the approximate position shown in Figure 1–79.

Q&A Why did I need to move the page number?
The dotted line near the right-hand edge of the screen indicates the right-hand border of the available space on the printed page, based on whatever margins and orientation are currently selected. A portion of the page number extends beyond this border. By moving the page number, it no longer extends beyond the border.

3

- Tap or click the Save button on the Quick Access Toolbar to save your changes to the report layout.

- Close the report.

To Print a Report

The following steps print the report.

 1 Open the Navigation Pane if necessary, confirm that the Customer Financial Report is selected, and then tap or click FILE on the ribbon to open the Backstage view.

2 Tap or click the Print tab in the Backstage view to display the Print gallery.

3 Tap or click the Quick Print button to print the report.

When I print the report, I have pound signs (####) rather than numbers where the totals should be for the Amount Paid and Current Due columns. The report looked fine on the screen. How can I correct it?

The columns are not wide enough to display the complete number. Open the report in Layout view and slightly increase the width of the Amount Paid and Current Due columns by dragging the right boundary of the column headings.

How can I print multiple copies of my report?

Tap or click FILE on the ribbon to open the Backstage view. Tap or click the Print tab, tap or click Print in the Print gallery to display the Print dialog box, increase the number in the Number of Copies box, and then tap or click the OK button (Print dialog box).

How can I print a range of pages rather than printing the whole report?

Tap or click FILE on the ribbon to open the Backstage view. Tap or click the Print tab, tap or click Print in the Print gallery to display the Print dialog box, tap or click the Pages option button in the Print Range area, enter the desired page range, and then tap or click the OK button (Print dialog box).

BTW

Exporting a Report as a PDF or XPS File

To export a report as a PDF or XPS file, display the EXTERNAL DATA tab, and then tap or click the PDF or XPS button (EXTERNAL DATA tab | Export group). Enter the appropriate information in the Publish to PDF or XPS dialog box and tap or click the Publish button.

BTW

Report Navigation

When previewing a report, you can use the Navigation buttons on the status bar to move from one page to another.

Database Properties

Access helps you organize and identify your databases by using **database properties,** which are the details about a file. Database properties, also known as **metadata,** can include such information as the project author, title, or subject. **Keywords** are words or phrases that further describe the database. For example, a class name or database topic can describe the file's purpose or content.

Five different types of database properties exist, but the more common ones used in this book are standard and automatically updated properties. **Standard properties** are associated with all Microsoft Office documents and include author, title, and subject. **Automatically updated properties** include file system properties, such as the date you create or change a file, and statistics, such as the file size.

Why would you want to assign database properties to a database?

Database properties are valuable for a variety of reasons:

- Users can save time locating a particular file because they can view a file's database properties without opening the database.

- By creating consistent properties for files having similar content, users can better organize their databases.

- Some organizations require Access users to add database properties so that other employees can view details about these files.

To Change Database Properties

To change database properties, you would follow these steps.

1. Tap or click FILE on the ribbon to open the Backstage view and then, if necessary, tap or click the Info tab in the Backstage view to display the Info gallery.

2. Click the 'View and edit database properties' link in the right pane of the Info gallery to display the Bavant Publishing Properties dialog box.

Q&A Why are some of the database properties already filled in?
The person who installed Office 2013 on your computer or network might have set or customized the properties.

3. If the property you want to change is displayed in the Properties dialog box, click the text box for the property and make the desired change. Skip the remaining steps.

4. If the property you want to change is not displayed in the Properties dialog box, click the appropriate tab so the property is displayed and then make the desired change.

5. Click the OK button in the Properties dialog box to save your changes and remove the dialog box from the screen.

To Sign Out of a Microsoft Account

If you are signed in to a Microsoft account and are using a public computer or otherwise wish to sign out of your Microsoft account, you should sign out of the account from the Account gallery in the Backstage view before exiting Access. Signing out of the account is the safest way to make sure that nobody else can access SkyDrive files or settings stored in your Microsoft account. The following steps sign out of a Microsoft account from Access. For a detailed example of the procedure summarized below, refer to the Office and Windows chapter at the beginning of this book.

1 If you wish to sign out of your Microsoft account, tap or click FILE on the ribbon to open the Backstage view and then tap or click the Account tab to display the Account gallery.

2 Tap or click the Sign out link, which displays the Remove Account dialog box. If a Can't remove Windows accounts dialog box appears instead of the Remove Account dialog box, click the OK button and skip the remaining steps.

Q&A Why does a Can't remove Windows accounts dialog box appear?
If you signed in to Windows using your Microsoft account, then you also must sign out from Windows, rather than signing out from within Access. When you are finished using Windows, be sure to sign out at that time.

3 Tap or click the Yes button (Remove Account dialog box) to sign out of your Microsoft account on this computer.

Q&A Should I sign out of Windows after signing out of my Microsoft account? [End Q]
When you are finished using the computer, you should sign out of your account for maximum security.

4 Tap or click the Back button in the upper-left corner of the Backstage view to return to the database.

To Exit Access

The following steps exit Access.

 Tap or click the Close button on the right side of the title bar to close the open database, if there is one, and exit Access.

2 If a Microsoft Access dialog box appears, tap or click the Save button to save any changes made to the database since the last save.

Special Database Operations

Additional operations involved in maintaining a database are backup, recovery, compacting, and repairing.

Backup and Recovery

It is possible to damage or destroy a database. Users can enter data that is incorrect; programs that are updating the database can end abnormally during an update; a hardware problem can occur; and so on. After any such event has occurred, the database may contain invalid data or it might be totally destroyed.

Obviously, you cannot allow a situation in which data has been damaged or destroyed to go uncorrected. You must somehow return the database to a correct state. This process is called recovery; that is, you **recover** the database.

The simplest approach to recovery involves periodically making a copy of the database (called a **backup copy** or a **save copy**). This is referred to as **backing up** the database. If a problem occurs, you correct the problem by overwriting the actual database — often referred to as the **live database** — with the backup copy.

To back up the database that is currently open, you use the Back Up Database command on the Save As tab in the Backstage view. In the process, Access suggests a name that is a combination of the database name and the current date. For example, if you back up the Bavant Publishing database on October 20, 2014, Access will suggest the name, Bavant Publishing_2014-10-20. You can change this name if you desire, although it is a good idea to use this name. By doing so, it will be easy to distinguish between all the backup copies you have made to determine which is the most recent. In addition, if you discover that a critical problem occurred on October 18, 2014, you may want to go back to the most recent backup before October 18. If, for example, the database was not backed up on October 17 but was backed up on October 16, you would use Bavant Publishing_2014-10-16.

To Back Up a Database

You would use the following steps to back up a database to a file on a hard disk or high-capacity removable disk.

1. Open the database to be backed up.
2. Tap or click FILE on the ribbon to open the Backstage view, and then tap or click the Save As tab.
3. With Save Database As selected in the File Types area, tap or click 'Back Up Database' in the Save Database As area, and then tap or click the Save As button.
4. Navigate to the desired location in the Save As box. If you do not want the name Access has suggested, enter the desired name in the File name text box.
5. Tap or click the Save button to back up the database.

Access creates a backup copy with the desired name in the desired location. Should you ever need to recover the database using this backup copy, you can simply copy it over the live version.

Compacting and Repairing a Database

As you add more data to a database, it naturally grows larger. When you delete an object (records, tables, forms, or queries), the space previously occupied by the object does not become available for additional objects. Instead, the additional objects are given new space; that is, space that was not already allocated. To remove this empty space from the database, you must **compact** the database. The same option that compacts the database also repairs problems that might have occurred in the database.

TO COMPACT AND REPAIR A DATABASE

You would use the following steps to compact and repair a database.

1. Open the database to be compacted.
2. Tap or click FILE on the ribbon to open the Backstage view, and then, if necessary, select the Info tab.
3. Tap or click the Compact & Repair Database button in the Info gallery to compact and repair the database.
   The database now is the compacted form of the original.

Additional Operations

Additional special operations include opening another database, closing a database without exiting Access, and saving a database with another name. They also include deleting a table (or other object) as well as renaming an object.

When you open another database, Access will automatically close the database that previously was open. Before deleting or renaming an object, you should ensure that the object has no dependent objects; that is, other objects that depend on the object you want to delete.

TO CLOSE A DATABASE WITHOUT EXITING ACCESS

You would use the following steps to close a database without exiting Access.

1. Tap or click FILE on the ribbon to open the Backstage view.
2. Tap or click Close.

TO SAVE A DATABASE WITH ANOTHER NAME

To save a database with another name, you would use the following steps.

1. Tap or click FILE on the ribbon to open the Backstage view, and then select the Save As tab.
2. With Save Database As selected in the Database File Types area and Access Database selected in the Save Database As area, tap or click the Save As button.
3. Enter a name and select a location for the new version.
4. Tap or click the Save button.

If you want to make a backup, could you just save the database with another name?

You could certainly do that. Using the backup procedure discussed earlier has the advantage that it automatically includes the current database name and the date in the name of the file it creates.

TO DELETE A TABLE OR OTHER OBJECT IN THE DATABASE

You would use the following steps to delete a database object.

1. Press and hold or right-click the object in the Navigation Pane.

2. Tap or click Delete on the shortcut menu.

3. Tap or click the Yes button in the Microsoft Access dialog box.

TO RENAME AN OBJECT IN THE DATABASE

You would use the following steps to rename a database object.

1. Press and hold or right-click the object in the Navigation Pane.

2. Tap or click Rename on the shortcut menu.

3. Type the new name and press the ENTER key.

Database Design

BTW

Database Design Language (DBDL)
Database Design Language (DBDL) is a commonly accepted shorthand representation for showing the structure of a relational database. You write the name of the table and then within parentheses you list all the columns in the table. If the columns continue beyond one line, indent the subsequent lines.

This section illustrates the **database design** process, that is, the process of determining the tables and fields that make up the database. It does so by showing how you would design the database for Bavant Publishing from a set of requirements. In this section, you will use commonly accepted shorthand to represent the tables and fields that make up the database as well as the primary keys for the tables. For each table, you give the name of the table followed by a set of parentheses. Within the parentheses is a list of the fields in the table separated by commas. You underline the primary key. For example,

Product (<u>Product Code</u>, Description, On Hand, Price) represents a table called Product. The Product table contains four fields: Product Code, Description, On Hand, and Price. The Product Code field is the primary key.

Database Requirements

BTW

Determining Database Requirements
The determination of database requirements is part of a process known as systems analysis. A systems analyst examines existing and proposed documents, and examines organizational policies to determine exactly the type of data needs the database must support.

The Bavant Publishing database must maintain information on both customers and book reps. The business currently keeps this data in two Word tables and two Excel workbooks, as shown in Figure 1–80. They use Word tables for address information and Excel workbooks for financial information.

- For customers, Bavant needs to maintain address data. It currently keeps this data in a Word table (Figure 1–80a).

- Bavant also maintains financial data for each customer. This includes the amount paid, current amount due, and return amount for the customer. It keeps these amounts, along with the customer name and number, in the Excel worksheet shown in Figure 1–80b.

- Bavant keeps book rep address data in a Word table, as shown in Figure 1–80c.

- Just as with customers, it keeps financial data for book reps, including their start date, salary, and bonus rate, in a separate Excel worksheet, as shown in Figure 1–80d.

Customer Number	Customer Name	Street	City	State	Postal Code
ASU37	Applewood State University	300 University Ave.	Greer	PA	19158
BCJ21	Brodkin Junior College	4806 Park Dr.	Greer	PA	19158
CSD25	Cowpens ISD	829 Wooster Ave.	Gossett	PA	19157
CSU10	Camellia State University	725 Camellia St.	Pleasantburg	NJ	07025
DCC34	Dartt Community College	3827 Burgess Dr.	Chambers	NJ	07037
FSC12	First State College	7300 Cedar Rd.	Quaker	DE	19719
FSU23	Farnham State University	1445 Hubert St.	Gaston	DE	19723
HSD05	Hammonds County ISD	446 Lincoln Blvd.	Chesnee	NJ	07053
KCC78	Key Community College System	7523 Penn Ave.	Adelphia	PA	19159
MCC45	Mauldin Community College	72 Montrose St.	Chesnee	NJ	07053
MEC56	Mehitable College	202 College St.	Gaston	DE	19723
PLI22	PrattLast Institute	236 Ashton Ave.	Pleasantburg	NJ	07025
SCC77	Stallone Community College	1200 Franklin Blvd.	Adelphia	PA	19156
SEC19	Seaborn College	345 Mather Rd.	Quaker	DE	19719
TSC02	Tri-State Consortium	3400 Metro Pkwy.	Adelphia	PA	19156

© 2014 Cengage Learning

Figure 1–80 (a) Customer Address Information (Word Table)

	A	B	C	D	E	F	G	H
1	Customer Number	Customer Name	Amount Paid	Current Due	Returns			
2	ASU37	Applewood State University	$41,530.98	$38,812.66	$12,008.02			
3	BCJ21	Brodkin Junior College	$0.00	$6,081.98	$0.00			
4	CSD25	Cowpens ISD	$12,750.00	$13,275.00	$2,000.00			
5	CSU10	Camellia State University	$63,246.88	$69,847.76	$14,967.98			
6	DCC34	Dartt Community College	$21,345.50	$23,467.75	$4,496.80			
7	FSC12	First State College	$34,557.25	$23,875.98	$7,234.99			
8	FSU23	Farnham State University	$18,268.00	$22,024.50	$3,496.23			
9	HSD05	Hammonds County ISD	$18,434.75	$0.00	$0.00			
10	KCC78	Key Community College System	$21,288.65	$11,367.49	$2,256.98			
11	MCC45	Mauldin Community College	$9,500.00	$5,000.00	$0.00			
12	MEC56	Mehitable College	$9,111.19	$7,310.76	$574.25			
13	PLI22	PrattLast Institute	$17,229.45	$11,769.75	$3,450.50			
14	SCC77	Stallone Community College	$7,525.98	$2,515.78	$0.00			
15	SEC19	Seaborn College	$9,225.34	$10,496.89	$2,017.67			
16	TSC02	Tri-State Consortium	$34,578.90	$9,432.56	$943.34			

Figure 1–80 (b) Customer Financial Information (Excel Worksheet)

Book Rep Number	Last Name	First Name	Street	City	State	Postal Code
42	Perez	Melina	261 Porter Dr.	Adelphia	PA	19156
48	Statnik	Michael	3135 Simpson Dr.	Pleasantburg	NJ	07025
53	Chin	Robert	265 Maxwell St.	Gossett	PA	19157
65	Rogers	Tracy	1827 Maple Ave.	Adelphia	PA	19159

© 2014 Cengage Learning

Figure 1–80 (c) Book Rep Address Information (Word Table)

	A	B	C	D	E	F	G	H	I	J
1	Book Rep Number	Last Name	First Name	Start Date	Salary	Bonus Rate				
2	53	Chin	Robert	6/1/2013	$26,250	0.19				
3	42	Perez	Melina	5/14/2012	$31,500	0.20				
4	65	Rogers	Tracy	7/1/2014	$7,750	0.18				
5	48	Statnik	Michael	1/15/2013	$29,000	0.20				
6										
7										

Figure 1–80 (d) Book Rep Financial Information (Excel Worksheet)

- Finally, Bavant keeps track of which customers are assigned to which book reps. Each customer is assigned to a single book rep, but each book rep might be assigned many customers. Currently, for example, customers ASU37 (Applewood State University), BCJ21 (Brodkin Junior College), FSU23 (Farnham State University), MEC56 (Mehitable College), and SCC77 (Stallone Community College) are assigned to book rep 42 (Melina Perez). Customers CSD25 (Cowpens ISD), CSU10 (Camellia State University), HSD05 (Hammonds County ISD), MCC45 (Mauldin Community College), and PLI22 (PrattLast Institute) are assigned to book rep 53 (Robert Chin). Customers DCC34 (Dartt Community College), FSC12 (First State College), KCC78 (Key Community College System), SEC19 (Seaborn College), and TSC02 (Tri-State Consortium) are assigned to book rep 65 (Tracy Rogers). Bavant has an additional book rep, Michael Statnik, whose number has been assigned as 48, but who has not yet been assigned any customers.

Database Design Process

The database design process involves several steps.

What is the first step in the process?

Identify the tables. Examine the requirements for the database to identify the main objects that are involved. There will be a table for each object you identify.

In a database for one organization, for example, the main objects might be departments and employees. This would require two tables: one for departments and the other for employees. In the database for another organization, the main objects might be customers and book reps. In this case, there also would be two tables: one for customers and the other for book reps. In still another organization's database, the main objects might be books, publishers, and authors. This database would require three tables: one for books, a second for publishers, and a third for authors.

Identifying the Tables

For the Bavant Publishing database, the main objects are customers and book reps. This leads to two tables, which you must name. Reasonable names for these two tables are:

Customer
Book Rep

After identifying the tables, what is the second step in the database design process?

Determine the primary keys. Recall that the primary key is the unique identifier for records in the table. For each table, determine the unique identifier. In a Department table, for example, the unique identifier might be the Department Code. For a Book table, the unique identifier might be the ISBN (International Standard Book Number).

Determining the Primary Keys

The next step is to identify the fields that will be the unique identifiers, or primary keys. Customer numbers uniquely identify customers, and book rep numbers uniquely identify book reps. Thus, the primary key for the Customer table is the customer number, and the primary key for the Book Rep table is the book rep number. Reasonable names for these fields would be Customer Number and Book Rep Number, respectively. Adding these primary keys to the tables gives:

Customer (<u>Customer Number</u>)
Book Rep (<u>Book Rep Number</u>)

CONSIDER THIS

CONSIDER THIS

What is the third step in the database design process after determining the primary keys?
Determine the additional fields. The primary key will be a field or combination of fields in a table. A table typically will contain many additional fields, each of which contains a type of data. Examine the project requirements to determine these additional fields. For example, in an Employee table, additional fields might include Employee Name, Street Address, City, State, Postal Code, Date Hired, and Salary.

Determining Additional Fields

After identifying the primary keys, you need to determine and name the additional fields. In addition to the customer number, the Customer Address Information shown in Figure 1–80a on page AC 59 contains the customer name, street, city, state, and postal code. These would be fields in the Customer table. The Customer Financial Information shown in Figure 1–80b on page AC 59 also contains the customer number and customer name, which are already included in the Customer table. The financial information also contains the amount paid, current due, and returns. Adding the amount paid, current due, and returns fields to those already identified in the Customer table and assigning reasonable names gives:

> Customer (<u>Customer Number</u>, Customer Name, Street, City, State, Postal Code, Amount Paid, Current Due, Returns)

Similarly, examining the Book Rep Address Information in Figure 1–80c on page AC 59 adds the last name, first name, street, city, state, and postal code fields to the Book Rep table. In addition to the book rep number, last name, and first name, the Book Rep Financial Information in Figure 1–80d on page AC 59 would add the start date, salary, and bonus rate. Adding these fields to the Book Rep table and assigning reasonable names gives:

> Book Rep (<u>Book Rep Number</u>, Last Name, First Name, Street, City, State, Postal Code, Start Date, Salary, Bonus Rate)

BTW
Additional Data for Bavant Publishing
Bavant could include other types of data in the database. The Customer table could include data on a contact person at each organization, such as, name, telephone number, and email address. The Book Rep table could include the mobile telephone number, email address, and emergency contact information for the book rep.

What happens as the fourth step, after determining additional fields?
Determine relationships between the tables. A relationship is an association between objects. In a database containing information about departments and employees, there is an association between the departments and the employees. A department is associated with all the employees in the department, and an employee is associated with the department to which he or she is assigned. Technically, you say that a department is related to all the employees in the department, and an employee is related to his or her department.

The relationship between department and employees is an example of a **one-to-many relationship** because one employee is associated with one department, but each department can be associated with many employees. The Department table would be the "one" table in the relationship. The Employee table would be the "many" table in the relationship.

When you have determined that two tables are related, follow these general guidelines:

Identify the "one" table.

Identify the "many" table.

Include the primary key from the "one" table as a field in the "many" table.

CONSIDER THIS

BTW

Certification
The Microsoft Office Specialist (MOS) program provides an opportunity for you to obtain a valuable industry credential — proof that you have the Access 2013 skills required by employers. For more information, visit the Certification resource on the Student Companion Site located on www.cengagebrain.com. For detailed instructions about accessing available resources, visit www.cengage.com/ct/studentdownload or contact your instructor for information about accessing the required files.

Determining and Implementing Relationships Between the Tables

According to the requirements, each customer has one book rep, but each book rep can have many customers. Thus, the Book Rep table is the "one" table, and the Customer table is the "many" table. To implement this one-to-many relationship between book reps and customers, add the Book Rep Number field (the primary key of the Book Rep table) to the Customer table. This produces:

Customer (<u>Customer Number</u>, Customer Name, Street, City, State, Postal Code, Amount Paid, Current Due, Returns, Book Rep Number)

Book Rep (<u>Book Rep Number</u>, Last Name, First Name, Street, City, State, Postal Code, Start Date, Salary, Bonus Rate)

CONSIDER THIS

After creating relationships between tables, what is the fifth step in the database design process?
Determine data types for the fields, that is, the type of data that can be stored in the field.

Determining Data Types for the Fields

See Pages AC 9 through AC 10 for a discussion of the available data types and their use in the Bavant Publishing database. That section also discusses other properties that can be assigned, such as captions, field size, and the number of decimal places.

Identifying and Removing Redundancy

BTW

Quick Reference
For a table that lists how to complete the tasks covered in this book using touch gestures, the mouse, ribbon, shortcut menu, and keyboard, see the Quick Reference Summary at the back of this book, or visit the Quick Reference resource on the Student Companion Site located on www.cengagebrain.com. For detailed instructions about accessing available resources, visit www.cengage.com/ct/studentdownload or contact your instructor for information about accessing the required files.

Redundancy means storing the same fact in more than one place. It usually results from placing too many fields in a table — fields that really belong in separate tables — and often causes serious problems. If you had not realized there were two objects, such as customers and book reps, you might have placed all the data in a single Customer table. Figure 1–81 shows an example of a table that includes both customer and book rep information. Notice that the data for a given book rep (number, name, address, and so on) occurs on more than one record. The data for rep 42, Melina Perez, is repeated in the figure. Storing this data on multiple records is an example of redundancy.

Customer Number	Customer Name	Street	...	Book Rep Number	Last Name	First Name
ASU37	Applewood State University	300 University Ave.	...	42	Perez	Melina
BCJ21	Brodkin Junior College	4806 Park Dr.	...	42	Perez	Melina
CSD25	Cowpens ISD	829 Wooster Ave.	...	53	Chin	Robert
CSU10	Camellia State University	725 Camellia St.	...	53	Chin	Robert
DCC34	Dartt Community College	3827 Burgess Dr.	...	65	Rogers	Tracy
...	...	...	...	...	...	...

name of Book Rep 42 appears more than once

Book Rep numbers are 42

© 2014 Cengage Learning

Figure 1–81

What problems does this redundancy cause?

Redundancy results in several problems, including:

1. Wasted storage space. The name of book rep 42, Melina Perez, for example, should be stored only once. Storing this fact several times is wasteful.

2. More complex database updates. If, for example, Melina Perez's name is spelled incorrectly and needs to be changed in the database, her name would need to be changed in several different places.

3. Possible inconsistent data. Nothing prohibits the book rep's last name from being Perez on customer ASU37's record and Perret on customer BCJ21's record. The data would be inconsistent. In both cases, the book rep number is 42, but the last names are different.

How do you eliminate redundancy?

The solution to the problem is to place the redundant data in a separate table, one in which the data no longer will be redundant. If, for example, you place the data for book reps in a separate table (Figure 1–82), the data for each book rep will appear only once.

Customer Number	Customer Name	Street	...	Book Rep Number
ASU37	Applewood State University	300 University Ave.	...	42
BCJ21	Brodkin Junior College	4806 Park Dr.	...	42
CSD25	Cowpens ISD	829 Wooster Ave.	...	53
CSU10	Camellia State University	725 Camellia St.	...	53
DCC34	Dartt Community College	3827 Burgess Dr.	...	65

Book Rep numbers are 42

Book Rep Number	Last Name	First Name	...
42	Perez	Melina	...
48	Statnik	Michael	...
53	Chin	Robert	...
65	Rogers	Tracy	...

name of Book Rep 42 appears only once

© 2014 Cengage Learning

Figure 1–82

Notice that you need to have the book rep number in both tables. Without it, there would be no way to tell which book rep is associated with which customer. The remaining book rep data, however, was removed from the Customer table and placed in the Book Rep table. This new arrangement corrects the problems of redundancy in the following ways:

1. Because the data for each book rep is stored only once, space is not wasted.

2. Changing the name of a book rep is easy. You need to change only one row in the Book Rep table.

3. Because the data for a book rep is stored only once, inconsistent data cannot occur.

Designing to omit redundancy will help you to produce good and valid database designs. You should always examine your design to see if it contains redundancy. If it does, you should decide whether you need to remove the redundancy by creating a separate table.

If you examine your design, you will see that there is one area of redundancy (see the data in Figure 1–1 on page AC 3). Cities and states are both repeated. Every customer whose postal code is 19158, for example, has Greer as the city and PA as the state. To remove this redundancy, you would create a table with the primary key Postal Code and City and State as additional fields. City and State would be removed from the Customer table. Having City, State, and Postal Code in a table is very common, however, and usually you would not take such action. No other redundancy exists in your tables.

BTW

Postal Codes
Some organizations with customers throughout the country have a separate table of postal codes, cities, and states. When placing an order, you typically are asked for your postal code (or ZIP code), rather than city, state, and postal code. You then are asked to confirm that the city and state correspond to that postal code.

Chapter Summary

In this chapter you have learned to create an Access database, create tables and add records to a database, print the contents of tables, import data, create queries, create forms, create reports, and change database properties. You also have learned how to design a database. The items listed below include all the new Access skills you have learned in this chapter, with tasks grouped by activity.

Database Object Management
    Delete a Table or Other Object in the Database (AC 58)
    Rename an Object in the Database (AC 58)

Database Properties
    Change Database Properties (AC 55)

File Management
    Run Access (AC 5)
    Create a Database (AC 6)
    Create a Database Using a Template (AC 7)
    Exit Access (AC 24)
    Open a Database from Access (AC 25)
    Back Up a Database (AC 56)
    Compact and Repair a Database (AC 57)
    Close a Database without Exiting Access (AC 57)
    Save a Database with Another Name (AC 57)

Form Creation
    Create a Form (AC 45)

Import Data
    Import an Excel Worksheet (AC 33)

Print Objects
    Preview and Print the Contents of a Table (AC 30)

    Print the Results of a Query (AC 45)
    Print a Report (AC 54)

Query Creation
    Use the Simple Query Wizard to Create a Query (AC 40)
    Use a Criterion in a Query (AC 43)

Report Creation
    Create a Report (AC 48)
    Modify Report Column Headings and Resize Columns (AC 50)
    Add Totals to a Report (AC 53)

Table Creation
    Modify the Primary Key (AC 11)
    Define the Remaining Fields in a Table (AC 14)
    Save a Table (AC 16)
    View the Table in Design View (AC 17)
    Change a Field Size in Design View (AC 18)
    Close the Table (AC 20)
    Resize Columns in a Datasheet (AC 28)
    Modify a Table in Design View (AC 37)

Table Update
    Add Records to a Table (AC 20)
    Add Records to a Table that Contains Data (AC 26)

What decisions will you need to make when creating your next database?

Use these guidelines as you complete the assignments in this chapter and create your own databases outside of this class.

    1. Identify the tables that will be included in the database.

    2. Determine the primary keys for each of the tables.

    3. Determine the additional fields that should be included in each of the tables.

    4. Determine relationships between the tables.

        a) Identify the "one" table.

        b) Identify the "many" table.

        c) Include the primary key of the "one" table as a field in the "many" table.

    5. Determine data types for the fields in the tables.

    6. Determine additional properties for fields.

        a) Determine if a special caption is warranted.

        b) Determine if a special description is warranted.

        c) Determine field sizes.

        d) Determine formats.

    7. Identify and remove any unwanted redundancy.

    8. Determine a storage location for the database.

    9. Determine the best method for distributing the database objects.

CONSIDER THIS

How should you submit solutions to questions in the assignments identified with a ✳ symbol?

Every assignment in this book contains one or more questions identified with a ✳ symbol. These questions require you to think beyond the assigned database. Present your solutions to the questions in the format required by your instructor. Possible formats may include one or more of these options: write the answer; create a document that contains the answer; present your answer to the class; discuss your answer in a group; record the answer as audio or video using a webcam, smartphone, or portable media player; or post answers on a blog, wiki, or website.

CONSIDER THIS

Apply Your Knowledge

Reinforce the skills and apply the concepts you learned in this chapter.

Adding a Caption, Changing a Data Type, Creating a Query, a Form, and a Report

Note: To complete this assignment, you will be required to use the Data Files for Students. Visit www.cengage.com/ct/studentdownload for detailed instructions or contact your instructor for information about accessing the required files.

Instructions: Cosmetics Naturally Inc. manufactures and sells beauty and skin care products made with only natural ingredients. The company's products do not contain any synthetic chemicals, artificial fragrances, or chemical preservatives. Cosmetics Naturally has a database that keeps track of its sales representatives and customers. Each customer is assigned to a single sales rep, but each sales rep may be assigned to many customers. The database has two tables. The Customer table contains data on the customers who purchase Cosmetics Naturally products. The Sales Rep table contains data on the sales reps. You will add a caption, change a data type, create two queries, a form, and a report, as shown in Figure 1–83 on the next page.

Perform the following tasks:

1. Start Access, open the Apply Cosmetics Naturally database from the Data Files for Students, and enable the content.

2. Open the Sales Rep table in Datasheet view, add SR # as the caption for the Sales Rep Number field, and resize all columns to best fit the data. Save the changes to the layout of the table and close the table.

3. Open the Customer table in Design view and change the data type for the Postal Code field to Short Text. Change the field size for the field to 5. Save the changes to the table and close the table.

4. Use the Simple Query Wizard to create a query for the Customer table that contains the Customer Number, Customer Name, Amount Paid, Balance, and Sales Rep Number. The query is a detail query. Use the name Customer Query for the query and close the query.

5. Create a simple form for the Sales Rep table. Save the form and use the name Sales Rep for the form. Close the form.

6. Create the report shown in Figure 1–83 for the Customer table. The report includes totals for both the Amount Paid and Balance fields. Be sure the totals appear completely. You might need to expand the size of the total controls. Move the page number so that it is within the margins. Save the report as Customer Financial Report.

7. If requested by your instructor, add your last name to the title of the report, that is, change the title to Customer Financial Report LastName where LastName is your actual last name.

8. Compact and repair the database.

9. Submit the revised database in the format specified by your instructor.

10. ✳ How would you change the field name of the Balance field in the Customer table to Current Balance?

Continued >

Apply Your Knowledge *continued*

| Customer Financial Report | | | | Monday, September 15, 2014 |
| | | | | 9:24:56 PM |

Customer Number	Customer Name	Amount Paid	Balance	Sales Rep Number
AS24	Ashley's Salon	$1,789.65	$236.99	34
UR23	U R Beautiful	$0.00	$1,235.00	39
		$14,786.17	$5,617.78	

Figure 1–83

Extend Your Knowledge

Extend the skills you learned in this chapter and experiment with new skills. You may need to use Help to complete the assignment.

Using a Database Template to Create a Contacts Database

Note: To complete this assignment, you will be required to use the Data Files for Students. Visit www.cengage.com/ct/studentdownload for detailed instructions or contact your instructor for information about accessing the required files.

Instructions: Access includes both desktop database templates and web-based templates. You can use a template to create a beginning database that can be modified to meet your specific needs. You will use a template to create a Contacts database. The database template includes sample tables, queries, forms, and reports. You will modify the database and create the Contacts Query shown in Figure 1–84.

Perform the following tasks:

1. Start Access.
2. Select the Desktop contacts template in the template gallery and create a new database with the file name Extend Contacts.
3. Enable the content. If requested to do so by your instructor, watch the videos in the Getting Started with Contacts dialog box. Close the Getting Started with Contacts dialog box.
4. Close the Contact List form.
5. Open the Contacts table in Datasheet view and delete the Fax Number field and the Attachments field in the table. The Attachments field has a paperclip as the column heading.
6. Change the data type for the ID field to Short Text, change the field name to Contact ID, and change the field size to 4. Change the column width so that the complete field name is displayed.
7. Save the changes to the Contacts table and close the table.
8. Use the Simple Query Wizard to create the Contacts Query shown in Figure 1–84. Close the query.

Figure 1–84

9. Open the Phone Book report in Layout view. Delete the control containing the date. Change the title of the report to Contact Phone List.

10. Save the changes to the report.

11. If requested to do so by your instructor, add your first and last names to the end of the title and save the changes to the report.

12. Submit the revised database in the format specified by your instructor.

13. ✳ a. Why would you use a template instead of creating a database from scratch with just the fields you need?

b. The Attachment data type allows you to attach files to a database record. If you were using this database for a job search, what specific documents might you attach to a Contacts record?

Analyze, Correct, Improve

Analyze a database, correct all errors, and improve the design.

Correcting Errors in the Table Structure

Note: To complete this assignment, you will be required to use the Data Files for Students. Visit www.cengage.com/ct/studentdownload for detailed instructions or contact your instructor for information about accessing the required files.

Instructions: Analyze SciFi Movies is a database containing information on classic science fiction movies that your film professor would like to use for teaching. The Movie table shown in Figure 1–85 contains errors to the table structure. Your professor has asked you to correct the errors and make some improvements to the database. Start Access and open the Analyze SciFi Movies database from the Data Files for Students.

Figure 1–85

1. Correct Movie Number should be the primary key for the Movie table. The ID field should not be a field in the table. The Rating field represents a numerical rating system of one to four to indicate the quality of the movie. Your instructor wants to be able to find the average rating for films directed by a particular director. Only integers should be stored in both the Rating and the Length (Minutes) fields.

2. Improve The default field size for Short Text fields is 255. Changing the field size to more accurately represent the maximum number of characters that can be stored in a field is one way to improve the accuracy of the data. The Movie Number, Director Number, and Awards fields should have a maximum size of 3 characters. The Year Made field should have a maximum field size of 4. The Movie Name and Studio fields should have a maximum field size of 50. If instructed to do so by your instructor, rename the Movie table as Movie Last Name where Last Name is your last name. Submit the revised database in the format specified by your instructor.

3. ✳ The Awards field currently has a data type of Short Text, but the only values that will be stored in that field are Yes and No to indicate whether the movie won any awards. What would be a more appropriate data type for this field?

In the Labs

Design, create, modify, and/or use a database following the guidelines, concepts, and skills presented in this chapter. Labs are listed in order of increasing difficulty. Labs 1 and 2, which increase in difficulty, require you to create solutions based on what you learned in the chapter; Lab 3 requires you to create a solution, which uses cloud and web technologies, by learning and investigating on your own from general guidance.

Lab 1: Creating Objects for the Dartt Offsite Services Database

Problem: Dartt Offsite Services is a local company that provides offsite data services and solutions. The company provides remote data backup, disaster recovery planning and services, website backup, and offsite storage of paper documents for small businesses and nonprofit organizations. Service representatives are responsible for communicating data solutions to the client, scheduling backups and other tasks, and resolving any conflicts. The company recently decided to store its client and service rep data in a database. Each client is assigned to a single service rep, but each service rep may be assigned many clients. The database and the Service Rep table have been created, but the Monthly Salary field needs to be added to the table. The records shown in Table 1–6 must be added to the Service Rep table. The company plans to import the Client table from the Excel worksheet shown in Figure 1–86. Dartt would like to finish storing this data in a database and has asked you to help.

Figure 1–86

Note: To complete this assignment, you will be required to use the Data Files for Students. Visit www.cengage.com/ct/studentdownload for detailed instructions or contact your instructor for information about accessing the required files.

Instructions: Perform the following tasks:

1. Start Access and open the Lab 1 Dartt Offsite Services database from the Data Files for Students.

2. Open the Service Rep table in Datasheet view and add the Monthly Salary field to the end of the table. The field has the Currency data type. Assign the caption SR # to the Service Rep Number field.

3. Add the records shown in Table 1–6.

4. Resize the columns to best fit the data. Save the changes to the layout of the table.

Table 1–6 Data for Service Rep Table								
Service Rep Number	Last Name	First Name	Street	City	State	Postal Code	Start Date	Monthly Salary
21	Kelly	Jenna	25 Paint St.	Kyle	SC	28797	5/14/2012	$3,862.45
45	Scott	Josh	1925 Pine Rd.	Byron	SC	28795	4/28/2014	$3,062.08
24	Liu	Mia	265 Marble Dr.	Kyle	SC	28797	1/7/2013	$3,666.67
37	Martinez	Mike	31 Steel St.	Georgetown	SC	28794	5/13/2013	$3,285.00

5. Import the Lab 1–1 Client Data workbook shown in Figure 1–86 into the database. The first row of the workbook contains the column headings. Client Number is the primary key for the new table. Assign the name Client to the table. Save the Import steps, and assign the name Import-Client Data to the steps. Assign Import Client Data as the description.

6. Open the Client table in Design view and make the following changes:

   a. Change the field size for the Client Number field to 5. Change the field size for the Client Name field to 30. Change the field size for the Street and City fields to 20. Change the field size for the State field to 2 and the field size for the Postal Code field to 5. Change the field size for the Service Rep Number field to 2.

   b. Add the caption CL # to the Client Number field.

   c. Add the caption SR # to the Service Rep Number field.

7. Save the changes to the Client table. If a Microsoft Access dialog box appears with the 'Some data may be lost' message, click the Yes button.

8. Open the Client table in Datasheet view and resize all columns to best fit the data. Save the changes to the layout of the table.

9. Create a query using the Simple Query Wizard for the Client table that displays the Client Number, Client Name, Amount Paid, Balance Due, and Service Rep Number. Save the query as Client Query.

10. Create the report shown in Figure 1–87 for the Client table. The report should include the Client Number, Client Name, Amount Paid, Balance Due, and Service Rep Number fields. Include totals for the Amount Paid and Balance Due fields. Be sure to change the column headings to those shown in Figure 1–87. Save the report as Client Financial Report.

11. If requested to do so by your instructor, change the address for Jenna Kelly in the Service Rep table to your address. If your address is longer than 20 characters, simply enter as much as you can.

12. Submit the revised database in the format specified by your instructor.

13. ✳ You entered the records for the Service Rep table in the order shown in Table 1–6 on the previous page, that is service reps 21, 45, 24, 37. What order will the records be in after you close and reopen the Service Rep table? Why?

Client Financial Report				Monday, September 15, 2014 9:09:35 PM
Client Number	Client Name	Amount Paid	Balance Due	Service Rep Number
BBF32	Babbage CPA Firm	$3,524.00	$567.85	24
WSC01	Wood Sports Complex	$2,250.00	$1,600.00	24
		$31,820.85	$21,923.97	

Figure 1–87

Lab 2: Creating the Tennis Logos Database

Problem: Tennis Logos supplies customized tennis clothing and accessories for clubs and tournaments. The company purchases these items from suppliers at wholesale prices and adds the customer's logo. The final item price is determined by marking up the wholesale price and adding a fee that is based on the complexity of the logo. Tennis Logos also does graphic design work for customers. Currently, the information about the items and the suppliers is stored in two Excel workbooks. Each item is assigned to a single supplier, but each supplier may be assigned many items. You are to create a database that will store the item and supplier information. You already have determined that you need two tables, a Supplier table and an Item table, in which to store the information.

Note: To complete this assignment, you will be required to use the Data Files for Students. Visit www.cengage.com/ct/studentdownload for detailed instructions or contact your instructor for information about accessing the required files.

Continued >

In the Labs *continued*

Instructions: Perform the following tasks:

1. Use the Blank desktop database option to create a new database in which to store all objects related to the items for sale. Call the database Lab 2 Tennis Logos.

2. Import the Lab 1–2 Supplier Data Excel workbook into the database. The first row of the workbook contains the column headings. Supplier Code is the primary key for the new table. Assign the name Supplier to the table. Do not save the Import steps.

3. Open the Supplier table in Datasheet view. Change the field size for the Supplier Code field to 2; the field size for the Supplier Name field to 30; and the field size for the Telephone Number field to 12.

4. Import the Lab 1–2 Item Data Excel workbook into the database. The first row of the workbook contains the column headings. Item Number is the primary key for this table. Assign the name Item to the table. Save the Import steps, and assign the name Import-Item Data to the steps. You do not need a description.

5. Open the Item table in Design view. Change the field size for the Item Number field to 4. Change the field size for the Description field to 30. Add the caption Wholesale for the Wholesale Price field. The On Hand field should be an Integer field. Be sure that the field size for the Supplier Code in the Item table is identical to the field size for the Supplier Code in the Supplier table. Save the changes to the table and close the table.

6. Open the Item table in Datasheet view and resize the columns to best fit the data. Save the changes to the layout of the table and close the table.

7. Create a query for the Item table. Include the Item Number, Description, Wholesale Price, Base Cost, and Supplier Code. Save the query as Item Query.

8. Create a simple form for the Item table. Use the name Item for the form.

9. Create the report shown in Figure 1–88 for the Item table. Do not add any totals. Save the report as Inventory Status Report.

10. If requested to do so by your instructor, change the telephone number for Last Merchandisers to your telephone number.

11. Submit the database in the format specified by your instructor.

12. ✳ If you had designed this database, could you have used the field name, Name, for the Supplier Name? If not, why not?

Item Number	Description	On Hand	Wholesale Price
3363	Baseball Cap	110	$4.87
3673	Cotton Visor	150	$4.59
4543	Crew Sweatshirt	75	$7.29
4583			

Inventory Status Report — Monday, September 15, 2014 9:37:32 PM

Figure 1–88

Lab 3: Expand Your World: Cloud and Web Technologies
Exporting Query Results and Reports

Problem: You and two of your friends have started a pet sitting business. You want to be able to share query results and reports, so you have decided to store the items on the SkyDrive. You are still learning Access, so you are going to create a sample query and the report shown in Figure 1–89, export the results, and save to the SkyDrive.

Note: To complete this assignment, you will be required to use the Data Files for Students. Visit www.cengage.com/ct/studentdownload for detailed instructions or contact your instructor for information about accessing the required files.

Customer Balance Report				Monday, September 15, 2014 9:39:02 PM
Customer Number	Last Name	First Name	Balance	Sitter Number
AB10	Alvarez	Frances	$45.00	103
BR16		Alex	$80.00	
	Santoro	Maria	$0.00	107
TR35	Trent	Gerry	$40.00	105
			$419.00	

Figure 1–89

Instructions:

1. Open the Lab 3 Pet Sitters database from the Data Files for Students.

2. Use the Simple Query Wizard to create a query that includes the Customer Number, First Name, Last Name, Balance, and Sitter Number. Save the query as Customer Query.

3. Export the Customer Query as an XPS document to your SkyDrive in the Access folder.

4. Create the report shown in Figure 1–89. Save the report as Customer Balance Report.

5. Export the Customer Balance Report as a PDF document to your Sky Drive in the Access folder. For information about how to use the Sky Drive, refer to the Office and Windows chapter at the beginning of this book.

6. If requested to do so by your instructor, open the Sitter table and change the last name and first name for sitter 103 to your last name and your first name.

7. Submit the assignment in the format specified by your instructor.

8. ✺ Based on your current knowledge of XPS and PDF documents, which one do you think you would use most frequently? Why?

✺ Consider This: Your Turn

Apply your creative thinking and problem solving skills to design and implement a solution.

1. Creating the Craft Database

Note: To complete this assignment, you will be required to use the Data Files for Students. Visit www.cengage.com/ct/studentdownload for detailed instructions or contact your instructor for information about accessing the required files.

Personal/Academic

Part 1: You attend a college that is renowned for its school of arts and crafts. Students who major in arts and crafts can sell their designs online through the college bookstore. The bookstore has used an Excel workbook to store data on wood-crafted items as well as the students who created the items. Because you are a major in computer science and also are studying woodworking, your senior project is to create a database of these wood-crafted items. The database must keep track of the wood-crafted items for sale and maintain data on the students who created the items. Each item is created by a single student, but each student may have created several items.

Based on the information in the Your Turn 1–1 Craft workbook, use the concepts and techniques presented in this chapter to design and create a database to store the craft data. Create a Wood Crafts for Sale report that lists the item number, description, price, and student code. Submit your assignment in the format specified by your instructor.

Part 2: ✺ You made several decisions while determining the table structures and adding data to the tables in this assignment. What method did you use to add the data to each table? Are there any other methods that also would have worked?

Continued >

Consider This: Your Turn *continued*

2. Creating the Mums Landscaping Database
Professional

Part 1: Mums Landscaping is a local company that provides landscaping and lawn maintenance services to commercial customers, such as businesses, housing subdivisions, and schools. You worked for Mums part-time in both high school and in college. Mums has used an Excel workbook to store financial data on its customers but now would like to create a database that includes information on its customers and crew supervisors. Each customer is assigned to a single crew supervisor, but each supervisor may be assigned many customers.

Based on the information in the Your Turn 1–2 Mums Landscaping workbook, use the concepts and techniques presented in this chapter to design and create a database to store the data that Mums needs. Submit your assignment in the format specified by your instructor.

Part 2: ✺ You made several decisions while creating the Mums Landscaping database in this assignment. What did you decide to use as the primary key for each table? Why?

3. Creating an Electronic Assets Database
Research and Collaboration

Part 1: In today's world, most college students will own at least one electronic device, such as a cell phone. Many students have multiple electronic devices. Microsoft Access includes a desktop Asset tracking template that you can modify to keep track of your electronic devices, such as cell phone, MP3 player, and computer. Get together with your group and make a list of the electronic devices that each of you own. Use the desktop Asset tracking template to create an Electronic Assets database. Watch the video to learn how the database works. As a team, review the fields in the Assets table and decide which fields to include in the database. Delete any unwanted fields. Decide how you will describe each device, for example, will you use the term cell phone, smartphone, or mobile phone? Have each team member enter at least two devices. Create a query to find one type of device, such as cell phone. Submit your assignment in the format specified by your instructor.

Part 2: ✺ You made several decisions while creating the Electronic Assets database. Which fields did you decide to delete from the Assets table? What terms did you use to describe each device? What was the rationale for these decisions?

Learn Online

Reinforce what you learned in this chapter with games, exercises, training, and many other online activities and resources.

Student Companion Site Reinforcement activities and resources are available at no additional cost on www.cengagebrain.com. Visit www.cengage.com/ct/studentdownload for detailed instructions about accessing the resources available at the Student Companion Site.

SAM Put your skills into practice with SAM! If you have a SAM account, go to www.cengage.com/sam2013 to access SAM assignments for this chapter.

Index

Quick Reference Summary

Microsoft Word 2013 Quick Reference Summary

Task	Page Number	Ribbon	Other On-Screen Element	Shortcut Menu	Keyboard Shortcut
All Caps	WD 19	Change Case button (HOME tab | Font group), UPPERCASE			CTRL+SHIFT+A
Bold	WD 29	Bold button (HOME tab | Font group)	Bold button on mini toolbar	Font, Font tab (Font dialog box) Touch mode: 'Show Context Menu' button on mini toolbar, Font on shortcut menu, Font tab (Font dialog box)	CTRL+B
Bullets, Apply	WD 23	Bullets button (HOME tab | Paragraph group)	Bullets button on mini toolbar		* (ASTERISK), SPACEBAR
Center	WD 15	Center button (HOME tab | Paragraph group)	Center button on mini toolbar	Paragraph, Indents and Spacing tab (Paragraph dialog box)	CTRL+E
Center Page Vertically	WD 43	Page Setup Dialog Box Launcher (PAGE LAYOUT tab | Page Setup group), Layout tab (Page Setup dialog box)			
Change Case	WD 19	Change Case button (HOME tab | Font group)		Font, Font tab (Font dialog box) Touch mode: 'Show Context Menu' on mini toolbar, Font on shortcut menu, Font tab (Font dialog box)	SHIFT+F3
Change Spacing before or after Paragraph	WD 42	Spacing Before or Spacing After box (PAGE LAYOUT tab | Paragraph group)		Paragraph, Indents and Spacing tab (Paragraph dialog box) Touch mode: 'Show Context Menu' button on mini toolbar, Paragraph on shortcut menu, Indents and Spacing tab (Paragraph dialog box)	
Color Text	WD 26	Font Color arrow (HOME tab | Font group)	Font Color arrow on mini toolbar	Font, Font tab (Font dialog box) Touch mode: 'Show Context Menu' on mini toolbar, Font on shortcut menu	

Microsoft Word 2013 Quick Reference Summary *(continued)*

Task	Page Number	Ribbon	Other On-Screen Element	Shortcut Menu	Keyboard Shortcut
Document Properties, Change	WD 44	Properties button (FILE tab | Info tab)			
Exit Word	WD 46		Close button on title bar		
Font, Change	WD 18	Font arrow (HOME tab | Font group)	Font arrow on mini toolbar Touch mode: 'Show Context Menu' on mini toolbar, Font on shortcut menu	Font, Font tab (Font dialog box)	CTRL+D
Font Size, Change	WD 17	Font Size arrow (HOME tab | Font group)	Font Size arrow on mini toolbar	Font, Font tab (Font dialog box) Touch mode: 'Show Context Menu' button on mini toolbar, Font on shortcut menu, Font tab (Font dialog box)	CTRL+D
Formatting Marks	WD 6	'Show/Hide ¶' button (HOME tab | Paragraph group)			CTRL+SHIFT+*
Graphic, Resize	WD 36	Shape Height and Shape Width boxes (PICTURE TOOLS FORMAT tab | Size group)	Drag sizing handle	More Layout Options, Size tab (Layout dialog box)	
Insertion Point, Move Down/ Up One Line	WD 12				DOWN ARROW/ UP ARROW
Insertion Point, Move Down/ Up One Paragraph	WD 12				CTRL+DOWN ARROW/ CTRL+UP ARROW
Insertion Point, Move Down/ Up One Screen	WD 12				PAGE DOWN/ PAGE UP
Insertion Point, Move Left/ Right One Character	WD 12				LEFT ARROW/ RIGHT ARROW
Insertion Point, Move Left/ Right One Word	WD 12				CTRL+LEFT ARROW/ CTRL+RIGHT ARROW
Insertion Point, Move to Beginning/End of Document	WD 12				CTRL+HOME/ CTRL+END
Insertion Point, Move to Beginning/ End of Line	WD 12				HOME/ END
Insertion Point, Move to Bottom of Document Window	WD 12				ALT+CTRL+PAGE DOWN/ ALT+CTRL+PAGE UP

Microsoft Word 2013 Quick Reference Summary *(continued)*

Task	Page Number	Ribbon	Other On-Screen Element	Shortcut Menu	Keyboard Shortcut
Italicize	WD 25	Italic button (HOME tab | Font group)	Italic button on mini toolbar	Font, Font tab (Font dialog box) Touch mode: 'Show Context Menu' on mini toolbar, Font on shortcut menu, Font tab (Font dialog box)	CTRL+I
Microsoft Account, Sign Out Of	WD 45	Sign out link (FILE tab | Account tab)			
Move Text	WD 49	Cut button (HOME tab | Clipboard group); Paste button (HOME tab | Clipboard group)	Drag and drop selected text	Cut, Paste	CTRL+X, CTRL+V
On-Screen Keyboard, Display	WD 6		Touch mode: Touch Keyboard button on Windows taskbar		
Open a Document	WD 47	Open (FILE tab)			CTRL+O
Page Border, Add	WD 41	'Borders and Shading' button (DESIGN tab | Page Background group)			
Picture Effects, Apply	WD 39	Picture Effects button (PICTURE TOOLS FORMAT tab | Picture Styles gallery)		Format Picture or Format Object Touch mode: 'Show Context Menu' button on mini toolbar, Format Object or Format Picture on shortcut menu	
Picture Style, Apply	WD 38	More button in Picture Styles gallery (PICTURE TOOLS FORMAT tab | Picture Styles group)		'Picture Quick Styles'	
Picture, Insert	WD 34	From File button (INSERT tab | Illustrations group)			
Print Document	WD 51	Print button (FILE tab | Print tab)			CTRL+P
Print Layout View	WD 53	Print Layout button (VIEW tab | Views group)	Print Layout button on status bar		
Read Mode	WD 52	Read Mode button (VIEW tab | Views group)	Read Mode button on status bar		
Redo	WD 24		Redo button on Quick Access Toolbar		CTRL+Y
Save	WD 12	Save (FILE tab | Save tab)	Save button on Quick Access Toolbar		

Microsoft Word 2013 Quick Reference Summary *(continued)*

Task	Page Number	Ribbon	Other On-Screen Element	Shortcut Menu	Keyboard Shortcut
Save Document, Same File Name	WD 33	Save (FILE tab | Save tab)	Save button on Quick Access toolbar		
Scroll, Up/ Down One Line	WD 12		Tap or click scroll arrow at top/ bottom of vertical scroll bar		
Scroll, Up/ Down One Screen	WD 12		Tap or click above/ below scroll box on vertical scroll bar		
Select Block of Text	WD 32		Click beginning, SHIFT+click end Touch mode: Drag selection handle(s)		
Select Character(s)	WD 32		Drag pointer through characters Touch mode: Drag selection handle(s)		SHIFT+RIGHT ARROW or SHIFT+LEFT ARROW
Select Entire Document	WD 32	Select button arrow (HOME tab | Editing group)	In left margin, triple-click		CTRL+A
Select Graphic	WD 32		Tap or click graphic		
Select Group of Words	WD 28		Drag pointer through words Touch mode: Drag selection handle(s)		CTRL+SHIFT+RIGHT ARROW OR CTRL+SHIFT+LEFT ARROW repeatedly
Select Line	WD 16		Click in left margin Touch mode: Double-tap to left of line		SHIFT+DOWN ARROW
Select Multiple Lines	WD 32		Drag pointer in left margin Touch mode: Drag selection handle(s)		HOME, then SHIFT+DOWN ARROW; or END, then SHIFT+UP ARROW
Select Multiple Paragraphs	WD 32		Drag pointer in left margin Touch mode: Drag selection handle(s)		SHIFT+DOWN ARROW
Select Nonadjacent Items	WD 32		Select first item, hold down CTRL key while selecting item(s)		
Select Paragraph	WD 32		Triple-click paragraph		CTRL+SHIFT+DOWN ARROW or CTRL+SHIFT+UP ARROW
Select Sentence	WD 32		CTRL-click		

Microsoft Word 2013 Quick Reference Summary *(continued)*

Task	Page Number	Ribbon	Other On-Screen Element	Shortcut Menu	Keyboard Shortcut
Select Word	WD 32		Double-tap or double-click word		CTRL+SHIFT+RIGHT ARROW or CTRL+SHIFT+LEFT ARROW
Select Words	WD 32		Drag pointer through words Touch mode: Drag selection handle(s)		CTRL+SHIFT+RIGHT ARROW or CTRL+SHIFT+LEFT ARROW repeatedly
Shade Paragraph	WD 21	Shading arrow (HOME tab | Paragraph group)			
Spelling, Check as You Type	WD 10		Tap or click word, 'Spelling and Grammar Check' icon on status bar	Press and hold or right-click error, tap or click correct word on shortcut menu	
Text Effect, Apply	WD 20	'Text Effects and Typography' button (HOME tab | Font group)		Font Touch mode: 'Show Context Menu' on mini toolbar, Font on shortcut menu	
Theme Colors, Change	WD 31	Theme Colors button (DESIGN tab | Document Formatting group)			
Underline	WD 29	Underline button (HOME tab | Font group)	Underline button on mini toolbar	Font, Font tab (Font dialog box) Touch mode: 'Show Context Menu' button on mini toolbar, Font on shortcut menu, Font tab (Font dialog box)	CTRL+U
Undo	WD 24		Undo button on Quick Access Toolbar		CTRL+Z
Zoom 100%	WD 37	100% button (VIEW tab | Zoom group)			
Zoom Document	WD 35	Zoom button (VIEW tab | Zoom group)	Zoom Out or Zoom In button or Zoom level button on status bar Touch mode: Pinch or stretch		
Zoom One Page	WD 30	One Page button (VIEW tab | Zoom group)			
Zoom Page Width	WD 7	Page Width button (VIEW tab | Zoom group)			

Microsoft PowerPoint 2013 Quick Reference Summary

Task	Page Number	Ribbon	Other On-Screen Areas	Shortcut Menu	Keyboard Shortcut
Document Properties, Change	PPT 48	Properties button (FILE tab | Info tab)			
Document Theme, Change Color Variant	PPT 5	Choose color variant (DESIGN tab | Variants group)			
Document Theme, Choose	PPT 5	FILE tab, New tab; More button (DESIGN tab | Themes group)			
Exit PowerPoint	PPT 55	Exit (FILE tab)	Close button on title bar	Right-click PowerPoint app button on taskbar, click Close window	ALT+F4 or CTRL+Q
Font Size, Increase	PPT 12	Increase Font Size button or Font Size arrow (HOME tab | Font group)	Increase Font Size button or Font Size arrow on mini toolbar	Font, Size arrows (Font dialog box)	CTRL+SHIFT+RIGHT CARET (>)
Font, Change Color	PPT 13	Font Color button or Font Color arrow or Font dialog box launcher (HOME tab | Font group)	Font Color button or Font Color arrow on mini toolbar	Font, Font Color button on Font tab (Font dialog box)	CTRL+SHIFT+F
Illustration, Placeholder, or Shape, Move	PPT 39		Drag		ARROW KEYS move selected image in small increments
List Level, Increase	PPT 19	Increase List Level button (HOME tab | Paragraph group)	Increase List Level button on mini toolbar		TAB
List Level, Decrease	PPT 19	Decrease List Level button (HOME tab | Paragraph group)	Decrease List Level button on mini toolbar		SHIFT+TAB
Move to Another Slide in Normal View	PPT 29		Next Slide or Previous Slide buttons on vertical scroll bar; drag scroll box on vertical scroll bar; click slide thumbnail in Thumbnail pane Touch Mode: Tap desired slide in Thumbnail pane		PAGE DOWN (next slide); PAGE UP (previous slide)
Move to Another Slide in Slide Show View	PPT 50		Click to display next slide; click Next Slide or Previous Slide icons on Slide Show toolbar Touch Mode: Swipe forward or backward on slide		PAGE DOWN (next slide); PAGE UP (previous slide); RIGHT ARROW or DOWN ARROW (next slide); LEFT ARROW or UP ARROW (previous slide)
Open Presentation	OFF 54	Open (FILE tab)			CTRL+O
Picture, Insert	PPT 31	Pictures button or Online Pictures button (INSERT tab | Images group)	Pictures icon or Online Pictures icon in slide		
Picture, Move	PPT 39		Drag		ARROW keys to move in small increments

Microsoft PowerPoint 2013 Quick Reference Summary (continued)

Task	Page Number	Ribbon	Other On-Screen Areas	Shortcut Menu	Keyboard Shortcut
Print a Presentation	PPT 52	Print button (FILE tab | Print tab)			CTRL+P
Resize	PPT 36	Enter height and width values (PICTURE TOOLS FORMAT tab | Size group or DRAWING TOOLS FORMAT tab | Size group or VIDEO TOOLS FORMAT tab | Size group)	Drag sizing handles	Format Picture or Format Shape or Format Video, Size & Properties icon	
Run PowerPoint	OFF 46, PPT 4		PowerPoint 2013 tile on Start menu; search for PowerPoint 2013 using Search charm on Charms bar		
Save a Presentation with a New Name	PPT 15	Save As (FILE tab)			
Slide, Add	PPT 15	New Slide button (HOME tab | Slides group)		New Slide	CTRL+M
Slide, Arrange	PPT 42	Slide Sorter button (VIEW tab | Presentation Views group), drag thumbnail to new position	Drag slide in Thumbnail pane to new position, click Slide Sorter icon on status bar, drag thumbnail to new position		
Slide, Duplicate	PPT 41	New Slide arrow (HOME tab | Slides group), Duplicate Selected Slides		Duplicate Slide	
Slide, Select Layout	PPT 23	Layout button or New Slide arrow (HOME tab | Slides group)			
Slide Show, Start	PPT 49	Slide Show button (SLIDE SHOW tab | Start Slide Show group)	Slide Show button on status bar; 'Start from Beginning' button in Quick Access toolbar		F5
Slide Show, End	PPT 51		Tap or click black ending slide	End Show	ESC or HYPHEN
Text, Bold	PPT 21	Bold button (HOME tab | Font group)	Bold button on mini toolbar	Font, Font tab (Font dialog box), Font style arrow, Bold	CTRL+B
Text, Change Color	PPT 13	Font Color button or Font Color arrow or Font dialog box launcher (HOME tab | Font group)	Font Color button or Font Color arrow on mini toolbar	Font, Font Color button (Font dialog box)	CTRL+SHIFT+F
Text, Delete	PPT 43	Cut button (HOME tab | Clipboard group)		Cut	DELETE or CTRL+X or BACKSPACE
Text, Italicize	PPT 11	Italic button (HOME tab | Font group)	Italic button on mini toolbar	Font, Font style arrow (Font dialog box), Italic	CTRL+I

Microsoft PowerPoint 2013 Quick Reference Summary *(continued)*

Task	Page Number	Ribbon	Other On-Screen Areas	Shortcut Menu	Keyboard Shortcut
Text, Select	PPT 11		Drag to select; double-click to select word; triple-click to select paragraph Touch Mode: Tap to position insertion point and drag selection handles		CTRL+SHIFT+RIGHT ARROW (select word); CTRL+SHIFT+DOWN ARROW (select paragraph)
Theme, Change	PPT 26	More button (DESIGN tab | Themes group)			
Theme, Download	PPT 77	Choose category from Suggested searches (FILE tab, New tab), choose theme, tap or click Create button			
Transition, Add	PPT 45	More button (TRANSITIONS tab | Transition to This Slide group)			ALT+A, T
Transition, Change Duration	PPT 46	Duration box or arrows (TRANSITIONS tab | Timing group)			
Undo Changes	PPT 8		Undo button (Quick Access toolbar)		CTRL+Z
Zoom for Viewing Slides	PPT 10	Zoom button (VIEW tab | Zoom group)	Zoom slider on status bar; Zoom In or Zoom Out buttons on Zoom slider; change percentage in Zoom level box on left side of slider Touch Mode: Pinch two fingers to zoom out; stretch two fingers apart to zoom in		

Microsoft Excel 2013 Quick Reference Summary

Task	Page Number	Ribbon	Other On-Screen Element	Shortcut Menu	Keyboard Shortcut
Accounting Number Format, Apply	EX 32	'Accounting Number Format' button (HOME tab | Number group)	'Accounting Number Format' button on mini toolbar	Format Cells	CTRL+SHIFT+DOLLAR SIGN ($)
Auto Fill	EX 16	Fill button (HOME tab | Editing group)	Drag fill handle		
Bold	EX 26	Bold button (HOME tab | Font group)	Bold button on mini toolbar	Format Cells	CTRL+B
Cell Style	EX 24	Cell Styles button (HOME tab | Styles group)			
Chart Style, Apply	EX 40		Chart Styles button		
Chart, Add	EX 38	'Insert Pie or Doughnut Chart' button (INSERT tab | Charts group)			

Office Quick Reference

Microsoft Excel 2013 Quick Reference Summary *(continued)*

Task	Page Number	Ribbon	Other On-Screen Element	Shortcut Menu	Keyboard Shortcut
Chart, Move to New Sheet	EX 41	Move Chart button (CHART TOOLS DESIGN tab | Location group)			
Clear Cell Entries	EX 52	Clear button (HOME tab | Editing group)	Drag fill handle back into selected range	Clear Contents	
Clear Entire Worksheet	EX 52	Clear button (HOME tab | Editing group), Clear All			
Column Width, Adjust	EX 34		Double-tap or double-click boundary or drag boundary	Column Width	
Comma Style, Apply	EX 32	Comma Style button (HOME tab | Number group)		Format Cells, Number tab	
Copy and Paste	EX 16	Copy button (HOME tab | Clipboard Group), select destination, Paste button (HOME tab | Clipboard group)	Drag fill handle	Copy, select destination, Paste Touch mode: 'Show Context Menu' button on mini toolbar, Copy, select destination, Paste	CTRL+drag or CTRL+C; CTRL+V
Document Properties, Change	EX 44	Properties button (FILE tab | Info tab)			
Entry, Complete	EX 7		Tap or click Enter box in formula bar		ENTER or ARROW keys
Font Color, Change	EX 28	Font Color arrow (HOME tab | Font group)	Font Color arrow on mini toolbar	Format Cells	
Font Size, Increase	EX 27	Font Size arrow (HOME tab | Font group) or 'Increase Font Size' button (HOME tab | Font group)	Font Size arrow on mini toolbar	Format Cells	
Font, Change	EX 25	Font arrow (HOME tab | Font group)	Font arrow on mini toolbar Touch mode: 'Show Context Menu' button on mini toolbar, Format Cells	Format Cells	

Microsoft Access 2013 Quick Reference Summary

Task	Page Number	Ribbon	Other On-Screen Areas	Shortcut Menu	Keyboard Shortcut
Back up Database	AC 56	FILE tab, Save As tab, 'Back Up Database', Save As button			
Close Object	AC 20		Close button for object	Close	
Column, Resize	AC 28		Double-click or double-tap right boundary of field selector in datasheet	Press and hold or right-click field name, Field Width	
Compact Database	AC 57	FILE tab, Info tab in Backstage view, 'Compact & Repair Database' button			
Criterion, Use in a Query	AC 43		In Design View, tap or click Criteria row, enter criterion		
Data, Import	AC 33	Button for imported data format (EXTERNAL DATA tab | Import & Link group)			
Database Properties, Change	AC 55	View and edit database properties link (FILE tab | Info tab)			
Database, Create	AC 6	Blank desktop database thumbnail (FILE tab | New tab)			
Database, Create using Template	AC 7		FILE tab, New tab, select template		
Delete Object	AC 58			Delete	
Exit Access	AC 24		Close button on right side of title bar		
Form, Create	AC 45	Form button (CREATE tab | Forms group)			
Open Database	AC 25	Open button (FILE tab)			
Open Table	AC 21		Double-click or double-tap table in Navigation Pane	Press and hold or right-click table in Navigation Pane, tap or click Open	
Preview or Print Object	AC 30	Print or Print Preview button (FILE tab | Print tab)			CTRL+P, ENTER
Primary Key, Modify	AC 11	Select field, Data Type arrow (TABLE TOOLS FIELDS tab | Formatting group), select data type			
Query, Create using Simple Query Wizard	AC 40	Query Wizard button (CREATE tab | Queries group)			
Rename Object	AC 58			Press and hold or right-click object in Navigation Pane, Rename, enter new name, press ENTER	

Microsoft Access 2013 Quick Reference Summary *(continued)*

Task	Page Number	Ribbon	Other On-Screen Areas	Shortcut Menu	Keyboard Shortcut
Report Column Headings, Modify	AC 50			Press and hold or right-click field name, Rename Field	
Report, Create	AC 48	Report button (CREATE tab | Reports group)			
Run Access	AC 5		Access 2013 tile on Windows Start screen or display Charms bar, tap or click Search charm, type Access, tap or click Access 2013		
Save Object	AC 16	FILE tab, Save	Save button on Quick Access Toolbar		CTRL+S
Save Object As	AC 45	FILE tab, Save As tab, 'Save Object As', Save As button			
Table, Modify in Design View	AC 37	Table Design button (CREATE tab | Tables group)			
Table, View in Design View	AC 17	View arrow (TABLE TOOLS FIELDS tab | Views group), Design View	Design View button on status bar		
Totals, Add to a Report	AC 53	Totals button (REPORT DESIGN TOOLS DESIGN tab | Grouping & Totals group)			

Important Notes for Windows 7 Users

The screen shots in this book show Microsoft Office 2013 running in Windows 8. If you are using Microsoft Windows 7, however, you still can use this book because Office 2013 runs virtually the same way on both platforms. You will encounter only minor differences if you are using Windows 7. Read this section to understand the differences.

Dialog Boxes

If you are a Windows 7 user, the dialog boxes shown in this book will look slightly different than what you see on your screen. Dialog boxes for Windows 8 have a title bar with a solid color, and the dialog box name is centered on the title bar. Beyond these superficial differences in appearance, however, the options in the dialog boxes across both platforms are the same. For instance, Figures 1 and 2 show the Font dialog box in Windows 7 and the Font dialog box in Windows 8.

Figure 1 Font Dialog Box in Windows 7

Figure 2 Font Dialog Box in Windows 8

Alternate Steps for Running an App in Windows 7

Nearly all of the steps in this book work exactly the same way for Windows 7 users; however, running an app (or program/application) requires different steps for Windows 7. The following steps show how to run an app in Windows 7.

Running an App (or Program/Application) Using Windows 7

1. Click the Start button on the taskbar to display the Start menu.
2. Click All Programs and then click the Microsoft Office 2013 folder (Figure 3).
3. If necessary, click the name of the folder containing the app you want to run.
4. Click the name of the app you want to run (such as Excel 2013).

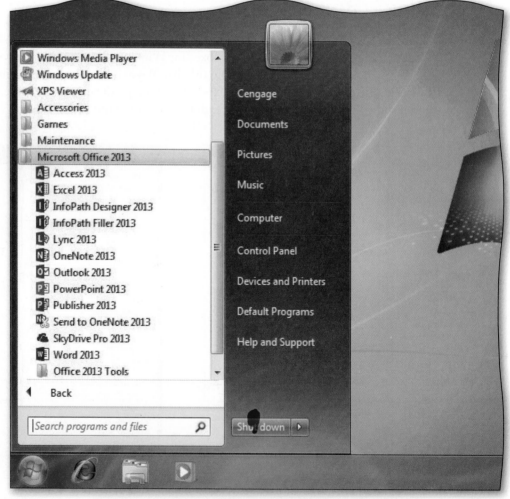

Figure 3 Running an App Using the Windows 7 Start Menu